Dear Kate,

Hope y

CW01023543

BANNED
HISTORY

What they didn't teach you at school

Lynsey Calver

**Grosvenor House
Publishing Limited**

The right of Lynsey Calver to be identified as the author of this
work has been asserted in accordance with Section 78
of the Copyright, Designs and Patents Act 1988

The book cover is copyright to Lynsey Calver

This book is published by
Grosvenor House Publishing Ltd
Link House
140 The Broadway, Tolworth, Surrey, KT6 7HT.
www.grosvenorhousepublishing.co.uk

A CIP record for this book
is available from the British Library

ISBN 978-1-80381-105-5

Acknowledgements

Thank you to my fiancé Aaron, for putting up with my prolonged absence from the living room. Thanks for all the food and feedback.

Thank you to my friends Anna and Polly for your never-ending support.

Thank you to my friends Amy, Clelia, and Lou for proofreading my chapters.

Thank you to Phil for allowing me to take a sabbatical from teaching to research and write the book.

Thank you to my family for spurring me on and encouraging my passion for writing as a child.

Thank you to all my students at Dover Grammar School for Boys for your ideas and encouragement. Special shout out to Oliver Q. for your critique on Churchill; Joshua B. for your non-stop encouragement and useful facts about WW2 planes; Georgie H. for pointing me in the direction of the cannibal Albert Fish; and Dan W. for coming up with the title: Banned History.

This would not be possible without you all.

Contents

Introduction

The national curriculum for History in secondary schools does the best it can with 70,000 years of humanity to get through in two-three years. Which, incidentally, is achieved by cheating and only doing a smidge of the ancient era and starting at 1066. Inevitably, this means a glossing over of events and huge number of omissions. The national curriculum is vague at best with the following topics described as "should be taught": the development of Church, state and society in Medieval Britain 1066-1509; the development of Church, state and society in Britain 1509-1745; ideas, political power, industry and empire in Britain, 1745-1901; challenges for Britain, Europe and the wider world 1901 to the present day (which includes a mandatory study of the Holocaust); the study of an aspect or theme in British history from before 1066; and at least one study of a significant society or issue in world history.[1]

The curriculum centres firmly on British history with one topic out of six focussing on somewhere else in the world. Because students are able to drop history (sharp intake of breath) when it comes to GCSE options time, many people leave school with a warped view of Britain's role in the world. A

---

[1] Department for Education, *History programmes of study: key stage 3 National curriculum in England,*2013, https://assets.publishing.service.gov. uk/government/uploads/system/uploads/attachment_data/file/239075/ SECONDARY_national_curriculum_-_History.pdf

warping which is facilitated by the school history textbooks completely ignoring things which don't paint the country in a good light. For example, one textbook has four pages dedicated to Britain's role abolishing the Atlantic Slave Trade[2], yet conveniently there is zero mention of Britain's role starting it. *Banned History* has no such rose-tinted view.

Banned History began life after a trip to Auschwitz as part of the Holocaust Educational Trust's (HET) programme. The HET opened my eyes to another side of the Holocaust – one that I had not come across in my lessons as a student. The HET taught us about the scale of collaboration from countries conquered by the Nazis, as well as the lack of help for Jews from Britain and her allies; both of which made the Holocaust possible. This other side of the story was also noticeably absent from the textbooks I had been using as a teacher and this got me pondering what else was missing. Soon enough I found myself down a YouTube rabbit hole of conspiracies and clickbait videos such as "Facts No One Knows". Whilst further research soon proved a lot of these videos to be utter codswallop, it set me off on a more academic journey to reveal the truth about Britain's role in the Holocaust. Churchill has long been a bone of contention for me – something which my students love to wind me up about by wearing badges with Churchill's face on it or by making bold statements about how he was a "diamond geezer". Whilst I concede he deserves credit for the Allies' victory in World War Two, I was also aware of other events, such as the Bengal Famine, which suggested he was not the "Best Prime Minister Ever" (a title he won in a 2010 poll by *The Times*). This famine occurred during World War Two in the jewel of the British Empire -India - yet is

---

[2] Colin Shephard, Andy Reid, Keith Shephard, *Peace and War*, (School History Project, John Murray publishing, London, 1993), PP. 82-85

ignored by British school history textbooks because any study into the event would soon reveal how Churchill's actions made the situation worse. With there being much debate about Churchill being a racist following his statue being defaced in June 2020, I was eager to uncover the evidence for and against. Thus began my quest to expose the propaganda about Churchill. This soon led me to consider how much other iconic English leaders are misrepresented in history textbooks, and so, Queen Elizabeth I, aka the Virgin Queen, and King Richard I, aka the Lionheart, also came under scrutiny.

Whilst the Holocaust, Churchill, Elizabeth I, and Richard the Lionheart will all appear in your history lessons at school (albeit in an unashamedly biased way) there are some topics which are too depraved and too horrifying for the classroom. But having taught thousands of students over the years, I was aware that these debased topics were the ones which got people interested in history because, lets be honest, learning how best to torture someone is far more engaging than learning about how farming changed in the 18th century (no offence to all the farmers out there). And so began my enquiry into human depravity which took me on a highly unpleasant (with lots of "ewww that's gross" moments) yet weirdly enjoyable trip through the history of torture, cannibalism, bestiality, and incest. Lastly, with the recent developments in same sex marriage in the Western world strongly contrasting with the death penalty for homosexuality in other parts of the world, I was curious where homophobia had come from in the first place. The answer was a definite surprise, that's for sure.

In the pages ahead you will discover why Churchill does not deserve to have won "Greatest Briton to have ever lived" and be able to decide for yourself whether he was a racist. You will be amazed at the extent of homosexuality throughout history and even more surprised to discover how little religion had to do with causing homophobia. You will find out why Elizabeth I is more virgin on being a blagger than she is being an actual virgin, and you will uncover her role starting the Atlantic Slave Trade as well as the *real* reason she never married. Richard the Lionheart will be shown to be more lying than lion and you will be shocked to discover how badly he treated England - *Disney* certainly has a lot to answer for in their misleading portrayal of Richard in "Robin Hood" that's for sure. You will learn valuable life lessons such as how to get away with torture; which family member the British law allows you to marry; and how to avoid being eaten by cannibals. Get ready to be disgusted by Albert Fish who describes exactly how he prepared and cooked his human meals. Can you guess which body part he threw away because it didn't taste as good as the rest? You may want to take some anti-sickness tablets before embarking upon the rollercoaster ride of incest and bestiality and get set to have your opinion on British Queen Elizabeth II changed by this chapter (no spoilers – you'll have to read on to see whether it's incest or bestiality she's a part of).

In addition to all these revelations there are also lots of random facts to enjoy such as who discovered dolphins (and who fell in love with one); why the Vietnam war began; why Russia turned communist; how many bombs were dropped in WW2, how Martin Luther King got his name; how many people Europe killed with their colonisation of the Americas; and when the British government legalised men hitting their wives.

With all this in mind, you best get your dramatic gasps of horror, surprised expressions, and sick bucket ready. Let's get going.

Churchill's Not So Finest Hours

"I wonder whether any historian of the future will ever be able to paint Winston in his true colours"[1]

Winston Churchill is Britain's favourite prime minister. This fangirling began in the 1940s when he won *Time* magazine's Man of the Year in 1940 and 1949. However, considering Hitler won this award in 1938 and Stalin also won this award twice (in 1939 and 1942), I'm not holding this accolade as evidence that he was a top bloke. The Churchill sycophancy truly took off in 1999 when BBC Radio 4 asked 20 prominent historians, politicians, and commentators who was the best British prime minister of the 20th century; all concluded Churchill.[2] This may be forgivable and somewhat understandable, considering the remit was just prime ministers. Less understandable is how in 2002, the British public voted him as the greatest Briton to have ever lived.[3] I mean, really? *Ever lived??* In September 2008, the BBC *Newsnight* programme asked voters who they thought was the greatest and worst of post-war prime ministers. 27,000 people took part, and it was, once again, decided that Winston Churchill was the greatest.[4] *The Times* did a poll of all British prime ministers in the lead-up to the 2010 general election. Churchill topped this one too[5] – of ALL the prime ministers ever. The furthest he came to NOT being first was when he came second. This poll was led by the University of Leeds and Ipsos Mori in 2004 and saw 139 academics who specialised in

20th century British history and/or politics vote Churchill as the runner up.[6] Modern-day prime ministers also like to sing Churchill's praises, which only adds to this falsification of history. PM David Cameron (famed for his love of pigs and hatred of the EU) called Churchill "the greatest ever Prime Minister"; and Boris Johnson loves him so much he wrote a book about his hero: *The Churchill Factor* and admits to trying to emulate the man while saying "all of us fall so very short" when attempting to do so.[7] Of course there is no one we can trust more than privately educated Tories praising another privately educated Tory.

Perhaps if the British public had known how much Churchill opposed their beloved NHS, they would have been less praiseworthy. Churchill was one of 172 Tories who voted against the NHS on its second reading in the House of Commons on 2 May 1946[8] and again on its third reading in July 1946. In one debate in the House of Commons, Churchill called Bevan (the man behind the NHS plan) a "curse". The Conservatives preferred a health service that wasn't centralised i.e., doctors, nurses and staff weren't employed and paid by the government – they wanted to rely on charity-run hospitals instead. In other words, they didn't want it to be free to the public, essentially opposing the whole premise of the NHS. Not that any Tory will admit to this opposition today, instead preferring to claim they are the reason the NHS existed. Yes, shockingly enough, politicians have lied to make themselves seem more appealing to voters. Jeremy Hunt claimed: "a Tory was the true founder of the NHS"[9] in 2017; Matt Hancock spouted the same drivel in 2019; and Boris Johnson wrote in his biography that: "Together with former PM David Lloyd George, he (Churchill) deserves the title of Founder of the Welfare State."[10]

Most of us have grown up with this opinion shoved in our faces. If it's not coming at you through the radio, TV, online polls, adverts for car insurance, or cuddly bulldogs in the tourist shops, it will get you with the history textbooks at school. British schoolbooks tell children 'Churchill is a Brave Bulldog' and that he should be celebrated for defeating the Nazis and spreading civilisation to indigenous people. The myth of Churchill is Britain's greatest bit of propaganda. And it's about to come crashing down.

The only decent Churchill was the first one.

Winston is the first-born of the fourth-born of the 7th Duke of Marlborough. Which almost sounds slightly impressive but in the eyes of Prime Minister Gladstone, who actually knew the family, "none of the Marlboroughs have morals or principles."[11] The only decent one was the first one, John Churchill, and it was down to him that the Churchills became dukes thanks to his military success in four battles in the 1710s. The second, third, and fourth dukes had nothing to contribute to history, while the fifth and sixth dukes contributed their time and effort in spending all the family's money. The seventh duke was Winston's grandfather, and Winston's father, Lord Randolph, was his fourth-born child. While Randolph and the seventh duke were respectable(ish) MPs, Winston's uncle – the 8th Duke of Marlborough, brought the family name into disrepute via an expulsion from Eton, two sex scandals, and a fist fight with the heir to the British throne. As you do. Queen Victoria was so appalled at the family's behaviour that she got rid of them by giving the seventh duke a job in Ireland.

Winston's mother was American: Miss Jennie Jerome. His parents married on 15 April 1874, having met the previous

August at a boat party at Cowes on the Isle of Wight. Clearly channelling the location of their first meet, the pair moo-ved so quickly Winston was born after just seven months of marriage. Winston was joined by a brother six years later called John Strange who, strangely enough, was called Jack by everybody. Talking of names, Spencer is actually Winston's proper surname. His full name is Winston Leonard Spencer-Churchill, but the Spencer bit is his proper surname. The fifth duke, in between spending the family money, added the Churchill bit to his name "George Spencer" in an attempt to grasp hold of some of the honour attributed to John Churchill. And the grasping stuck.

Winston was brought up in a household with principles of prejudice, parental neglect,[12] and sponging off other people. His parents' income came not through work but from his grandfathers. Jennie's father contributed £2,000 a year to the couple, and Randolph's father, the 7th Duke of Marlborough, contributed £1,000 a year.[13] This is roughly equivalent to £150,000 a year in today's money, a decent amount for sure, but when you've got a mansion to maintain, a reputation to grasp onto, and two boys to put through private school, the money soon goes, and so the family lived permanently in debt. Churchill's father died in 1895 at the early age of 45 on January 24th, a death date which was also shared by Churchill himself 70 years later. It wasn't just career choice and date of death father and son shared; Winston also picked up his father's racism and dislike of Indian people. During a public speech in Birmingham, Randolph referred to the Indian delegation as "three Bengalee baboos",[14] and 60 years later Winston was allowing the Indians to starve to death while being the only MP opposed to Indian Independence.[15]

there. He was at the races (Goodwood) with the Prince of Wales. When he heard there was action where he may be able to obtain some glory, he raced back. Unsurprisingly, the three brigades sent to fight the Pashtun, led by Commander Blood (could this name be any more appropriate?!) had gone on without him and there were "no vacancies". Blood was a friend of his mother's, but even pulling these strings couldn't change the fact they had already set off with men who were actually in the country and not betting on horses in London. Maybe if Blood had read Churchill's letters to his mum, he may have realised the value of this invincible man: "I am intended to do something in the world."[22] Blood advised that if Churchill really wanted to come then he would have to come as a journalist. And so, the only flag Churchill was operating under was that of the *Daily Telegraph* and *Pioneer* newspapers.

Upon arrival in India, he went to auction and bought himself a dead man's blanket as well as something every little girl dreams of – a white pony. Despite the warnings from the other commissioned men in his brigade (i.e., the ones who had actually been asked to be there), Churchill carried on riding this highly visible animal. The risk posed to those he was travelling with did not matter as reported by *Harper's Magazine* afterwards: "He rode on a white pony, the most conspicuous of all marks, and all the prayers of his friends could not make him give it up for a more safer beast."[23] When questioned about it afterwards, Churchill admitted it was not a great idea: "Foolish, perhaps…" but his justification was that it's more important to be noticed than to be considerate of others: "…but given an audience there is no act too daring or too noble. Without the gallery things are different."[24] Certainly not the attitude of a team player. Battle commenced on 16 September 1897, and it became a two-month siege of Malakand ending with British success as the Pashtun tribes retreated. Churchill's contribution is strangely vague; he sure as hell didn't know what he'd done. "I cannot be certain, but I think I hit four men. At any rate they fell."[25] At any rate, he was claiming it.

It was a small victory in a longer war that was fought because the Indians were opposed to British rule. Much to the British government's surprise, all the railways they had built failed to make up for all the atrocities they caused. Obviously, his audience in India was limited to the men who were there, but Churchill made sure everyone in Britain knew about it by writing a 268-page book: *The Story of the Malakand Force* published in 1898. Interestingly, the battle fails to get a mention on any websites describing the actions of the 4th Hussars. Churchill learnt early on that if he was to be seen as a hero, he would need to be the one writing the reports; "For my part, I consider that it will be found much better by all Parties to leave the past to history, especially as I propose to write that history." Basically, saying history books will be favourable to him because he'll be the one writing it, literally HIS story.

After the Malakand campaign, Churchill was hungry for more glory and so set about trying to get in on the war in Sudan (1891–1899). He was unsuccessful to start with because the commander of the British forces in Sudan, Lord Kitchener, rejected his request. This obviously would not do, and so Churchill, who was in England at the time on leave from the 4th Hussars, utilised his upper-class contacts to lobby Kitchener to change his mind – even dragging in Prime Minister Lord Salisbury to help. Still Kitchener refused, and so Churchill turned to the man who oversaw appointments back in England, General of the Horse Guards, Sir Evelyn Wood. After the death of an officer in the 21st Lancers on 24 July 1898 there was a space to fill, and Wood gave it to Churchill.[26] However, by the time he arrived, that position had been given to another man so once again Churchill was side-lined.

Incidentally, he didn't wait to receive the official OK from the 4th Hussars before abandoning his commitments there and going to Sudan; such desertion would have a man killed in other circumstances.

The War Office declined to pay for Churchill's trip to Sudan as well as refusing to accept any liability for him should he be killed or injured while out there. And so, just like in India, Churchill got a journalist commission – this time from *The Morning Post* who gave him £15 for each of the 13 articles he wrote about the war in Sudan.[27] Churchill arrived in Luxor on 5 August 1898, and was there for the battle of Omdurman on 2 September 1898. He had slightly more impact here and killed six men.[28] Once again, he wrote a book: *The River War*, this time it was 1000 pages! After Omdurman, the 21st Lancers were assigned other duties and Churchill returned home. He could now put his name to two colonial campaigns, and he decided his time in the army was done; he resigned and left the army in March 1899. This decision was heavily influenced by a new rule which prohibited serving officers from being war correspondents. A rule which ironically enough only came about because of Churchill's criticism of Lord Kitchener while he was a serving officer and war journalist.[29] Writing earnt him five times the amount the army could offer,[30] so it was undoubtedly the write decision to stick with this line of work.

His first commission in his new writing role was the Boer War in South Africa (11 October 1899–31 May 1902). The Boers were descendants of 17th century Dutch and French migrants, and they came into conflict with the British when the Brits decided they'd like a piece of the South African pie. Having left the army, Churchill sought a journalist commission to get out there near the fighting. He was by this point a well-established and sought-after writer, and he managed to secure a four-month £1000 commission, which made him the best paid war correspondent in England.[31] He arrived in Cape Town on 30 October 1899, accompanied by his valet Thomas Walden, and 18 bottles of Scotch.[32] Two weeks later, the armoured train on which he was travelling was ambushed by the Boers. By all accounts, during the ambush, Churchill acted bravely and put himself in the line of fire many times to try and get the men to safety. However, he made the schoolboy error of leaving his pistol on the train and thus was forced to surrender when confronted by the Boers. Churchill was captured, and given his "upper-class" background, was made a high-profile POW in a camp in Pretoria. The fate of his 18 bottles of Scotch is unknown. On December 12th, Churchill escaped the camp. A daring feat for sure, but one that was undertaken to the detriment of his two friends who had helped plan the whole thing but were left behind (luckily, they were able to make their own escape a few months later). Once out, Churchill made his way across 300 miles of enemy territory, helped by an Englishman named John Howard who smuggled him onto a freight train en route to Portuguese East Africa. This was an embarrassment for the Boers who put out Wanted posters – dead or alive – offering a £25 reward for his capture.

This escape made him a hero in Britain – he had finally got the glory and fame he had been searching for. He stayed in South Africa a bit longer, covering the war and, although it was against the rules, he was able to get a commission from Sir Buller into the army again! Buller had been impressed with Churchill's ballsy escape and made him a lieutenant in the South African Light Horse. A month later Churchill escaped death again when "a bullet severed a feather on his hat"[33] in the Battle of Spion Kop. This battle was lost by the British, so naturally there was no 1000-page book written about this one. He was still there in June 1900 when Pretoria fell to the British and as a result, he was able to claim some more glory leading the liberation of his former POW camp and freeing 180 men. After this, he returned home safe in the knowledge he was now considered a national hero; an opinion which would carry him forwards in his quest for greater things.

Full of MP promises

Riding high on his glorious tale of escape and victory in South Africa, Winston set his sights on becoming an MP. And there was nowhere better to take his first leap than in Oldham, the hometown of one of the men who had helped in his escape – Dan Dewsnap. Dewsnap had said to him "they'd all vote for you next time"[34] and while this wasn't quite the case (he got 25.3% of the vote and this was actually a 0.8% loss from the Conservative's previous hold on Oldham), he still managed to win a seat in the House of Commons as a 26-year-old first timer. At the time, MPs were unpaid. They were men from the upper classes who already had money, and the job was more of a status thing than a money maker. Churchill, being of the fake Upper Class, did not have money and so spent his first few months as MP travelling around England and America giving lectures instead of tending to his constituents' needs. He did well out of it – earning just under £4000 in England and £1600[35] in America (roughly totalling £280,000 in today's money).

One person who was immune to Churchill's allure and tales of courageous acts was American president Teddy Roosevelt who, after meeting him in 1901, commented: "I do not like Winston Churchill."[36] Living up to his name, Teddy found Churchill so un-bear-able, he refused to meet with him on a visit to England in 1910 and again in 1914; although he did concede Churchill had done some pretty good stuff: "I have never liked Winston Churchill, but… extend to him my congratulations".[37] And Teddy's not the only US President to resist the Churchillian charm – Barack Obama also refused to toe the "Hero" line. A bust of Churchill has been in the White House since 1965, but upon taking office in 2009, Obama had the bust removed. This was likely due to the fact Obama's Kenyan grandfather, Hussein Onyango Obama, was imprisoned without trial and tortured for two years for resisting Churchill's empire as part of the Mau-Mau uprising.[38] Obama's decision was criticised by Boris Johnson in 2016, and perhaps sensing there'll be hell toupee if he did the same thing, Donald Trump reinstated the bust when he took office in January 2017.

After a Conservative start to politics, Churchill switched to the Liberals in 1904 because he disagreed with the free trade ideas the Tories were promoting. Plus, the Liberals were doing rather well while the Conservative government were flailing, and Churchill didn't want to be on the losing side. This flip lasted 20 years until Churchill flopped back to the Conservatives in November 1924. During his 64 years as an MP, Churchill represented Oldham, Manchester NW, Dundee, Epping, and Woodford, suggesting little loyalty to any particular area other than his own career. But he wasn't always successful. He was defeated at MP elections four times, and in the general election just after WW2, he lost out to Clement Attlee in becoming the prime minister. As an MP, there are few achievements, mostly because this was a steppingstone role, and it wasn't his main focus – he always held other jobs (either in the military or government) at the same time. In the British government, he fulfilled the roles of Secretary of State for the Colonies; President of the Board of Trade; Home Secretary; First Lord of the Admiralty (twice); Chancellor of the Duchy of Lancaster; Minister of Munitions; Secretary of state for War and Air; Chancellor of the Exchequer; and Prime Minister (twice). He was basically Michael Gove before Michael Gove even existed.

Tanking in WW1

In the history textbooks, all the content on Churchill centres on WW2 but he also went to the frontline in WW1. Before going to the trenches in November 1915, his role in WW1 was the First Lord of the Admiralty. He started well by modernising the navy and establishing the Royal Flying Corps, which is even more impressive when you consider flying itself was only invented in 1903. However, things took a serious downturn with the Gallipoli campaign in February 1915. The idea itself was pretty solid and certainly looked good on paper – he proposed launching a naval attack on the Ottoman Empire with the hope they would be knocked out of the war, and a sea route could then be established from the Mediterranean to Britain's ally, Russia. The first part of the plan was to attack the Gallipoli peninsula and then steer the navy through the thirty-eight-mile Dardanelles strait up to the capital city of Constantinople (now called Istanbul). It started well enough on the morning of 19 February 1915, but then the weather turned, and the Ottomans returned heavier fire than was expected (although… being a war… the enemy giving it all they've got really should have been expected, right?!). Churchill, being the fearless pusher he was, pressured the British naval commander in the region – Admiral Sackville Carden – to such an extent the poor guy suffered a nervous breakdown and had to sack the whole thing off. He was replaced by Vice-Admiral John de Robeck.

They tried again on March 18th, but once again they were held back by mines. Robeck was clearly more robust than Carden – he refused to acquiesce to Churchill's demands to keep pushing and instead he stopped to await the arrival of fresh troops. Unfortunately, this gave the Ottomans plenty of time to re-enforce their defences and move more troops to the area. The Allies tried one more time, on April 25th with a land invasion this time. But it was not a case of third time lucky, and the battle of Gallipoli became a slaughter, with the Allies losing 45,000 men in the first month. By the time they evacuated the last of their men in January 1916, 46,000 Allies had been killed and 204,000 had been injured.[39] While the Ottomans fared similarly badly (65,000 killed and 185,000 wounded), it was definitely a defeat for the Allies as they gained no land for all the blood spilt while the Ottomans managed to hang on to their territory. Churchill, as the orchestrator, was fired by Prime Minister Asquith when he returned to Britain in May 1915. The Gallipoli campaign would hang over him for the rest of his political life, but Churchill refused to see it the way everyone else did (e.g., disaster/military failure/slaughter). When heckled about it in 1923, he said: "Don't imagine I am running away from the Dardanelles. I glory in it." Shame those 46,000 men killed weren't around to bask in his imagined glory. However, Gallipoli did cause Churchill to doubt himself and his future: "I am finished," he remarked to a friend in May 1915. But after six months of wallowing, he came up with a new plan to win favour and glory. Go to the trenches.

The International Churchill Society (ICS) describe Churchill's move to the Western Front as: "…giving up his government post to go out to the horrific battlefields of Flanders…"[40]

Oh, how admirable… get the guy a medal already.

The truth is the government post he so nobly "gave up" to go to the trenches was a job he didn't even want. It was the role of Chancellor of the Duchy of Lancaster which he was demoted to after being sacked as the First Lord of the Admiralty. You see, whilst being a chancellor sounds fancy schmancy, this role was basically requiring Churchill to be a glorified landlord; he had no official duties, no power, and no chance for glory. Of course, he's gonna give that up. Incidentally, he remained the MP for Dundee, meaning that in reality there was no giving up on anything he actually wanted. The whole move to the trenches was just a tactic to gain him likes. And despite his age of 41 (the age limit of conscription), the War Office agreed he could go. One can only assume they had heard about him maybe killing four men.

Churchill arrived in France in November 1915 and spent some time observing trenches and learning from the Grenadier Guards before he was given command of the 6th Battalion, Royal Scots Fusiliers on 5 January 1916. In true Churchill style, he arrived at the frontline with two servants, a bathtub, and a water heater. Unsurprisingly, coming with all this baggage did little to endear him to the troops; they were already not best pleased at being led by some sacked politician. He didn't really like them either and wrote to his wife: "This regiment is pathetic."[41] His first three weeks were spent on team-building exercises, sports, and declaring war on lice. Soon enough, the Scottish regiment warmed to him like a naughty class warm to a lax supply teacher. He didn't bother much with discipline, but if they *were* caught doing something wrong, they quickly figured out all they had to do was say they fought and survived the Battle of Loos (40% of them didn't survive) and Churchill would let them off. To be fair, he did manage to secure them decent food, steel helmets, and what every soldier needs on the frontline – a new football kit.[42] Fun fact: Churchill and Hitler were both in the trenches at the same time only a few miles apart! Churchill served at the front in Flanders from January to June 1916 and during that time, Corporal Adolf Hitler's 16th Bavarian Reserve Regiment served in the Aubers Ridge-Fromelles Salient sector.

So how did Churchill do in the trenches? The ICS say he took "… some active part in beating the Germans" and

"Churchill demonstrated again the courage he'd displayed in those battlefields of the Northwest Frontier and Sudan."[43] But a less biased view on the matter reveals that Churchill played *no* active part in beating the Germans, and the only courage he displayed was foolish courage which endangered his and his men's lives.

Front line duty began when his regiment took over their 1000 yards of front-line territory in Ploegsteert, Belgium on January 27th and they remained here until May 7th. During these four months, no offences were launched here. It's true that they were under constant shellfire (which killed 15 of his 600 men) but there was never the call for him and his men to go "over the top". Once again, Churchill was able to put his name to a war with barely lifting a trigger finger.

The ICS go on to describe his experience in WW1 as: "he certainly experienced the horrors and dangers of the trenches first-hand".[44] Erm… I certainly don't think the experience of an officer could ever be the *full* experience of horrors and dangers available to the soldiers. For a start, while other soldiers and officers had to stay till the bitter end of war (11 November 1918), Churchill was there for a total of six months – two of which he was in training – so it was really only four months on the frontline. None of the six were spent actually fighting. It's true he did have to contend with the "horrors and dangers" of dirt, lice, and rats but considering he had a bathtub and stayed in a house, these negatives weren't even close to what others suffered. A typical soldier's experience saw him witness the death or injury of comrades and/or suffer PTSD' trench foot, syphilis, trench fever, and horrific injuries from shelling or gunfire which usually became infected. In fact, as proof of the horrific conditions, more WW1 British soldiers died from infection than from the wound itself (not everyone had a bathtub to wash themselves in). Interestingly,

Churchill doesn't seem to agree with the 'horrors and dangers' his namesake society ICS claims he experienced. In one letter to his mum from 24 November 1915, he wrote: "I am happy here."[45]

You know, like no WW1 soldier said… ever.

Continuing the theme that Churchill played an active role in WW1, the ICS state: "Churchill came near to death several times."[46] But taking a closer look at what they want you to see as a near-death experience only highlights his upper-class privilege further.

Was he on the front line, rifle in hand?

No.

Was he leading his regiment on an offence?

No.

Was he in no man's land, or in the trench, under artillery fire?

Nope.

He was having breakfast when their dining room got hit.

Was this at least a dining room in the trench system used by the soldiers?

No.

This was an actual dining room in an actual house – a farmhouse behind the lines which Churchill had set himself up in. I guess missing breakfast must have been one of the 'horrors and dangers' Churchill experienced first-hand. To be fair, this level of shelter behind the lines was common; too many officers had died on the front lines in the first years of war and the War Office needed to keep as many alive as possible. It was so out of the way of danger (most of the time) that he was able to spend many of his days blissfully painting or listening to records.

"The Dining room Experience" is the only example given by the ICS to support the idea he came close to death because the other two occasions are even more embarrassing. The first was an artillery strike on his sector which saw him retreat to the safety of an underground cellar, which would be more accurately described as a "nowhere near-death experience". The second was his own fault for accidentally turning his torch on and giving away their position to the Germans. "Put out that bloody light," Churchill shouted before realising that HE was "that bloody light". Churchill came near to death several times because, quite frankly, he went looking for it. Forty times in 125 days to be exact. Basically, one risky walk for every year he had survived so far. Unsurprisingly, the men who had to go with him on these patrols into no man's land were not as up for it as he was. Subtlety and stealth were not Churchill's strengths; one commander brazenly likened him to "a baby elephant… that shouted a lot,"[47] suggesting Churchill was really not up for the tusk ahead.

The ICS present the ending of Churchill's service as if he had no choice but to leave: "When his battalion was amalgamated with another, rendering his command redundant, he returned to London, honour intact." In reality, Churchill was ready to come home just two months into his time at the frontline, as he made clear when he came back to Britain for two weeks leave in March 1916. Luckily for him, his wife and other advisors pointed out how leaving now would make him look like the opportunist he was. And so, he returned to paint another day. It is true that his battalion was amalgamated with another, but Churchill wasn't made redundant. The truth is he chose to not seek another position in command, saying instead he needed "to attend to my Parliamentary & public duties which have become urgent". You know, the parliamentary duties which he happily put on hold (when he got fired from his Admiralty post) to go in search of glory at the frontline. How convenient that these duties became "urgent" just as he tired of trench life.

Honour being intact is a matter of opinion. I would say leading zero offences and being a lax disciplinarian while painting and reading Shakespeare behind the lines leaves little opportunity to gain or lose honour. One thing he should be credited with though is the tank. It was an idea he thought of before going to the front line and one he developed after seeing the muddy conditions, although he nearly didn't invent it at all after losing his plans during a particularly bad night of shelling. Thankfully, after searching high and low, it turned out they were just in his pocket – a fact he must have missed thanks to being brought up on the principle of not putting one's hand in one's own pocket if one can help it. Churchill was officially credited with the creation of the tank on 17 November 1919, by the Royal Commission on Awards to Inventors. They said it was "primarily due to the receptivity, courage, and driving force of the Rt. Hon Winston Spencer-Churchill that the general idea of the use of such an instrument of warfare as the Tank was converted into a practical shape." He was at least honour roll with that one!

Hitler was more democratically elected than Churchill

Churchill led Britain to victory in World War Two. No one is denying that. But the reality is Britain's victory was more down to external factors than Churchill's decisions. And it's not even like people at the time saw him as a great leader; he lost the election immediately after World War Two to Labour leader Atlee who was promising people free healthcare in the form of the NHS. He was known to be a wartime leader but not one for times of peace.

He wasn't even elected prime minister in 1940. Churchill was simply handed the job because no one else was suitable! And why was he suitable? Because the other MPs were united in disliking him and they desperately needed a coalition with a leader everyone agreed upon. Not even King George VI wanted him to be PM due to all of Churchill's meddling trying to allow the king's brother (the ex-King Edward VIII) to remain on the throne after he married Wallis Simpson. King George VI preferred Lord Halifax, but because Halifax was not a member of the House of Commons, Churchill became prime minister because he was the only realistic choice. There was certainly no democratic vote. Fun Fact: Hitler got to his position as chancellor more democratically than Churchill got to his position as prime minister! Hitler won the majority of votes in the two 1932 elections preceding his appointment as chancellor in January 1933 (37% and 33%). Not that this democratic start stopped Hitler from becoming a genocidal dictator, but you can't have everything.

In another coincidental move, both leaders enacted legislation that removed basic freedoms within their first few months of power. Churchill took over on the 10th May, and on the 22nd he strengthened the Emergency Powers (Defence) Act to allow internment *without trial* of anyone deemed to show sympathy to an enemy power. Habeas Corpus (the law in place since 1679 which ensured no one could be imprisoned unlawfully) was suspended, and no appeal was allowed either. This was an obvious dishonour to the values of freedom and justice that Britain stood for. Those targeted were fascists and pacifists (fascists believe in dictatorship and oppression; pacifists believe in peace over war).[48] The justification for this act was "war" – the removal of freedoms, such as speech, was deemed necessary for the safety of Britain. Of course, this clampdown did not extend to Churchill's chums who had called for peace with Germany and/or shown a level of sympathy with the fascist Nazis such as the Dukes of Buccleuch and Westminster and Marquis of Tavistock.[49] While the defence of "necessity in war" is valid because vocal opposition to the British war effort could be damaging to British morale, it is still rather disturbing how Churchill considered pacifists as the same level of threat as fascists. I know who I'd rather have dinner with anyway.

Empire is a State of Mind

Churchill had a helluva lot of help winning WW2 courtesy of the biggest empire history has ever seen. By 1939, the British Empire covered 30% of the world and controlled 25% of the world's population (458 million people out of 2 billion).[50] This gifted the British a relentless supply of men. Even more conveniently, these men/soldiers were already positioned in the far corners of the world, which saved money on paying people's bus fares to the various front lines. The British Empire and commonwealth contributed between 8.5 and 10 million men[51] to Britain's 3 million.[52] Churchill could not have paid any of the Empire army or funded military supplies if it were not for loans from USA and Canada. By the end of the war, a casual £42.5 million was owed to the USA and £11.6 million to Canada.[53] Yes, borrowing money to win a war is a shrewd and necessary move from Churchill, but maybe he could have pushed for a better interest rate because by the time the money was paid back in December 2006 the loan had doubled in size.

Dominions which were not under direct rule, such as New Zealand and Australia, were allowed to declare war on the Axis powers in their own time. Nevertheless, both countries joined with Britain on 3 September 1939. New Zealand contributed 140,000 men and Australia 400,000 for overseas campaigns. But the "all in this together" thing was not a two-way street. Ten months after both countries had gone to war, they were kindly informed by Churchill, in June 1940, that Britain would NOT be helping them should their countries be attacked by the Japanese. They were instead advised to turn to the United States,[54] who, by the way, weren't even in WW2 yet. Great advice.

One of the biggest contributors to the Empire army was India with 2.3 million men, of whom 89,000 lost their lives.[55] But it wasn't like they had a choice in the matter or joined because Churchill was so inspirational – they were forced into the conflict because they were directly ruled by Britain. Churchill was firmly against giving responsibility for the governance of the country to "men of straw".[56] India was not well treated by Churchill during the war, despite their heavy contributions in terms of manpower, munitions, and food resources. Supporters of Churchill may like to draw our attention to the fact he helped maintain British control of northern India in 1897, and so perhaps he should have some credit for ensuring Britain still had India as part of her empire. And yes, he was there for the Malakand campaign, but his contribution was limited to just a couple of months (he wanted to go fight in the Sudan instead) and, in his own words, "I think I hit four men."[57] And I'm fairly sure Britain didn't manage to hold onto India as the result of one guy maybe shooting four men. Without the help of the British Empire, the Polish, the Soviets, and the Americans, Churchill would have lost the war, and we'd likely learning about him as an undemocratic loser who spouted racist claptrap.

Lacking in Dunkirk Spirit

Churchill's first big action in WW2, and possibly his most famous move, was saving the British army from defeat at Dunkirk between 26 May and 3 June 1940. The Germans, thanks to their Blitzkrieg tactics, had moved through Europe quicker than anyone expected, and the British were now cornered on the north-eastern coast of France. I say quicker than expected but if anyone had actually bothered to study the history of WW1, they would have seen this coming as the Germans essentially did the exact same route of invasion through Holland and Belgium… except this time it worked because they had tanks. (Tanks a lot for that, Churchill!)

The first important fact to digest is that Dunkirk was an embarrassing retreat that saw the Germans win the Battle of Dunkirk and conquer most of France. The second critical fact is that Churchill was only successful in this retreat because of a strategic mistake made by Hitler. And the third fact which is left out of the textbooks is that the "Miracle of Dunkirk" led to the British annihilating the French navy. When the question was posed about how Britain could do this to their French ally when they had promised to have their back, the British presumably replied "Allied". The only victory the British can really claim is a propaganda victory because the government managed to dress it up so well and keep the real horrors hidden. Although it must be said, on the surface of it all, it was a success – 198,000 British and 140,000 Belgian and French troops were saved. But the time needed to make these rescues a reality only came about because Hitler made the dumb/fortuitous decision to *not* push on to the beaches and destroy the troops. Hitler's reasoning was, well, quite reasonable actually: "I did not want to humiliate the British with a crushing military defeat, but on the contrary finally bring them to an armistice".[58] He must have führerious when Britain did not respond with peace talks.

In reality, Hitler's decision to not push forwards with the tanks came about due to his lack of foresight. The whole thing unfolded as the German forces were heading towards France from neighbouring Belgium and a "Halt" order was made on

May 23rd by General von Kleist. Kleist took this decision because he believed the tank division should not be too far ahead of the on-foot infantry soldiers. Another general (who understood warfare), cancelled this request and ordered all Panzer tank divisions to close in on Dunkirk from the north. A complaint was made to Hitler and, being no military genius but rather a massive egoist, he took offence to the change and issued his own "Halt" order on May 24th. The Panzers did not start moving again until the morning of May 27th and by this point the perimeter around the beach was secured and the evacuation of troops had begun.[59] Hitler failed to capitalise on the vulnerability of the British and French troops because he was more interested in proving he was the one in charge.

As a result of Churchill and Admiral Ramsay's planning, 338,000 lives were saved, and the film *Dunkirk* does a wonderful job in showing how this was possible. But this is not the whole story. At least 80,000 soldiers were left behind – half French and half British. Some were executed by the Nazis, like the Le Paradis Massacre where 97 British prisoners who had been defending their position in a farmhouse were killed by the SS. Others were made POWs and moved around various camps for the rest of the war. There was no rescue plan for these guys. There were also huge losses of equipment in the hasty retreat: 76,000 tons of ammunition, 64,000 vehicles, 400,000 tons of supplies, and 2,500 guns. While attempts had been made to destroy some of these, most were perfectly useable.[60] Christmas came early for the Germans in 1940. Ultimately though, the rescue at Dunkirk was possible because Hitler's priority was to force France out of the war; he deliberately spared the British.[61] So, however much propaganda is produced to make a hero out of Churchill for this, the truth is we should also (begrudgingly) give Hitler a lot of the credit.

Leaving France to surrender to the Nazis then created another opportunity for Churchill to be a bit of dick. France had the second largest naval fleet in Europe, and since they signed an armistice with Germany on 22 June 1940, their navy could now be taken over by the Germans and used against the British. The British were now, just a few weeks after Dunkirk, enemies of Nazi-occupied France. The French had been given a choice by the British – sail their fleet to UK waters and give it up to them, or sail it and scuttle it elsewhere so the Germans couldn't get at it. Admiral Darlan assured Churchill that should the Germans come close to seizing the French fleet, then he would scuttle them, but Churchill instead decided to destroy the French fleet in a move more commonly known as "F You". And this really was a plan of Churchill's doing; it was opposed by naval officials from the get-go, although when the French repeatedly turned down the British requests to hand over their fleet, this swayed a lot of senior naval officers round to Churchill's way of thinking. The real reason Churchill was so keen to destroy his ally of a week ago was because, according to his secretary Eric Seal, "[Churchill] was convinced that the Americans were impressed by ruthlessness in dealing with a ruthless foe…"[62] Yes, the British really did destroy the French fleet to make Churchill look 'ard.

The executions were given the fun name of Operation Catapult because it really was a stretch of the imagination to see this move as fair. The French navy was based in three different areas in July 1940 – about 40% was in France, near Marseilles; another 40% was in North Africa; and about 20% was split between Britain, Alexandria, and the French West Indies.[63] The fleet near Marseilles was unreachable so that was left out of the equation and the ships docked in British waters could be dealt with later. That only left the issue of the fleet in North Africa where there were two battle cruisers (the *Dunkerque* and the *Strasbourg*) stationed at Mers el-Kebir, Algeria; and two modern battleships, the *Richelieu* in Senegal, and the *Jean Bart* in Morocco. The Dunkirk evacuation was about to become the Dunkerque explosion.

Force H (three battleships, one aircraft carrier, two light cruisers, and eleven destroyers), led by Admiral Sommerville, arrived at Mers el-Kebir at 7am on 3 July 1940. The French were given a final chance to surrender with the choice of sailing to the UK or the French Caribbean or scuttle themselves anywhere out of reach of the Nazis, but French Admiral Gensoul refused all options. The British kicked off proceedings by mining the harbour at 12.30pm but held off their full-scale attack until they could have maximum impact on a larger fleet (which was due to arrive). At 5.54pm they fired on the French who were sitting ducks being unable to turn their ships and return fire in the shallow waters. After just twenty minutes, 1,300 Frenchmen had been killed[64], and the French asked for a ceasefire which the British honoured. Three days later, on July 6th, British aircraft finished off the *Dunkerque* (there were no men on board by that point); and the French ships in British waters were impounded with the French crews imprisoned in British jails. On July 7th, British torpedo bombers destroyed the *Richelieu* and put it out of action for a year while also making the decision to leave the *Jean Bart* alone because it wasn't armed, and stuck in Casablanca port nothing could be done with it anyway. Only the *Strasbourg* was able to get away damage free.

The French refer to Operation Catapult as "our Pearl Harbour"; Churchill supporters meanwhile call it a "turning point" because it hindered Hitler's plans to invade Britain. The ends justified the means, so all good, yeah? But if Churchill had trusted the French to scuttle when the expected pressure from the Germans finally came, then the ends would have still been the same (no French boats for the Nazis) and the means would have been a lot less like a war crime.

He'll Polish off the Nazis easily

The Polish were instrumental in spying on the Germans, and their early work decoding German radio messages[65] helped the Brits crack the infamous Enigma code of the Nazis. On 25 July 1939, the Poles shared with Britain and France their work in cracking the Enigma code. This enabled the codebreakers at Bletchley Park, at an early stage in the war, to provide Churchill with the "Ultra" decrypts which undoubtedly helped the Allies' war effort and hasten the end of the war. It was also due to Polish pilots that Britain was able to hold off the German air invasion known as the Battle of Britain. In fact, while the Battle of Britain is credited to the RAF, the fighting force was made up of pilots from 15 other nations; British pilots only made up a third of the total force. So it should really be known as the "Battle on behalf of Britain".

After France fell to the Nazis in June 1940, 8,500 Polish pilots came over to Britain, where the Polish PM was staying in exile. Churchill recognised the value of having extra men, and two Polish fighter wings were established to fight with the RAF: No. 302 Poznan Squadron and No. 303 Kosciuszko Squadron. Churchill reassured the Polish PM that they would conquer together or die together, but he failed to mention they would not be credited together. British Fighter Command was shamefully taken in by German propaganda that the Polish air force was not up to much; after all, Poland had fallen in just three days. Sticking with the idea that Hitler tells the truth, Polish pilots were not deemed operational and upon arrival were tasked with training exercises such as riding tricycles around airfields in practice formations. Polish requests to "give them a brake" fell on deaf ears.

The Battle of Britain began on 10 July 1940, and lasted until 31 October, but the Poles weren't allowed up in the skies until 1 September. It wouldn't even have been this early if it were not for the disobedience of one Polish pilot (Paszkiewicz) who broke ranks from a training formation (planes, not tricycles, by this point) and successfully took down a German aircraft. In total, 145 Polish Pilots fought in the Battle of Britain and they were split into three groups with 79 flighting with RAF squadrons, 32 in the 302 squadron, and 34 in the 303.[66] The two Polish squadrons went on to have great success, with 66 men (4% of the total) downing 10% of the total number of Luftwaffe planes destroyed in the battle. A fact that is even more impressive considering they were only in action for half of the battle. The 303 Squadron achieved three times more kills than the average British fighter squadron with only one-third the casualty rate.[67] Commander-in-Chief of Fighter Command, Sir Hugh Dowding, who once was so reluctant to allow Polish pilots into battle, summarised their contribution in probably the most telling way: "Had it not been for the magnificent work of the Polish squadrons and their unsurpassed gallantry, I hesitate to say that the outcome of battle would have been the same."[68]

Churchill's way of saying thank you to the Poles was to sign a treaty with Stalin at the Yalta conference (February 1945) which made Poland a satellite communist country of the USSR and all those who had fought with Britain to be punished as traitors should they return home. They weren't exactly welcome in Britain either what with the high competition for few jobs once the war was over, combined with the lack of public awareness of the Poles' contributions to Allied victory in WW2.

The ICS downplay this move by claiming: "The reality was that Poland's fate had been sealed by the fact that the Soviet Red Army… there was nothing that could be done to save our gallant Polish allies."[69] *Nothing*… hmmm… I disagree because even when given the opportunity to publicly recognise their contribution, Churchill looked the other way and did not allow Polish troops to participate in the Allied Victory Parade. His official reason was to avoid aggravating Stalin, which is utter poppycock. If aggravating Stalin was *such* a concern, then surely he wouldn't have kept the development and planned use of the atomic bomb a secret from his ally. A move which 100% aggravated Stalin and ended up leading to the forty-five-year-long Cold War. But publicly thanking the Poles would have been much worse, yeah?

Did Churchill cause a famine?

In Britain, the Bengal famine is a neglected part of history because it doesn't support the heroic storyline of Churchill. During World War Two, in 1943, a famine ravaged the Bengal region of India and at least three million[70] people died. Those who defend Churchill cite the causes of the famine as: the Japanese invasion of Burma in WW2; population booms in India (251,167 million in 1911 to 317,042 million by 1941);[71] the Midnapur cyclone; price increases (the official rice price per mound rose from 12 Rupees in February 1943 to 32 Rupees by July);[72] and Indian mis-governance. Churchill meanwhile blamed the Indians: "It's their fault for breeding like rabbits" he said in a war cabinet meeting.[73] Ultimately, there is no single solitary cause of the famine[74] but Churchill needs to be included in the list because his actions caused the famine to be more deadly than it should have been.

It is likely that the Japanese takeover of Burma in January – May 1942 was the most influential cause of the Bengal famine. This had a negative impact on the Bengal region of India because Burma supplied 60%[75] of their rice. But now they didn't. Also, very important was the devastating Midnapur cyclone which hit the Bengal region in October 1942. The cyclone killed thousands of people and destroyed the rice crops up to 40 miles inland.[76] Because the crops were destroyed, people then ate the rice which should have been planted for the following year. A report from 1944 stated the cyclone led to a two-million-tonne rice deficit[77] – around 10% of the rice needed to feed India. However, this was not enough to cause a famine alone.[78] The cyclone definitely reduced the amount of food available and indirectly caused the price of food to go up, but it did not play as decisive a role as Churchill.

Churchill's policies made the famine worse. The actions Churchill took in 1943, such as his scorched earth policy; his diversion of food-carrying ships; and sluggish moves towards providing inadequate relief, caused millions of deaths. It's worth knowing that in India, it *is* Churchill who is blamed for the famine. Indian politician Shashi Tharoor explains why he won't be winning any Indian polls for being a great leader: "This is the man who the British insist on hailing as some apostle of freedom and democracy, when to my mind he is really one of the more evil rulers of the 20th century, only fit to stand in the company of the likes of Hitler, Mao and Stalin".[79] Ouch.

So, what did he do? Well, at the start of 1943 he started with a bit of scorched earth policy which meant burning fields of crops in the Bengal region as well as destroying all viable land that could be farmed in the future. A secondary aspect of his scorched earth policy was to get the police to destroy local fisherman's boats.[80] This meant many people's livelihoods and an alternative way of getting food (other than the fields of crops) was cut off. Churchill's reasoning was that if Japan invaded, they would be left with nothing of value. Rather like the whole Machiavellian approach to the French fleet in 1940, Churchill felt that the ends would justify the means. Problem was, the "means" resulted in the Bengal people being the ones left with nothing of value, an impact which he either didn't think about or chose to ignore. Churchill's policy made the famine worse. A fact which has since been confirmed by the Nobel Prize-winning economist Amartya Sen who stated that the policies of the British were to blame for millions of deaths.[81]

So, what could be done at this stage? The burning had happened, and India, as part of the great and glorious British Empire, should surely be entitled to some relief at this point.

Nope.

Instead, Churchill diverted ships with food supplies *away* from India and declined foreign aid from other countries which could have saved millions of lives. He and his war cabinet ordered Australian ships to go directly to Europe to store 170,000 tons of wheat there. Yes, that's right, STORE. This food wasn't even needed in Europe at this time. The idea was that it would be stockpiled for European civilians after they had been liberated.[82] Possible European lives in the future were prioritised over starving Indians in the present. A decision likely made due to his prejudice: "I hate Indians. They are a beastly people with a beastly religion"[83] (stated to Secretary of State for India, Leopold Amery, in the midst of the famine in summer 1943). Prejudice which didn't go unnoticed at the time as Wavell, the Viceroy of India, agreed that Churchill put Indian lives at the bottom of the priority list.[84]

Meanwhile, the Bengalese were pleading with the British for food, firstly requesting 1.5 million tonnes of wheat before trying their luck with a lower 0.5 million tonnes. Both requests were declined by the war cabinet.[85] Clearly in the mood for declining things – Churchill also rejected help offered by Canada, Australia, and America. Canada offered 100,000 tonnes of wheat[86] but Churchill didn't think Indian lives were worth the effort of committing so many vessels to carry this 100,000 tonnes of life-saving food. I mean, obviously, we can see that diverting that original ship with 170,000 tonnes would have just been the simplest and most effective way to help people without the need to "find" ships. But it is hard to see solutions when your vision is clouded with prejudice.

If you thought it couldn't get much worse than preventing available food getting through then you're in for a shock because Churchill also forced the Bengal region to export 70,000 tonnes of wheat. Unbelievably, just months after the cyclone destroyed rice fields and in the midst of a food crisis, Churchill took their food away like a big fat bully at lunchtime. This action caused up to 400,000 deaths. Or, as a Churchill supporter cleverly phrased it (to look less like murder), "preventing the potential survival of 400,000 people for a year".[87]

In 1944, Churchill did (finally) allow some relief for the Indians. He agreed that America could help, and 350,000 tonnes of wheat were sent as well as some barley from Iraq (which he was most displeased to hear that the Indians did not want to eat).[88] But let's put this into perspective, one year into the famine and following various actions which have made the situation worse, he agrees to let 2/3 of the lowest requested amount find its way to India. How generous.

Don't let the Churchill supporters fool you into thinking this famine was inevitable. While it is true that food shortages had been an issue in India since 1941, these shortages were mostly due to the fact Burma had been taken over by the Japanese – shortages were not normally a common feature. Bengal is a fertile place and, until the British got involved, the region accounted for 12% of the world's economy and had better living conditions and wages than most of Europe.[89] Two hundred years of Britain siphoning off the money and forcing the region to de-industrialise saw Bengal forced to rely on agriculture – putting them in a precarious position. But still, India had done well up until WW2 avoiding famines, ironically enough thanks to the British and their installation of railways. According to the *Imperial Gazetteer of India*: "Railways have revolutionised relief. The final horror of famine, the absolute dearth of food, is not known".[90] But India had not bargained for the malevolent attitude of Churchill. And if further proof were needed that this famine was not natural or inevitable, the official cause of the famine has now been decided in the 21st century as "conflict". [91] Although it would probably be more accurate to label it as "Churchill".

It is the argument of "conflict" that Churchill supporters use to defend his murderous policy. "It was a horrendous event, but it needs to be seen within the context of global war... there are always going to be conflicting priorities and demands. It's an incredibly complex and evolving situation – and he's not always going to get everything right."[92] Well, Packwood is right on that last bit at least; he certainly did *not* get this right. Or even close to it. But that's still not a good justification because Churchill was given plenty of advice at the time on how he could have "got it right". Advice which he ignored. As for the idea this famine should be seen in the context of global war, well that's just about the worst excuse I've ever heard. Should we just see the Armenian genocide in the context of WW1? Should the Holocaust be relegated to the side-line because that's in the context of a global war? It is true there are conflicting priorities in war but keeping your people alive shouldn't be a conflicting choice, it should be an obvious one. The only conflict was Churchill giving a rat's arse about people who weren't white.

Others who are less biased than Packwood see it more as a: "failure of prioritisation. It's true that Britain's resources were stretched, but that's no excuse given the relatively small effort it would have taken to alleviate the problem".[93] Ultimately Churchill did not want to make this small effort because he thought providing food to India was unjustifiable. India was on the brink of becoming independent from Britain while losing millions of pounds a day in debt;[94] Churchill feared he would never see a return on this "investment", so why invest more?

One outrageous idea put forwards by Churchill's official biographer, Martin Gilbert, is that without Churchill the famine would have been worse.[95] Apparently, once he was fully aware of the famine's extent, "Churchill and his cabinet sought every way to alleviate the suffering without undermining the war effort".[96] The cabinet part may be true enough – British officials *did* beg Churchill to direct food supplies to the region. But *he* bluntly refused while raging it was their own fault for "breeding like rabbits" and praising how it was "merrily" culling the population.[97] His government could not get him to take the issue seriously[98] because Churchill saw the famine as nothing more than a distraction from winning the war. It is also argued that Churchill was unaware of the full impact of famine on the Indian people, but numerous letters and meeting records prove the opposite. [99] In his defence, it certainly didn't help matters that Churchill's man on the ground in India – Cherwell – had told Churchill that aid would have minimal impact.[100] Nevertheless, Churchill has gone against advice before and so this alone is not a good enough excuse for his inaction.

British school history textbooks do not include the Bengal famine in their coverage of WW2. And you can't even argue that this was because it was an indirect consequence of war and so maybe isn't relevant because they're happy enough to go to town on the Soviets and the famines suffered by their civilians during WW2. That story fits the accepted party line of

Communism = bad and Capitalism = good. But even when an effort is made to educate young people about what happened, the language used cleverly masks Churchill's responsibility. For example, on the *CBBC Newsround* website they state: "He is accused of not doing enough to prevent during a famine in the region of Bengal, in southeast Asia in which millions of people are thought to have died… some experts say his focus was on fighting the war in Europe and that when he became aware of the true seriousness what was happening, he ordered grain to be sent there."[101]

Firstly, the word *accused* implies wrongful responsibility, and even we accept that word, it is completely wrong to say "not doing enough to prevent it" considering he helped make it worse than it would have been. That's like saying Hitler didn't do enough to prevent anti-Semitism. Secondly, millions are not *thought* to have died, they *did* die. At least three million, with some Indian sources putting the figure as high as 7.5 million.[102] And thirdly, Churchill did not order grain to be sent there when he became aware of the seriousness. *Other* people in his government made that request whereas Churchill's reaction upon "becoming aware of the true seriousness" was to ask: "Why hasn't Gandhi died yet?"[103] (Gandhi was the one heading up the Indian Independence movement). While Churchill did eventually allow other countries to supply the much-needed grain – this is not the same thing as ordering it to be sent there.

Churchill's policies, influenced by his racism towards Indians, caused the deaths of at least three million people. Slow, agonizing deaths from starvation which could have been prevented if Churchill had been less imperialist and more humane. His own defence from March 1943 is like that which a mother gives when explaining why one child can't have a sweet; "if a concession is made to one country, others will also make demands".[104] Which makes no sense considering no other part of the British Empire was suffering a famine – therefore there were no other demands to expect. And so what if there were? He could have just said "no" like he did to India anyway. Even more ridiculous than this sentence about concessions is the statement which followed: "they must look after themselves as we have done." [105] What… Britain? The country which imported twice as much as it exported in the 1930s?[106] Yeah, that's really looking after ourselves, isn't it?

Churchill's policies of scorched earth and diverting food supplies made the famine a lot worse than it should have been. His lack of action during the entirety of 1943 then made it akin to murder. Ultimately, prioritising finances over people's lives is dark. In some people's eyes, this event is a genocide due to the combination of deliberate policy and deliberate prejudice. While this may be a step too far, it's certainly a lot closer to the truth than those who claim the famine would have been worse if it were not for Churchill. Don't let his victory in WW2 cloud the truth of what really went on in India in 1943–44.

Whitewashing the past

Was Churchill racist? Seems likely, yes.

This debate really heated up in 2020 in line with the Black Lives Matter campaign. Churchill's statue was graffitied and defaced twice in one week in June 2020, and this wasn't the first time. In 2000, red paint was sprayed on his face to look like blood dripping from his mouth and in 2007, red paint was thrown onto the feet of his statue. I'm sensing a bloody theme here…

The accusations of racism are not new either. In April 2014, Labour candidate Benjamin Whittington tweeted that

Churchill was "a racist and white supremacist".[107] Rather than start a discussion that looked fairly at the statement, he was criticised for being "ignorant" by Churchill's grandson Nicholas Soames and the Conservative politician Ben Wallace. The tweet had to be deleted (no room for freedom of speech when it comes to Churchill), and the Labour Party said: "[It] does not represent the view of the Labour Party. He apologises unreservedly if it has caused any offence."

Unlike Churchill or his family, who have never apologised unreservedly for causing offence. Which is not beyond the realm of possibility considering in December 2020 we saw Roald Dahl's family apologise for an anti-Semitic statement the much-lauded children's writer made in 1983. And while the Bank of England were happy enough to ignore every single racist statement Churchill ever made in favour of whacking his face on a fiver in 2018, the Royal Mint refused to issue a commemorative coin for Roald Dahl due to his anti-Semitism.[108] Money talks, and the conversation is clearly pro-Churchill.

So what evidence is there of Churchill's racism? Is there enough to definitively label him a racist? A racist, according to the *Cambridge English Dictionary* is: "coming from or having the belief that people who belong to other races are not as good, intelligent, moral, etc. as people who belong to your own race."[109]

Churchill personified the dictionary definition in 1937 when he said to the Peel Commission (a British panel investigating the causes of unrest in Palestine): "I do not admit for instance, that a great wrong has been done to the Red Indians of America or the black people of Australia... by the fact that a stronger race, a higher-grade race, a more worldly-wise race to put it that way, has come in and taken their place."[110] So yeah, according to Churchill, the policy of removing the natives from their land is not *a bad thing* because the white people who replaced them were better. This quote could literally be used as an exemplar in the dictionary. His belief that Indians were inferior is also clear from statements such as he hated people with "slit eyes and pig tails".[111] To him, people from India were "the beastliest people in the world next to the Germans".[112] And if neither of those statements was quite convincing enough about his belief in white superiority, then perhaps his faith that "the Aryan stock is bound to triumph"[113] should swing it for you. This shocker was made during a speech at the University of Michigan in 1902, and while it may seem rather Hitler-esque, Churchill was championing the Aryan race while Hitler was still a fourteen-year-old boy dreaming of being an artist.

In his defence, Toye says: "Although Churchill did think that white people were superior, that didn't mean he necessarily thought it was OK to treat non-white people in an inhumane way."[114] Yes, fair enough. But even he doesn't sound that convinced with his phrasing "necessarily". Clearer still is a statement Churchill made to the cabinet in January 1955 where he suggested they "Keep England White"[115] when pushed to accept immigration from the British Caribbean islands.

The dictionary goes on to provide further clarification: "… Relating to policies, behaviours, rules, etc. that result in a continued unfair advantage to some people and unfair or harmful treatment of others based on race."

Yep, tick. His policies in the Bengal famine nicely covers this.

Some people still strongly defend Churchill with the notion "well, everybody thought that way back then". But you don't hear that touted as an excuse for Hitler even though lots of people were anti-Semitic in the 1930s and 40s. Yes, it's undeniable that Hitler's crimes towards non-whites were on another level to Churchill's, but we shouldn't dismiss

Churchill's views as an anachronistic misunderstanding just because we like him. In truth, his thoughts and comments *were* seen as racist at the time and thus should be still viewed like this today. In his lifetime, Churchill was seen as at the "most brutish end of the British imperialist spectrum" [116], and Prime Minister Stanley Baldwin was warned by cabinet colleagues not to appoint him because his views were so outdated. Even Churchill's own doctor, Lord Moran, had heard enough racist vitriol during his check-ups to be able to chime in with: "Winston thinks only of the colour of their skin."[117]

Other people may defend Churchill by saying that the chosen quotes have been taken out of context, or he didn't really mean it in the way it sounds. Richard Langworth, whose bias may be gleaned from his authorship for The Churchill Society; The Churchill Project; and a few books dedicated to promoting the Churchill myth, believes that suggesting Churchill is racist shows "ignorance".[118] He thinks clinging onto a few things Churchill has said is *not* good enough evidence to convict him. Interestingly, he then clings onto a few things Churchill has said to evidence the idea he wasn't racist. Funny how that argument is good enough to disprove the critics but not applicable to *his* choice of quotes.

In his article "Was Churchill a White Supremacist?" Langworth states: "Those who call Churchill a racist will have to explain to me why he harangued his Boer captors in 1899 defending equal rights for native Africans."[119]

OK, Richard, well, I think I can explain that one with the fact the Boers were Churchill's opposition in the war and therefore the "Common Enemy" theory comes into play. The only reason he is saying "black is to be proclaimed same as white" is because that goes against what the *Boers* believe. Churchill is able to put aside any level of difference in order to defeat a common enemy – just look at his alliance with communist Stalin in WW2. And if he is as passionate about black equality in South Africa as Langworth likes to make out then why, seven years later, did he argue for a Peace Treaty which would allow self-rule for Afrikaners but exclude black Africans from the vote?[120]

Rather than acknowledge this racist treaty of 1906, Langworth clutches onto some other straws. This time choosing a fleeting moment when Gandhi praised Churchill to prove Churchill isn't racist (no, I'm not sure how this proves a lack of racism either). And because this clearly wasn't good enough evidence, Langworth then points out that Gandhi, too, was not fair to black Africans. (I guess the idea here is someone else's racism is proof of another person's lack thereof?!) Continuing the Gandhi theme, Langworth chooses a quote where Churchill praises Gandhi: "Why in 1935… did he (Churchill) say, "Mr. Gandhi has gone very high in my esteem since he stood up for the Untouchables"?" This time I think we're meant to believe that a bit of praise for a non-white person is proof Churchill isn't racist. You know, like the people who claim they're not racist because they have a black friend.

Langworth then postures: "Why in 1943 did he say this to India's representative on the War Cabinet? 'The old idea that the Indian was in any way inferior to the white man must go. We must all be pals together.'" Well, the reason *why* this time is because Churchill wants the Indian Independence movement to calm the hell down while WW2 rages. "Pals together" was useful for him in 1943. And let's not forget that this "pals together" moment came during the Bengal famine – clearly Churchill didn't think they were pally enough to save their lives.

If Langworth is happy to use a few quotes to defend Churchill, then he should accept the same method for the opposing argument instead of childishly labelling those who question him as "ignorant". In truth, all quotes are taken "out of context". We weren't there, and so all we have are the recorded words from the people of the past. If we were to go down the route of scrapping all quotes through fear the person "didn't really mean it that way", then what are we left with to judge them on, their actions, right? Well, luckily for us we also have plenty of actions and policies which back up his racist quotes. His scorched earth policy and diversion of grain from Bengal India to benefit whites over non-whites. His refusal to grant Indian Independence so that whites could remain dominant. His refusal to allow more Jewish immigrants into Britain because he prioritised the feelings of whites over the deaths of Jews. His refusal, in the 1950s, to allow immigrants from the British Caribbean islands into Britain (despite the fact Britain had been the one to force their ancestors there during the slavery era) in order to keep Britain white. The conclusion of racist, at least to some extent, seems the white one to come to.

Ultimately, there is proof Churchill was seen as racist by his contemporaries. That he favoured Aryans over all others. That he disregarded native lives, Indian lives, and black lives, in favour of whites. We know that he is currently viewed as racist by billions of people around the world. We have seen that his actions and his words fit the dictionary definition of a racist to a tee. Any defence of him can be neatly overruled by delving deeper into his real motivations for that fleeting non-racist moment.

It is dangerous to overlook a person's flaws in favour of their successes, that is to ignore history. Even Boris Johnson, aka Churchill's number one fan, doesn't go that far. Boris' statement on the issue, against the backdrop of Churchill's statue being vandalised, may have been the only sensible thing he said in 2020: "We cannot now try to edit or censor our past.

We cannot pretend to have a different history."[121] And he's right. It's no good trying to ignore the racism and only remember the victories. No one is completely good or completely bad and this is how we now need to view Churchill. Admitting he was a racist does not cancel out his other achievements. But it does allow us to see him more accurately without the rose-tinted nationalism that Britain is renowned for. Whitewashing the past like this is exactly what Churchill would have wanted.

The Rise of Homophobia

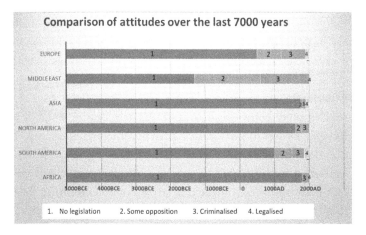

*Figure 1: Graph detailing attitudes towards homosexuals
by charting the existence of legislation against it.*

Men have been having sex with men since the beginning of
time.[122] Before the invention of writing, homosexuality was
recorded in cave wall paintings such as those of the San people
in Zimbabwe[123] with some examples dating as far back as
8000 years. Proving not only the long-term existence of male-
male sex but also the fact that the urge to draw penises is not
the sole remit of 21st-century schoolboys. Homosexuality has
occurred in all nations, in all social strata, and in all eras of
human history[124] despite the fact the word *homosexual* did not
appear until the 19th century.

Homophobia has not existed as long as homosexuality. Surprisingly, it is more difficult to be homosexual in the modern world than at any other time. Humans have populated earth for around 200,000 years; they existed for 195,800 of these years without any laws at all and 196,700 years without homophobic legislation. The amount of time the world has been homophobic, at the same moment, accounts for only 0.15% of human existence. Humanity has gone backwards on this issue, a reversal beginning in 1300 BCE, but not really catching on until 1300 CE. But this process did not happen everywhere. Twenty-two countries and ten territories around the world have never legislated against it.[125] Thirteen of the twenty-two are in Africa, eight are in Asia (including the much-feared North Korea), and the last one is Poland in Europe. However, just because they never legislated against it, this doesn't mean gay rights exist. It may be the case that legislation is not needed because it is already socially accepted that homosexuality is forbidden while in other countries there may not be legislation AGAINST it but there is also no legislation FOR it – like the right to marry or hate crime laws to stop discrimination.

There is less evidence of homophobia against lesbians than that recorded against gay men. Unfortunately, this is not for any moral reason but instead because most people didn't believe lesbianism existed. A bit like the clitoris which was not "discovered" until the 17th century[126]… though I'm pretty sure half the population knew about it already. The plus side of this ignorance and casual sexism was that lesbians were low priority when it came to prosecution by the law. The downside is they have been largely ignored in historical records and so our understanding of their lives is very limited (it's called *his*tory for a reason). There is, however, evidence from the South African Basotho culture between the years 500 and

1914, which proves women were able to form a socially accepted relationship, with or without sex, which was called *motsoalle* (special friend).[127] And there is also circumstantial archaeological evidence of lesbianism with "sex aids" found all over the world – some dating as far back as 30,000 years.[128] And although we don't know for sure the purpose of these 6-inch tools, the fact they were made from smooth and precious materials such as the 1000-year-old Jade dildos from Japan,[129] and women chose to be buried with them (like a lover) strongly suggests they had a sexual purpose. However weird they were back in time, it's highly unlikely women would choose to be buried with some random kitchen utensil.

When was homophobic legislation introduced and what was it like to be homosexual before this?

The Assyrians (2500 BCE – 609 BCE) were the first people to make laws regulating sex 4200 years ago, and their *Code of Ur-Nammu*, (2200 BCE) is the oldest documented law code in the world.[130] They had many laws concerning heterosexual sex, but the first lawmakers did not criminalise same-gender sex. Female virginity was prized by all ancient civilisations (bar the Egyptians who preferred their virgin daughters to be enjoyed by everyone); so, while there were laws that allowed a father to sue the rapist of his virgin daughter for three times the value of her hand in marriage, there were no Egyptian laws against male-male sex.

The first ever laws against homosexuals came from the Hebrews in 1200 BCE, but widespread homophobic legislation did not really begin in the Middle East until the 9th century CE. In Europe, the Romans were the first to legislate against homosexual sex in 342 CE, but this did not have a huge impact considering the Roman Empire crumbled just 100 or so years later. Europe did not make homosexuality a state crime again until the 16th century, at which point they also exported the prejudice to South America. North America made sodomy a crime in 1792 and most African countries followed suit in the nineteenth century due to the influence of imperialism. The last continent to embrace homophobia was Asia which turned against its homosexual citizens in the 20th century. Up until these points in time, the experience of homosexuals varied from open acceptance (China and Ancient Egypt) to acceptance with restrictions (Ancient Greece, Ancient Rome, and Japan) to acceptance but only if it was practised within clearly defined roles (Native American and African tribes). Only a few civilisations, such as the Aztecs and Mayans of central and southern America, promoted homophobia before the arrival of secular law (laws made by government).

Rather ironically, considering its current stance on homosexuality, China has been the best place to be gay throughout most of history. China is one of the oldest civilisations in the world[131] , and for most of its 5000-year history bisexuality has been seen as the norm.[132] Ancient Chinese literature is littered with references to same-gender sex. Chinese Children grew up hearing the story of *The Yellow Emperor* (2712–2599 BCE), who is credited with being the first to have a male bedmate while also being married to a woman. While historians point to the fact that this guy is more likely to be a mythical character than a real man (he did live to be 113 after all), the attitude of acceptance is clear. I mean, there was no tale of Goldilocks rocking up to a house with two daddy bears for us growing up, was there?

The earliest records of same-sex relations in China come from the Shang dynasty (1600 BCE–1001 BCE).[133] Many early Chinese emperors had homosexual relationships alongside heterosexual ones; for example, in the western Han region between 206 BCE and 8 CE, ten out of the eleven emperors had at least one male lover.[134] They had some great names for it too, for example, "allied brothers"; "the male trend"; "the southern custom"; and "sharing the remaining peach" (the last of which has possibly inspired the emoji used to represent a bum in the modern day). Official Chinese historical records show that between 770 BCE, and 24 CE, male homosexuality was considered neither a crime nor immoral behaviour.[135] In fact, homosexual relationships were so common, Chinese women became rather pissed off, as suggested in this 5th century CE source; "All the gentlemen and officials esteemed it. All men in the realm followed this fashion to the extent that husbands and wives were estranged. Resentful unmarried women became jealous."[136]

China has a long history of male homosexuality and the same is true for females. This is evident during the Han dynasty between 200 BCE and 200 CE because it is during this period (but probably not during theirs) that one of the first mentions of female homosexuality appears – called *duishi* (對食). During the Han dynasty, Imperial Palace women were forming homosexual relationships and acting like a married couple – hopefully the honeymoon phase rather than bitter-end phase. Archaeologists exploring tombs in China from the Han dynasty also discovered several bronze dildos. The Hans believed their afterlife would continue in the tomb and it's good to see that these women were planning to have a jolly clear time.

Some opposition to homosexuality in China began in the medieval era during the Tang Dynasty (618–906 CE) due to the influence of neighbouring states' adoption of Christianity or Islam.[137] After 1000 CE, exclusive homosexuality was not openly tolerated and faced some opposition.[138] This opposition is evident in medieval literature which, while still having homosexual protagonists, now saw the main characters being caught and punished for their actions like in the story: *Yi-Chun Xiang-Zhi* (Pleasant Spring and Fragrant Character).[139] But unlike in Europe, high-profile persecutions of Chinese homosexuals did not occur[140] , and any literature suggesting homosexuality should be punished was counterbalanced with a proliferation of nonfiction and fiction books about homosexuality that were published between 1368 and 1911.[141] During these Ming and Qing dynastic eras there were also an enormous number of paintings which strongly suggested homosexual behaviours were taking place unpunished. One such painting from the late Qing period, which depicts a young male actor and a male scholar explicitly making love, even has the added dimension of promoting literacy as one of the pair is also casually reading during the event.

Even after 1740, when voluntary homosexual intercourse between adults was made illegal in China (but involuntary isn't… so you can slip into it?!), the punishment prescribed was the lightest available. If caught, you could go to prison for one month and receive 100 hits with heavy bamboo, which certainly isn't pleasant but at least you didn't lose your tackle like some European laws recommended.

The second oldest civilisation in the world, the ancient Egyptians (from 3100 BCE until the death of Cleopatra in 30 BCE), had zero qualms with homosexuals. To be brutally honest, it is hard to find qualms about anything sexual from the ancient Egyptians. Fornicating with a goat was seen as a divine act;[142] it was common for Egyptian women to marry their brothers or fathers;[143] and girls who had not yet entered puberty were offered up as prostitutes in the temple of Zeus.[144] Considering incest, bestiality, and paedophilia were all a normal part of Egyptian life, it's no surprise that male-male sex existed without condemnation. The only thing the ancient Egyptians did find heinous was a husband being mugged off by his wife. As such, the crime of female adultery brought various options of retribution for the cheating woman, ranging from having her nose cut off to being chopped up and fed to the dogs.[145]

Funnily enough, homosexuality in ancient Egypt is a real shocker for modern Egyptians. Zahi Hawass (a famous archaeologist who discovered the Tombs of the Pyramid Builders and the Valley of the Golden Mummies) claimed that the ancient Egyptians denounced homosexuality. Hawass bases his claim on a papyrus which tells the story of King Pepi I secretly leaving his home to "drop in" and have sex with an army commander. Rather than point out this story proves homosexual relationships existed, Hawass believes the sheer *existence* of the story is proof of denouncement; "The ancient Egyptians were dissatisfied with the King's action, so they repeated the story twice, to raise people's awareness and warn them of such an inappropriate action."[146] And with homosexuality being illegal in Egypt since the year 2000 and penalised with fines, deportation, and up to 170 years hard labour,[147] it's no surprise to see a respected Egyptian archaeologist saying such things.

Another fact conveniently ignored by Hawass and modern Egyptians is that ancient Egypt gave us the first recorded homosexual couple in history[148] – Niankhkhnum and Khnumhotep (2494 to 2345 BCE). Their tomb was discovered in 1964 with the two men having been buried embracing each other with their noses touching. This was an unusual pose for any Egyptian couple, let alone a male-male pairing. They also had their names intertwined above the entrance to the inner chambers of the tomb and an inscription which can be translated as "joined in life and joined in death". Engravings in the tomb also identified both men as *hm*, (a gender-neutral pronoun… not the engraver thinking aloud), and there were paintings across the walls of the tomb showing the two men holding hands, sitting arm in arm, and embracing. But they were just friends, right, Hawass?

The fact that the Hebrews were so quick to rule against homosexuals to be different to the ancient Egyptians also attests to the idea homosexuality was common in the land of the Pharaohs. As does the evidence found in rock carvings, in tombs, and in literature such as the stories of Egyptian gods. For example, *The Contending's of Horus and Seth* describes homosexual sex erstwhile revealing it was important who the dominant one was in ancient Egyptian homosexual relations. While not a story for before the watershed, it's quite the thriller with the involvement of Horus' mother and a humble garden lettuce in the sex act – and so the suggestion of acknowledged homosexuality and lack of condemnation in ancient Egypt romaines (in honour of the lettuce, I guess).

Ancient Greece (circa 700 BCE-146 BCE) had homosexual relations out in the open in various groups in society. Considering how long it took modern armies to officially allow homosexuals in their ranks (the year 2000 in UK and 2011 in USA), perhaps the most surprising place to find them in ancient Greece was the military. While the Americans pursued a policy of "don't ask, don't tell" as recently as the 1990s, conversely in the Greek military, male-male affection was prized.[149] The army of Thebes went so far as to set up a specifically gay unit consisting of 150 pairs of lovers in 378 BCE. And they were amazing – remaining undefeated for 40 years until they encountered Philip and Alexander the Great in 338 BCE, (he wasn't called *Great* for nothing). But such was the level of respect given to male-male relations at the time, even their victorious opponents were impressed. Philip said (after he had killed everyone) "perish any man who suspects that these men either did or suffered anything that was base."[150] He really did Phil the love. Perhaps Philip's opinion wouldn't have been quite so accommodating had he lost… but the fact he said this, and it was then recorded in the annals of history, suggests an absence of homophobia in ancient Greece.

In addition to the original G-Unit, a lack of homophobia is clear from tales of Trojan warriors. Trojan war hero Achilles and younger warrior Patroclus openly loved each other, and this relationship was admired by many at the time. Another tale recounts how when the king's fiancée Lavinia is attracted to the Trojan warrior Aeneas (pronounced *Anus*… I mean, the signs were there), she is warned by her mother that "all Trojans are averse to women".[151] Advice to stay faithful to her fiancée might have been more prudent, but there you go.

Nevertheless, there were some caveats to ancient Greek homosexuality. Outside of the military, male-male sex was only acceptable if there was an appropriate difference in age and social status between the pair. The idea of a relationship was not taken up in ancient Greek society because it wasn't practical in terms of reproduction, and you could be punished if you took the "wrong" male to be your partner. The older man was meant to be the dominant one while the younger man represented a female, and you *definitely* didn't give in order to receive. This caveat did not reduce the popularity of homosexuality and in fact led many Greek communities to include male-male sex as part of their education. In Crete, for example, young boys went to the countryside for "manly" training. An integral part of the training to become 'A Real Man' was to have sexual relations with their (older) tutor. They were so serious about this that if the teacher did not please the student sexually, the student could fire him![152] A similar method of education existed in Sparta where boys were sent to elders at age 12, and penalties were incurred if the elder refused, or performed their sexual duties badly. The elders were often over the age of 40 as the Greeks believed men were less sexual by then and therefore would focus more on the teaching than their own pleasure.

This attitude of acceptance, when pairing old with young, went beyond the classroom. Influential older men such as the politician Aeschines, and philosopher Socrates, openly sought attractive young boys as sexual partners and described how they went to the gym to find them because they couldn't weight to get involved.[153] If you couldn't find yourself a willing young man to be your partner, then there were plenty of male prostitutes in Greece known as *pornai* (just be careful typing the first half of that word into Google). Happily, for the married and single men of Greece, there was no shame or punishment for using *pornai* and they were such an ingrained part of society they even paid taxes on their earnings. However, there was shame in being a *pornai*. While the Greek state was conveniently able to see them as taxable citizens, they did not see them as actual citizens with legal rights. Homosexuals therefore were only acceptable in certain roles, and the Greeks certainly didn't view full-time homosexuals as equal to other men. Homophobia was beginning to take shape.

Ancient Greece was also a pretty good place for lesbians and in fact the word *lesbian* originated here thanks to the 7th-century writer Sappho who wrote poems about female homosexuality and lived on the island of Lesbos.[154] Sappho wrote about how she was susceptible to the charms of younger women, yet it seems she married a man, had children, and then killed herself over a male lover. Nonetheless, she became a gay icon, and the term *lesbian* was used forever more. A fact which three modern-day Greeks living on the island of Lesbos are not too happy about. In 2008 they went so far as to file a request to stop LGBTQ groups using the word *lesbian* in their names. Leader of the trio, Dimitris Lambrou, explained that: "international dominance of the word in a sexual context violates our human rights because it is insulting and disgraces us around the world"[155] (I'm getting a homophobic vibe here). Due to the fact you can't own a word, and this was most definitely *not* against their human rights, they lost the case.

Evidence of lesbianism in ancient Greece comes from literature and art. The speech of Aristophanes in Plato's *Symposium* comments on female homosexuality while Plutarch writes about women in Sparta forming relationships with each other which had big age gaps just like the male homosexual relationships. Greek art also pictures female-female relationships, such as a plate from archaic Thera which shows two women dating, and a vase in the collection of the Tarquinia national museum in Italy which is adorned with an image of women having sex with each other. Ancient Greece even had a sex manual to help newbies navigate their way through lesbian etiquette. However, at the time, the book was regarded as obscene because lesbianism was actually a bit taboo. You see, ancient Greeks loved their penises. They prized male sexuality above anything else and so any notion that men and their penises were not needed was met with hostility. The seeds of lesbian homophobia were being sowed based on the fear that men may not be able to plant their baby seeds. One Greek male (circa 270 BCE) described women partaking in lesbian sex as "disgracing themselves".[156] Him and Dimitris of Lesbos would have got on like a house on fire.

Chronologically next in line after the Greeks were the Romans. The Romans were basically massive copycats, and they adopted a lot of the same practices as the ancient Greeks; thus, when it came to homosexuality, male-male sex was legal but it was important who was the dominant one. This attitude is clear from their language and laws. The Latin for a male being penetrated is *muliebria patitur,* which means "having a woman's experience".[157] It was shameful to be the passive one, as pointed out by Roman philosopher Seneca who said being on the receiving end was a crime for the free born. Roman men got around this problem by choosing slaves, non-Roman citizens, and prostitutes to be their partners (there were male prostitutes in every Roman city). Conversely, being the passive one was seen as "a necessity in a slave,"[158] i.e., it's in the job description. How much the slaves were up for it is unknown, but we do know it was not OK to force yourself on a Roman man; a law dating from Caesar's reign defined rape as: "forced sex against boy, woman, or anyone" and the death penalty was applied which was a rare punishment in Roman times.[159] Talking of Caesar, 14 of Rome's first 15 Emperors (i.e., Caesar onwards) enjoyed sex with other men, Claudius was the only one to abstain.[160] There was even a bit of banter about Caesar among soldiers of the Roman army (who incidentally were allowed to bring their sex-slaves away with them on campaign). Soldiers chanted: "Caesar got on top of the Gauls, but Nicomedes got on top of Caesar".[161]

You could even have a gay marriage in Roman times! If you were to go to ancient Rome from 100 BCE onwards, you would be able to witness male couples engaging in traditional marriage rites. Emperor Nero, while not a great example of most things due to all the craziness, is a shining example of gay marriage. He married not just one, but two men in his lifetime – Pythagoras and Sporus (presumably the Pythagoras measuring triangles theory was inspired by this original love triangle). With Sporus, Nero was the groom; but with Pythagoras, Nero was the bride showing Nero was Far-o way from gender conformity. Sporus didn't have the balls to argue against this arrangement (because Nero had his testicles removed) but he does get the prize of being the first drag queen when he appeared in public dressed like a Roman empress in 67 CE. [162] You win some, you lose some. However, while one may be able to take part in such marriages, they were not respected unions due to the inability to produce children, and once Christianity took hold of the empire in the 4th century CE, you could kiss such privileges (but not your partner) away.

The prevailing attitude in ancient Rome was of male supremacy and therefore male-male sex was viewed simply as another option. There was no explicit homophobia, and with the ancient's obsession with penises (just take a look around Pompeii!), it was no wonder that men having sex with one another was seen as a normal part of everyday life. Unfortunately for lesbians, the Roman love affair with their penises and using them willy-nilly did not work out quite so happily for them. The extra whammy against lesbians in Roman times was the fact there were clearly defined gender roles to follow. The idea of women forming sexual relationships but not needing a man, or his member, was well beyond the comprehension of a Roman male. So, while men were relatively free to have sex whenever and with whomever they wanted, women were expected to stay at home. A bit like the 1950s but without all the Tupperware. A prolific writer from the 2nd century CE – Lucian – describes a conversation two men had about homosexuality in his book *Dialogues of the Courtesans*. They were debating which is better – male love or heterosexual love. The conclusion they drew was that you best stick to heterosexual because if male-male relationships were made legit, then lesbianism would have to be too. And that was simply absurd![163] Also in Lucian's book is a story of one woman seducing another, but Lucian could not describe the encounter in detail because apparently it was too disgusting for words. Not such a great writer after all then, are you, Lucian?

This acceptance of (male) homosexuality did not last for the whole of the Roman era, and the 4th century CE brought the first decree against same-sex relations. This prohibition was followed up in the 6th century with a more explicit law against gay sex which also came with the death penalty. Fortunately for most of Europe, the Roman Empire had been reduced to a shadow of its former self and so this ruling had no impact on those living in northern or western Europe.

The indigenous tribal cultures of North America and Africa (prior to European colonisation) accepted homosexuality, but people were restricted with specific roles in their societies. They were not completely free, and it was not always a nice experience. Over in North America, before the Europeans claimed the land as "theirs" in the 16th century, it was populated with at least 573 different native tribes.[164] In traditional Native American culture, same-sex relations were accepted[165] and existed alongside heterosexual relationships. The people who led a gender non-conforming life were known as *Two-Spirit*. However, while lacking what we understand to be homophobia, the Native Americans blurred the lines of transvestism and homosexuality, and in a lot of tribes, the *Two-Spirit* people had specific roles in everyday life and during ceremonies. In his records of expeditions across America, Nicholas Biddle observed: "Among the Mamitarees, if a boy shows any symptoms of effeminacy or girlish inclinations he is put among the girls, dressed in their way, brought up with them, and sometimes married to men."[166] Among the Crow tribe, it was noted that: "men who dressed as women and specialised in women's work were accepted and sometimes honoured."[167] In one tribe, the role given to homosexual young men was that of a glorified sex doll – open for use by the rest of the tribe whenever they fancied it. So, while their sexual preference was accepted, they were not afforded the right to a relationship or choose their sexual partners. However, it was still a better situation than facing death for committing a capital crime.

In some African tribes, provisions were made which gave homosexuals certain names (not the nasty sort) and a certain role in society. Like the blurred lines found in Native American tribes, a common theme in African tribal culture was that one man would assume a female role – thus mirroring a heterosexual relationship. In the 5000-year-old Hausa culture (whose people cover one-quarter of modern-day African counties), they have the term *yan daudu,* which is used to describe "effeminate men who are considered to be wives to men".[168] This transgender approach to homosexuality also existed in Southern Ethiopia. Here they were called *ashtime,* and "these (biological) males dressed like women, performed female tasks, cared for their own houses, and apparently had sexual relations with men."[169] In Kenya and Uganda there was a similar set-up with the *mugawe* and *mudoko dako* who wore women's clothes, had feminine hairstyles and were able to marry a man. The Shangaan of southern Africa called same-sex relations *inkotshane* (meaning male-wife). Like the ancient Greek education, in various South African communities, adolescents would experiment with each other on their quest to manhood.[170] Of course, these sorts of relationships are not like homosexual relationships of the 21st century. Clearly, some of these men had little choice but to live as women to be accepted; but it's pretty crazy to see such a level of gender fluidity and acceptance of same-sex relations in a continent that now houses countries with a draconian level of homophobic legislation.

Beyond the gender fluid roles homosexuals could live under, there was also a belief in some African cultures that taking part in same-gender sex would provide spiritual security.

Tribes in Zimbabwe, Sudan, Congo, Nigeria, Rwanda, and Burundi all believed that this type of sex would give them increased power to control their lands. Similarly, homosexual acts were used in rituals because of the belief that same-sex relations were a source of magical powers. To engage in such acts was not seen as unnatural or immoral, rather it would guarantee a good harvest of crops and/or hunting would be successful. It was believed good health would follow, and to top it off, evil spirits would be abated. For example, in Angola and Namibia, a group of male mystics were believed to have powerful female spirits that they could pass on to other men through sex, and so the act itself was desirable.

In some places, such as Japan, homosexuality has been accepted for hundreds of years with minimal interruption. Japanese culture features homosexuality as part of the Buddhist lifestyle and the Samurai lifestyle. An expert on Buddhism confirms: "It is in Japanese Buddhism that male love became most visible and came to designate... an ideal of man".[171] Homosexuality in the Buddhist monasteries was known as *shudo* or *nanshoku,* and it came to Japan via a man named Kuukai who visited China in the 9th century and observed their *nanshoku* practices. He then set up the Shingon School which became the blueprint for other Buddhist monasteries. Following the *nanshoku* tradition, in Buddhist monasteries the older partner would be a monk, priest, or abbot (called the *nenja*), while the younger partner was a boy called the *chigo*. Both males were expected to take the relationship seriously and be nice to each other, sometimes the *nenja* even went so far as to create vows of commitment. The relationship would be dissolved once the boy reached adulthood (or left the monastery) and the *nenja* would then be free to find another *chigo*. These relationships were celebrated rather than judged and there is a huge array of paintings and literature documenting their lives. There were even guidebooks, written by Buddhist monks, to help men navigate these homosexual relationships with supportive chapters such as these from a 1657 edition: "on kissing" and "when the feelings change". The latter of which would have been most helpful when the *nenja* were inevitably feeling bummed out when the relationship came to an end.

The Samurai were the aristocratic warriors of Japan between the 12th century and late 19th century; they're like European Knights but with much cooler swords. Male-male sex was common in the Samurai class because of practicalities. There was a small number of females around during these periods of war and, like in the ancient Roman and medieval Persian armies, men met their sexual needs with each other. Like ancient Greece, boys in the Samurai class were apprenticed to older men, and the man was allowed to take the younger boy as his lover until he came of age. As well as learning how to be a lover *and* a fighter, the boys were also taught martial arts, life skills, and how to have a good relationship. These Samurai relationships were serious stuff, and they were expected to be exclusive to each other with no other male lovers.[172] However, just as in ancient Rome, these homosexual relations were only acceptable with an age difference and sexual relations became inappropriate once the boy was older.[173] It also seems like homosexuality existed within the Samurai because they enjoyed it because even when peace was obtained, and the Samurai were instructed to live in the cities from 1600 onwards, they took this practice named *wakashudō* with them.

One interesting explanation for the differing development of homophobia across the world is geography. Peter Avery asserts that: "where the environs are far more lush than in the little watered countries of West Asia and Northern Africa, it makes for a naturally tolerant lackadaisical people."[174] While he then goes on to explain that other factors may then come along and trump this "anything goes" mindset, it is a pertinent point when we consider the relaxed approach witnessed in China and Japan for most of their history.

Not all cultures have been so accepting of homosexuality in the past. You wouldn't want to be gay in medieval Mexico, that's for sure. The Aztecs of Mexico (1000–1521CE) were undoubtedly homophobic and probably had the worst punishment for homosexuals. The man accused of being the dominant one would be impaled, while the passive receiver would have his intestines extracted through his anus. Gutting. Lesbians, while happy they were being recognised, swiftly had the smile wiped off their faces when they were strangled to death.[175] Bizarrely, despite this strict opposition, homosexual acts still featured in many Aztec rituals; but it was made clear that only here, in the "theatre", were such actions tolerated. Sodomy was officially a capital offence, as was transvestism, and lesbianism. Like the Hebrews, the Aztecs were keen to criminalise sodomy because the "others" (in the Aztec's case the "others" were the Toltecs they conquered) were open towards it, and like the Greeks and Romans, the Aztecs promoted "manly" behaviour and condemned "submissive" behaviour.

The Mayan culture (2000 BCE – 1697 CE) of Central America also had homophobic principles which were set down in their *Chilam Balam* books. Lacking basic sex education, they believed that sodomites (men who had sex with men) would be responsible for destroying Mayan society by producing illegitimate and inept children through their anuses. Sodomites were thus condemned to death in a fiery furnace. However, just like the Aztecs, they still allowed homosexual sex if it had a ritualistic purpose. For example, some shamans (magical doctors) would engage in sodomy with their patients to "help" them be cured. Outside of this selectively applied treatment, homosexuality was also found in the Mayan aristocracy, where parents would provide their sons with male slaves to satisfy their teenage sex drive and keep them away from pre-marital heterosexual sex.

Overall, it is the ancient era (pre-Jesus) where male-male sex was most considered acceptable. How could it not be? Practicably the peg fits in the hole and philosophically it was greatness merging with greatness. Ancient European societies had provision for it in the sex trade and slave trade while their militaries and education systems promoted it. However, an undercurrent of homophobia was developing due to the notion that it was vital who was the dominant "manly" one. Interestingly, it is this theory that still influences modern homophobia where derogatory terms are based around the idea that those engaging in gay sex are feminine. While lesbian sex (and a manual on how to do it) certainly existed in ancient Europe, lesbian relationships were harder to find. But this was not the case in other parts of the world. So, what really pushed these ancient civilisations away from acceptance into the arms of homophobia?

Homophobia comes from Religion… right?

Religion certainly has a lot to answer for, but it is not solely responsible for the development of homophobia. For a start, not all religions are homophobic, and even those that *were* did not go on about it to a huge extent. Other factors were necessary to ingrain this prejudice into people's psyche and spread homophobic attitudes around the world. More important than religion was the impact of individuals and imperialism. People's obsession with the infrequent references to homosexuality as a sin in religious texts, followed by imperialism spreading these influential people's views into five out of six continents (there's snow homophobia in Antarctica) and did more damage than religion in its original form.

The oldest religion in the world, Hinduism (circa 2300 BCE – 1500 BCE), is not homophobic and instead was accepting of gender fluidity and homosexual acts. Traditional Hinduism was far less homophobic than modern Hindu cultures because contemporary civilisations have been negatively influenced by western imperialism. The Hindu scriptures describe homosexuals without judgement. Three Hindu scriptures explicitly deal with homosexuality – the *Narada-smriti* (a 1st century BCE text of religious codes), the *Sushruta Samhita* (a 7th century BCE medical book) and the *Kama Sutra* (a 3rd century CE book about lovemaking). The *Narada-smriti* lists 14 different types of men who are "impotent" with women; for example, the *mukhebhaga* has oral sex with other men, the *sevyaka* is sexually enjoyed by other men, and the *irshyaka* is a voyeur who watches other men have sex. All three types are declared "incurable" and forbidden to marry women. And while this label "incurable" is reminiscent of modern gay conversion camps in USA and China, what was really meant was to leave these people the heck alone. You can't change them. They just didn't want them marrying women, leading them on, and then not producing any children.

Stories of Hindu deities also promoted homosexuality without condemnation; for example, the water-gods Varuna and Mitra are openly homosexual in their behaviours. In the ancient *Shatapatha Brahmana* text, Mitra is described as "implanting his seed" in Varuna on every new moon night in order to secure the moon's waning.[176] And ancient Hinduism wasn't just focussed on male-male homosexuality – in a story found in two texts (the *Padma Purana* and *Krittivasa Ramayana*), the god Siva commands two queens to make love together and blesses them to thus conceive a child. Many Hindu deities were gender non-conformist, and so this gender fluidity and sexual freedom was also acceptable for their people. The *Vedas* (6000 BCE) is considered to be the oldest scripture in the world and it refers to the concept of a third gender, which is roughly defined as those who lack a desire for the opposite sex or those for whom procreative sex is not possible.[177] These people were sometimes considered to have divine powers and they were not ostracised from society. This open-mindedness within Hinduism is supported by a recent report from The Gay & Lesbian Vaishnava Association (GALVA) who state: "Vedic culture allowed transgender people of the third sex, known as *hijras*, to live openly according to their gender identity."[178]

There is no law in Hindu scriptures that punishes homosexual behaviour between men or women of the third gender. However, there were limitations among the elite and those who identified as clearly male or female and *then* engaged in homosexual acts. A typical punishment for an elite male was to pay a fine or take a ritual bath. If he continued or if it was deemed he had not atoned, then loss of status was prescribed.[179] If you were a young and unmarried female, then an even lower fine was your atonement, although the ancient texts did also allow corporal punishment to be applied.[180] For the lower classes, homosexual behaviour was not a punishable offence because it was considered harmless to them. In a pattern which was repeated across the ancient world, what mattered in the ancient Hindu culture was *who* was being homosexual, *not* the act itself. And with gender fluidity evident in the scriptures and in everyday life, even the 'who' was not punished too harshly.

Attitudes began to shift away from such laissez-faire loveliness when monotheism (religion with one God) became a thing. The Hebrews were the first to rule against homosexuals in 1300 BCE. The Hebrews took such a harsh view on homosexuals because God told them to. The story goes that after Moses led the Jews out of Egypt, God spoke to him and laid down some rules for his new people. These are more commonly known as the Ten Commandments but there were actually 613 in total (that is some in-ten-sive streamlining). Within these commandments, a basis for morality was set regarding sex, a base which lasted a whopping 3000 years and managed to impact most of the globe thanks to imperialism.

God instructed Moses: "Do not lie with a man as one lies with a woman; that is detestable."[181] A punishment of death by stoning was recommended. However, God was only homophobic a couple of times, and so one bright spark/early homophobe who later re-wrote the book of Genesis decided to include a story whereby God destroyed the homosexual friendly cities of Sodom and Gomorrah. This, it was believed, would add serious weight to the notion that God disapproved of same-sex love.[182] This story was put forward firstly by the Jews in their holy book, the Torah, and was later taken up by the Christians in their Bible. The impact of these stories was huge and soon became a 'justification' to punish people, with the aptly named Justinian using the stories to explain his persecution of homosexuals in the 6th century CE. He believed that homosexuals were why things like earthquakes and volcanic eruptions occurred. Aside from the fact Justinian clearly never went to his geography lessons, this meant he promoted a homophobic theory of best kill 'them' before all the natural disasters kill 'us'. Worryingly, even as recently as 70 years ago, these biblical stories were used to foster homophobia; in 1966 and 1968, American courts who were prosecuting men for sodomy referred to "the savage horror practised by the residents of Sodom".[183] Of course, there is no evidence that either of these cities were the homosexual meccas implied by the Great Book; but there was evidence of Sodom being a hotbed for incest. Which, incidentally, God was fine with.

Putting aside the idea "God told them to", the Hebrews banned male-male sex for two reasons. Firstly, it was for practicality – this type of sex didn't produce children. The absence or reduction of children being born would restrict their population growth and therefore weaken the nation of Israel[184] at a time when the Hebrews were starting out. They needed more Hebrews to flourish away from their Egyptian oppressors. The second reason was because they wanted to be different to the Egyptians they had just escaped from. God even issues a specific commandment to Moses to NOT "do as they do in Egypt, where you used to live".[185] A *straight*forward way to be different was to take a serious stance against gay sex because the Egyptians and other ancient civilisations were largely unconcerned by it. The Hebrews were taught to see sodomy as a filthy foreign practice, thus nailing two levels of prejudice (xenophobia and homophobia) in one easy step. Between the years 1047–597 BCE, the Hebrews developed their laws and extended their control over the coastal region in Palestine, thus slowly building a community of people who were homophobic. Because Judaism went on to spawn Christianity and Islam, the followers of these two religions followed suit with the homophobia vibe. Free loving homosexuality was now ancient history.

Next on the religious scene was Buddhism originating between the 6th and 5th century BCE. Buddhism is a non-theistic religion (no belief in a creator god) and it is also another non-homophobic religion. Buddhism's leniency towards homosexuals derives from the doctrine of *hooben* whereby people's actions are not judged in isolation but in terms of their motivation and outcome.[186] In fact, Buddhism promoted the idea of sex as a pleasure in itself and not solely connected to producing children, which meant there was nothing to fear from non-procreative sex. Buddhism even somewhat encouraged homosexuality through the male-only way of life found in Buddhist monasteries and their practice of *nanshoku* (homosexual relations). This commonality was commented upon by a 16th-century Catholic missionary who had travelled to Japan with the purpose of converting everyone to Christianity. He said that "this evil" was so normal that the people "are neither depressed nor horrified",[187] suggesting that male-male sex was so acceptable that it drew no opinion at all.

Buddhism became a major religion in Japan from the 7th century CE, and it is in Japan where homophobia has been the hardest to find. In total, Japan has only criminalised homosexuality for eight years. This absence is due to religion – partly the Buddhist influence – but also because of the 'sex positive' vibe of Japan's indigenous religion, Shintoism.[188] Some of the Shinto gods, especially Hachiman, Myoshin, Shinmei, and Tenjin were regarded as guardians of *nanshoku,* and this belief was especially popular between the 17th and 19th centuries.

Around the same time as Buddhism, another non-homophobic religion was developing – Confucianism. The origins of Confucianism are in the 6th century BCE and it was widely adopted across China by the 7th century CE, lasting until 1905.[189] This belief system, like Buddhism, saw people as inherently good and did not set out to punish people for their sexual preferences. There was no God to judge you. In fact, just like Buddhism, Confucian ideology may have indirectly facilitated homosexuality[190] as it emphasised the value of male-male friendships. However, same-sex relationships were only accepted if they existed alongside heterosexual relationships which produced children because, much like a mother-in-law, Confucianism believes not having children is one of the greatest sins. Other Asian countries such as Taiwan, Hong Kong, Korea, Japan, Singapore, and Vietnam were strongly influenced by Chinese Confucianism, which is why most East Asian nations, for most of history, have had an attitude of toleration and acceptance towards homosexuals. There was no Confucion for them about whether same-sex love was a sin.

Then came one of the greatest influences of them all – Christianity. But while it's got a bad rep, original Christian teachings were ambiguous, and the few parts that were explicitly homophobic were simply copied from what the Hebrews said. Christianity in its original form never intended to be homophobic.

Homophobia can be found once in the Old Testament and four times in the New Testament. The Old Testament (written between 1200 BCE and 165 BCE)[191] is made up of five books, known as the Pentateuch and they are the first books of the Christian Bible and the Jewish Torah: Genesis, Exodus, Leviticus, Numbers and Deuteronomy. Leviticus is where the homophobic reference resides with the infamous: "Do not lie with a man as one lies with a woman; that is detestable."[192] After Jesus died (yes, he was a real man[193]… son of God bit unconfirmed), the Christians then produced their own religious text – The New Testament – written during the 1st century CE. In this part of the Great Book, the four references to homosexuals can be found in Romans, Corinthians, Timothy, and Jude. Yet nowhere do we find out What Would Jesus Do as he made no clear declarations against homosexuals. Christians *assumed* he was against it because the one time he talked about marriage, he only referred to it in terms of between a man and woman.[194] You know, like you would assume a person wanted to punish vegetables if they only referenced meat when talking about dinner.

The four references are as follows:

Romans 1: 26-27: "…for even their females exchanged the natural use for that which is contrary to nature, and likewise also the males, having left the natural use of the female, were inflamed by their lust for one another, males with males, committing what is shameful…"

1 Corinthians 6: 9–10: "Know ye not that the unrighteous shall not inherit the kingdom of God? Be not deceived: neither fornicators, nor idolaters, nor adulterers, nor effeminate, nor abusers of themselves with mankind."

1 Timothy 1:9–10: "… for them that defile themselves with mankind ".

Jude 1:7: "Even as Sodom and Gomorrah, and the cities about them in like manner, giving themselves over to fornication, and going after strange flesh, are set forth for an example, suffering the vengeance of eternal fire."

Reading these, it is incredible how Christian preachers completely ignored the implication that homosexual acts were reasonably common with both men and women partaking "…even their females… likewise also the males". But they sure as heaven made sure they didn't miss the criticism of homosexual acts. Words such as "shameful" and "error" meant denunciation.[195] Modern readings of this passage prefer to think that what is being denounced is homosexual acts between heterosexuals,[196] or that the condemnation is limited to male prostitution,[197] or that the rules were only meant for priests and not the normal everyday folk.[198] These defences imply that Christianity had no intention of creating homophobia.

But unfortunately, these are moot points because by the time these 'interpretations' came to light in the 20th century, the damage had already been done. Armed with their four references in the Bible, Christian priests were able to preach against homophobia from the 1st century CE onwards, meaning that essentially homophobia arose because a few individuals wanted it to.

Christianity led to the first decree (in 342 CE) against homosexuality in the Roman Empire.[199] By this point, Christianity had made it official with the Roman Empire while enjoying a "friends with benefits" relationship with homophobia and the 4th century saw the trio travel across Europe together. Once the Roman Empire fell in the 6th century, homophobia kept travelling thanks to the Christian Penitentials (religious guidebooks on what is a sin and how best to punish it). Christianity was relegated to the role of influencer once government laws took over in the 13th century, but its impacts were visible in how strict a stance governments took as sodomites were blamed for "bringing down the wrath of God" upon the land. The remedy for all this wrath was fire, which led to individuals being burned at the stake or impaled with hot iron rods. The earliest recorded execution following secular law comes from France and is that of John de Wettre on 8 September 1292. John, "a maker of small knives", was burned at the pillory next to St. Peter's for the crime of sodomy,[200] which undoubtedly left his family pretty cut up.

In the end, neither Christianity nor secular law made much difference to people's choices. Punishments do not deter people. In fact, in Venice, officials acknowledged that the "abhorrent vice" was on the rise[201] (as were some other things…). They found that sodomy was *so* popular, female prostitutes were going out of business![202] Interestingly though, despite this popularity, there were few executions such as de Wettre's taking place, and those found guilty were given less harsh punishments such as a fine or a lifetime of bread and water. It's possible this leniency was because executing someone would draw attention to the fact it was happening in your city, or maybe because the high society and law-enforcers were also having relationships with men – as evidenced by numerous male-male, side-by-side burials (the traditional way for husbands and wives to be laid to rest) of knights, nobility and clerics.

Christianity's final throw of the homophobic dice came via the Protestant Reformation. This kicked off in Germany in 1517 when Martin Luther nailed a list of 95 issues with the Catholic church to a church door. Incidentally, this is THE Martin Luther who Martin Luther King Jr. was named after (Fun Fact: Martin Luther version two was named Michael for the first five years of his life and his dad changed *both* their names to Martin once he learnt about this reforming OG). Anyway, Martin and the list went viral. Turned out lots of people agreed that the Catholic church was too powerful and corrupt, and before people could think of something good to call their protest religion, Protestantism was born. Christianity was thus split in two – Catholics were Christianity with the Pope, wine, colour, and bling; and Protestants were Christianity without the Pope, without the wine, without the colour, and without the bling. Obviously these two denominations couldn't take a hint from their shared Bible and love thy (gay) neighbour, and instead, both sides chose to focus on outdoing each other in condemning homosexuality. Considering this hatred didn't even have a name yet (the term homophobia was coined in 1965 by Dr George Weinberg) you could say they were ahead of their times. Just imagine the lovely world we may have inherited if both sides competed in who could be the best "good Samaritan". Instead, we got the Spanish Inquisition. The Catholic Spanish Inquisition was originally intended to hunt down Protestants, but Pope Clement VII thoughtfully expanded their remit by adding homosexuals to the list in 1524. The Protestants meanwhile made homophobia part of their new laws in countries which converted from Catholicism. In this reformation era, man became the judge of men. And because man was most definitely here in front of you instead of being whimsically omnipresent – tolerance and acceptance were swiftly ended and individuals' ideas of morality usurped the role of religion.

In England, the Protestant Reformation led to the first law which specifically outlawed gay sex. Henry VIII started the Protestant Reformation in England so that he could get a divorce, marry a younger model, and have a male heir. As well as being famous for not stopping there – this law is also one of his claims to fame. While history textbooks will fall over themselves to tell you about his impact on religion, or his invention of tennis, this deuce-y fact about creating the first anti-gay law is left out. The 1533 beautifully unsubtle "*a*cte for the punyshement of the vice of buggerye" allowed, for the first time, the government of England to persecute individuals for sodomy. However, it was a bit of a flop. Henry wasn't actually homophobic – he just wanted to take the power away from *the church* to be homophobic and punish people. Homosexuality continued unabated in England as recorded by Samuel Pepys, the 17th-century diarist: "buggery (sic) is now almost grown as common among our gallants as in Italy".[203] Pepys is not famed for sensible decisions (during the Great Fire of London he was more concerned with hiding his cheese than escaping to safety) and this was an edam-ing and risky statement to make about the lack of compliance from the English public.

It was a different story elsewhere in Protestant Europe. Every religion has a group who take it too far – aka the radicals. In Protestantism, the radicals were the Puritans and Calvinists.

Geneva was a Calvinist city, and in the 125 years before Calvinism took hold, there were six sodomy trials; in the 125 years after – there were sixty. And… hold onto your hats for this one… they even acknowledged women and punished lesbianism. A fact which saw one woman drowned in 1568 for having sex with men *and* women. However, they weren't fully embracing gender equality just yet and with lesbianism still not fully recognised, the conviction was deliberately ambiguous: "detestable and unnatural crime, which is so ugly that, from horror, it is not named here".[204]

Islam, beginning in Arabia, was the last religion to surface in the monotheist love triangle that is Judaism, Christianity, and Islam. About 25%[205] of the Quran's verses are about prophets and other people from the Jewish and Christian faiths, and because of this shared content, homosexuality was also classified as a sin in Muslim doctrine. However, there is not as much as modern Islam may have you believe, and it can be argued that traditional Islam is devoid of homophobia.[206]

There are more frequent references to homosexuals in the Quran (610–632 CE) than in the Bible (nineteen versus five) and yet the opportunity to be homophobic was still avoided. All 19 mentions refer to homosexuality as equal to other crimes such as highway robbery or the unforgivable misdemeanour of not being a decent host at your dinner party. Clearly Islam views homosexuality as a sin, but it is no worse than any other sin, and so the punishments are the same as if the person had committed adultery or uncleanness[207] i.e., being stoned to death or crushed to death beneath a wall.[208] There are two places in the Quran where homosexuality is explicitly mentioned and there are 17 references to Lot and the destruction of his city Sodom,[209] which, in the Quran is always associated with homosexual acts. The first reference in the Quran is in Surah XXIX, 56, where it says: "Do you come to men in lust instead of women?" which is followed by the statement "you are a people ignorant" (ignorant is translated as without faith). And the second reference in Surah VII, 79 uses the same question, except this time the follow-up is "You are an intemperate (wasteful) people."[210] So, there is a suggestion that to lust after men is seen as non-Islamic and something to criticise; however, there is no marking out of these people as a separate group open to abuse and subject to persecution. Incidentally, lesbians were left alone too; Khaled El-Rouayheb, an academic at Harvard University, has discovered that while sodomy was judged a sin by Muslim law makers, lesbian sex was not.[211]

The Hadith is another text which is a pillar of Islamic law, and this helpfully provides a real-life example of how Imám Alí ordered a sodomite to be stoned to death and then cremated in a pit. It was ruled in the Hadith, as in the Quran, that sodomy (and heterosexual adultery) should elicit both guilty parties to be punished with elimination of the culprit as the intended outcome; it's likely that readings of these parts has caused homophobic attitudes to develop in the Muslim world.

However, Islam provided some loopholes to these punishments. Firstly, there was some leniency on grounds of age and mental health. More significantly, provisions made in the Hanabalite Law could nullify these punishments completely; for example, should the culprit sincerely repent (express regret and say sorry type thing) before conviction, he would be acquitted. It seems that, unlike the Christian God, Allah wanted to forgive *all* people – not just the straight ones. Even if the accused didn't repent, the law required four witnesses to have seen the sodomy take place. And, ostensibly, a pretty big bedroom to accommodate this audience.

Overall, the impact of monotheistic religion on the development of homophobia is negligible. Even when Judaism, Christianity, and Islam did start teaching and preaching homosexuality was bad – people ignored it. The few ambiguous references found in the Torah, Bible, and Quran were brushed aside in favour of allowing homosexual partnerships in real life. For example, in Catholic southern Europe between 600–1200 CE, homosexuals could get married. In churches. By actual Catholic priests. They even used the same prayers and rituals employed in heterosexual marriage ceremonies, although there were some adaptations to the wording to reflect the male-male aspect, such as in Ukraine where you would be "bound as brothers".[212] Over in England, where canon law (laws from the church) was supreme until 1534, they also failed to practice what they preached. In London, between 1470 and 1516 there was only one sodomy case out of the 21,000 crimes prosecuted by the church courts.[213]

The Quran also had a limited impact in the Islamic world; 9th century CE writer Al-Jáhiz commented how: "homosexuality spread in the Muslim world owing to the army life of the Persians,"[214] showing how practicality and horniness trumped religion. Islam's lack of impact on homophobia is also evident from an Iranian manual from 1082 CE; the *Qábús Náma* advised men to enjoy *both* young men and women so as not to annoy the other one (early version of equal rights), and it is further recommended that one should focus on men in the summer and women in the winter.[215] Literally blowing hot then cold. Similar advice, which ran contrary to the sin the Quran it was declared to be in, came from the 9th century CE erotic poet Abú Nuwás. He explained that boys were preferred to girls because boys were purer and didn't come with the risk of pregnancy; girls were also seen as a bloody bad choice because of all their inconvenient menstruating.[216] As time has gone on, Muslim lawmakers have moved further and further away from such attitudes, meaning that in the modern-day Islamic countries of Saudi Arabia, Sudan, Yemen, Mauritania and Iran, sodomy is still punished with death.[217] This has the effect of making Islam seem more homophobic than it ever intended to be.

Religion is the starting point for homophobia, but it has not been the most damaging factor. Even this starting point (with Judaism 3300 years ago) wasn't properly homophobic in its intentions – the Hebrews were against homosexuals because their oppressors (the Egyptians) were *not*. It was more about being different than truly believing in homophobia. The other oldest religions – Hinduism, Buddhism, Shintoism, and Confucianism did not teach or preach homophobia. Instead, there was acceptance of a third gender and acceptance that some people may partake in homosexual and/or heterosexual sex. Monotheistic religion is responsible for tying people's sex lives up with their morality and teaching people to punish those who did not conform to procreative sex, but religion as a whole should not shoulder the blame for hate against homosexuals. People's selective interpretation and obsession with certain aspects of some religious doctrine is what's really behind the development of homophobia.

So, who is to blame for homophobia?

Never underestimate the power of an individual. One person can change the course of history. One person can also ruin it for everyone else. In terms of homophobia, there are the religious lot and the law-making lot who have a lot to answer for.

In the religious corner we have, of course, Moses for giving people the homophobic word of God. Then there's Paul, Jerome, and Augustine, who all did a marvellous job of making everyone in the Christian world think sex was a terrible thing, which made it a nice easy leap to convince people that male-male sex was an even *terribler* thing. Saint Jerome (c.347–420 CE) came out (no, not like that) with such gems as: "Everything is poison which bears within it the seeds of sensual pleasure." Saint Augustine (354 CE-430 CE) meanwhile introduced us all to the concept of sex shame using the story of Adam and Eve. Sex was permissible only within marriage. Only when aimed at procreation. Only if you did not enjoy it too much. And only if you washed vigorously afterwards. Incidentally Augustine only came up with this theory after he had enjoyed many sexual relationships, a variety of extra-marital affairs, and an eleven-year-old wife.[218] How convenient.

The apostle Paul (5–64 CE), who saw marriage as preferential only to death: "it's better to marry than to burn,"[219] had the biggest influence of these early religious individuals. This particular hater of love established 13 churches across Europe and wrote at least seven books of the Bible[220] which enabled him to spread the homophobic word better than butter on Jesus' miraculous loaves. Originally a Hebrew (which helps explain his hatred of homosexuals), Paul literally found Jesus. And they started hanging out. Paul liked Jesus so much he even stopped his hobby of persecuting Christians (Paul had previous for stoning Saint Stephen to death) and he began preaching Christianity instead. Paul took the lead in spreading the word that all who partook in homosexual acts would be barred from the kingdom of heaven. His killer statement saw him describe homosexuality to be as bad as murder.

As a keen proponent of equal discrimination, Paul is also responsible for initiating homophobia against lesbians. Christianity did not condemn lesbians; there is no reference to it as a sin in the Old Testament, and the Jewish Talmud viewed lesbianism as: "a mere obscenity".[221] All that changed with the New Testament (the bit he helped to write). Paul successfully Paul-ed a fast one on Christians everywhere by adding his own thoughts about lesbians which, unsurprisingly, were condemnations of women who "exchanged the natural sexual relations for unnatural ones".[222]

While Paul's cheeky bit of ad-lib had zero impact at the time on legislation, his homophobia was resurrected in the Middle Ages better than Jesus ever was. This resurrection came about in England due to three men and was strongly directed at lesbians. Firstly, there was the 7th-century Archbishop of Canterbury, Theodore of Tarsus, who wrote the English Penitentials, which recommended women caught using sex aids with each other should be punished with three years of penance (just bread and water), or one year of penance if she was caught using it on her own. I'm guessing the theory here was that after one or three years, you'd barely have the strength to lift a sex aid, let alone use one. Conversely, a man using a sex aid got 40 days. Incidentally, this punishment for lesbians of three years of bread and water was also the penalty given to a man who raped a virgin. Because, clearly, that's the exact same level of deviance.

Theodore's theories were followed up in the 12th century by St. Anselm, who wrote a book describing lesbian sex as: "shameful deeds".[223] Other books by Christian leaders then continued to spread and clarify the word of St Paul. Gratian's *Decretum* of 1140 placed lesbianism on the same level of evil as male sodomy, and this remained part of canon law (what the church deemed legal/illegal) until 1917. *The Summa Theologica,* written by St. Thomas Aquinas in 1267–1273, confirmed for any doubters that St Paul was slating lesbians and helpfully described four forms of "unnatural vice". The third vice was: "copulation with an undue sex, male with male, or female with female, as the Apostle states (Rom. I, 26–27): and this is called the vice of sodomy".[224] Thanks to all these homophobic ideas being written down – they stuck around like maggots on rotting meat and contaminated Christian's opinions for hundreds of years.

The Penitentials, which condemned homosexuality in men and women, were the work of individuals. These guidebooks were written by different people and so varied from one area to the next, depending on what the locals preferred to do and how common certain misdemeanours were. It was basically a postcode lottery approach towards punishing homosexuals. A lottery which also depended on the predilections of other individuals – i.e., the local priests who enforced the rules. There was no secular law at this time (legislation from governments rather than the church) and so the local priest, as well as preaching to you from the pulpit every Sunday, was also your judge and jury, your police, your educator, and your moral compass. And to top it all off, he could read, and you couldn't, so you were at his mercy as to what the Bible or the Penitential *really* said about your sin. One consequence no one saw coming (nudge nudge wink wink) was how these guidebooks describing the full range of sexual acts were akin to soft porn. A consequence which was later remedied with the addition of a section on how priests should punish themselves if they had "erupted" while doing their bedtime Penitential reading. And there was even a separate punishment if they erupted in their sleep because being able to do it with their eyes closed was not an achievement to celebrate.

While the priests and Penitential writers justified themselves as correcting people in a way God would have liked, the Penitentials were certainly not a respectable form of Christian scripture. Inspired by Paul, Jerome, and Augustine, the Penitentials agreed *all* sex was corrupting, to the extent that women giving their husband fellatio was deemed to be worse than killing him. Not sure he'd agree, but there you go. Punishments for homosexuals varied based on the perpetrator's age or frequency of the act. For example, in an Irish Penitential, a boy caught having sex with a boy his own age was punished with two years' fasting, but a man who did it with a youngster got seven years. Fully blown (sorry) homosexual sex between two adults resulted in 15 years of a bread and water diet. Which, considering the water was pure filth, was really a death sentence in disguise.

Amusingly, it was the Christian Crusaders of the 12th century who turned out to be more influential in causing homophobia than any of these early religious guys. The Crusaders caused a canon law against homosexuals to be created. A law which stemmed from them being losers. Unable to defeat the Arab Muslims in the Crusades and unable to pray away the plague at home – rather than question themselves, they looked for others to blame and a neat group of scapegoats was formed. If anyone were to blame for the tough times in medieval Europe, then it was sure to be either Muslims, Jews, or women. To tie everything together nicely, word was put out that these groups of people also practised homosexuality. Especially the Muslims. Which was actually sort of true but of course the Crusaders took it too far, and Medieval Fake News went into overdrive with stories such as Muhammed getting Muslims hooked on sodomy in the 7th century and bishops being raped to death by Muslim mobs. Such was the strength of belief that even those who fought against the Muslims for too long could be accused of becoming homosexual. The Knights Templar were executed en-masse based on this stupid "guilty by association" theory. The fact they were only there in Muslim territory because the Crusaders wanted them to defend Christian territory didn't matter. Influenced by the strength of view from the Crusaders, the Christian church sensed an angle that could be exploited and issued a canon (a law created by the church) in the late 12th century which required excommunication and exile for homosexuals. They also included Jews and Muslims in this law as the church doesn't like to discriminate.

However, it was the advent of secular law and the influence of a few key individuals in creating these state laws which had more impact than religious leaders and canon law. This began with Justinian, who is likely the world's first homophobe – and an extremely enthusiastic one too. The Laws of Justinian in 533CE were the first secular laws against homosexuality in the Christian world, but Justinian was torturing and executing homosexual bishops for 10 years prior to this law being approved. One particularly horrendous story sees a man castrated and carried through the streets until he bled to death. The 533 law allowed executions of those who "perform actions contrary to nature herself".[225] Death through castration became his choice of punishment, but there were also torture methods such as "insertion of sharp reeds into the pores and tubes of most exquisite sensibility"[226] (tube is code for penis). Incidentally, Justinian wasn't concerned with getting evidence – children and servants were killed off the back of an accusation, and if no crime could be found for a person he wanted dead then he used this law and convicted them of Pedastry (male-male prostitution).[227]

Secular law was brutal to homosexuals. A Castilian law (Spanish province) of the 13th century stated: "both be castrated before the whole populace and on the third day be hung up by their legs until dead".[228] And genitals weren't just for cutting off – some European lawmakers liked to tie the castrated genitals around the necks of the accused while others would hang the men up using their genitals as the rope. Those who faced the latter punishment must have been well hung in all respects. In Venice, they went for the traditional burning at the stake while other cities added a bonus element that your family HAD to watch you burn. Fun fact: the homophobic insult *faggot* originates from this execution method because *faggot* was the name given to the bundle of wooden sticks used in the burnings of gay men.[229] In England, a live burial was prescribed as the remedy for those having same-gender sex. The same punishment was also applied if you were caught having sex with an animal or a Jew. Once again, it was a bit of a postcode lottery, but by 1300, the only lottery element was the execution method because these laws were in place all across Europe. Secular law had entered a whole new period of disgust. Granted, the church had set the tone, but it was the individual governments and individual leaders around Europe that began the process of condemnation, ghastly punishments, and homophobia.

No one was completely immune to these laws, as seen with the English King Edward II (1307–1327). Edward did father four children, but he also lavished gifts and privileges on his male lovers, and it didn't go unnoticed by the nobility. Or his wife. Who then all plotted to depose him. In 1326, Edward's lover, Hugh le Despenser, was despensed with – he was castrated and then made to watch his genitals be burnt in front of him before being beheaded. One year later Edward was deposed and then murdered in the tower with a red-hot poker shoved up his bottom. The method of execution was no coincidence.

Secular law did not forget to include lesbians in their prohibitions. Lawyers across Europe were trained in Roman law and swiftly picked up on the Roman's condemnation of lesbians, and so they also wrote provisions for killing women into the codes they drafted for various states. In France, Spain, Germany, Italy, and Switzerland, lesbians were deemed equal to male sodomites (yay equality) and as such were punishable with death.[230] The earliest reference to legal punishment for lesbianism is from 1270 courtesy of the French legal treatise: *Li livre de justice et de plet*.[231] It is likely to have only applied in Orleans, but it is still a revealing snapshot of medieval attitudes …and their lack of anatomical knowledge.

22. He who has been proved to be a sodomite must lose his testicles. And if he does it a second time, he must lose his member. And if he does it a third time, he must be burned.

23. A woman who does this shall lose her member each time, and on the third must be burned. (Feme qui Ie jet doit a chescune joiz perdre membre et la tierce doit estre 6 arsse.)[232]

The translation of "member" (*perdre membre*) could mean loss of an arm or leg, but because the same phrase was used for the men's punishment, it implies that female genitalia was to be removed. The suggestion we're left with is a clitorectomy, but still… there's not two of those… and they haven't officially discovered it yet anyway. France was undoubtedly homophobic against lesbians because even after sodomy was decriminalised in 1791, the authorities still went after gay women. The 19th century saw lesbian pornography seized and the publishers and writers were harshly punished. And while you now only need to go to a French beach to see a billion boobies, at the start of the 20th century, the Moulin Rouge manager was fined 200 Francs and sent to prison for three months for allowing a performance where two women exposed their breasts and acted sexually towards each other. Ooh la *nah*!

Henry VIII brought homophobia into English law in 1533 with An Acte for the Punyshement of the Vice of Buggerye. The law explained it was needed because: "there is not yet sufficient & condigne punishment appointed & limitted by the due course of the lawes of this realme for the detestable & abominable vice of buggeri committed with mankind or beest."

Henry's legislation remained in place until 1828 when it was rebranded as The Offences Against the Person Act. For the first time in England, the crime of sodomy was moved away from the church courts and became a capital crime. No longer was this something the priest would assign you penance for; now, thanks to Henry, the priest was only needed to assign you a space in the graveyard. Shit just got real.

However, Henry's motives for the act were not homophobic but the impacts definitely were – this is the beginning of the fear of 'them' as the public became wary of being associated with homosexuals. His real motivations behind the law were money and power – the Buggary Act was simply a superficial attempt to assert his power over the church. If he had this act in place, then he had something to charge monks and nuns with and then he had a "moral" imperative to shut down the monasteries and make money by selling off their land. And his motives were handsomely rewarded. In 1535, his Principal Secretary Thomas Cromwell was sent out to the monasteries to investigate the goings-on and within 175 entries in the report there were 180 monks deemed as sodomites.[233] Perhaps inspired by the male-male sex acts of the monks, the MPs in parliament responded with shouts of: "Down with Them!" when the report was read out. And down they went; by 1540, 563 houses out of 800 had been dissolved with the resale value of the monastic land estimated at a not too shabby £1.3 million.[234]

The first person to be executed under the law didn't happen until 1540 and intriguingly it was just one man on his own – Walter Hungerford, 1st Baron Hungerford of Heytesbury. In truth, the act was just used to discredit him and he was also charged with treason and witchcraft, which were much more acceptable death penalty offences. Ironically, Hungerford was a friend of the man who made the Buggary Act a reality – Thomas Cromwell. In the end, the two men ended up being executed together on 28 July 1540, as Cromwell was also charged with treason (which in Henry VIII's tenure meant he took a disliking to you that day). In true Tudor gory style, their heads were mounted on spikes and displayed on London Bridge. But don't feel too sorry for Hungerford, he was known to be an abusive husband and locked up his third wife (Elizabeth) in his castle for four years with so little food and drink that she was forced to drink her own urine to survive.[235] Offences against your wife, however, were not seen as worthy of prosecution in the Tudor era, or for that matter until well into the 20th century.[1]

The first person to be properly charged under Henry's Buggery Act for committing actual buggery was the headmaster of Eton College, Nicholas Udall, in 1541. An historical first which is curiously absent from the school's prospectus. However, Udall did not get the death penalty; in his case the sentence was commuted to imprisonment, and he was released in less than a year. With no DBS checks in place, he was then able to go on to become headmaster at Westminster School. Showing that status and connections have always been a viable route out of trouble (*cough *cough *reader is free to insert whichever Conservative politician this applies to on this particular day).

While in England, Henry VIII's Buggery Act was very much a "boys only" club, it was a different picture in Europe[236] where lesbians were harshly prosecuted under secular law. The first recorded execution of a lesbian happened in Germany in

---

[1] Whilst the 19th century saw the penalty for sodomy reduced, English law made a provision ALLOWING men to hit their wives. You may have heard of "the rule of thumb"? This idiom comes from an English law of 1847 which allowed husbands to hit their wives - so long as the implement used in the beating was no wider than their thumb. Incidentally, the reasoning behind this change was not, as you may innocently assume, to protect women. It was to prevent the screams of injured women disturbing their neighbours and causing complaints to be raised which the police then had to deal with.

1477. Katherina Hetzeldorfer was found guilty of "lesbian love"[237] and was drowned in the river Rhine. She had been turned in by a person whom she had confided in about her living arrangements (she was posing as a man living with his "sister"), and she had also paid to have sex with two other women using a red leather dildo, both of whom subsequently claimed to have no idea she was female.[238]

Homophobia really took hold after 1532 when capital punishment for lesbians began across most of Europe. Once something is deemed evil enough to warrant the death penalty it is hard to avoid disliking it. At that time, a large portion of Germany, Austria, Spain, and the Netherlands were under the control of one man: Charles V as the Holy Roman Emperor (an empire which ironically enough did not include Rome nor any part of Italy). In 1532, Charles issued Section 116 of the Constitutions of the Holy Roman Empire which said: "if anyone commits impurity with a beast, or a man with a man, or a woman with a woman, they have forfeited their lives and shall, after the common custom, be sentenced to death by burning."[239] And no one was exempt with two Spanish nuns burned for using "material instruments" after this ruling.[240] Following the trend, other European states, such as those that make up modern-day Italy, also made laws which condemned lesbians. For example, the Italian town of Treviso, near Venice, stated that if any woman over the age of 12 was caught having sexual relations with another woman, then: "she shall [also] be fastened naked to a stake in the Street of the Locusts and shall remain there all day and night under a reliable guard, and the following day shall be burned outside the city".[241] In Geneva, Switzerland, the Calvinists (radical Protestants) took over and reformed the law as well as the religion. In 1568 they drowned a woman who was found guilty of "Fornication" (lesbian sex), "Sapphism" (lesbian sex) and "Blasphemy" (she probably said "for God's sake, this is ridiculous" at some point).[242]

The last lesbian execution in Europe was Catharina Linck in 1721, and, just like the first, it took place in Germany. Linck, an orphan, wasn't one for half measures and took on at least nine different male identities in her life. However, her first identity was not the best start– she became a preacher in a Christian cult which required the members to repeatedly hit their heads against walls. Linck spent two years travelling with these headbangers until she was forced to flee after telling two men they could walk on water. The fools believed her (having previously knocked the sense out of themselves) and drowned. Following this ridiculousness, she took it easy for a while, looking after some pigs and making a leather penis for herself; she was even so ballsy as to add two testicles to the contraption. Presumably she also used this time to practice peeing standing up as her next move saw her join three different armies: the army of Hannover, the Polish army, and the German Hessians. Tiring of the military life, Linck then became a dyer of clothes and married a young woman who was also called Catharina (surname Műhlhahn). Incidentally, Linck was not a good "husband", nor a good dyer; she beat her wife, and the couple ended up begging for money. One night, Műhlhahn decided to take a closer look at Linck's "member" and discovered it was fake, but she agreed not to say anything (presumably for fear of being punched again). Luckily, Műhlhahn's mother was the interfering type and she, with another woman's help, attacked Linck, stole her leather penis and turned her in to the law enforcement, leading to Linck's execution in 1721.[243] And here's us thinking *Disney's* Mulan was a good story of girls pretending to be boys…

Meanwhile, in the newly formed United Kingdom (1707), lesbians still didn't exist. Twenty-five years after Linck's execution, Mary Hamilton aka Dr Charles Hamilton (why just be a man when you can be a doctor!), found herself in a similar predicament. Hamilton was caught two months into her second (!) marriage to Mary Price after being recognised by someone from her wife-number-one days. Incidentally, Mary Price had no idea she was being penetrated with a bit of leather and she was kindly described as "naïve" by the courts. But unlike in Germany, there was no provision for women in the UK's sex laws and so there was no crime to charge her with. Obviously, they couldn't just let her go, she had dared to imitate a man, and so Hamilton was charged with deception under the Vagrancy Act but got to keep her life. Even when presented with an eyewitness, the UK authorities still couldn't believe there were such people as lesbians. In 1811, two mistresses of a boarding school were accused of "improper conduct" by a student who had witnessed the women in bed together. However, when investigated there was no evidence of sex aids and, without a fake phallus, the 19th-century lawmakers ruled that sex between the two women was as likely as "murder by hocus pocus".[244] The women's status added further doubt to the accusation; it was literally unbelievable in the judges' eyes that two middle-class women were capable of such a thing.

Just as religious doctrine failed to have an impact on people's behaviour, so too did the attempts of these individuals. The most significant reason why homophobia did not develop from the legislation is because of how popular homosexuality was at every level in society. The closet door was particularly wide open for the rich and powerful. A Parisian lawyer in 1725 described how: "All of the young noblemen of the court were wildly addicted to it;"[245] which was also the case across other royal courts of Europe. Homosexuality flourished in the court of Henry III of France; Queen Christina of Sweden; James I and William III of England; Queen Anne of England; and Frederick the Great of Prussia. Homosexuality was also incredibly popular out at sea. Tellingly, the English navy waited nearly 130 years after Henry VIII made homosexuality an offence to make it punishable at sea: "If any person or persons in or belonging to the Fleet shall commit the unnaturall (sic) and detestable sin of Buggery (sic) or Sodomy with Man or Beast he shall be punished with death without mercy".[246] But it was so commonplace, men were rarely punished; court martial records show just 45 hangings in the British Navy from 1703 to 1829.[247] As one officer explained, "executing all the homosexuals would have led to a very small navy,"[248] so you can sea why they held back. This popularity wasn't just limited to the realms of the legal seamen. A lot of 17th-century pirates were also homosexual.[249] Obviously, these ships weren't the sort of organisations to be having rules, and so by the 17th century it was the only safe place a homosexual could guarantee their life. And it wasn't a case of "making do" and then having heterosexual relationships on land – men had exclusive and long-term relationships with each other aboard the boats.[250] Arrrr, how sweet.

Back on land and further down the food chain, homosexuality was so popular in some European cities that special clubs were set up and specific etiquette had developed for homosexuals to find each other. In the Dutch city of The Hague, gay men would signal they were up for it by stepping on each other's feet; while in Stockholm, a visit to the urinal indicated you were up for a quickie. In 17th and 18th century London you didn't even need secret signals because there were numerous gay sex clubs and brothels called "Molly Houses" which men could go to. It was called a Molly House because *Molly* was the term used to describe homosexuals, so it wasn't even like they were trying to be subtle. Imagine a street of clubs called "Coke Clubs" where you could go and take cocaine and you'd be on the right lines. These Molly Houses were run by men with wonderful names such as Miss Muff, Plump Nelly, and Mother Clap (STD link unconfirmed). While male prostitutes were the norm, all tastes were catered for in such establishments. One club near the Strand offered a "real life" service where gay couples married in a chapel, then went into a room to "conceive" a baby, and then were able to "deliver" this baby (a large doll) in a birthing room complete with accessories such with towels and warm water.

Equally important as the popularity of homosexuality, the fact that those enforcing the law were not *actually* enforcing the law also stagnated the development of homophobia. In France, the authorities didn't want to prosecute because they believed homosexuality was contagious and so didn't want to draw any extra attention to it. So, while the French police caught 40,000 men in the act during the first half of the 18th century, there were only four executions by 1750.[251] In other cases, the authorities were happy to take bribes and ignore the goings-on; for example, at least 20 UK Molly Houses were under investigation by 1720[252] but the enquiries did not lead to them shutting down. However, this lack of prosecution did not sit well with everyone, and a group of individuals set about trying to instil the homophobia they thought should exist. This vigilante group was created by a bunch of self-righteous rich men and MPs who gave themselves the most humdrum name ever: Society for the Reformation of Manners. Because clearly it was bad manners to be homosexual. This group only lasted for 40 years because they lacked support from the non-homophobic public. But my goodness did they achieve a lot in those forty years –100,000 people were prosecuted thanks to the Mind your Manners campaign, which was approximately 3.5% of the adult male population of England and Wales.[253] An impressive feat considering that even today, with homosexuality legal, only 2.7% of the UK population identify as lesbian, gay or bisexual.[254] They manner-ged to find, not just ALL of them, but one quarter more than the estimated number!

It was not until the 19th century that homophobia really took hold in the UK – a change which came about not because of religion but due to the sudden application of Henry VIII's Buggery Act and the influence of three law-making individuals: Prime Minister Robert Peel, Judge Lord Penzance, and busybody Henry Labouchere. By 1806, Henry's Buggery Act was being used far more than he ever intended, and Britain was executing more sodomites than murderers;[255] there were 60 homosexual hangings in Britain during the years 1806–1835.[256] Contrastingly, there are no known executions for the crime of homosexuality, of men or women, in continental Europe during the nineteenth century.[257]

In 1828, Prime Minister Robert Peel re-peel-ed Henry's Buggery Act and replaced it with his Offences Against the Person Act. Peel's new law specifically focussed on male-male-sex activity (leaving out the bestiality bit). Peel believed that laws define "the moral habits of the people",[258] and to this end he was keen to clarify in people's minds that homosexuality was an immoral act by placing the words "abominable crime" before the word *Buggery*. According to Peel and his 1828 Act, consensual male-male sex was worse than raping an eleven-year-old girl. Accordingly, his law prescribed the death penalty for homosexuals while rapists of girls aged between 10 and 12 got prison and hard labour. Peel could now sleep easy, safe in the knowledge his law would define the moral habits of the people. Homophobia:1 – Little girls: 0.

As well as ensuring Britain had legislation to condemn homosexuals, Peel also made sure there was the machinery to enforce it by establishing the Metropolitan Police of London as well as local police forces (the "Peelers") between 1829 and 1850. Bribes could not be taken so easily with a united force of police. While executions under the 1828 law were not long applied (the last executions for homosexual acts were James Pratt and John Smith on 27 November 1835);[259] Peel's law, in one sweeping move, made homosexuality a collective social threat. Homophobia had begun.

Lord Penzance is responsible for starting opposition to gay marriage by ruling that marriage is solely for the union of men and women in 1866. Gay marriage remained illegal in Britain until 2014. He used that bit in the Bible where Jesus spoke only of men and women in terms of marriage to justify his decision: "I conceive that marriage, as understood in Christendom, may for this purpose be defined as the voluntary union for life of one man and one woman, to the exclusion of all others".[260] Ironically, this law didn't come about because of two men trying to get married – it was the result of a court case about a heterosexual polygamous marriage: the 1866 case of Hyde v. Hyde and Woodmansee.[261]

It's a shame that all Penzance's time in private education and two degrees from Trinity College, Cambridge, didn't afford him the opportunity to educate himself on what "the historical nature of marriage" factually was in Christendom. As we have seen, male-male unions were a long-time part of Christendom, but he preferred to focus on what one man *might* have once said rather than evidence from the last 5000 years of human history and marriage. Penzance's witterings remained the common-law definition of marriage throughout the British Empire until the 21st century. His ruling prevented equality in marriage and became the basis of homophobic arguments against gay relationships, arguments which insisted the sacrament of marriage has ALWAYS been between a man and a woman. Which is Fake History – there were Christian men getting married in churches for *hundreds of years* up until the 13th century. Penzance even managed to influence American homophobia as President Bill Clinton used his theory in 1996 to justify *his* Defence of Marriage Act (a bizarre move for someone who had an affair and clearly didn't give a rat's arse about defending any sort of marriage). Clinton's act stated that marriage was "only for a man and a woman"[262] and this was not overturned by federal law until 2015.

In 1885, *all* homosexual acts were criminalised thanks to Henry Labouchere. The Labouchere Amendment (his last-minute addition to The Criminal Law Amendment Act aiming to protect young girls from sex slavery) made Every. Single. Type. of homosexual act illegal and enabled courts to charge people with the crime of "gross indecency" when penetrative sex (buggery) could not be proven. Up until this point, the law had been focussed on condemning public liaisons and punishing men who had been judged to be corrupting young boys. But now, even in your own home and with a partner your age, who you loved – you were a criminal facing two years imprisonment. Once this law was in place, Britain began exporting it to all their colonies and other western nations copied, seemingly thinking that Great Britain knew what it was doing. Great. The amendment remained in law until 1967 and was used against the WW2 codebreaker and computer scientist Alan Turing in 1952. Turing was convicted of "gross indecency" and was given a choice between imprisonment or chemical castration via 12 months of injections of oestrogen hormones (which aimed to reduce his libido). He was found dead, caused by cyanide poisoning in 1954 – possibly suicide, possibly an accident or possibly an assassination by the secret services because of all he knew.

One individual who indirectly caused a rise in homophobia in Britain was Oscar Wilde. Wilde was an Irish writer, most famed for his book *The Picture of Dorian Gray* (1891) and his play *The Importance of Being Earnest* (1895). He was homosexual and, due to the Labouchere Amendment, found himself prosecuted with gross indecency at the trial which began 26 April 1895. The judge, Sir Arthur Charles, described it as "the worst case I have ever tried,"[263] (I would like to think that this was his first day and he'd never tried a murderer but unfortunately his comment was due to homophobia rather than inexperience). There were cries of "shame!" from the public around the courtroom but Wilde was not forced to walk naked down the streets *Game of Thrones Style*. Wilde did not deny the charges and instead (accurately) likened his actions to those of the Ancient Greeks as a sort of defence: "The 'love that dare not speak its name' in this century is such a great affection of an elder for a younger man as there was between David and Jonathan, such as Plato made the very basis of his philosophy, and such as you find in the sonnets of Michelangelo and Shakespeare."[264]

This did not go down well. Wilde's blasé attitude in admitting his actions made him seem arrogant and immoral and although the first trial resulted in a hung jury (after three hours of deliberation) a second trial, three weeks later, saw him convicted and sentenced to two years imprisonment – the maximum allowed. Wilde's reaction to the conviction saw him sway slightly in shock and his face turned a shade of (Dorian) grey. England's top prosecutor, Solicitor-General Frank Lockwood, took the case the second time around and successfully persuaded the jury that Wilde was a criminal because the men he had engaged in sexual relations with were "illiterate boys"[265] and not his equals. These years in prison saw Wilde face hard labour, such as separating the fibres in scraps of old navy ropes and forced exercise such as walking on a treadmill for hours at a time[266] which undoubtedly led to his early death at the age of 46 in 1900.

The case garnered huge publicity and created the stereotype of what a gay man was – effeminate. He was seen to be unmanly because he wore a fashionable coat with a flower in his buttonhole and had long hair ("maybe he'll get it cut now" was one response to his conviction). Due to Wilde being the cultured sort, the British public began associating art and culture with homoeroticism and effeminate men were assumed to be gay. This stereotype enabled homophobes to come up with a whole new vocabulary of homophobic slurs based around the idea that gay men were not "real" men. The trials also led to public attitudes to become harsher towards homosexuals because they were now seen as predators and viewed as a threat. The British public's tolerance of same-sex relationships was over. As a result, the 20th century saw huge numbers of homophobic attacks and abuse which, ironically enough, eventually led to the decriminalisation of homosexual acts which took place in private.

While religious individuals are to blame for starting homophobia, the people with the most impact in Britain are the two Henrys – the VIII and the Labouchere. King Henry was the first to criminalise homosexuality and bring homophobia into English law. As time went on, people saw the law was there, thought they better follow it, and changed their attitudes of acceptance accordingly. Updates to Henry's law only made things worse as homosexuality was deemed as akin to raping a child – which does kind of create a negative association. If Henry had never made the law in the first place, the 19th-century governments might not have come down so harshly on male-male sex because, after all, it was bloody popular. Labouchere's amendment is to blame for criminalising homosexual relationships and infecting the British Empire and other parts of the world with this homophobia. Homophobia was created by Henry means necessary.

How did homophobia spread around the world?

Imperialism (the policy of creating an empire) caused homophobia to increase and spread around the world. Same-gender sex was common around the globe until European and Arabian empires conquered and made the rules change.[267] British colonists regularly recorded the homosexuality they encountered while exploring, such as Sir Richard Francis Burton, who talked of a "Sotadic zone" in Northern Africa, parts of Asia and most of North and South America.[268] These relationships between men were celebrated and permitted, which clearly shows how far away from homophobia these parts of the word were. Britain, along with her European imperialist mates ensured this didn't last for long and managed to infect most of the world with homophobia in just a few hundred years.

The Spanish were the first to bring homophobia with them as part of the colonisation package when they conquered southern and Central America following Columbus' 1492 discovery of "India" (sidenote: NOT India – they were Caribbean islands). Upon arrival, the Spanish conquistadors were mortified to discover sodomy being openly practised by the natives. Hernan Cortes landed in Mexico in 1519 and somewhat exaggerated the situation with his description of the people as "all sodomites".[269] The Spanish and Portuguese then set about imposing their Catholic beliefs on the native populations, ignorantly believing they were doing God's work. These new sex laws were imposed upon the natives with a backdrop of raping the native women without consequence; after all, there's no need to implement *every* sex law that existed in Europe, least of all the ones which might ruin their "fun". The traumatic result for the natives was public execution (burning alive or being ripped apart by dogs) for something they had no idea was a crime. In a sneaky move no one saw coming, the Europeans then used the existence of homosexuality in the New World as their *reason* to conquer – these people "needed" to be saved. Violently of course.

European imperialism and homophobia came to North America in the 16th century; the first known case of homosexual activity receiving a death sentence was in 1566, when the Spanish executed a Frenchman in Florida.[270]

The British colonised most of the East Coast from 1619 (aka the Thirteen Colonies) until the American War of Independence put an end to that in the 1770s. Other parts of America were claimed by France, Spain, and the Netherlands. Fun fact: New York used to be called New Amsterdam until the British bought the land from the Dutch in 1664. The British law makers of the Thirteen Colonies copied their laws from back home and imposed them in their settled colonies and on conquered people. One positive of this was British ignorance about lesbians came too. Despite the best efforts of the Rev. John Cotton to bring forth a punishment of death for these women,[271] there was only one conviction for lesbianism in the whole of the Thirteen Colonies' history. This first and only known conviction was in Plymouth, Massachusetts, in 1649, when Sarah Norman was charged with "Lewd behaviour with each other upon a bed" with Mary Hammon. However, the conviction did not result in death for either woman. Mary was cleared of all guilt and Sarah was made to publicly acknowledge her crime and then basically told to not do it again. This attitude prevailed into the 20th century so that by the 1920s lesbian life was openly celebrated in cultural centres such as New York's Harlem and Greenwich village. African American women sung the blues with lyrics about lesbian desires and their struggles and there were also performances with male and female drag stars.[272] Homophobia did not develop against lesbians because it never really got the chance to start due to Britain's failure of acknowledgement (yay patriarchy).

However, while the British Thirteen Colonies were not so active in pursuing homosexuals, their influence on the morals of Americans meant male sodomy was made a capital crime in 1792, just nine years into America's existence. Once the Americans kicked Britain out in 1783, they began expanding westwards by buying land from other European countries who got there first (such as Louisiana from France in 1803) or stealing it from the natives who resided there (such as the other 32 states). Over the next 150 years, homophobia spread across America as the newly added states adopted the same sex laws. There was no interest in debating the origins or morals of these sex laws. The native's *Two-Spirit* attitude was forced to change – they were pushed off their land and either forced to live on reservations or stay put and adopt the Christian ways of their overlords. Native children were forced into boarding schools, get their hair cut, and change their clothes so that they learnt the "accepted" morals rather than those held by their cultures for thousands of years. It was out with the old *Two-Spirit* and in with the Old Testament *Three Spirit* of the father, son, and homophobic ghost.

Before Africa came under the influence of European imperialists, it had a long history of homosexual relations. European conquest of the continent began in the 16th century with the establishment of slave ports in western Africa. The "Scramble for Africa" began in 1877 as European nations competed to claim territory and influence – a process which continued in earnest until the Europeans found something else to fight about – World War One.

Egypt, since the death of Cleopatra, has come under the rule of four different empires: the Roman Empire (30 BCE–649 CE); the Arab Empire (649–1517); the Ottoman

Empire (1517–1882); and the British Empire (1882–1952). Imperialism brought homophobia but strangely not until the British came along. Prior to this, homosexuals were tolerated in Egyptian society so long as it wasn't the religious leaders who were at it.[273] Gustave Flaubert commented in an 1850 letter how homosexuality is freely accepted in Egypt and openly discussed in public[274] (a letter which our friend Hawass of earlier in the chapter fame clearly did not consider before making his statement about the absence of homosexuals in Egypt). When the British killjoys took charge, they put an end to such tolerance and instigated private inspectors[275] to go after the "culprits". Britain's policies in other colonies such as India strongly influenced what they put in place for Egypt; in 1860 Britain had enacted Section 377 of the Indian Penal Code and banned sodomy – this was the first ever anti-sodomy law to exist in a penal code. British imperialism has impacted on Egyptian attitudes to such an extent that homosexual acts are still illegal to this day.

However, elsewhere in Africa, European imperialism has had less of an effect. Even as recently as the early 20th century, male-male sex existed openly and without punishment in Somalia. Britain and Italy colonised Somalia and established British Somaliland in 1884 and Italian Somaliland in 1889, and yet in 1909, traveller F.J. Bieber (First Justin Bieber?!) observed that: "sodomy is not foreign to the Harari. Albeit not as commonly, it also occurs among the Galla [Oromo] and Somal[i]".[276] Nonetheless, European influence won in the end, and colonial pressure has resulted in such a huge change in attitudes that even today, homosexuality is seen as an evil which must be punished in more than half of the 54 countries. Even Somalia eventually fell victim to the homophobic trend, and it is now a crime that carries a prison sentence of three years or possibly death if you're caught by a militant group.

In Asia, European imperialism had a more indirect effect and homophobia appeared, not because of western colonisation but due to the western influence around them. For example, some opposition to homosexuality in China began in the medieval era during the Tang Dynasty (618–906 CE) due to their neighbouring states' adoption of Christianity or Islam.[277] Western influence had a more direct impact from the 19th century onwards, and homophobia became an entrenched part of Chinese culture when the latter half of the Qing dynasty (1644–1912) deliberately attempted to become more westernised.[278] This change was long lasting, and homosexual sex was banned in China until 1997. Progress since then has been slow. Although homosexuality was removed from the official list of mental illnesses in China in 2001, this declassification has not been recognised by the Chinese Ministry of Health. Homophobia is still prevalent as evidenced by the existence and acceptance of gay conversion therapy.[279] Japan also fell victim to the influence of western culture, albeit fleetingly. While for most of Japan's history homophobia has not existed due to the influence of Buddhist and Samurai lifestyles, between 1872 and 1880, male-male sex was criminalised as the ruling elite became seemingly inspired by western laws. However, unlike in China, this particular western "value" was short lived, and the Japanese Penal Code of 1880 repealed their legislation and furthermore introduced an equal age of consent for homosexual and heterosexual sex. Since then, Japan has had no laws against homosexuality.

Intertwined with imperialism is the need to be different to what came before. A newly formed empire needs to be distinct from the rulers it displaced; otherwise who would know the difference? This cause of homophobia began with the newly forming Hebrew state in 1300 BCE; was then employed by both the Arab and European empires; and most recently, the aspiration to be visibly anti-western has inspired the harsh penalties imposed in post-revolution Iran.[280] By the time the Iranian revolution took place in 1979, Britain and most of Europe had legalised homosexuality, and so it was seen by the radical Muslims as a form of western indulgence and corruption which must be stamped out.

The need to be different to define oneself in opposition to who ruled before is responsible for the emergence of the homophobic *Sharí'a law* between the 8th and 9th centuries. In the 21st century, Sharí'a law is still the basis of the oppressive regimes in Iran and Saudi Arabia and explains why these countries punish homosexuality with death. But Sharí'a law would never have even existed if it were not for imperialism. Running an empire which stretched from central Asia across to Spain and down into Northern Africa brought them into contact with the existence of same-sex relations in these newly conquered lands.[281] With the backdrop of consistency in the empire and need to be different to what came before, it was then necessary to create a standardised set of laws to be implemented in their new territory. And so, two centuries after the death of the Prophet Muhammed, the Hadith and the Quran were codified into laws named after the founders: Malikite, Hanabalite, Hanafite, and Shafi'ite. Sharí'a law was chosen to be established as the law in the conquered lands once the takeover was completed. Imperialism, therefore, not only led to the creation of these homophobic laws, but it also caused them to be spread all over the Middle East and Northern Africa.

To be fair, imperialism did have one positive impact once. The Code Napoleon, imposed by (guess who?) in France and across her empire from 1804, was a set of new laws based on freedom, equality, and fraternity. A big part of this freedom and fraternity was legalising gay sex. Although it was not such good news for women who found themselves ruled to be the property of men. The Code Napoleon then became a moderating influence in their conquered territories in North Africa, Syria, and Lebanon. But while this *egalite* theory is still in force in France, it was a short hiatus elsewhere due to the empire soon crumbling under independence movements. Still… it's nice to know that, despite being a sexist military dictator who was unable to make sensible decisions (such as the right time of year to invade Russia), at least Napoleon wasn't a homophobe.

The biggest twist in the tale of imperialism is how everything ended. Once Europe was done with all their conquering and had hung up their imperialist jackets in the latter half of the 20th century, they then changed their minds about the whole homophobia thing. Ignoring the fact *they* had been the ones to impose laws against homosexuality around the world in the first place, Europe then condemned countries with homophobic legislation for not being open-minded like them. You cheeky sods, EU.

Why are people homophobic?

Homophobia has arisen due to the influence of law-making individuals and has spread around the world due to imperialism and globalisation. Although it sure does look like religion was to blame, what with the first homophobic word on the street coming from God (apparently). Religious texts gave certain individuals the backup they needed when they wanted to spread homophobia but, religion does not condemn homosexual relationships – it condemns sodomy because this was not a form of pre-creative sex. In the modern world, it *seems* like religion is homophobic due to the draconian punishments in Islamic countries and the fact that the bestselling Bible in the world (the New International Bible of 1973) has tweaked the original text so that it now explicitly condemns: "those who practice homosexuality".[282] Which is most definitely not the word of God – this is the word of the American publishing company, Biblica. Most concerning about this tweak is the fact Biblica chose to use these inflammatory words *after* homosexuality had begun the process of decriminalisation in Europe. America lagged far behind and did not legalise homosexuality until 2003, so basically it is American values we are getting in the New International Bible of 1973 – not Christian values.

Individuals have been more impactful than religion because people have the power to make laws which *force* societies to behave and think in certain ways. Religious doctrine certainly affected these laws but, ultimately, without the homophobic views of Roman Emperor Justinian, Europe might never have thought to legislate against homosexuality. Without Henry VIII, the Protestant leaders of Europe, or Pope Clement VII – Europe would not have legal prohibitions against homosexuals. Without Robert Peel, Britain would have continued to do bugger all with Henry VIII's Buggery Act. Without Henry Labouchere, British law enforcement would not have gone all Big Brother on us and embarked on an era of snooping into people's private sex lives. If all of these people had not taken the actions they did, homophobia would not have had the chance to develop, and it would have been contained within religious doctrine instead of being written into secular law.

Imperialism caused homophobia to be exported around the world because those doing the conquering wanted to be clearly different from what came before and to have consistency across their newly conquered territories. The Europeans impacted those living in North and South America from the 16th century onwards and Africa from the 19th century onwards, and the Arabs impacted upon their territory across the Middle East and Northern Africa from the 9th century onwards.

Globalisation enabled European homophobia to also have an indirect influence in Asia. Some rulers, such as those in 19th century China and (fleetingly) 19th century Japan, adopted homophobic attitudes to be the same as the West and thus seen as political equals. Conversely, in the 20th century, China and Iran came down *more* harshly on homosexuals to be seen as different to their Western counterparts.

Homophobia against women arose from male fear. Fear of being replaced and fear of losing the prescribed gender roles which kept men in power. In a nutshell, if you didn't use a fake penis, then the authorities were uninterested, but as soon as a woman pretended to have her own member, lesbianism was a serious crime. It really didn't sit well with the patriarchal law makers to discover they could be replaced with a stuffed bit of leather. But then, ironically enough, patriarchy meant this homophobia was less visible, less pursued, and less harsh than that directed against gay men – especially in Britain. Women were an afterthought in religious doctrine – Eve was made from Adam's rib after all (though I prefer to think this happened because, after God made man, he thought "I must be able to do better than that"). Women were therefore also an afterthought in the law. Without the influence of individuals such as the Apostle Paul and the books from Archbishop Theodore of Tarsus, St. Anselm, Gratian, and St. Thomas of Aquinas, lesbians might have escaped condemnation completely.

By the 20th century, most countries around the world had carefully cultivated their homophobia to be backed up with religious texts (look carefully and you'll find it) and endorsed with legislation. As a result, homophobia was ingrained into society. The misconception that homosexuality was a mental illness really didn't help matters either. This lasted from the 19th century all the way up to 1990, when the World Health Organisation announced that, actually, it wasn't. Ultimately, people's misinterpretation of religion combined with people's need to set themselves apart from others (those who came before and those being conquered) has caused homophobia. Homosexual acts remain illegal in 73 sovereign states around the world, and it is punishable with death in 13.[283] The countries in bold are the ones with the death penalty still: **Afghanistan**, Algeria, Angola, Antigua & Barbuda, Bangladesh, Barbados, Bhutan, Botswana, Brunei Darussalam, Burundi, Cameroon, Comoros, Cook Islands, Dominica, Eritrea, Ethiopia, Egypt, Gambia, Gaza, Ghana, Grenada, Guinea, Guyana, India, Indonesia, **Iran**, **Iraq**, Jamaica, Kenya, Kiribati, Kuwait, Lebanon, Liberia, Libya, Malawi, Malaysia, Maldives, **Mauritania**, Mauritius, Morocco, Myanmar, Namibia, **Nigeria**, Oman, **Pakistan**, Papua New Guinea, **Qatar**, Saint Kitts & Nevis, Saint Lucia, Saint Vincent & the Grenadines, **Saudi Arabia**, Senegal, Sierra Leone, Singapore, Solomon Islands, **Somalia**, Samoa, South Sudan, Sri Lanka, **Sudan**, Swaziland, **Syria**, Tanzania, Togo, Tonga, Trinidad & Tobago, Tunisia, Turkmenistan, Tuvalu, **United Arab Emirates**, Uganda, Uzbekistan, **Yemen**.

These 13 countries are still so vehemently homophobic due to their application of Sharí'a law, proving that the most influential cause of homophobia has been imperialism and the need to be different from what came before.

King Richard I – More Lyingheart than Lionheart

Richard was born in England and spent his childhood in the country, but he never learned the language and would not have described himself as an Englishman. He was an Angevin, and to him, England was just one part of their Empire. The Angevin Empire encompassed much of France, and it was here that Richard would have most felt at home. Being the third son of five, he was never expected to be king. Richard the Lionheart is special because he is one of the few monarchs of England remembered by his epithet rather than his number[284] (Tudor Queens: The Virgin Queen and Bloody Mary are the others). But that's where his specialness ends.

Richard the Lionheart is a legend – just look at his name, right?

What makes someone a legend in history? Traditionally, things like winning a war, defeating an evil foe, leading a revolution, successfully completing a heroic mission, or simply making people's lives better in some way. Richard didn't manage any of these things.

Apparently, Richard received the title *Coeur-de-Lion* (Lion Heart) due to his reputation as a great military leader. But this, ladies and gentlemen, is nothing more than one of the greatest bits of spin you ever will see. Firstly, this judgement of "great military leader" did not come from someone in the know... or as the result of a democratic referendum... it came from his mum (Eleanor of Aquitaine). And she based her opinion on the fact he had killed his father, aka the King of England Henry II. An act which, admittedly, must have required the courage of a lion but considering Henry II was not a tyrant who needed displacing for the good of the country, it was also an act that was completely unnecessary. Sure, Henry made mistakes, such as accidentally inciting the murder of Thomas Beckett and levying an unpopular new tax so that he may go to Jerusalem and reconquer the Holy Land. But in truth, the former was a storm he had weathered, and the latter (a "surprise" tax) was a common occurrence in medieval England. Richard and his brothers had basically got a bit bored waiting for dad to die (he had been on the throne for 35 years – the selfish scoundrel) and so they took up arms against him. Richard also allied himself with France against his father. Uniting with the French was a very clever plan, and the armies of Phillippe II of France and Richard I were able to defeat King Henry II at Le Mans in July 1189. If asked about it in heaven, Henry II may argue that he was ill and going to die anyway so it wasn't *really* a defeat but regardless of how it happened, Richard was made heir apparent on his deathbed. So, it's easy to understand why the French agreed with Richard's mum and awarded the title *Coeur-de-Lion* – he was their main man for defeating the English king. Still difficult to see why the English have run with it for over one thousand years though.

One thing the ol' Lionheart *did* manage to do was get kidnapped. He fell out with his Christian ally, the King of France, while on Crusade in Jerusalem fighting against the Muslims. Likely due to the fact he was now Billy-no-mates, Richard changed his mind about conquering Jerusalem and began his journey home. Only problem was, his journey home was through huge swathes of Europe that were ruled by monarchs who now, in allegiance with the King of France, didn't like him either.[285] That's right, Richard had managed to wind up so many people during his crusade campaign he even turned his fellow Christian allies in Europe against him.[286] Even evil dictators have managed to hang onto their foreign alliances longer than this wally. King Phillipe, meanwhile, had already returned home to start plotting his revenge on Richard, and following the Angevin family tradition of double-crossing, Richard's younger brother John also joined in with the scheming.

To be fair to Richard, he did try to avoid capture by travelling through Europe disguised as a peasant. To be even more fair to Richard, he was an absolute idiot for not removing the HUGE gold ring which completely gave him away as a king. Richard was captured by the duke of Austria near Vienna in December 1192 and handed over to Henry VI, the Holy Roman Emperor (the big dog of Europe). A huge ransom of 150,000 silver marks or £60,000 was promptly demanded for his safe return – a big sum even by today's standards, and at the time this represented double the annual income of England (it would be like demanding £4 trillion today).[287] The payment was *sooo* huge that even the guys from the Holy Roman Empire (HRE) were embarrassed about it; the German chronicler, Otto of St Blasien, wrote: "I prefer not to give the exact weight (of gold and silver) that he paid because if I did, it would be thought incredible and I would be accused of lying."[288] It took two years to pay the ransom, which is actually pretty impressive when you compare it to Germany only paying back their WW1 reparations in 2010.

Richard's biggest fan, his mum, was the one ensuring the ransom was paid. It's unclear how enthusiastic the rest of the country was. And so, perhaps in honour of his dead father, a "surprise" tax of 25% was levied on every free man in England.

The cathedrals were emptied of their gold and silver crosses which were melted down to help make the payment. It's what God would have wanted. Especially after Richard had failed to win back the Holy Land (Jerusalem) for the Christians. In 1194 Richard was released. And if only he could have spoken English, he might have thanked his people. He did at least forgive his brother. And then – as a truly grateful Lionheart of legend status would do – he left England after a few months and went to battle in France. Never to return. He died a few years later while besieging a castle in France (I don't think he forgave the French king so easily).

But isn't he a hero of the Crusades?

Richard's objective in the Crusade was to recapture Jerusalem and defeat Saladin. If he had done either of those things, then he would have deserved hero status. In reality, he had a successful start with two victories ON HIS WAY to the Crusades and then during the fourteen-month campaign he won three battles. Essentially Richard did well but he didn't succeed in either of his objectives, though I'm sure his mother still gave him a "good effort" sticker and reassured him he was mummy's brave little soldier. In the process of all this not winning malarky, Richard at least managed to successfully multi-task by spending most of England's money while turning the leaders of Christian Europe against him. The whole truth about his crusade campaign is not told in English history books because it doesn't fit with the romantic notion of a Lionheart Hero. There is no mention of some of the less heroic things he did out there (what goes on tour stays on tour).

Saladin, of Iraqi origin, captured Jerusalem in 1187 because he thought the holy city should be in Muslim hands. Jerusalem is, rather awkwardly, the epicentre of three religions – Christianity, Islam, and Judaism. It's where Christ was crucified, where Muhammed ascended to heaven and where Abraham offered his son Isaac to God. What a city! Richard's first success was on his way to the Holy Land, but it had nothing to do with the Crusade against Saladin. He landed in Sicily and captured the city of Messina in October 1190, which allowed him to fulfil his mum's wishes and free his sister, Joan. This wasn't exactly a quick stage, though, and he spent around eight months on the island, which caused some tension between him, King Phillippe of France, and their respective soldiers. Maybe if somebody had told him he only had another nine years to live he might have hurried the hell up.

After Sicily he travelled to Acre, a city on the coast of modern-day Palestine. While en route, a storm blew his ships adrift and three of them were shipwrecked off the coast of Cyprus. The Cypriot king, being loyal to Saladin, refused to let Richard's people go and so Richard took a small diversion to the island and conquered it. It's likely that this victory added weight to the "Lionheart" cult that his mother had started as, admittedly, it was one of Richard's finest moments. The conquering was quick and chivalrous. He achieved his victory in under two months; he rescued his new fiancée and his sister who were together on one of the ships held hostage, *and* he was gallant enough to heed the King of Cyprus' request to not be held in common-as-muck irons with Richard chaining him with silver instead. What a top bloke. In addition to all these positives, Cyprus, even though it wasn't on his "To Do" list, was worth having. It was strategically important – laying off the coast of the Holy Land – and Richard was able to use it to raise some much-needed cash as he sold the island to the Knights Templar soon after (it didn't go too well for them but that's another story…).

After occupying Sicily, rescuing his sister (twice), conquering Cyprus, and then using the island as his wedding venue to marry Berengaria of Navarre, Richard must have felt on top of the world. And he hadn't even started the Crusade yet! He left Cyprus on 5 June 1191, and landed at Acre three days later. Acre had been controlled by Saladin and under siege by Christian forces for two years, but within a month Richard had captured the city. Another success. Go, Richard! Except Richard was sick with scurvy and is unlikely to have had much impact on the fighting. One (rather favourable) report describes him as firing a crossbow at some Muslims while being carried on a stretcher. But I'm calling that.

Luckily his allies were there to help, and the triple entente of the 12th century (Phillipe of France, Richard of England, and Leopold of Austria representing HRE) claimed victory by displaying their banners over the walls of the conquered city. It was from this point that things took a turn for the worse due to Richard having a bit of a strop. He fell out with Leopold because he thought Leo shouldn't be hanging *his* banner of Austria but rather the banner of the HRE. And then he fell out with Phillipe because Richard didn't want to share Cyprus with him. Leopold and Phillipe both left the Crusade because of this tiff, likely muttering something about not getting their "Lion's share" of the goodies.

After Acre, we see a more sinister side to Richard. He was left in charge of the Muslim hostages – a group of between 2700 and 3000 people made up of soldiers, men, women, and children. On 16 August 1191, Richard ordered this group to be taken to a small hill called Ayyadieh. This location was chosen because it was in sight of the opposing Ayyubid army as well as Saladin's headquarters and Richard wanted them to see exactly what was about to occur. He ordered for ALL the hostages to be killed. Beha-ed-Din was a member of Saladin's court who (along with much of the Saracen army) witnessed the massacre: "Then the king of England, seeing all the delays interposed by the Sultan to the execution of the treaty, acted perfidiously as regards his Muslim prisoners… They numbered more than three thousand and were all bound with ropes. The Franks then flung themselves upon them all at once and massacred them with sword and lance in cold blood."[289] Tellingly, not even Richard's enemies considered him an Englishman by calling him one of the Franks (French).

This is known as the Massacre of Ayyadieh, but it's unlikely you'll read about it in any British history textbook. Sneaky massacres of innocent people tend to not make the cut. Richard felt justified in the massacre due to the fact Saladin had not kept to the deal they had brokered after the battle of Acre. Saladin had promised, and failed, to hand over 1500 Christian prisoners, 200,000 gold coins, and part of the True Cross (the cross Jesus was crucified on). He also felt justified due to the impracticalities of keeping so many prisoners. And while we must be careful not to judge people of the past with our modern ideas of right and wrong, it is fair to say that the killing of innocents has never been seen as heroic.

After the massacre, Richard carried on with his quest and achieved another almighty victory at the Battle of Arsuf on 7 September 1191. In this battle he inflicted major casualties on the Muslim army and their morale. As a result, he was able to establish mighty castles and Christian bases for future use in the cities of Tyre, Ascalon, and Jaffa (minus the cakes). But still, he couldn't capture Jerusalem. The Holy Grail of Holy Lands was holy unobtainable. He came very close, twice, but there are no medals for that. The first time it was the bad weather of hailstorms and rain that forced him and his men to turn back. (If he'd spent a bit more time in England, he may have been more used to such things. Just saying.) The second time was because Richard and the new guy Hugo (who was replacing Phillipe from France) couldn't agree on a strategy, and neither army was strong enough to follow their own strategy on their lonesome. Richard wanted to invade Egypt to capture Jerusalem (it's in the other direction but I'm sure he had a marvellous plan), whereas Hugo thought it might be better to just, you know, invade Jerusalem. They retreated to the coast to argue some more, and it was near here that Richard had his fifth victory against Muslim forces at the Battle of Jaffa on 8 August 1192.

At this point everyone was knackered. Richard had been fighting for the Holy Land for 14 months and had been away from England for two years. Saladin's forces had been decimated but not defeated. The Christian forces had been divided but not defeated. It was a weird sort of stalemate that eventually led to a settlement being reached on 2 September 1192. The terms of the settlement favoured neither side really – Richard had to lose the castles and fortifications he had built in the city of Ascalon; Saladin had to allow Christian pilgrims and merchants access into Jerusalem, and both had to agree to give it a bloomin' rest (for three years). Richard essentially gave up having got within 12 miles of Jerusalem and acted all Terminator-like saying: "I'll be back." He was keen to get home to stop his brother plotting with his ex-boyfriend and new enemy – Phillippe. Richard didn't win the Crusades. He didn't capture Jerusalem. He didn't kill Saladin. He did win five battles and conquer Cyprus. He did spend all the money England had. Hero? Err – no.

But wasn't he really popular with his people?

Yes.

So was Hitler.

Popularity doesn't mean you're a hero. Besides, the only reason Richard was liked was because the church supported him (due to all the crusading and killing the infidel business), and priests then relayed these "isn't he wonderful" messages to their congregations on a weekly basis. And then to fool the rest of us in the future, the history books (or as they called them at the time – "books") were written by some other church people: monks. Unsurprisingly, they toed the church line of "isn't he wonderful" perfectly. Monks writing chronicles/history books was customary practice back then – they were some of the only people who could write. Therefore, it has always been in the monarch's interest to not upset the church. They were the only ones (before the *Daily Mail*) who could turn public opinion against you.

The church influence would have been hard to avoid, but the people of England supported their king for another reason that our 21st-century minds may find hard to understand – he was popular because he went to war. If he wasn't fighting the infidel in the Holy Land, he was fighting the French for territory, and both things endeared him to a 12th-century civilian.

Another reason for his popularity was the fact that his mum held him in such high regard. After the death of his father, Richard had released her from the captivity her husband King Henry II had held her in for 16 years (she was, after all, supporting a rebellion against him). Once released, Eleanor embarked upon a tour of the country, singing his praises everywhere she went. It is customary for a new monarch to undertake a tour of their realm upon ascending the throne and its normally called a Royal Progress. But meeting his people was not a priority for Richard – he had bigger plans and so he left his mum to do it. Eleanor encouraged the barons (the rich and important landowners) to support her son and announced a general amnesty of prisoners, which doesn't sound great to me but at least ensured the support of some of the dodgier elements of society. Roger of Howden claims she went from "city to city and castle to castle", holding "queenly courts", releasing prisoners and exacting oaths from all freemen to "be loyal to her son as their as yet uncrowned king".[290] Imagine if Charles had killed the Queen and his dad had gone round the country releasing all the criminals while telling us to support Charles?! Oh… hang on… yeah, you'd be scared senseless into agreeing. Well played, Eleanor, well played.

The rose-tinted message has endured – look at how he is described in his bio on the Westminster Abbey website: "He joined the Third Crusade to the Holy Land but returned to England when he heard of his father's death in 1189".[291] I mean… what the hell? Firstly, he wasn't even on Crusade yet (he didn't leave until summer 1190), and secondly, Richard was *literally there* on his father's deathbed ensuring he was given the crown. After he had helped kill the poor guy. More Westminster Shabby than Abbey in terms of research.

Having said that, there was one aspect of Richard's private life that he and his mother did not openly acknowledge – the fact he was likely in love with the French king. Yes, in another shocking twist, the union between England and France against his dad King Henry II was the result of a homosexual love affair between the two kings! Richard was gay[292]. Richard and Phillippe had apparently shared a bed for years, which certainly helps explain why Richard spent so much time over there, and why he avoided England and his mum's various plans to marry him off. To be fair, Eleanor had a few weird suitors lined up such as his dad's old mistress, but she did eventually persuade him to marry Berengaria of Navarre – a union she was keen on because Navarre bordered Aquitaine, and the marriage would therefore help secure the border of her ancestral lands. In fact, she was *so* keen to get her son married off and buy a new hat, she literally brought Berengaria to Richard while he was travelling south to Jerusalem. Despite Tricky Dicky immediately leaving England after his coronation instead of hanging around to secure his dynasty, it seems Eleanor did not get the hint. Mums obviously know best, so she secured it for him. Eleanor picked up Berengaria from Navarre in southern France and the two women undertook the long journey to catch Richard up in Sicily. Bet he was super pleased to see them. Even putting Berengaria on a different ship when they left Sicily failed to scupper his mother's plans because she had been placed in the care of Richard's sister, and so when the ship got taken hostage, Richard had to rescue them. He was loyal to the women in his family at least.

While Richard played ball with the marriage, Berengaria did not get to play with any balls at all, and the marriage remained childless. After the Crusade and his kidnapping, the pair never saw each other again. Richard instead preferred to chase after Phillippe who had engineered the kidnapping and hefty ransom, rather than go see his wife who had been working behind the scenes in Western France to collect said hefty ransom. I think we can scrap that "loyal to the women in his family" bit.

Well, he must have been a chivalrous knight at least?

Richard was good at being a knight and fighting; I'll give him that. But chivalrous is another thing entirely. These days chivalry is played out in moments such as a man opening a door, but back in Richard's day there was a bit more to it. The Knight's Code of Chivalry set ground rules for knightly behaviour.[293] Men would have to swear an oath to follow these rules upon becoming a knight and the system was understood by all. But it seems like things weren't really "alright on the Knight" during this medieval period, and historian Jennifer

Goodman Wollock describes these guys as: "hired thugs".[294] Towards the end of Richard's reign, these 17 ideas were written down in "The Song of Roland". Let's see how Richard fares…

1. ***To fear God and maintain His Church*** (mostly nailed it: he put church above everything and went on crusade to honour God. Though melting all their gold and silver probably didn't help with the whole long-term maintenance of the churches thing).

2. ***To serve the liege lord in valour and faith*** (failed it: he rebelled against his "liege lord" – his father – and then killed him).

3. ***To protect the weak and defenceless*** (failed it: he didn't protect the interests of the English peasants by charging them 25% surprise tax, and he murdered women and child hostages).

4. ***To give succour (aid) to widows and orphans*** (failed it: murdered women and children as part of the Massacre at Ayyadieh. He didn't even ensure his own widow got her dowager payment – Berengaria had to fight for this for 17 years after his death).

5. ***To refrain from the wanton giving of offence*** (failed it: he offended all his Christian allies and English Crusaders with his Massacre of Ayyadieh, not to mention the offence felt by Jews and women at being barred from his coronation. Then of course there's all the Muslims of the world who he called "infidels" because they dared to claim the land he wanted. And I'm pretty sure his wife felt more than a little offended when he abandoned her in favour of King Phillippe).

6. ***To live by honour and for glory*** (failed the first bit – see previous examples plus the fact he needed his mum to do the hard work for him is not exactly an honourable thing.

But he certainly nailed the living for glory bit. That's literally all he did).

7. ***To despise pecuniary (money) reward*** (failed it: he demanded 200,000 gold pieces from Saladin to compensate himself for not getting the Holy Land).

8. ***To fight for the welfare of all*** (failed it: he would only fight for you if you were Christian. And it really helped if you were French).

9. ***To obey those placed in authority*** (failed it: rebelled against his father).

10. ***To guard the honour of fellow knights*** (failed it: tarnished their reputations with his massacre of Ayyadieh and refused the reward the contributions of Leopold and Phillippe to the victories they shared in Acre and Cyprus).

11. ***To eschew (shun) unfairness, meanness, and deceit*** (failed it: he epitomised unfairness by refusing to share the spoils of war, demonstrated meanness with the treatment of his wife and Muslim hostages, and was 100% deceitful to his father, mother, Christian allies, English people, and wife).

12. ***To keep faith*** (nailed it… if you ignore the commandments to honour thy father and not kill people).

13. ***At all times to speak the truth*** (failed it: "yeah, Dad, I think you're doing great…"/ "of course I will release the hostages"/" yes, I'd love to marry you").

14. ***To persevere to the end in any enterprise begun*** (failed it: he dodged out of the Crusades when victory looked impossible, did not persevere with his marriage, and couldn't even see it through being king of England past 10 years).

15. ***To respect the honour of women*** (mostly nailed it through his actions in rescuing his sister but he couldn't secure her inheritance money. He did respect his mother and left her in charge of England while he went crusading

so chivalry points should be awarded for that. Not so respectful of the honour of Muslim women. Or his wife. Plus, banning all women from his coronation does strongly suggest he did not respect them enough to let them attend).

16. ***Never to refuse a challenge from an equal*** (nailed it: the guy literally couldn't stop himself from accepting challenges from other monarchs and leaders).

17. ***Never to turn the back upon a foe*** (failed it: he left Saladin very much alive. And in charge of Jerusalem).

Richard scores a total of four and a half out of the seventeen criteria. Chivalry is definitely dead.

But there's a statue of him outside the Houses of Parliament – doesn't that mean he's an English Icon?

Iconic blagger that's for sure. Richard was a mostly absent king (he was in England for approximately six months); he failed in his one aim of recapturing the Holy Land; and he used England as a bank to fund his crusading armies[295] and save his ass when he got kidnapped. Yet this shamefully low level of success and loyalty somehow qualified him for a statue of honour. The statue was constructed during the reign of Queen Victoria and started life in clay form as part of the Great Exhibition of 1851. It was so well received that Queen Vic and other rich Victorian folk clubbed together to get it made into bronze and become a more permanent fixture. Richard was chosen because, at the time, it was trendy to have sculptures of romantic historical figures (translation of romantic = lies). This may be forgivable then; it was a different time. However, work was also undertaken in 2009 to restore the statue when they could have just taken it down and chosen a less "romantic" historical figure, maybe one who didn't spend everyone's money to go on a *jihad*.

Apparently, there was a bit of discussion as to where the statue should be placed after it was shown off at the Great Exhibition of 1851, but quite why outside parliament was chosen is anybody's guess considering Richard had absolutely diddly-squat to do with the institution. Having died 16 years before the Magna Carta, Richard ruled England in the days of absolute power and before any changes to the king's supremacy were made. That first piece of democracy in 1215 was his brother King John's doing, and even then, a parliament of sorts didn't appear until 1264 – a good 65 years after Richard popped his clogs. It would be like trying to credit Queen Victoria with the creation of NATO. Not A Thing OK? Richard did nothing to further democracy or "power to the people" so maybe he now sits in front of the Houses of Parliament as a reminder of the last king to truly rule without the people? If so, they should really install a plaque saying that.

But we like him cos he stood up for England?

When was that? In between selling off parts of our land to the Scots and taxing people 25%? He once said he would sell London if only he could find a buyer.[296]

Richard was so headset on going on crusade that he didn't think to save up first and instead taxed the English and sold off bits of the country that he wasn't planning on visiting (i.e., all of it). In another shocking move, he made a deal with William, the King of Scotland, whereby he formally acknowledged the independence of Scotland from England. He literally gave away England's power – the deal was called the "Quit-Claim of Canterbury" and it gave him £6000 for his travels as well as short-term peace with Scotland (like... *really* short term – until

1215). However, it would be more accurate to call it the "Twit-Claim of Canterbury" because the twit that he was, ended up causing four hundred years of war between the two nations *and* enabled the Scots to ally themselves with the French in 1238 in the "Auld Alliance". Which really did NOT help England as the two nations then ganged up on England at every opportunity they could for the next 500 years, leaving England as nothing more than the poor piggy in the middle.

Not content with just selling off England's power, Richard also sold the town of Berwick to the Scottish. Berwick was extremely important to the wool trade (England's main export back then). But this long-term economic benefit was of little concern to Richard because he wanted the short-term gain of money for his crusade. Once more, this action led to future problems for England as the two countries fought over the town numerous times over the next few hundred years. However, Richard's stint as an estate agent for the Scots did give us the film *Braveheart* so, you know, swings and roundabouts.

In his reign as King, Richard's dad Henry II created the role of a Sheriff – this job was all about reducing crime and corruption by having a police officer of sorts in every county. Richard sold these jobs to the highest bidder, which must have really helped with the whole corruption thing. He also sold the Archbishop of York job for £2,000 (3% of England's annual income). Roger of Howden, who saw it all unfold, claimed that: "he (Richard) put up for sale all he had: offices, lordships, earldoms, sheriffdoms, castles, towns, lands, everything".[297] To be fair it was not unusual to sell job titles and offices, but the speed at which he sold everything *was* unusual and very risky. Not content with just selling stuff that shouldn't be sold, Richard also used more dubious means of making money such as taking rich people hostage. He put Ranulf de Glanville, the former Chief Justiciar of England and one of the richest men in the country, in prison and only released him when his family paid Richard £15,000[298] (25% of England's annual income). Which, while his mum likely lauded as showing initiative, was downright illegal. Inevitably, all these dodgy dealings led to people positioned in influential jobs who felt zero loyalty towards him. This came back to bite him in the bum when his brother John started a rebellion in England with these people's support while Richard was gallivanting overseas. Someone with the country's best interests at heart would have taken a bit more care in their job allocations. Unfortunately for England, the only thing pounding in Richard's chest was pound signs.

To really add salt to English wounds, Richard didn't even want to be buried here. His body was interred at Fontevraud, France, with his father (sure his dad loved that). Aorta tell you that his heart was also buried in France – at Rouen in Normandy; and he lovingly bequeathed his bowels and entrails to Poitou, in, yep you guessed it, France. Richard really did not want to leave any part of himself in England. Shame the Victorians didn't take this hint.

Ultimately Richard just wanted to fight. Didn't really matter against who – whoever was trending at the time was fine by him. His loyalties were fluid and shallow, and his priorities were skewed. He could have had children with his wife and secured the dynastic future of England, but his priority was going to Jerusalem. He had some success in some battles but failed in the aims of the Crusade. He was only popular at the time because he was living up to 12th-century expectations of a warrior king, but even this popularity waned as people were crushed under taxation and corruption. By the end of his reign, only his mum and the church had his back, and even *that* proved temporary as his back ended up being buried in France with the rest of him. He visited England only twice once appointed king and viewed the country as a piece of property from which he could raise money for the Crusades. This myth of him being a good guy started with his mum in the 12th century, was bolstered by his statue in the 19th century, and further perpetuated by *Disney* portraying him as some sort of saviour in their cartoon version of "Robin Hood" in the 20th century. Despite a whole host of evidence to the contrary, Richard's legend endures as England's Lionheart. History's weird, isn't it?

Britain's Role in the Holocaust.

*The only thing necessary for the triumph of
evil is that good men do nothing.*[299]

The teaching of the Holocaust is banned in 28 countries
around the world. The United Arab Emirates, New Zealand,
Egypt, Palestine, Iraq, and Thailand make no mention of the
Holocaust in their curricula at all. The UAE even go as far as to
ban all mention of Israel (they have a similar stance on
Communism). Out of 272 curriculums from 139 countries
around the world, only 57 enforce the teaching of the
Holocaust.[300]

   In the UK, the topic is compulsory only in England. In
Wales, Scotland, and Northern Ireland, the Holocaust is
suggested as a teaching topic but not enforced.[301] In
England, the topic is taught at the end of a student's
compulsory learning of history i.e., before they take their
GCSE options. But the government do not state which
aspects of the Holocaust must be covered. It is included as
part of the module: *Challenges for Britain, Europe, and the
wider world 1901 to the present day,* but what English
students learn about the Holocaust is at the behest of their
teachers and it could end up being just one lesson. The
focus of school textbooks is the experience in the death
camps, and there is no exploration of Britain's awareness or
their lack of action.

What is the Holocaust?

The Holocaust is the genocide of European Jews undertaken by the Nazis between 1941 and 1945. In 1933, the Jewish population in Europe stood at nine million[302] and there were around 525,000 Jews in Germany (1% of the total German population).[303] By 1945, there were three million[304] Jews in Europe, none in Germany.

But 1941 is not when Jews first began to be slaughtered by Nazis. The systematic murders began on 1 September 1939, when killing patrols made up of German Order Police and SS units (the *Einsatzgruppen*) followed behind the German army as they invaded Poland. Their method of killing Jews was to round up whole villages at a time, force them to dig a massive pit and line up around the edge. The Jews would then be shot, sometimes two with one bullet to save ammunition for the war effort and fell straight into the pit which now became a mass grave. Those that didn't die straight away would be suffocated to death by the soil or the people piled upon them. By the end of 1941, at least 1.5 million people had been killed in this way.[305] Those who were not killed were forced to leave their homes and live in ghettoes (an area of a city that has been walled off from the outside which you can't leave).

The term *Holocaust* comes from the Greek words *holos* (whole) and *kaustos* (burned). Interestingly, the term *Shoah* (catastrophe) is preferred by Hebrew speakers as it is more particular about the Jewish experience. *The Final Solution* is another term which is frequently used because it was 'a final solution to the Jewish question' that the Nazis were looking to solve when they produced the idea of gas chambers. The Nazis were always anti-Semitic, but their early plans for the Jews involved displacement and removal (either to Eastern Europe or to Madagascar). When they could no longer pursue these plans due to WW2, they looked for another solution to their 'problem'. Ergo: The Final Solution. The Final Solution refers specifically to the period 1942–1945 where there was organised extermination of Jewish people in camps using gas.

The Nazis killed Jews from Germany and the countries they conquered. Some countries suffered more than others; it all depended on the speed of the Nazi invasion, the ease at which people could escape, and the level of collaboration between European governments and the Nazis. Poland, for example, had 91% of their Jewish population killed because they were the first to be invaded using Blitzkrieg tactics, and their government surrendered after just 26 days. Due to high levels of cooperation with the Nazi's, Greece lost 87%. Conversely, Italy (Germany's ally until 1943) refused to hand over their Jewish population and "only" 17% of their Jewish population were killed in the Holocaust.[306]

The Nazis operated concentration camps in Germany and The Netherlands and death camps in Poland. The two types of camp had different purposes. Concentration camps were greater in number – there were 980[307] of these (such as Bergen-Belsen where Anne Frank died) with an estimated 90,000 smaller camps in German territory which held "undesirables" until the Nazis decided into which larger concentration camp they should go.

Dachau was the first concentration camp to open on 10 March 1933, just five weeks after Hitler became Chancellor of Germany. The original intention of concentration camps was to hold opponents of the Nazi regime such as Communists or people who liked democracy. It was easier to put people in a camp than to send them to jail because the justice system required, well, some level of justice. There would have to be trials and evidence and that sort of fairness is not very Nazi. In the camps, people were subjected to meagre rations, hard labour, and isolation, but they were not deliberately killed (although people did die due to the harsh conditions). Once WW2 started, the concentration camps were used to hold prisoners of war (POWs) such as Stalin's son, Yakov Dzhugashvili, who was held at Sachsenhausen camp, just outside Berlin from 1941 until his death there in 1943[2].

Death camps meant certain death, they were fitted with gas chambers and run by the SS, headed up by Heinrich Himmler. There were six death camps: Auschwitz-Birkenau, Sobibor, Belzec, Treblinka, Chelmno and Majdanek.

Auschwitz opened as a concentration camp in June 1940 and was in the Polish town of Oswiecim. The first transport of 728 Polish political prisoners and some Jews arrived on 14 June 1940 from Tarnow Prison, and by August, the camp held 1000 people.[308] In its first six months, 15,000 people entered Auschwitz; by the end of 1940, only 8500 were still alive.[309] Chelmno was the first dedicated death camp to open on 8 December 1941, and is also the first location gassings of Jews began. At Chelmno, there were no gas chambers – instead, people were put in the back of vans and gassed using carbon monoxide from the van engine. There were three gas vans in operation by the end of that first month; each van would kill ten loads of 60 people in one day. The Nazis were murdering 1800–2000 people a day in this way.

Jews were not the first to be gassed – experimental gassings of Soviet prisoners had taken place at Auschwitz in August 1941. Based on the success of these experiments at Auschwitz and Chelmno, the first few months of 1942 saw Belzec, Sobibor and Treblinka death camps open with specially constructed gas chambers. Auschwitz was the last to become a death camp in spring 1942, and larger gas chambers were built

---

[2] The Nazis did offer to trade Yakov with German POWs held by the USSR but, Stalin being Stalin, said "nah, you're alright".

on a second site (Birkenau) next door. From this point it was known as Auschwitz-Birkenau.

Auschwitz is the most well known because it was first to be liberated, and, despite being the camp to record the most murders, far more Jews from Auschwitz survived to tell the world what happened than at any other camp. Several thousand lived to tell the horrors of Auschwitz-Birkenau; two people survived Belzec, Chelmno had three, from Treblinka there were less than 40, and Sobibor had 64 survivors.[310] Just over half of the six million murders took place in the death camps; Auschwitz 1.1 million; Treblinka 750,000;[311] Belzec 550,000;[312] Sobibor at least 200,000;[313] and Chelmno 150,000–320,000.[314] The rest of the deaths came from: shootings in Poland (at least 220,000); deaths in concentration camps (at least 150,000); shootings and gas wagons in German-occupied Soviet Union (at least 1,355,000); shootings and gas wagons in Serbia (15,088); shot or tortured to death in Croatia (25,000); deaths in ghettoes (at least 800,000) and at least 500,000 died via an "unknown method".[315]

So how much of this was Britain aware of?

The traditional narrative is that the British were unaware of the true nature of Auschwitz camp until June 1944.[316] The scarcity of documents in the British National Archives helps promote this myth as there are only seven significant pieces of information about the killing of Jews dated before summer 1944.[317] This has also become the accepted date for British knowledge because summer 1944 is when the rest of Europe found out about the purpose of Auschwitz via the *Vrba-Wetzler Report*.

However, this narrative is not true. News of the systematic murder of Jews was known "all over Europe" in 1942,[318] and there were actually at least 48 different pieces of information to reach Britain before summer 1944 which confirmed the Nazi's extermination policy.[319] Britain was well aware of what was happening at the camp throughout 1943.[320] So why did Britain not bomb Auschwitz or the railway lines leading to it as soon as they got wind of the camp's purpose? What exactly and when did Britain know about the extermination of the Jews? And most importantly, why did Britain fail to act to stop the Holocaust?

When did Britain find out about Jews being deported?

The first deportation of German Jews from ghettoes into occupied Poland took place on 12 February 1940, and the British were aware that same month. They knew what was going on with the Jews in Germany and occupied territory[321] thanks to British intelligence agents being sent to France to pick up radio signals in February 1940. While their work failed to provide the tactical information they wanted, the intercepted messages gave the British real-time awareness of the Nazi's plan to deport Jews into their freshly conquered Polish territory.[322] There were at least 1000 Jewish ghettoes established in Nazi territory during WW2, the biggest was in the Polish capital – the Warsaw ghetto.

Construction of this city-prison began on 1 April 1940, and in October all Warsaw Jews were ordered to go there; it was sealed off in November 1940 with 350,000 Jews (30% of the population) confined to 2.4% of the city's space.[323] Confirmation of the deplorable conditions inside reached the ears of British leaders in December 1942 after Polish underground operative Jan Karski managed to get in and out of the Warsaw ghetto and see what was really going on inside the high walls.[324] He reported back on the mass starvation, epidemics of disease, random violence, cramped and filthy living conditions, and plethora of corpses lying on the ground. Living in a ghetto was slow murder.

This knowledge was made public during the first two weeks of September 1942, *The Times* in London published full reports of the deportation of Jews from France. Its source was their own correspondent who was at the border between Vichy France (the chunk of France taken over by the Nazis) and neutral Spain. On September 7th, the headline on the imperial and foreign page was "Vichy's Jewish victims, children deported to Germany".

When did Britain find out about the Nazi's plan to murder the Jews?

Britain first got wind of the Nazi's plan to exterminate the Jews in 1936 when the Foreign Office received a new translation of Hitler's autobiography, *Mein Kampf*. While an English translation had existed since 1931, they clearly suspected it was an abridged version (it was) to make Hitler seem less extreme (good luck). The new translation revealed Hitler's plan to use gas: "If at the beginning of the war or during the war twelve or fifteen thousand of these Hebrew corrupters of the people had been held under poison gas… the sacrifice of millions at the front would not have been in vain".[325]

It's possible Britain knew as early as 1933 because the plan to annihilate the Jews was publicly announced, firstly by Hitler and then by his second-in-command Himmler. Britain had an ambassador living in Berlin – Horace Rumbold – whose job was to report back on political goings-on. He was there until May 1933, and he regularly reported back on the rising anti-Semitism, likely also referencing these two speeches. Hitler made his announcement when he took power on 30 January 1933, and on 21 March 1933, Himmler stated: "Germany will experience the greatest mass murders and pogroms in world history, and no state power and no police will be able to halt this murder".[326]

It was January 1942 when the Brits truly understood the extermination policy. Funnily enough, this was also the month the Nazis fully understood their extermination policy too. On 20 January 1942, there was a meeting attended by 15 high-ranking Nazi officials (but not Hitler), now known as the Wannsee Conference. The meeting had been called to inform people of the proposals to physically exterminate the Jews using gas, and Heydrich wanted to tell everyone that he was the chosen one who had been tasked with coordinating the operation.[327] Just two days after the Wannsee Conference, the British government acknowledged their awareness of the planned annihilation. The Ministry of Information's *Reports on Jewry* explicitly stated that the wholescale murder of European Jews was Nazi policy: "The Germans clearly pursue a policy of extermination against the Jews… (an official German document states) the only things Jewish that will remain in Poland will be Jewish cemeteries."[328] Sadly, it turned out that even this bleak forecast was overly optimistic, with numerous Jewish graves being desecrated in the town of Oswiecim (location of Auschwitz) in the years following 1945.[329]

More significantly, a speech from Hitler on 30 January 1942, brought confirmation straight from the horse's (teetotal) mouth. The Allied Monitoring Service secretly heard and recorded this speech where Hitler said: "…the result of this war will be the complete annihilation of the Jews."[330]

So that clears that up then.

Verification of the plan came in August 1942 from Gerhart Riegner, who was secretary for the World Jewish Congress (WJC). Riegner was based in Geneva, neutral Switzerland, and had been told about the Final Solution plan by a well-placed source – German industrialist: Eduard Schulte. Shocked by what he had heard, Riegner sent a message to two of his contacts in the WJC – Samuel Wise in America and Sydney Silverman in Britain. These messages were seen by the British Foreign Office and the State Department in Washington. The Riegner Telegram was sent on 8 August 1942, and it said: …all Jews in countries occupied or controlled by Germany numbering 3½ to 4 million should, after deportation and concentration in the East, be at one blow exterminated."[331]

The British war cabinet (all the top politicians including Prime Minister Churchill) were told about the Nazi's extermination policy on 14 December 1942, via the Foreign Secretary, Anthony Eden. In his presentation about Britain's knowledge of the Holocaust, he stated: "it might well be that these transfers were being made with a view to wholesale extermination of Jews."[332] If we ignore the subtle implication that all the intelligence, eyewitness accounts, report from the Ministry of Information, Polish underground sources, and articles from foreign correspondents were not true ("might well be"), this can be considered good progress. Following this, Britain made their knowledge public with the Joint Allied Declaration (with America and other Allies) on 17 December 1942. Just over two years after Britain became aware of the killings of Eastern European Jews, they acknowledged and condemned them. Better late than never, some might say. And if it had actually led to some action, it would have been better late than never. In reality, the follow up was more like an Arianna Grande song ("Thank you, next") than any sort of Grande action.

When did Britain find out about the systematic slaughter of Jews?

Britain was aware of the Jewish pogroms (a violent massacre of one ethnic group) as they were happening from 1939 thanks to an intelligence breakthrough at the start of the war. A replica German coding machine had been given to them by the Polish resistance just as the Germans began *Blitzkrieg*-ing their way through Poland. As a result, the German code "Double Transposition" was broken by brigadier John Tilman, and Britain was able to decode German Order Police messages on a regular basis. Tidy. By the time Churchill became PM on 10 May 1940, decoding was well advanced, and a group of British intelligence agents was established at Bletchley Park (Britain's code-breaking HQ) in August to work solely on decoding German police messages. These guys were the dogs' bollocks – in the last five months of 1940, they intercepted 10,600 messages and broke codes in 83% of all attempts.[333] The messages revealed transfers of Jews into Poland and a requirement for executions to be reported[334] which gave the Brits a huge red flag that there would be a sizable number of executions to come.

By the end of summer 1941, the British government were aware of phase one of the Holocaust – the shootings and killings of (thus far) 500,000[335] undertaken by the German Order Police and Einsatzgruppen death squads. In June 1941, British intelligence learnt about the beginnings of the Holocaust in the USSR.[336] On 22 June 1941, Hitler did the dirty on Stalin and invaded the Soviet Union (they had agreed to do precisely NOT this in the *Molotov-Ribbentrop Pact* in August 1939). The USSR had a Jewish population of three million, and just as in Poland in 1939, SS Einsatzgruppen and the German Order Police followed the soldiers and acted as Jewish killing patrols. Bletchley Park cryptographers had been listening in to some of the messages coming in from this invasion, and they noted that the Order Police units were recording long lists of Jews they had shot alongside communists and partisans (civilian opposition).[337] At least 1.3 million Soviet Jews were murdered in this way[338] and "the volume of such reports increased with time".[339] There was no delay to this intelligence; the British knew what was happening exactly as it happened.

In August 1941, British intelligence learnt about the massacres of Jews in Eastern Europe. Intercepted and decoded reports from Bach-Zelewski (a high-ranking SS commander) to Himmler revealed the scale of killing, such as the message from 4 August 1941, where he told his boss about a liquidation the day before of 3,274 partisans and "Jewish Bolsheviks". The Nazis used the terms *partisans* and *Bolsheviks* (the name for Soviet communists) to imply they were justified in killing them. Tellingly, all 3,274 deaths were achieved without the Germans suffering ANY losses in return; the absence of a single German casualty in all this killing indicates the victims were not partisans, and this was a massacre.[340] No army is *that* good at fighting. Bach-Zelewski's radio message on August 7th then boasted: "the figure of executions in my area now exceeds the 30,00 mark".[341] An obscene number to be partisans but a logical number of citizens from a town. Decodes from August 8th told of 8000 Jews liquidated in Pinsk with a few thousand more just days later.[342] The analysts clearly knew the tone of the killing was savage butchery rather than defence as they reported how the Nazis in charge were attempting to outdo each other with numbers killed: "the leaders of the three sectors stand somewhat in competition with each other as to their "scores"."[343]

But obviously analysts don't make policy, and politicians don't decode messages, so how much did the British government know? Well, Churchill knew all about it, that's for sure. Throughout 1941, intelligence summaries with information from the police decodes were sent to PM Churchill on a weekly basis.[344] On 24 August 1941, Churchill made a public speech where he explicitly acknowledged that the British government knew Jews were being indiscriminately murdered: "Whole districts are being exterminated. Scores of thousands – literally scores of thousands – of executions in cold blood are being perpetrated by the German police-troops upon the Russian patriots who defend their native soil… merciless butchery... We are in the presence of a crime without a name."[345]

Unfortunately, the speech drew headlines but no action. The problem was, despite knowing Jews were the target, Churchill failed to mention this to the public. It's possible that this was deliberate because Churchill was trying to not give away the fact they were listening in on German police radio messages. But this is giving him too much credit. Because the information he gave about the use of "German police-troops" *did* give away the fact they were successfully earwigging. If anything, mentioning the Jews would have been a *better* thing to do than mentioning the police because everyone was aware of the Nazi's anti-Semitism, but it was not public knowledge (even in Germany) that the German police were being used as killers. Churchill had given away the fact that British intelligence was able to crack the German's code AND that they were intercepting the police's messages in one fail swoop. A fact which was immediately picked up on by the Chief of the German Order Police, meaning that on 13 September 1941, an order was sent to stop giving the game away by reporting execution numbers and to also switch from using the Double Transposition code to Double Playfair. Ironically, this planned switch was intercepted by the British and even more ironically, Playfair turned out to be even easier to crack than Transposition, which meant the British could listen to more messages than ever before.[346] All's (play)fair in love and war!

September 1941 turned out to be a funny old month for knowledge. While there was progress on the one hand when, on September 12th, British intelligence concluded that the

Nazis were deliberately annihilating the Jews: "a policy of savage intimidation if not of ultimate extermination".[347] On the other hand, on this exact same day, the Secret Intelligence Service (SIS) decided to stop reporting executions of Jews to Churchill. Their reasoning was he knew now, so best not go on about it: "the fact that the police are killing all Jews that fall into their hands should be now sufficiently well appreciated. It is not therefore proposed to continue reporting these butcheries specially, unless so requested."[348] Unofficially, the SIS took this decision because they didn't want to give Churchill information that he might stupidly use in a speech like he did back in August. The British Foreign Office were instructed to handle Holocaust matters from now on. Incidentally, Churchill did not request any more information and the Foreign Office showed no inclination to believe the reports, let alone act.[349]

By March 1944, the British were aware of the logistics of genocide, and they understood the Nazi's tripartite extermination policy. The Political Warfare Executive's (PWE) report: *Special Annex on the persecution of Jews* was circulated among its staff on 24 March 1944.[350] The document explained: "the German policy of extermination was planned and executed in three stages" – firstly build ghettoes and camps; secondly transport Jews to these places and thirdly; liquidate them there.[351] Twenty months before these details would be known to the world through the Nuremberg Trials (the post-WW2 prosecution of Nazis for war crimes), Britain understood the measures being taken to exterminate the Jews. Not that this spurred them into any action to stop the measures from succeeding.

Did Britain know the scale of the genocide?

1941 saw an estimated 355,142 Jews killed; in 1942, 1,496, 052 were murdered; and in 1943, 1,462,000 Jews were slaughtered.[352] In 1944, the number killed was 570,000,[353] but this lower figure wasn't good news – it was because by 1944, 90% of all those killed in the Holocaust were already dead.[354]

The scale of the genocide was understood by British intelligence and Churchill in August 1941. British intelligence had police decodes which revealed 40,000 executions in just a few days[355] and contained specifics such as the 12,361 Jews who were killed by the SS and Order Police between 23 and 31st August.[356] Between 2nd and 4th September, decoded Order Police messages revealed the horrors of the Kamianets-Podilskyi massacre, where 23,600 Jews were killed between 27 and 28th August. [357] Clearly British intelligence did not think this was the full story as a report in September 1941 concluded that the number of Jews being killed was likely to be DOUBLE what the analysts had recorded so far. Churchill was first made aware of the scale on August 28th, when he found out that Police Battalion 314 had shot 367 Jews. On the 30th he read about Battalions 45 and 314 shooting 355 Jews and the Police killing 113, and the next day he read about the 1st SS brigade killing 283 Jews and the Police Regiment South killing 1,342. He had just discovered that 2,460 Jews had been murdered over just four days. There's no doubt Churchill read these statistics because, just like a student idly revising, he circled the numbers of Jews killed in the reports handed to him.[358] A big effort which must have really helped stop all the killing.

External sources then verified the scale. In October 1941, a Ukrainian newspaper testified that in Zhitomir only 6,000 out of 50,000 Jews were still alive.[359] At the beginning of 1942, the British minister in Bern, Switzerland, informed the Foreign Office that 1.5 million Jews in the former Soviet Zone of Poland had simply disappeared, nobody knew what had happened to them.[360] During the war, the British were regularly supplied with information from the Polish intelligence group: Bureau VI –

their reports on what was going on in Nazi-occupied Poland were called *Aneks*. On 23 August 1943, the British intelligence group, Special Operations Executive (SOE), received *Aneks 57*, which revealed that most of Europe's Jews had now been killed and the camps were now moving on to murdering Europe's Gypsies.[361] Which is HUGE news, right? They were saying that out of nine million people – most had been killed. A few months later, in November 1943, *Aneks 58* told British intelligence that 468,000 Jews had been murdered at Auschwitz by the end of 1942,[362] and on 19 June 1944, the Polish revealed 100,000 Hungarian Jews had been killed at Auschwitz so far that year.[363] That's 2.34 million litres of blood on British hands (468,000 x five litres) because by 1944 they were well aware of the extermination policy and purpose of Auschwitz and yet did nothing to stop the killings going ahead.

When did Britain know about Auschwitz and the other death camps?

At the end of 1940, just six months after it opened, knowledge reached Britain about Auschwitz via the Polish resistance. This group were set up to oppose the Nazi invasion of Poland and subsequent implementation of Nazi policy. They were curious about what the camp was like and so, looking for evidence that could incriminate the Germans on an international stage, a recruit was sent in on 21 September 1940 (voluntarily) to investigate. That man was Witold Pilecki. Yes, someone really did get into Auschwitz on purpose.

His first message was sent out in October 1940 via a released prisoner named Aleksander Wielopski. The message detailed the conditions of the camp and stated: "The Prisoners beg the Polish Government, for the love of god, to bombard these warehouses and end their torment. Should they die in the attack, it would be a relief given the conditions. This is an urgent and well thought out request of the prisoners."[364]This was then passed to the Musketeers (a Polish resistance cell), who gave it to Julia Lubomirska to carry to neutral Switzerland. Upon arrival in Geneva, Switzerland, she delivered it on to Stanislaw Radziwill (in charge of Polish affairs at the League of Nations), and it was then smuggled through Vichy France to reach neutral Spain on December 10th. The Polish station chief in Madrid then got it across to the exiled Polish government (led by Sikorski) who had set up a temporary HQ in the Rubens Hotel in London. The report arrived at Christmas 1940.[365] Pretty good going considering the stealth mission it went through. Quicker than a Hermes parcel getting from Europe to Britain these days, that's for sure.

Britain learnt the location of Auschwitz in March 1941 and Sobibor camp in October 1943. On 1 March 1941, Himmler (head of SS) made his first visit to Auschwitz and ordered expansion with new buildings at nearby Birkenau to hold 100,000 prisoners. This was the start of Auschwitz-Birkenau, and the British government were made aware of the camp's activities in the same month with the arrival of a second report: *Report on the internal situation until January 30th, 1941*. Along with further descriptions of what was happening in Poland, this document revealed the location of Auschwitz and specifically the location of warehouses in the camp which could contain weapons and ammunition. There was also an extra bit: *Part III: the camp at Oswiecim* which revealed more of the horrors of what Pilecki had witnessed at Auschwitz. The location of Sobibor was discovered in 1943 via decoded radio messages which had information about the Nazi's plan to find the 700 Jews who had escaped the camp. The messages revealed that Sobibor lay 5km from the Bug River, between Cholm and Wlodawa, in the Lublin district.[366]

Britain first found out about the killing purpose of Auschwitz in May 1942. While they had been intercepting radio traffic from Auschwitz since the start of 1942, which confirmed the death statistics Pilecki smuggled out in 1940;[367] this still wasn't enough to convince them the camp was a killing centre. Fortunately, in mid-May 1942, a 6th report from escapees of Auschwitz arrived in London,[368] which explicitly described the mass killings of Jews and backed up Pilecki's previous report about French and Slovakian Jews arriving at Auschwitz in March 1942.[369] The reporters specifically stated they wanted to inform London so the world could come and rescue the Jews. Unfortunately, it was less Lond*on* and more Lond*off* in terms of action.

Archival evidence proves that Polish intelligence routinely passed on information about Nazi atrocities and the purpose of Auschwitz from November 1942.[370] Between January and May 1943, the British Foreign Office received four independent reports of Jews being killed at Auschwitz. Firstly, on 10 January 1943, they received a letter from a Polish citizen which told of the deliberate slaughter of Jews she had seen;[371] secondly, on March 12th, when the Polish ambassador informed Alec Randell at the Foreign Office;[372] thirdly, on April 7th via a report from the Movement of the Polish Working Masses;[373] and fourthly, on May 4th when the Foreign Office and PWE both read the *Salski Reports* which told of the mass killings of Jews and the use of gas chambers at Auschwitz to do this.[374]

In autumn 1942, the British government were made aware that other killing centres existed (Sobibor, Belzec and Treblinka)[375] and that Jews were also being systematically murdered at these camps.[376] Different sources then confirmed the systematic killing of Jews in all death camps. On 8 December 1942, a memo from Jewish representatives based on a variety of eyewitnesses (which was only found in 1999 by

Barbara Rogers – go Babs!) was received by President Roosevelt and the British Foreign Office.[377] On page 11 of 20, the report described the death camps: "centers (sic) have been established in various parts of Eastern Europe for the scientific and cold blooded mass murder of Jews…concrete buildings on the former Russian frontiers are used by the Germans as gas chambers in which thousands of Jews have been put to death".[378] On 18 May 1943, Alec Randell at the Foreign Office received reports from the Polish underground which described mass killing at Treblinka and described Oswiecim as a similar camp. All these sources confirmed the same thing – Jews were being killed in death camps. Most importantly, they came from different groups and thus should not have been dismissed as isolated or sensationalist information.

It was not just the killings the British were aware of; they also knew about the further expansion of Auschwitz in 1943. While other death camps were ceasing operation in 1943 (Chelmno stopped in April, Treblinka stopped in August, and Sobibor in October), Auschwitz was increasing its capacity to kill. Between 22nd March and 4th April, three newly built gas chambers (IV, II and V) and crematoria opened at Auschwitz. With its completion, the four crematories at Auschwitz had a daily capacity of 4,756 bodies. Just four days after these had been completed, the British knew about it thanks to the Polish underground informing the PWE. Their report also contained information about the sterilisation of women which was occurring in the camp.[379] Therefore, by the end of 1943. Britain knew about the existence of four of the six death camps, the exact locations of two of them, and their genocidal purpose. While the term *genocide* was not yet in popular use (it was only invented in 1941 by Polish lawyer, Raphael Lemkin, combining the ancient Greek word *genos* (race, tribe) and the Latin word *cide* (killing));[380] semantics did not hinder Britain's understanding of what was going on.

All of Britain's knowledge about the existence, purpose and methods of the death camps was completely verified in summer 1944 with the *Vrba-Wetzler Report* and liberation of Majdanek death camp. The report came from two Auschwitz escapees, Slovak Jews, Rudolf Vrba and Alfred Wetzler. They escaped in early April 1944 and fled to Czechoslovakia where they wrote their eyewitness accounts of the whole extermination process from arrival to death in the gas chambers. The first page of the report stated: "It is a fact beyond denial that the Germans have deliberately and systematically murdered millions of innocent civilians – Jews and Christians alike – all over Europe."[381] The report included numbers killed, the different categories of prisoner, the geography and location of the camp, how the camp functioned, and what the daily routine was like. They recounted how prisoners were selected for "work" (and then tattooed) or selected for immediate death in the gas chamber. There was also a request to bomb the camp and the railway lines leading to it from Hungary, as masses of Hungarian Jews were then being deported to the camp. Richard Lichtheim (German-born Jewish politician) sent a message with the report confirming the numbers: Hungarian Jews were "sent to the death camp of Birkenau near Oswiecim…where in the course of the last year 1,500,000 Jews from all over Europe have been killed."[382]

The information from the *Vrba-Wetzler Report* was validated when Soviet troops liberated Majdanek on 24 July 1944. At least 360,000 Jews had been murdered here, but a few hundred were still alive when the Soviets arrived. The camp still had its gas chambers and barracks, although the Nazis did try to cover their tracks by destroying the crematorium chimney. Nevertheless, there were now allied eyes on the ground confirming all previous intelligence about the purpose of these camps.

In summer 1944, the allied world also found out about the genocidal purpose of Auschwitz. The *Vrba-Wetzler Report,* unlike previous intelligence, was not solely shared with the British and overpowered their control of knowledge about Auschwitz.[383] From May through to July 1944, copies of the *Vrba-Wetzler Report* were sent to neutral Switzerland's War Refugee Board; to the War Refugee Board headquarters in Washington, D.C.; to the Vatican; to all the Allied leaders; and it was also published in the non-Nazi countries in Europe. The British received their copy of the report on 27 June 1944. Suddenly, a huge swathe of people were privy to facts which the Foreign Office, PWE, SOE, intelligence agencies and war cabinet had known since January 1943 (and likely known since November 1942).[384]

When did Britain find out about the use of gas?

The first gassings at Auschwitz took place in August 1941 with Soviet POWs as the victims of the Nazi's experiment with Zyklon B.[385] The gassing of Jews at Auschwitz began from January 1942, although thousands had already been murdered using carbon dioxide pumped into vans prior to this.

News of the gassing of Jews at Auschwitz first reached London on 12 November 1942.[386] This came from the Polish underground, sent on September 4th, and is the first known report to describe the use of gas chambers at the camp:[387] "There are different methods of execution. People are shot by firing squads, killed by an air hammer/ Hammerluft/ and poisoned by gas in special gas chambers…the gas chamber is employed for those who are ill or incapable of work and those who have been brought in by transports especially for the purpose /Soviet prisoners of war, and recently Jews/."[388]

However, there is no evidence proving anyone in British intelligence or the Foreign Office read this report until 23 January 1943, (when Foreign Secretary Anthony Eden read it). This documented evidence of knowledge of gassings can be found in the archives of PWE, SOE, Foreign Office, America, and Israel. Further verification came from a second report received by the Foreign Office in March 1943, which described the gassing method of Jews at Auschwitz.[389] Therefore it would be fair to say that early 1943 is likely when Britain was first aware of the use of gas.

In May 1943, the *Salski Reports* provided the Foreign Office, PWE, and various branches of British Intelligence with proof that gas chambers were being used to kill Jews on a mass scale at Auschwitz.[390] The Foreign Office were also privy to intelligence from the Polish underground, which described the mass murders at Treblinka camp and described Oswiecim as a similar camp in term of purpose.[391] Conveniently, there is no written documentation confirming Eden read any of these reports because the Foreign Office were being deliberately cautious in their written communications and thus it is likely Eden was made aware verbally.[392]

In November 1943, British intelligence got confirmation of gas from two different sources. Firstly, they received *Aneks 38* from Polish Intelligence which described the use of gas in the extermination process at Auschwitz; this was also sent to the Foreign Office. Secondly, captured ex-Einsatzgruppen member and Nazi defector Robert Barth confirmed that the Jews were always shot, without question, and he told them that gassings were taking place.[393] It is most likely, due to the dates of his service, that his idea of gassing was limited to the gas vans rather than the purpose-built gas chambers at the extermination camps. But still, here it was from someone literally in the centre of it all.

They were so sure of the gassing that in March 1944, the PWE put together a report: *Special Annex on the persecution of Jews.*[394] It included the 31 August and 7 September 1943 reports from the Polish underground, which described how the slaughter of Jews at Auschwitz "goes on incessantly" and the fact that 7300 Jews from Greece had been gassed at the camp.[395]

While January 1943 is the evidenced date of awareness, there were snippets of information about gassing in 1941 thanks to a second report from the volunteer spy at Auschwitz, Pilecki, and more intercepted messages by British intelligence. In Pilecki's second report he detailed the gassing experiments and sudden influx of Soviets, but this information was not considered worthy of further discussion by those who saw it.[396] British intelligence also intercepted radio messages between Himmler and Rudolf Querner (Police leader for the North Sea Region in Germany) where the two men discussed the use of gas[397] (likely in relation to the gas vans that began to be used in December, not the gas chambers). On the 15th of December, another decrypted radio message divulged the posting of SS Officer Magill to Oranienburg camp to receive instructions about use of Zyklon B.[398] The British didn't know the full plans at this point as, to be fair, neither did the Nazi's until January 1942. But it's important to recognise that in the same month as gassings of Jews began, the British had some awareness gas was being experimented with. Knowledge which future revelations could then be linked to.

When did the British public find out about the Holocaust?

The British public were mostly kept in the dark about the ongoing genocide of European Jews. The first inkling the British public got about the Nazi's systematic killing came from Churchill's speech in August 1941. But they still did not know the Jews were the target because Churchill chose to name the perpetrators rather than the victims. Some stories were published in *The Times*, *The Daily Telegraph*, and *Daily Mirror*, but the British policy was to marginalise such stories and place them deep within a newspaper or at the end of a news broadcast. In 1941, the British government even went so far as to warn British newspapers against running stories about Auschwitz because they thought they were too horrific[399] (but not horrific enough to try and put a stop to it of course). While the Polish were allowed to publish details of Auschwitz (using most of Pilecki's first report) in their English-language fortnightly government newspaper, the British government did not endorse their statements, thus implying to the wider reading public that this may be Fake News. The Jewish newspapers available in Britain did carry a lot of the news about the Holocaust, but even they were forced to bury these reports within the pages, and unfortunately these were quite obscure publications not read by the wider British public.

The first topic to be public knowledge were the deportations of German and Austrian Jews with widespread reporting in October and November 1941, beginning with *The Times*.[400] The *Jewish Chronicle* in London took up the story from a Ukrainian newspaper that only 6000 out of 50,000 Jews were still alive in Zhitomir,[401] and they published articles about the pogroms in Ukraine throughout late October and early November.[402] The following year, *The Times* published full reports of the deportation of Jews from France in September. Within the article the violence used against these people was clear; it reported how there was no time for people to prepare and how one train left with four thousand children aboard, none of whom had ID cards, belongings, or parents. Their geographical destination was unknown.

The first British newspaper to report on Auschwitz was *The Scotsman* on 8 January 1942.[403] However, it was buried in the pages of the newspaper, which indicated the information was not 100% certain and was less important than news about WW2. Readers of *Polish Jewish Observer* were told about Auschwitz in 1942, but it's unlikely it was read by many people because it was a supplement to the *City and East London Observer* and was so obscure it wasn't even registered in the Willings Press Guide (a list of all newspapers published in Britain).[404] Readers of *The Jewish Chronicle* were made aware Auschwitz was a death camp in 1943.

However, once again, these stories were buried within the pages, such as the 520,000 killed at Auschwitz published on 10 September 1943, found on page eight.[405] *The Times* and *The Daily Telegraph* sporadically published information about the Holocaust, such as *The Daily Telegraph's* report that 700,000 Jews had been killed in Poland in June 1942.[406] News that a crematorium at Oswiecim could kill 3000 people a day, most of whom were Jews, was published in the *Polish Jewish Observer* on 3 September 1943. While this fact was not reported in the British press, the *Daily Mirror* did reveal that 468,000 Jews were killed at Auschwitz in a report on 16 November 1943, and then again on 22 March 1944. By the end of 1943, while the government was aware millions of Jews were missing, the British public may have only been aware of numbers in the hundreds of thousands. And even this level of knowledge would have only been gleaned by those who had the time to read multiple newspapers in the midst of a war.

On 17 December 1942, *The Joint Allied Declaration* ensured everyone in Britain and America was aware of the atrocities. This declaration was significant because it was the first official allied government statement acknowledging and denouncing the killing of Jews. It was a clear confirmation of the extermination policy and did not require the public to "read between the lines" as was the case with Churchill's speech of August 1941. It was announced in the House of Commons like a movie scene which needed a big dramatic build up to be interesting. Sidney Silverman asked Anthony Eden: "whether he has any statement to make regarding the plan of the German Government to deport all Jews from the occupied countries to Eastern Europe and there put them to death before the end of the year"[407] and like some sort of hero, Eden read the declaration:

> *"The attention of the Governments… has been drawn to numerous reports from Europe that the German authorities… are now carrying into effect Hitler's oft repeated intention to exterminate the Jewish people in Europe. From all the occupied countries Jews are being transported, in conditions of appalling horror and brutality, to Eastern Europe. In Poland, which has been made the principal Nazi slaughterhouse, the ghettoes established by the German invaders are being systematically emptied of all Jews except a few highly skilled workers required for war industries. None of those taken away are ever heard of again… (we) condemn in the strongest possible terms (in words not actions) this bestial policy of cold-blooded extermination…"[408].*

Following Eden's speech, MP James de Rothschild (who had been requesting Churchill speak to the British Jews) made an emotional speech, and the House of Commons observed a moment of silence to indicate they had a heart.[409]

But don't get too excited.

Despite stating they would: "press on with the necessary practical measures,"[410] the declaration made no indication there would be rescue efforts. It seemed to be just about enough that they were accepting the facts they had been aware of for two years. And let's not forget that this declaration only came about because of the work of the Polish underground and the pressure applied from Jewish organisations in Britain and America. A fact not missed by the British Foreign Office who had the cheek to complain that while the Poles were the driving force, the Foreign Office had to do "most of the work".[411] Poor things. Having to do work they were paid for.

The problem with the Declaration for the British government was the reaction from the British public. In a move which clearly no one in the government foresaw (else they may not have done it), the public cared that innocent people were being murdered, and the statement led to a huge number of complaints that the British government were not doing enough to help. Eden was particularly surprised that people had such strong feelings and wrote in his diary that the declaration: "had a far greater dramatic effect than I had expected".[412] Because in his mind a genocide of Jews isn't big news. They didn't make this mistake again – the British public were deliberately kept in the dark about the lack of action to help the Jews which was later agreed at the 1943 Bermuda Conference.

Summer 1944 brought public awareness of the Holocaust in Britain, Europe, and America. The *Vrba-Wetzler Report* was widely shared and published, plus there were two other reports: *The Polish Major's Report* written by Jerzy Tabeau (who escaped in November 1943 and created the report between December 1943 – January 1944) and the *Death Camp at Oswiecim* by Arnost Rosin and Czeslaw Mordowicz, (created after their escape from Auschwitz on 27 May 1944). These reports combined with the *Vrba-Wetzler Report* became known as *The Auschwitz Protocols,* and they had a particularly positive impact in neutral countries. In Switzerland, their legendary neutrality Swissly changed into an anti-Nazi stance[413] which resulted in 383 articles about Auschwitz being published in their press between 23 June and 11 July 1944.[414] And in Sweden, the king straight up offered help to the Jews after reading the *Vrba-Wetzler Report.* Now there's a thought...

America and Britain were more cautious with their response to the newly published reports. In America, the information from the reports was published in *The New York Times* in July 1944, but before they released the *Vrba-Wetzler Report* to the American public, it was rebranded to sound less Jewish. Yes, you did read that right. A churchman called Paul Voght took the contents of the original report, plagiarised the hell out of it, and then gave it a snazzy new rhyming name: *The Voght Report.* This was done to make it more believable because, apparently, Christians don't lie. Meanwhile in Britain, censorship rules prohibited the publication and referencing of the *Vrba-Wetzler Report.*[415] In an early honouring of Voldemort, naming the report was also banned. The British government had received their copy of the *Vrba-Wetzler Report* on 27 June 1944, and yet on July 4th *The Manchester Guardian* stated: "No further reports have been received about the extermination of Hungarian Jews in the Polish death camp at Oswiecim."[416] Aside from the blatant lie about no further reports, the problem with the articles in the British media was all the sneaky semantics that hindered the public's understanding; for example, it was not a *Polish* death camp – it was a Nazi death camp located *in* Poland. This hindrance was exactly what government wanted so that they were not inundated with requests for action[417] such as those which had happened following *The Joint Allied Declaration* of December 1942.

But withholding of information, censorship, and clever semantics could only last so long. On 7 July 1944, the British public were informed for the first time that the camp at Oswiecim was an extermination centre via a BBC Home Service News bulletin at 9pm. While previously the BBC had been deliberately vague (such as calling Auschwitz a "notorious German camp");[418] they now reported that more than "400,000 Hungarian Jews (had been) sent to the concentration camp at Oswiecim" [419] and most had been killed in gas chambers. The report clarified that both adults and children were transported to the camp with the ruse they would be exchanged for prisoners of war. They even revealed that the gas chambers were installed in 1942 and were able to kill 6000 people a day.[420] However, they still did not name the camp as Auschwitz (harder to make a protest sign if you don't know the name of the camp). Most significantly, the report was not mentioned in the "coming up tonight" introduction of the bulletin, AND it was the last of nine reports that night (seven reports on the progress of war and one report on the seventh anniversary of war in China were deemed more important than the ongoing genocide of millions). In addition to this lack of priority, once the BBC broadcast had gone out on July 7th, there was no follow up on subsequent bulletins.

Clearly there had been *some* leeway in censorship of the genocide, but the press was still forced to rely on Polish sources rather than the eyewitness testimony in *The Auschwitz Protocols* that the rest of the non-Nazi world were publishing left, (far) right and centre. This change in censorship likely came about because by July 1944 most of Europe and America were aware of what was happening – the British government had lost control of the flow of information. This change was nothing more than damage limitation.

Why is it thought Britain lacked knowledge?

By the end of 1940, the British knew German and Polish Jews had been forcibly evicted from their homes into ghettoes and that thousands of Polish Jews had been murdered by the German

Order Police and SS Einsatzgruppen killing regiments. By the end of 1941, the British government knew about the Nazi's extermination policy to kill innocent Jews and that Jews were being gassed using vans.[421] By mid-1942, they understood this extermination policy was "The Final Solution", and in December 1942 all members of the British government were aware of the scale of the Nazi's extermination policy due to *The Joint Allied Declaration*. This would have also been the first explicit confirmation of what was going on for the British public. Ultimately, by January 1943 the British government knew everything there was to know. They knew there were millions of victims; they knew about the existence and purpose of Auschwitz, Sobibor, Treblinka, and Belzec death camps; and they knew gas was being used to kill Soviets and Jews at Auschwitz.

But the extent of Britain's real-time awareness is not common knowledge due to the fact there is little evidence proving this in the British archives or media. Luckily, the Brits weren't the only ones keeping records and British newspapers weren't the only publications available. By trawling through Polish documents and seeing what they SENT (even though we conveniently have no record of receiving) we know that information about the Holocaust from the Polish underground reached London from 1942 onwards. The fact that most of these reports (which confirmed Auschwitz was a place where European Jews were taken to be murdered) no longer exist in the archives of the Foreign Office, PWE, British Intelligence or the National Archives in Kew shows how hard these departments have worked since 1945 to eradicate such evidence.[422]

There is also evidence which we know *did* exist but now doesn't. Many sources from the Polish government in exile have since been destroyed. Other files have gone "missing" such as all the information Britain received about Jewish persecution and the atrocities at Auschwitz which was collated by Roger Allen. The unimaginatively named "Allen files" may have been deliberately destroyed or they may still reside with those who want to hide their contents – the British Foreign Office and British Intelligence services – because of the "sensitive" (i.e., damning) nature of their contents.[423] In fact, the Foreign Office were *sooo* desperate to cover up the extent of their knowledge they didn't even admit to having the intercepted Police decodes *after* the war when they could have been used as evidence in the Nuremberg Trials to convict and punish those Nazis responsible.[424] Something else which is handily missing from the British archives are the papers of the Minister of Information, Brendan Bracken. He was well informed about Auschwitz[425] and oversaw telling the press what *not* to publish. His notes would have provided a thorough understanding of what exactly was known and how far Britain went to hide the truth. But he literally took this to his grave. His papers were burnt upon his death at his request. Which I'm sure you'll agree is completely not suspicious at all…

Between November 1942 and July 1944, there were at least 48 separate sources shared with British government departments about Auschwitz which led to at least 50 British reports based on this data. Britain also had intelligence from their own decoded Nazi radio messages; eyewitness accounts; confirmation from a member of the Einsatzgruppen; smuggled reports from ghettoes; speeches from Hitler and Himmler explaining their plan to kill the Jews; media reports of the deportations; and photographic evidence of a liberated camp and the conditions there. These 50 reports about Europe's Jews being exterminated at Auschwitz were distributed to the press in the UK and USA; to the PWE; to Jewish representatives in Britain, USA, and Palestine; and to the top dogs of the political and military establishments in Britain.[426] So why, considering the extent and timing of all their knowledge, did the British government take no action to stop the Holocaust?

Why didn't they bomb Auschwitz?

The request to bomb Auschwitz had been first mooted by the Polish PM Sikorski on 4 January 1941and the Brits had the location details for Auschwitz since December 1940 from Pilecki's report.[427] This initial request was turned down by the British authorities with the excuse that it could not be bombed because the planes did not have the necessary range or precision. The prisoners themselves then requested Britain bomb Auschwitz in 1941: "The prisoners of the concentration camp in Oswiecim implore for a bombing of the camp in the shortest possible time."[428] Britain even had a legitimate motive to carry out a bombing raid on the camp because they had international law on their side; the 1907 *Hague Convention* protected the rights of prisoners of war and defended civilians against mistreatment and arrests for no reason. But in the end, the only bomb they dropped was a big fat "NO".

Britain chose not to bomb Auschwitz and officially refused the request on 15 January 1941, for a few reasons. Firstly, because not all the information got through to the Air Ministry about the real motivation behind this bombing campaign i.e., saving innocent civilians. For some reason, head of Bomber Command, Richard Peirse, did not mention the suffering faced by the prisoners and by the time the message reached Charles Portal at the Air Ministry, Pilecki's words had been condensed to just a single line. Secondly, and undoubtedly influenced by not getting the full story, the Air Ministry saw the bombing of Auschwitz as not vital to the war effort, with Portal brutally explaining it would be an "undesirable diversion". Portal was also worried that if they fulfilled this request, then other governments might ask them to do something similar, and obviously, he could only find the strength to say "no" once. Thirdly, it was deemed too difficult to bomb the camp due to difficulties with precision and resources.[429] Conveniently it was not too difficult to bomb the German chemical plant IG Farben which was located just four miles from Auschwitz. Proving that the real reason underpinning the Air Ministry's decisions was because saving the Jews was not Britain's aim in World War Two.

It is valid that favourable results were not guaranteed. Until 1943 that is. It is unlikely that military action in the form of bombing raids between 1939 and September 1943 would have worked because Britain was ill-equipped. While the Brits received specific requests to bomb Auschwitz in December 1940, the reality was they had precious few planes to spare, the distance was too far with planes leaving from airfields in Britain, and the technology was not good enough to hit precise targets. It is also true that bombing the gas chambers would have been an extremely complicated operation, requiring very direct hits. 220 bombs would need to be dropped on each of the four crematoria at Auschwitz-Birkenau (quick maths… 880 bombs in total) to have a 90% chance of one of them hitting each of its targets.[430] On top of this, completely destroying the gas chambers was unlikely because the chambers were on the bottom floor of buildings built with concrete. Doubts about success bolstered by Britain's previously unsuccessful bombing raids on French railways after France fell to the Nazis in June 1940. Living up to their stereotype of efficiency, in just two days, the Germans managed to repair every kind of damage the Allies had inflicted. According to British logic, if they couldn't do it in France, then they certainly couldn't do it in Poland.

Britain also chose not to bomb Auschwitz because it was feared such reprisal action might lead the Germans to take revenge on any captured British airmen and/or massacre even more Poles and Jews. The Foreign Office completely ruled out the possibility of reprisal raids in January 1943 and decided that in future, a stock denial would be issued to all incoming requests to the camp.[431] The idea was closed down faster than Churchill poured his breakfast whiskey.

Another unfavourable result which was feared was that bombing the camps may have negative consequences for Britain's reputation. Portal (Air chief Marshall aka head of the RAF) was worried such an attack would make Britain look like the Nazis in terms of brutality.[432] To be fair, it was entirely conceivable that the Nazis may twist the events and end up being able to claim the Allies were the ones to kill the Jews. But if these fears really *were* the justification for not taking military action, then why did they not change their stance in 1944 when the *Vrba-Wetzler Report* brought widespread knowledge of the extermination process at Auschwitz? It wouldn't be possible to twist events and make Britain seem bad now most of Europe knew the truth. Yet still, in 1944, Britain stated bombing may do more harm than good by inciting the Nazis to take revenge in some way, and Britain did not want to be held responsible for the killing of innocent civilians.[433] Far better to do nothing and allow the Nazis to kill them instead, apparently.

However, the truth of the matter is that by the end of 1943, favourable results *were* possible, and Britain was no longer ill-equipped. By this point, America, with all her resources, had joined the war; and from September 1943 the British had the use of air bases in Italy which brought their planes within range of the camps in Poland. While they kept plugging the excuse that the railway lines, gas chambers, and crematoria could not be bombed because the planes did not have the necessary range or precision, this was a load of BS. And they proved themselves to be liars in July 1944 when they sent planes to bomb factories and oil refineries which were just 4–6 miles from Auschwitz. That's like 20 seconds in a plane. A synthetic fuel factory north-east of the camp was bombed 10 times between 7 July and 20 November 1944.[434] As part of the planning for this bombing raid, planes flew directly over Auschwitz several times between spring and autumn on a reconnaissance (photography) mission, giving them even *more* detailed information.

And the British could be precise enough when they wanted to be – just look at how they managed to avoid hitting American owned factories in Germany during previous bombing raids. If they can *avoid* a factory-sized building, they can definitely *hit* a target of 15.44 square miles. The successful bombing of the underground gas chambers could have been achieved with 500-pound bombs, and by 1944 there were planes that could deliver those bombs: the Thunderbolt, the Beaufort Blenheim, the Sunderland, B17s, B29s, B24s, and B25s. It is not plane to see why they kept insisting it was not possible.

In 1943, the same year that Churchill and Eden learnt Auschwitz was an extermination centre (likely in January but definitely in April),[435] and bombing Auschwitz became a realistic proposition, more requests came in for this to happen. These came from the Polish government, the Czechoslovakian government, the American War Refugee Board, and Isaac Gruenbaum from the Jewish Agency in Jerusalem, who insisted that the Allies give the bombing of death camps in Poland the same priority as their military objectives.[436] Fully aware that Britain was only prepared to use military force against military or industrial targets (the British were not in the business of ending human suffering), the Polish government thought they phrased their bombing request just right. Their proposal focussed on bombing the industrial targets (factories) within the Auschwitz boundary, a military action which would damage the Nazi war effort. It could also liberate the prisoners as defences were destroyed and guards were distracted.[437] Wisely, the Poles did not lead with this last part.

However, once again, no action was taken. What is most frustrating about this lack of action is that 1943 was prime time for the bombing. Firstly, because in June 1943, the geographic section of the British General Staff had created their own detailed Polish map showing the town where Auschwitz was located (Oswiecim) as well as all the railway routes leading to it.[438] They didn't need to rely on the information provided by Auschwitz prisoners or the Polish government. This was also the year when the assistance of the Home Army (of Poland) could have been utilised as there was support of the plan to attack Auschwitz within these ranks.[439]

Further countering the lame British excuses, in 1944 it was PROVED that favourable results could be achieved. Firstly, the Americans managed to have a significant impact with a bombing raid on the railway yards of Budapest, Hungary, on 2 July 1944. Admiral Horthy (in charge of Hungary) was already under pressure from neutral states and the Christian church to stop the deportations of Hungarian Jews – with a threat of allied bombing raids if he didn't. While the Americans didn't bomb the railways with this in mind, Horthy interpreted the raid as American intervention against the deportation of the Jews. This raid was one of the main reasons behind the decision of the Hungarian government to stop the deportations on 6 July 1944, with the last deportation on July 25th.[440] Demonstrating that bombing could stop deportations to Auschwitz and could lead to lives being saved.

Secondly, on 13 September 1944, some bombs accidentally fell on Auschwitz-Birkenau during a bombing raid on the Buna-Werke synthetic rubber plant at Monowitz. The result was the death of some prisoners, but also some SS men were killed and the railway spur to the Birkenau camp was damaged.[441] All this without even trying! If they had properly planned the whole thing, it is likely they would have achieved their desired results. According to SS reports, there were still more than 700,000 prisoners registered in the concentration camps in January 1945.[442] There was definitely opportunity to save these people in 1944, but the British did not want to even try.

While Britain was aware of the role of Auschwitz in the Nazi's extermination policy from May 1942, they did not change their minds. Auschwitz went on to become the centre for killing and deportations, and 1942 became the year that more Jews were killed (1.5 million) than in any other year of the Holocaust.[443] Even if the two gas chambers were not completely destroyed, the Nazis may have been put off the idea of opening other death camps (the other five were not operational until 1942) due to the fact Auschwitz had been located and bombed so easily. A bombing raid would have also set back the Nazi's plans as they would have had to rebuild Auschwitz before continuing with the genocide. Obviously one bombing raid is unlikely to have stopped the Final Solution, but it sure as hell would have made it more difficult and would have been an action they did Nazi coming.

More bombing requests (from Jewish organisations in Slovakia, America, Poland, and Israel) reached Britain's desk in June 1944 due to the publication and spread of the *Vrba-Wetzler Report*. This report confirmed everything the British already knew – people were being systematically gassed at Auschwitz. It also contained lots of useful information such as maps of the site.

The *Vrba-Wetzler Report* spurred everyone who read it into agreeing that the camp should be bombed. And hold onto your hats… even the British agreed! The British government received their *Vrba-Wetzler Report* on the 27 June 1944. With it, Churchill and the Foreign Office also received a request from Richard Lichtheim for the railway lines and death camp to be bombed.[444] Churchill and Eden seemed all for it on paper. Churchill wrote to Eden on 7 July 1944 saying: "You and I are in total agreement. Get anything out of the air force you can and invoke me if necessary."[445]

So why did they still not bomb Auschwitz?

That old chestnut of "practicalities" was cited again, but the reality was Eden didn't try to follow through. Eden got nothing from the air force because the Secretary of State for Air, Sir Archibald Sinclair, told him bombing the railways was not possible. But the only reason Sinclair thought this was because Eden had failed to provide him with the maps the Ministry of Air had asked for! Then before anyone else might have had the chance to share the information Sinclair needed, Eden and the Foreign Office took the decision on 1 September 1944, to tell Sinclair that the bombing proposal was now off the agenda.[446] "Technical issues" was the official explanation. As in, they technically didn't want to help solve the issues faced by the Jews.

Churchill was not to be invoked. Nor did he see fit to invoke himself and check in on how the situation was developing – a weird response considering he was "in total agreement" bombing should go ahead just two months before. I guess he had grown tired of drawing all those circles. Actions speak louder than words, and there was no action taken from either man to ensure the bombing requests were fulfilled. It seems Churchill and Eden were more concerned with getting some documented evidence (such as the terrifically "supportive" statement of July 7th) which painted them in a favourable light and put them on the right side of history[447] than they were about actually seeing it through. Both men had their own reasons for acting in this way – there is evidence to suggest Eden held anti-Semitic views himself and thus did not want to help the Jews, and Churchill was obsessed with winning the war and did not want to be distracted.

Ultimately, Britain did not bomb Auschwitz at any point because winning the war was the priority and anything to do with saving Jews obstructed the war effort.[448] They argued that such bombardment would not slow down the murder operation but would instead divert resources from battles and endanger the pilots. The only way to rescue Jews, they said, was by winning the war stating: "rescue through victory".[449] To add to this terrible catalogue of avoidance, the Brits didn't even have to be the ones to take military action as the US pilots were well up for it! The pilots who had run bombing raids on Nazi factories close to Auschwitz in 1943–44 actually asked for permission to bomb the concentration camp while they were there. Their request was denied by the British War Department.[450] This rebuff was not based on any logistical analysis (because this would have shown it were possible) but rather because the War Department had a policy not to use armed forces to rescue refugees. And this policy was not for turning.

So why didn't America just bomb Auschwitz themselves then? Well, because Britain never learnt to share properly. America did not plan her own raid because the government had no confirmation of the horrors happening at Auschwitz until summer 1944 despite the fact her ally, Britain, knew full well what was going on from early 1943. Britain did not share this information because they feared that if Bletchley Park revealed their deciphering success, then word would get back to the Nazis and they would change their method of communication. Leading to zero decodes at all. Even after the Joint Allied Declaration had been made in December 1942 the Americans were clueless, as demonstrated by this memo from January 1943: "the State Department has never received any information from official sources and therefore it is not in a position to furnish official confirmation to these allegations."[451] The British did not share their knowledge that Jews were being gassed to death at the camps with the Americans until 8 June 1944.[452] No one's suggesting sending a "Reply All" to everyone in the American government, but why couldn't their knowledge be shared in a private meeting with President Roosevelt? This would have been enough to get the bomb ball rolling. But rolling balls was not part of Britain's war effort. The Americans were never going to approve significant bombing raids for something they had no proof was occurring (they knew the Nazi's were enacting a ruthless campaign against Polish Jews but little else had been confirmed by official sources). And this is exactly what the British government wanted: "no diversion from the war effort".[453]

Why didn't they warn the Jews of Europe in time to save them?

Warning the Jews could have been achieved through announcements on the BBC foreign service radio broadcasts. This would have had the benefit of stopping people believing they were being "relocated" and encouraged people to go into hiding or escape. While it was illegal in Nazi territory to own a radio which could pick up these shortwave BBC broadcasts;[454] the Gestapo estimated there were still 1 million radios out and about by the end of 1941 which could pick up these broadcasts immune to the Nazi's jamming attempts.[455]

The first warnings came in December 1942. The PWE and BBC made the decision on December 10th to announce Hitler's plan to exterminate the Jews, regardless of whether there would be an announcement by the Allied powers.[456] A week later they advised: "In giving the facts soberly, stress … The deliberate plan of Jewish extermination… Main languages should include this week at least one message of encouragement to the Jews".[457] Following this, a few times a day for a week, the BBC aired the Joint Allied Declaration of 17th December as part of their European broadcasts.

January 1943 could be considered "Holocaust awareness month" as this month saw the RAF agree (due to pressure from British Jewish representatives) to drop 1.2 million leaflets about the Nazi extermination programme during their January bombing raids. In Berlin alone, 150,000 leaflets were dropped which contained excerpts of the Joint Allied Declaration.[458] This month also saw BBC radio broadcasts increase their coverage of Nazi atrocities. The broadcasts may have saved some lives but more importantly they helped counter Nazi propaganda with some Germans aware of the atrocities for the first time[459] as they learnt what had really happened to their neighbours who had "gone to live in the East".

Regrettably, the warnings were too late. More Jews were killed in 1942 than any other year of the Holocaust – so the warnings which came in December 1942 and January 1943 were largely futile. The Poles were warned even later – the first BBC broadcast on the Polish service that referred to transportation and gas chambers came on 11 April 1943. Three-and-a-half years after the murders began. Warnings were also delayed for the Hungarian Jews. The Nazis invaded Hungary on 19 March 1944, but the British waited 11 days before warning collaborators against helping the Nazis.[460] There was no mention of death camps in the PWE's broadcasts into Hungary until June 8th – seven weeks after the PWE first suggested releasing such information and just over two months after the Nazi invasion. All these delays only served to help the Nazis – late minds think alike and all that.

Britain did not warn the Jews of Europe of the Nazi's plan of extermination or give public denouncements in the early years because they did not want to give away the fact they were successfully listening in on the German Order Police's radio messages. Openly acknowledging the atrocities they had discovered would have put their code-breaking success at risk. This is a valid reason for not making an early public statement as was made clear by the Nazi's switch to the Double Playfair code following Churchill's "give it all away why don't you" speech in August 1941. However, this excuse of keeping their secrets a secret was null and void from early 1942 once the *Reports on Jewry* were published and the Foreign Office received the 160-page report *Jews in Nazi Europe: February 1933 to November 1941* in February 1942.[461] These reports confirmed the information from the German Police decodes about the path the Nazis were taking but most significantly, they provided the British with a source which was not hush hush because these reports were based on material from foreign publications and journalists. If the British government had *wanted* to react publicly to the killings of Jews and give warning to those at risk, early 1942 was their chance.

For example, while the BBC Polish service broadcast news in April 1943 about the Cracow liquidation and Jews being sent to Oswiecim where there were gas chambers;[462] listeners had to hear between the lines about the fate awaiting these people. By naming the *town* instead of Auschwitz death camp and by mentioning gas chambers but not their purpose, people were not getting the full reality. More specific reports of the killing of Jews and Poles at Auschwitz were not broadcast on the BBC Polish service until October 1943. The publication of the *Vrba-Wetzler Report* in summer 1944 led to all allied governments becoming aware of the genocide and role of Auschwitz. This was an opportunity for Britain to change her censorship policy on the matter because, with the truth out there, censorship was pointless. Yet the British were still opposed to broadcasting warnings on the Hungarian BBC service and were lethargic in changing this policy position.

One individual who heavily influenced the delayed warnings to the Hungarian Jews was George Hall (Under-Secretary of State for Foreign Affairs). He believed the British had "done all we can". Hall thought: "it seems superfluous to inform the Jewish population in Hungary" because this would cause "unnecessary alarm amongst the Jews of Hungary".[463] While I'm pretty sure learning about your impending death is 100% *necessary* alarm, British policy stood firm that it wasn't. The whole of Europe and the USA knew of the fate awaiting Hungary's Jews, but no one said anything to them. Worst surprise ever. Even the prisoners already at Auschwitz couldn't believe the Hungarian Jews knew nothing of their fate as recorded by Holocaust survivor Elie Wiesel who was asked upon arrival: "didn't you know what was in store for you at Auschwitz? Haven't you heard about it? In 1944?" Wiesel noted sadly: "No we had not heard. No one had told us."[464]

While the PWE and BBC deserve some credit for their broadcasts about the Final Solution, the information was not always clear enough to be effective. Ultimately, the British did not warn the Jews early enough, or explicitly enough, for two reasons: rigid wartime censorship rules; and a distinct lack of empathy or urgency from British officials.

Why didn't they allow more Jewish refugees into Britain and/or Palestine?

No action was taken to help refugees because, firstly, the British thought it would be too difficult to house large numbers of Jews in Britain; and secondly because they feared upsetting the Arabs by allowing them into Palestine.

However, these refusals and fears were not shared by everyone in the British government and the lack of action is mostly down to the Foreign Office and Home Office. There were requests for the British government to help refugees from Viscount Herbert; the Archbishop of Canterbury; and various MPs from 1938 onwards. The first of which came from MP and all-round humanist Eleanor Rathbone. As a member of the British Non-Sectarian Anti-Nazi Council (why wasn't *everyone* a member of this?!), she was one of only a few MPs to directly promote the Jewish cause.[465] In 1938 she pressurised parliament to grant entry for Jews, and in 1942 she was pushing for them to publish their knowledge of the Holocaust meanwhile publishing her own pamphlet informing the public of what was going on. She also suggested the British government pressure the Nazi-occupied countries of Europe to evacuate their Jews to safe havens. Not that she is remembered for any of these noble acts – her blue plaque instead refers to her as a pioneer of "the family allowance".

Following the Joint Allied Declaration of December 1942, Viscount Herbert naively raised the question of whether the West may now do something to help during a discussion in the House of Lords. He suggested that they help neutral countries around the Nazi empire take in Jewish refugees. [466] Archbishop Temple was similarly inspired by the declaration and suggested the Allies take in all Jews who made it out of Nazi-controlled territory.[467] Both great ideas. Neither of which were pursued by Great Britain. By 1943, over a third of British MPs were in favour of some sort of action beyond merely saying "oh that's pretty naughty" and there were various lobbying efforts in parliament.[468] At the start of the year, MPs put forward a motion suggesting Britain enact: "immediate measures on the largest and most generous scale... providing help and temporary asylum to persons in danger of massacre".[469]

Despite the fact this was a popular motion (260 out of 650 MPs signed it) and had high-level support from the Archbishop of Canterbury – it was shut down when it got to the House of Lords on 23 March 1943.

Britain did not allow more Jewish refugees into Britain because they thought there was no space, as evidenced by the minutes of a committee meeting on 31 December 1942: "the accommodation problem was already most difficult".[470] They had already eased their policy in 1938, meaning 70–80,000 Jewish refugees had been accepted into Britain by September 1939.[471] The British therefore thought they had done enough. Once war began, the Home Secretary Herbert Morrison suggested they could accept 1000–2000 refugees "but certainly no more." He thought they should all be sent to the Isle of Man and be made to stay there as long as necessary. It's unclear whether he had gotten wind of the Nazi's plan of 1941 to send all the Jews to the island of Madagascar, but the similarity of segregation is concerning. Out of the nine million Jews in Europe, 10,000 made it into Britain during the war.[472] Essentially, the British immigration policy, made by the Home Office, aimed to keep European Jews OUT.[473]

Britain also didn't help Jewish refugees because those in charge of doing exactly this didn't think Jews deserved special treatment. A new group was established at the end of 1942: "The War Cabinet Committee on the Reception and Accommodation of Jewish Refugees." Heading up the group was the Foreign Secretary Anthony Eden, the Home Secretary Herbert Morrison, and the Secretary of State for Colonies Oliver Stanley. Their job was to consider possible arrangements for Jewish refugees who escaped. Unfortunately, none of the three read their job description...

At the very first meeting they vetoed the idea of resettling Jewish refugees who had escaped to neutral countries. In a further WTF moment, Stanley argued that they shouldn't be distinguishing Jews from other refugees because that wasn't fair to everyone else (who wasn't being murdered). Despite the onslaught of evidence to the contrary which Eden had been privy to during 1942, the committee rebuffed the idea Jews were suffering more than other people and thus needed targeted help. So, they deleted the word *Jewish* from their title, and the War Cabinet Committee on the Reception and Accommodation of Jewish Refugees rejected the whole point of their group. Eden, Stanley, and Morrison are very much comparable to the "All Lives Matter" crowd in the present day.

All totally missing the point.

By 1943, there was a new excuse to not help refugees – it was "too tricky". This was the justification given to the 260 MPs who had voted to help refugees in the House of Commons on February 24th. Government spokesman Viscount Cranborne explained that they could not possibly help because it was too difficult due to the constraints on food and shipping. He also fobbed the MPs off by claiming that the upcoming Bermuda Conference would sort things out once and for all.[474] This childish excuse of not doing something because it seemed difficult was not just reserved for parliament. When, in 1943, a member of the public requested the Foreign Office do something (anything!) to help the Jews, Foreign Secretary Eden's response was: "Even if we were to obtain permission to withdraw all Jews, transport alone presents a problem which will be difficult of solution."[475] Just a shame the Nazis didn't adopt this closed mindset when they, too, were faced with the difficulty of transporting nine million Jews.

This idea of difficulty is valid to some extent. Money was tight and it would have been incredibly difficult to organise the transportation required, especially as some of it would have to take place in enemy territory. But by September 1943, the difficulty had been reduced somewhat by the fact Italy were now on the allied side – boats could have transported refugees across the Mediterranean from Italy to Palestine. Yes, the boats of refugees ran the risk of being blown up in the sea, but the likelihood is, in 1943, the Nazis would not want to divert their limited resources to a goal which was being realised on their behalf. After all, the Jews were leaving Europe, and this exodus was what Hitler wanted one way or another, (to quote Blondie – as in the seventies singer – not Hitler's dog).

Proof that helping refugees was in fact, not so difficult, came from a few different sources, including ironically enough, Churchill. Firstly, Germany's ally, Japan, had been proving how easy it was to help refugees since the start of the war, and refugees were allowed to enter Japan until the spring of 1941. More people made the 5000–6000-mile trip over there in two years (17,000 people)[476] than made the 20–30-mile trip across the English Channel into Britain in five years. Let's not forget, Japan were Germany's ally since 1936 but they still managed to find it within themselves to allow Jewish refugees to enter and refused to take stringent measures against them as the Nazis demanded. Then in April 1943, Churchill had success with asking the Spanish ambassador to reopen the Spanish border to Jewish refugees fleeing Nazi persecution. This cost nothing and was immediately effective. The border was reopened within a few days, showing that the previous years' lack of requests to neutral countries was a mistake. But this tactic was not tried again. Lastly, when neutral Sweden found out on 29 September 1943 that Germany intended to deport all Jews from Denmark, they acted. By October 9th they had successfully transferred nearly all the Danish Jews into Sweden.[477] Yes, the distance was shorter than the distance from Britain to France (three miles versus twenty-one), but this is still an inspiring feat over a risky stretch of sea. By December 1943, the British were forced to explain what was "so difficult" about helping and the Foreign Office, with little awareness of how bad this sounded, explained it was: "the difficulties of disposing of any considerable number of Jews".[478] It was far easier for the British to condemn these people to death than to put a plan in place to "dispose" of the Jews themselves.

The Home Office refused visa applications from Jewish refugees trying to get into Britain because they believed there was a high level of anti-Semitism in the country. Shortly before the Home Secretary, Herbert Morrison, went to celebrate the New Year in 1942, he made sure that the British public were blamed for the Home Office's refusal to admit Jewish refugees: "there was considerable anti-Semitism under the surface of this country. If there was any substantial increase in the number of Jewish refugees or if these refugees did not leave this country after the war, we should be in for serious trouble".[479]

The Home Office believed Jews brought anti-Semitism with them, much like a bully blames his victim for being an easy target. They assumed the public would react with horror because horror was *their* reaction to the idea. Any evidence to the contrary, such as the numerous requests for action from the "anti-Semitic" British public which flooded in during early 1943,[480] was ignored. A letter from Lady Reading dated 16th January implored: "England surely cannot sink to such hypocracy (sic) that her members of parliament stand to show sympathy to the Jewish dead and meanwhile her officials are condemning those same Jews to die?"[481] Erm… Have you ever met the British, Lady Reading?! They are the kings of hypocrisy: just look at the Crusades (fine and dandy for us to invade the Holy Land but the Muslims defending it were immoral) or the building of the British Empire (we'll take your land and enforce our culture, but the indigenous people are the bad guys for rebelling).

The Home Office knew they were in the wrong turning all these applications down because they desperately tried to seek an excuse to hide the ruthlessness of their refusals. They asked the Foreign Office on 5 January 1943, if, maybe, they could use the cover of the upcoming Bermuda Conference as an excuse. Their thinking was they could say the Allies were trying to figure out an *even better* plan than simply allowing Jews safe refuge in Britain ergo the rejection was for their benefit.

Naturally, the Foreign Office agreed.

But they advised the Home Office to use specific wording so that when, inevitably, the Bermuda Conference came to nothing, they could not be criticised. "We would prefer the substitution of the word 'consultation' for 'discussions'… and it might be better if, instead of mentioning a "joint scheme" you said (that the Allies were consulting to see) whether there is any prospect of overcoming the great difficulties in the way of any substantial relief."[482] A real smack in the face for those who had endeavoured to escape then managed to find a pen (hard enough at the best of times), and then taken the time to fill out the paperwork. Jewish applicants were told that they weren't allowed in *now* because the Allies would rather discuss if there was *a chance* they *might* be able to help in the future. All the while ignoring the chance right in front of their faces! A fact not missed by the political correspondent of *The Manchester Guardian* who commented that the British government had "thrown up the sponge" about Jewish refugees.[483] And they threw the sponge even further the following month when they (and America) ignored a proposal from the Romanian government to transfer 70,000 Jews to Palestine.

Britain did not allow significant Jewish immigration into Palestine due to fear of upsetting the Arabs who lived there. Britain was controlling Palestine under a mandate from the League of Nations since 25 April 1920, following the defeat of the Ottomans in WW1 (who had control of it prior). The mandate included a request that the British establish a "national home" for Jewish people in Palestine. The awkward thing was, to secure Arab support against the Ottomans in WW1, Britain had *already* promised the Arabs the territory of Palestine (and Jordan) as a way of saying thank you, (bloomin' cheap thank you considering the land wasn't even theirs to gift away in the first place). Therefore, the British government couldn't allow mass emigration to Palestine because their two-timing would have been revealed. This fear of creating major political problems with the Arabs became the go-to excuse for the Foreign Office for the entirety of the Holocaust. [484] When Alexander Easterman (director of the World Jewish Congress) asked Britain to help Jewish refugees on 7 January 1943, Richard Law of the Foreign Office told him that an influx of Jews into Britain or Palestine was too risky, and it was safer to avoid such initiatives. Not so sure the Jews would have agreed.

Churchill was asked in January 1943: "is it possible, is it really possible, to refuse sanctuary in the Holy Land?"[485]

The answer was yes.

Although this wasn't of course how Churchill's secretary phrased the answer in the response letter, and instead the classic "difficulties" of transportation was cited. But this wasn't true. Because even when Jewish refugees had overcome the transport issues themselves (i.e., they made their own way there without British help) Britain still didn't allow them in. They prioritised border regulations over saving lives.

Instead of being proactive about protecting lives, the British were proactive in stopping Jews reach safety, such as when they prevented the ship *Struma* from getting to Palestine. The *Struma* left Romania on 12 December 1941, with 769 Jews on board. However, upon reaching Istanbul their boat was halted and kept there for two months because the British were trying to persuade the Turkish government not to let the boat through. Only one person was allowed to leave the ship – a heavily pregnant lady called Medea Salamovitz. While Britain did eventually engage their conscience and conceded to let 70 children onboard proceed to Palestine, the negotiations had taken so long the Turks had already ordered the boat to turn back into the Black Sea. There, on the night of February 24th, it was sunk by a Soviet torpedo and all but one person (David Stoliar) drowned. Even when people had created their own means of escape, without British help, they were denied, with British help.

For those who did overcome "transport difficulties" and the difficult British government and managed to make it into Palestine without a visa, Britain still ignored their plight and treated the Jews like criminals. In fairness, illegal immigration is not OK, but considering the British were aware of the dangers faced by the Jews, AND they had signed up to the League of Nation's definition of a refugee as someone who needed to be protected due to threats being made on their life – they should have recognised their status as refugees and offered protection. But rather than process the arrivals as the refugees they were, the British Colonial Office put them in Atlit detention camp, such as when the *Darien II* arrived in March 1941and the 792 people (mostly Jewish) on board were imprisoned for at least 15 months. The people were split up and segregated by gender, sprayed with DDT, and the grounds had watchtowers around the perimeter with the people imprisoned behind barbed wire fences.[486] Curiously, while the *Darien II* was confiscated by the British Mandate government, the British did not think to use said ship to help overcome the "transport difficulties" which had been thus far preventing them from helping. The Brits kept a stiff upper ship when it came to sympathising with the refugees, although pleasingly Churchill criticised this process calling it "an act of inhumanity".[487]

While fear about the Arabs reaction was present and valid, it's possible that underpinning their refusals to allow Jewish refugees into Palestine was an anti-Semitic attitude. Ultimately, the British did not want to save these Jewish lives – a lack of desire which can be proved by the fact they didn't even let in the 75,000 allowed by *The White Paper* of 1939! This agreement had a deadline of 1944 giving them five years to save lives; after March 1944, Arab consent would be needed to allow more.[488] Yet by the start of 1943, there were still 41,000 places available.[489] Britain had accepted only 45.4% of the number while using up 80% of the time allowance. In the end, there were more than 500,000 case files of Jews who were not admitted to Palestine according to British Jewish associations.[490] That's 8.3% of all those killed who could have been saved had Britain taken it upon themselves to grant permission. However, there were some positive moves in the right direction as the war cabinet later approved an extension to the White Paper limit on Jewish immigration into Palestine.[491] An extension to the time, that is, which meant the original 75,000 limit still needed to be adhered to, but it could be reached after March 1944. Somewhat helpful, but time wasn't exactly on the Jews' side.

A significant reason why Jewish refugees were not helped by Britain or America is because these two were more concerned about *looking* like they were going to do something rather than actually doing something. As well as squabbling among themselves about who was pulling this farce off better.[492] Concerns raised for Jewish refugees in 1941 were quietened with the upcoming St James' Conference in January 1942; requests to help refugees were shot down in 1942 with the promise of the *Joint Allied Declaration* in December 1942; and from the first week of March 1943, the Foreign Office was able to deflect any requests to do something towards the fact there was the Bermuda Conference coming up where a chat about events *would* constitute them doing something. All these meetings presented opportunities for joint allied action to help refugees. All opportunities were passed up on. St James' saw an agreement on punishment for war crimes but ignored the plight of the victims of those war crimes; the Joint Allied Declaration was an open condemnation of the Nazi's persecution but failed to provide a way to escape said persecution; and Bermuda was just an absolute farce.

The Bermuda Conference failed to help Jewish refugees because the whole purpose of the conference was to *stop* other countries from changing their refugee policies (and helping Jews). Despite fobbing off Jewish refugees for months and months with the promise Bermuda would result in action to help them – the leader of the British delegation, Richard Law, thought the most important goal of the conference was to get a joint agreement on what should NOT be done.[493] As a result, American immigration quotas were not raised, and the British prohibition on Jewish refugees seeking refuge in Palestine was not lifted either.

The British did have a secondary aim for the conference. But this wasn't to help the Jews either. They aimed to enlist American help to get the Anglican church and British archbishops to stop publicly criticising their inaction so far.[494] The only proper agreement made at Bermuda was that the war must be won against the Nazis. I mean… really? They took 11 days to come up with that?! However, they did verbally agree to give humanitarian aid to neutral countries, and they called for all the Allied nations to club together to ensure the return of refugees after the war.[495] They did not, of course, create a document which guaranteed either of these things.

The pointless nature of the conference did not escape scrutiny from British MPs who questioned the lack of action.[496] Unfortunately, everyone else in Britain was not afforded the opportunity to criticise because the agreement (to continue doing as little as possible) was deliberately kept secret.[497] But to be fair, there was one agreement of action which Churchill personally intervened in to ensure it happened. The construction of small concentration camps. Yes, really. Churchill was a big fan of the idea because he believed concentration camps "produce the minimum of suffering" based on his experience of them in the Boer War (where, incidentally, 42,000 people died because of this minimal suffering).[498] The camps were intended to house Jewish refugees from Europe and be located in North Africa. Yes, this does also involve a sea crossing but conveniently this transport wasn't too difficult to organise. And "concentration camps" was literally how Lord Halifax described them at the time. A home from home maybe, Lord Halifax?

When opportunities came, in the months after Bermuda, to honour their agreement to provide aid to refugees in neutral countries, Britain turned the other way. Firstly, when Britain was given the chance to help evacuate Bulgarian Jews to the Near East in June 1943, the British explained they'd rather wait for the construction of their concentration camps in North Africa.[499] These camps were dodgy enough as it was, but even more ridiculously, they were not even big enough to hold the number of Bulgarian Jews who needed helping so what was the point in waiting?! The second opportunity came in July 1943 when Britain and the Allies were asked to provide the food and fuel required to support Switzerland in taking in up to 100,000 refugees from Germany, France, and Italy. Britain did not help because one man didn't think it would work. Clifford Norton was the British minister in Switzerland, but he took it upon himself not to bother the Swiss with the proposal because he *assumed* they would say no due to the fact most of the adult refugees were Jewish.[500] The Foreign Office did not dispute his reluctance or encourage him to, you know, try anyway. In a show of difference between the Allies, when US President

Roosevelt was presented with a similar opportunity in the same month (to help with the relief and evacuation of Jewish refugees in Romania and France), his response was "go ahead" and the plan was approved by the American Treasury in August.[501] Britain's promises had presumably got lost in the Bermuda Triangle.

Prioritising the war was a significant reason why Britain did not do more to help Jewish refugees into Britain or Palestine. This focus blindsided an alternative way of helping Jewish refugees (by negotiating with the Nazis for the release of certain groups). SS leader and Nazi second-in-command Heinrich Himmler had made it clear he was prepared to release some small numbers of Jews in return for money; in fact, part of Bergen-Belsen camp had been set up to specifically hold those they thought suitable for such an exchange.[502] If money were the issue, then Britain could have exchanged Jews for German civilians held in Allied countries.[503] This option was viable in June 1943 when Himmler (mostly) agreed to Britain's request to allow 5000 Jewish children from Nazi territory in the East to go to Palestine. Himmler's conditions were that the children go to Britain (the Nazis also feared upsetting the Arabs); and that they should be exchanged for young, imprisoned Germans at the ratio of four Germans to one Jew.[504] But nothing came of it. Negotiations whimpered on into 1944[505] before being completely dropped as by this point an Allied victory was now in sight. Ultimately, Britain had a Machiavellian approach; they believed that the ends would justify the means i.e., destroying the Nazis and winning the war would stop the killing of Jews. A joke about men's inability to multi-task would work here if it were not so heartbreakingly true.

The fact it would have been difficult to help is valid. But it shouldn't have stopped the British politicians from trying. It was difficult for the Nazis to murder six million Jews, but they managed it. The difficulties Britain acknowledged (money, logistics, and housing) could have been overcome with the support of other nations. Support, which was there for the taking at the St James conference in 1942; the 1943 Bermuda Conference; from the Swedish King and American War Refugee Board in 1943; and from Switzerland, various Jewish groups in Palestine and America, the American War Refugee Board, and the Czechoslovakian president Edvard Benes in 1944. Benes wrote directly to the British Foreign Office on 4 July 1944, saying he was happy to: "associate himself with any protest that might be organised".[506] Edvard must have Benes under the false impression that Eden was a nice guy, whereas he and the Foreign Office are seemingly the ones most responsible for the lack of British action.

Overall, Britain did not help Jewish refugees because they didn't want to deal with the logistics and the expense. They got away with this for so long because they were able to fob people off with the promise of future action. On the surface of it all, refusals could be justified with the priority of winning the war, but the reality was Britain feared that if she did push for Jews to be released from the Nazis – the Nazis might actually say yes.[507] When Alexander Easterman of the World Jewish Congress suggested to Richard Law in the Foreign Office that the Nazis might release 100,000 Jewish children if the Allies pressed for it, Law declined to make the offer explaining: "we could not take the risk of the German's calling our bluff".[508] Erm… it wasn't a bluff, Richard – pretty sure Easterman was serious about saving those kids. Two months later, in March 1943, in response to a request to do something about the 60–70,000 Bulgarian Jews at risk of death, Eden responded that they wouldn't offer help because: "Hitler might well take us up on the offer".[509]

Why didn't Britain act to stop the Holocaust?

The killing of Jews began in September 1939, and the Holocaust began in January 1942 with the systematic use of gas. In the early years of war, Britain had few resources to spare and, to be fair, they did not yet know the full extent. Yet from November 1942 until June 1944, news of Jews being killed at Auschwitz reached London at an average rate of two reports a month.[510] So why did they not help?

1. Britain prioritised the war effort

The main reason why Britain did not take action to stop the Holocaust or help European Jews escape is because they prioritised the war effort. Churchill's strategy to win World War Two was threefold: use Allied bombing to destroy military resources to wear down the resolve of the people and government; use invasions and troops to create a shrinking circle around Nazi territory; and use economic measures to starve Germany into collapse.[511] Money and effort were put towards these aims but he was deaf to any request which did not fit this plan.

Prioritising war also meant prioritising funds towards this end rather than any rescue missions or directing funds towards neutral countries (such as Spain, Sweden, or Switzerland) to help them look after refugees. Yes, this is war and money is tight, but considering the British found the money to fund Churchill's hairbrained scheme to drop anthrax cakes into Germany, I'm sure the money could have been found. This 1942 idea was called Project Vegetarian – possibly in honour of Hitler – the vegetarian murderer. The "logic" was to bake a load of cattle cakes (made of linseed and anthrax) and drop them into the German fields. Cows would eat the cakes, get infected and spread it to the Germans. There was even enough money in the wartime kitty to test the plan out in Guinard Island, Scotland, before ploughing even more money into the scheme in 1943–44 with five million anthrax cakes cooked up and RAF planes customised to drop cakes instead of bombs (you couldn't make this stuff up). The plan was discarded when the British were instead presented with the genuinely logical idea of D-Day (an invasion of Nazi Europe using soldiers instead of cakes) and because they realised they'd be the ones clearing up the anthrax mess once Germany lost.[512] But, the point stands, money was there.

Winning the war was the priority and anything to do with saving Jews obstructed the war effort.[513] This is why Britain did not bomb Auschwitz and explains why Churchill decided punishment for the Nazis once the war was over was the best course of action: "When the hour of liberation strikes Europe, as strike it will, it will also be the hour of retribution".[514] The British government believed that an Allied victory was the only real remedy for the Nazi's racial and religious persecution,[515] rather than actual action which would have saved actual lives at the actual time. And boy did they literally stick to their guns. At the Bermuda Conference in April 1943, the British made it clear they wouldn't do anything which stopped their blockade of Germany; their steadfast commitment to this war tactic closed down any suggestions of shipping food to the Jews of Europe.[516] A note from the Foreign Office explained: "our requirements are predominantly military".[517] The Foreign Office weren't even ashamed of their obstruction and boasted in 1943: "His Majesty's Government took every possible measure to discourage the hope that very-far reaching measures of relief were practicable at the present crisis of war."[518] This lack of shame is even more shocking considering the naval blockade on Germany from 1939–45 was illegal under international law.

From joining the war on 8 December 1941, until spring 1943, the Americans also agreed winning the war should be the priority. Even the guy in charge of helping those flee from persecution – the refugee specialist at the American State Department agreed: "…our main purpose is the winning of the war and other considerations must be subordinate thereto".[519] This guy really was a bad egg as he went on to make it abundantly clear how little he cared about the people he was tasked to care about: "whether the number of dead amounts to tens of thousands or, as these reports state, to millions is not material to the main problem."[520] Turns out *he* was the main problem.

The American's blinkered view on the war and saving the Jews did not last. From March 1943, the Americans (under pressure from their citizens and the World Jewish Council) were keen to send food and medicine to provide relief for women and children in Belgium and Norway. Even without official confirmation, the Final Solution was taking place (due to Britain's withholding of intelligence), the American president was keen to do something. Roosevelt spoke with Churchill between March and June of 1943 with the intention of stopping the British blockade to allow the relief to get through. But even with official confirmation of the Final Solution taking place in this year, Churchill would not budge. A US State Department official commented on the unsuccessful conversation saying: "The public reason given is that Germany would probably interfere, but the actual reason is not that. It is Churchill's insistence on the primacy of the military consideration."[521]

Churchill remained as stubborn as a three-year-old at bedtime throughout the rest of the war, telling the Americans again, in spring 1944, that there would be no shipments of food to Europe. Eden helpfully added that blockading had historically been a mainstay of British war policy.[522] It would have been more pertinent for him to acknowledge that ignoring the rights of non-British people was also a mainstay of British policy.

It is disturbingly clear that war trumped all rescue efforts because in April 1944, Adolf Eichmann (head of Reich Security) was in talks with Joel Brand from the Aid and Rescue Committee to swap Jews for trucks, or money, or other helpful wartime commodities. Eichmann told Brand: "I am prepared to sell you one million Jews... you can take them from any country you like, wherever you can find them – Hungary, Poland... from Auschwitz".[523] So here was a leading Nazi, offering to save the lives of one million Jews – he was even proposing to hand over those already at Auschwitz! But the British were not interested in the blood for trucks deal[524] because giving the Nazis what they were asking for would have helped the Nazi war effort and done nothing to aid the Allies. The plan was deliberately thwarted by the Foreign Office who leaked details of the proposal to the press on July 19[th,] with the BBC first to report on it. This leak was not what the Nazis wanted because it made them look weak asking for resources and letting Jews go free and so the deal was cancelled. On the positive side, the possibility of a deal had seen Eichmann allowing 1685 Jews to go free; nevertheless, the focus on military objectives prevented any more people from being saved.

To be fair, the logic behind the British decision was sound; if they helped the people in Nazi territory then that took responsibility away from the Nazis who could then direct more food and resources to their soldiers. It would have benefitted the Axis war effort and resulted in their slower collapse. However, by spring 1944, the collapse of the Nazis was inevitable. The Allies were closing in from the south (via Allied victories in North Africa and Italy); the east (via the Soviets relentless fighting); and they were aware that June 1944 would bring D-Day, allowing them to close in from the west. Helping people and alleviating some suffering from spring 1944 onwards would not have countered this Allied progress.

2. The British government didn't believe it

The British government found the Holocaust impossible to believe because it was such a unique event.[525] *So unique* Churchill managed to predict it would happen in April 1933: "There is a danger of the odious conditions now ruling in Germany, being extended by conquest to Poland and another persecution and pogrom of Jews being begun in this area".[526] Eight years later, in August 1941, Churchill also openly acknowledged that killing of a specific ethnic group had, actually, been seen before: "Since the Mongol invasions of Europe in the sixteenth century, there has never been methodical, merciless butchery on such a scale, or approaching such a scale."[527] Rather awkwardly, it seems no one told Viscount Samuel about this future line of defence either and in December 1942 he compared the Jewish genocide with the Armenian genocide (1915–17) during a debate in the House of Lords: "The only events even remotely parallel to this were the Armenian massacres of fifty years ago."[528] The British prime minister and House of Lords clearly understood the genocide was not an unprecedented event. Plus, let's not forget the small fact that Britain had been responsible in the past for killing large ethnic groups themselves. Their takeover of America had genocidal intent with seven different massacres of natives in the British Thirteen Colonies in the first 100 years alone.[529] There were also more underhand tactics, such as the Pamunkey peace talks on 12 May 1623, where the Brits poisoned the wine which killed two hundred people;[530] or the "gift" of smallpox infected blankets to the natives in 1763.[531] The Holocaust was definitely not the first time that specific ethnic groups could be targeted and killed.

A big reason why the government found it hard to believe Jews were the specific target was because British intelligence officers (whose job is to take meaning from what they decipher), took the wrong meaning from the decodes which explicitly described Jews being killed. Whereas you or I would take these descriptions of Jews being murdered to mean Jews were being murdered, they chose instead to interpret these messages meant it was unlikely *all* the deaths could be Jews.[532] An interpretation which is hard to fathom considering… the British government had known Jews were the target of Nazi persecution and at threat of death since at least May 1939 when MP James Rothschild stated in the House of Commons: "For the majority of Jews who go to Palestine it is a question of migration or of physical extinction."[533]

The distrust of Polish information and Polish informants had a huge impact of the British government's belief. Victor Cavendish-Bentinck, chairman of the British Joint Intelligence Committee (JIC), wrote in August 1943 that the Poles and the Jews exaggerated Nazi atrocities "in order to stoke us up".[534] He even went so far as to criticise the PWE for publicising such "exaggerated" information about the atrocities during 1943.[535] Even crazier is the fact Cavendish-Bentinck's prejudiced assumption came AFTER the British government publicly acknowledged the atrocities in the Joint Allied Declaration in December 1942 i.e., proving the Polish sources to be truthful and not exaggerated. Not every Pole was considered unreliable; for example, Polish courier Jan Nowak-Jezioranski was judged to be trustworthy by Cavendish-Bentinck because he was: "not a Jew, but quite an intelligent middle-class Pole."[536] But if you didn't have money and were a Polish Jew then your integrity was in doubt which explains why the British took no action off the back of Pilecki's report in December 1941. However, this was a selective approach and British intelligence conveniently had no problem believing these Polish sources could give them some military insight.[537]

A lack of sharing information between British government departments also hampered widespread certainty. A limited number of government offices received copies of the decodes: the military intelligence experts in MI 8; the intelligence specialists on Germany in MI 14; the Air Ministry, the Ministry of Economic Warfare; the Joint Intelligence Committee; and some were also shared with Churchill.[538] Lack of sharing was not just limited to within the British government. When Pilecki's second report arrived in London at the end of November 1941, it was vetted by the British authorities before being handed to the Polish PM Sikorski.[539] The report was an important turning point in knowledge of the Holocaust as it was the first to describe the gassing experiments in Auschwitz.[540] Sadly, Sikorski failed to see the significance and did not share the information about the gassings when addressing the British and American governments in January 1942.

British disbelief was further heightened by a report from The Red Cross which indicated life in Nazi concentration camps was rather jolly. The International Red Cross and Danish Red Cross were allowed to visit Theresienstadt ghetto-camp in June 1944 after a request was put forward at the end of 1943. But of course, as masters of propaganda and with six months to prepare, the Nazis did not let them see what was really going on. The ghetto-camp was renovated with new paintwork, fresh plants and grass, and repaired buildings. There was even a football match accompanied with a cheering crowd and a singing performance by children. Jewish inmates were forced to play different roles and act happy; and while there were signs that all was not well, such as a bruise under the eye of the "town mayor" (a part played by Jewish inmate Paul Eppstein), the three Red Cross delegates believed the elaborate hoax and produced a favourable report.[541] How they managed to come to this conclusion when there was so much public evidence to the contrary (Joint Allied Declaration; BBC foreign service broadcasts; newspaper reports; *Mein Kampf*; and little things like Hitler's speeches saying the Jews will be destroyed) is beyond comprehension.

Disbelief certainly wasn't down to a lack of information. By 1941, British analysts knew more about the displacement and murder of Poles and Jews and the role of the German Order Police in the East than anyone else would for years![542] By the end of 1942, the British government had intelligence from a variety of sources (Polish prisoner at Auschwitz – Pilecki; the Swedish government; the Ukrainian press; the Jewish Press; the underground Polish government still in Poland; the *Aneks* from the Polish intelligence agency Bureau VI; the Polish resistance; and, of course, the plentiful decodes from their own intelligence agency). You would think there would be no room for disbelief, considering all this information matched the speeches made by Hitler and Himmler as well as their statements of genocidal intent made in *Mein Kampf* and the *Völkischer Beobachter* Newspaper. You would think…

Rather than being caused by a lack of information, it is more accurate that the British government *chose* not to believe it was happening.

To be fair, it is understandable that the Holocaust was hard to believe due to its scale and methods. Millions of people systematically killed using gas had not been seen before and it takes a while for such news to sink in. Even those hearing from reliable sources expressed doubt due to the horrific nature of the information.[543]

What is not understandable is how the British government, Foreign Office, and intelligence officers were unable to see the links between: a) their knowledge of Nazi persecution of Jews; b) their intelligence from 1940–1941 detailing the massacres in Nazi-occupied Europe with c) the news that came in later about the systematic executions. Perhaps if the reports about the executions at Auschwitz had come before 1933 then the whole "can't believe it" thing may have actually had some weight to it. But they didn't. The reports from Auschwitz about the slaughter of Jews came to London in early 1943; this was *after* Nazi extermination policy was known, *after* Hitler had made his promises of destruction, *after* British intelligence had listened in on reports of mass murder in 1940, *after* Pilecki's 1941 eyewitness account of Auschwitz, *after* the St James' Conference in January 1942 saw agreement that some form of retribution would be needed (for crimes they didn't believe were happening) and *after* news of mass killings in other death camps began arriving in 1942. If anything, the news about Auschwitz in early 1943 should have been undeniable rather than unbelievable. It literally confirmed every other piece of information the British had been receiving for the last three years. To then say that the idea of persecution and murder of the Jews was "unbelievable" is in itself unbelievable.

3. Britain failed to act because of anti-Semitism

There is evidence of anti-Semitism in the Foreign Office (led by Anthony Eden); the Home Office (led by Herbert Morrison); PWE (led by a committee governed by Anthony Eden, Brendan Bracken the Minister of Information, and Hugh Dalton, the

Minister of Economic Warfare); and the War Cabinet Committee on the Reception and Accommodation of Jewish Refugees (led by Anthony Eden, Herbert Morrison, and Oliver Stanley). Between them, these government departments sought to downplay the Holocaust and prevented news about the atrocities from appearing in the press.[544] They were unwilling to act upon the data they received because they openly suspected the informants of not being truthful, a suspicion rooted in xenophobia and anti-Semitism.

Incidentally, there is little evidence of anti-Semitism from Churchill, although historian Toye has described his attitude towards Jews as "inconsistent",[545] a view partly based on an article titled: "How the Jews can combat persecution" from 1937. In the article, Churchill was quoted as saying: "It may be that, unwittingly, they are inviting persecution – that they have been partly responsible for the antagonism from which they suffer."[546] Because, according to Churchill, it is the victim's fault they are victims. However, the article was never published. And, sensing this statement was destined to put him on the wrong side of history, Churchill's office refused permission to print it in 1940 when a newspaper tried to – wisely saying this was "inadvisable".[547] While he was described by one contemporary as being ""too fond of Jews,"[548] this fondness did not lead to him initiating action to stop the Holocaust.

Anthony Eden headed up three out of the four departments which stand accused of anti-Semitic induced avoidance. Not a great start for anybody choosing to defend him. After serving as a Major in the British Army in WW1, Eden became a Conservative MP and went on to hold the position of Foreign Secretary on three different occasions, as well as being prime minister between 1955–1957. However, it seems Eden must have flunked the "how to be a good Prime Minister" class at Eton (educators of 20 out of the 55 PMs) because he has since been voted the least successful prime minister of the 20th century. Not just once – but in two different polls.[549] He was forced to resign just two years into the job due to, rather ironically, a huge blunder in foreign policy (regarding the Suez Canal). Clearly those three stints in the job had taught him as little as Eton had. Eden met Hitler in 1934 and deemed him to be nicer than the Italian dictator Mussolini.[550] While he was too early to see the full picture of Hitler exterminating 11 million people, including 6 million Jews, (Mussolini went on to kill 430,000); by 1934, Hitler had already turned Germany into a dictatorship by banning all political parties other than the Nazis and imprisoning those who disagreed. So it wasn't as if Hitler was going through a nice patch. Eden also thought the internal policies of a country were of no concern to the Foreign Office, which is like saying criminal acts committed out of sight are of no concern to the police. And, of course, there are his opinions on helping the European Jews.

Eden had a dismissive attitude towards the plight faced by the Jews. He actively tried to avoid any discussions that may have highlighted the dangers they faced, which undoubtedly had a huge impact on the scale of British action. For example, he advised Churchill not to respond when Polish Jews protested at the continuation of the Nazi exterminations in 1943. Eden said it was better to say nothing at all because if Churchill reacted in any way, they would have to take action.[551] Far better to ignore these people than to dignify them with a conversation.

Even when Eden *did* dignify people with a conversation, he was rude to them and displayed a flippant attitude. One of these shocking encounters was with Jan Karski (the man responsible for bringing information about the Final Solution to British ears in 1942) on 4 February 1943. Eden oh-so-generously agreed to meet with him for 30 minutes whereby

Karski gave a presentation about the work of the Polish underground and requested a retaliatory bombing campaign and the dropping of more leaflets to inform civilians of the Nazi's extermination policy. It was at this point Eden cut him off and said: "The Polish report on atrocities has already reached us… The matter will take its proper course".[552]

An *almost* polite way of saying "shut up".

Eden's favoured plan was to avoid the subject completely. When he travelled to Washington the month after meeting Karski, he told his colleagues at the Foreign Office he *wouldn't* initiate any discussion of Jewish refugee issues during his trip.[553] A statement which initiated this blunt response from his under-secretary Richard Law: "I am sorry to bother you about Jews… I know what a bore this is but… it will look very queer… to say you have never mentioned the subject".[554] Law's choice of words such as "I know what a bore this is" are very telling of Eden's previous comments and thoughts on the matter. In the end, Eden did bring up the subject (because he had to), but he steered the conversation towards pressing America for guarantees to Spain, Portugal, Switzerland, and Sweden that they would NOT have to support refugees. Rather than using the opportunity to discuss financial help which would have allowed these neutral nations to help Jewish refugees, Eden instead alleviated them of any responsibility while avoiding having to organise a plan of action for Britain.

Later that month, in March 1943, Eden was given another opportunity to look sympathetic. An opportunity which he also passed up on. Clearly having a thirty mind – another 30-minute meeting was arranged. This time with Joseph M. Proskauer of the American Jewish Committee and Rabbi Wise, who was co-chair of the Joint Emergency Committee for European Jewish Affairs. Every suggestion the two men came up with was shot down by Eden.

Wise and Proskauer: "Ask Hitler to permit Jews to leave occupied Europe?"

Eden: "Fantastically impossible." (It wasn't. The Nazis actually agreed to this idea three months later.)

Wise and Proskauer: "Can adult Jews from Bulgaria be allowed to go to Turkey?"

Eden: "Turkey does not want any more of your people." (Eden did not know this, he had not even asked Turkey.)[555]

Their other ideas of shipping food to starving Jews in Europe or arranging shipments of Jewish refugees from Spain and Portugal to Palestine were also turned down in the limited time he had so graciously afforded them. He explained that it was too dangerous in the Mediterranean to ship refugees safely. The obvious fact that it was more dangerous to stay in Europe was evidently not so clear to Eden.

Eden was not the only person in the Foreign Office to show contempt towards the Jews and their plight. One official even had the audacity to complain about the deluge of reports they were receiving about the Jewish atrocities: "the Foreign Office is never short of would-be do-gooders sending us lots of information".[556] And in December 1942 a refugee specialist in the Foreign Office called the potential release of 70,000 Jews from Bulgaria a: "frightening prospect".[557] Evidently this specialist did not specialise in understanding what a *genuinely* frightening prospect was, i.e., death.

As a result of their leadership and personal beliefs, the Foreign Office were responsible for a variety of measures which prevented Britain from taking action to stop the Holocaust. Measures that all took place after the British government had openly acknowledged their awareness of the Holocaust in December 1942 with the Joint Allied Declaration.

On 20 January 1943, the Foreign Office sent a message to Washington stating their intention to create common ground and begin a dialogue about the refugee problem. Sounds good. But then they vetoed the idea of treating the refugee situation as a purely Jewish crisis because they thought there would be a rise in anti-Semitism if they were to focus on the truth.[558] They thought (using their crystal ball-shit) that if they highlighted the fact Jews were the target, it would draw criticism for showing favouritism. Then they had the cheek to ask whether America considered it "advisable" to initiate joint action to help the Jews. By asking this, they were suggesting that the promise of action in the Joint Allied Declaration of December 1942 didn't have to happen. They were basically testing the water to see if the Americans would join them in opposing those previous decisions. The Foreign Office wanted to forget the declaration and instead present British MPs with "Joint Allied Doubt" and thus convince them to not rush into action which might help the Jews.[559] Luckily, the Americans did not respond; they didn't trust the request or the British Foreign Office (due to previous disagreements) and instead agreed to the Bermuda Conference which would take place in April 1943.

The Foreign Office also hindered other groups' efforts to help the Jews such as editing a message from Richard Lichtheim sent in May 1943. Lichtheim's message, sent from his base in Geneva, Switzerland, described the persecution of Jews in Bulgaria and Romania; he urged that this information and warnings to the Bulgarian and Romanian governments that they would be held accountable for their actions should be broadcast by the BBC.

Fair enough.

The Foreign Office didn't think so. They removed Lichtheim's urging of publicity before forwarding it, as requested, to the Jewish Agency representative in London. An internal memo explained: "it was better not to put such ideas into the heads of the Jewish Agency in London."[560]

The Foreign Office refused to change their policies regarding immigration and publicity. Spurred on by the promise of the Bermuda Conference (weren't we all), campaigns had begun in earnest in 1943 with requests sent to the Foreign Office for a relaxation of the refugee limits and appeals for publicity and warnings.[561] But these campaigns and lobbying attempts in parliament were worn down by the Foreign Office's stubbornness to alter their policy.[562] In December 1943, Ignacy Schwarzbart from the World Jewish Congress found his appeals "dismissed as propaganda".[563] Activism had zero chance of affecting change in government policy with the Foreign Office's anti-Semitic attitude.[564]

Towards the end of June 1944, the Foreign Office struck again by stopping the publication of an appeal to the Christian world for action, sent from the Federal Council of Churches of Christ in America. The appeal told how 450,000 Hungarian Jews had been taken "to Auschwitz in Upper Silesia".[565] But it stopped sharply at the British Foreign Office's door on June 27th and was not shared with the British press.[566] Furthermore, the Foreign Office tried to prevent the information from this appeal being debated in parliament by telling MP Silverman on 4 July 1944, that he should NOT ask about the issue of the deportations of Hungarian Jews because: "this question could not do any good and might do harm".[567] Harm to the Jews was fine but harm to the Foreign Office's reputation was not.

Luckily, Silverman was not the sort of person to listen to such claptrap, and on the 5th of July he straight-up asked Eden in parliament: "to confirm the figures which have been given in some quarters, namely, that in recent days the number deported amounted to 400,000". Eden gave your typical politician response and avoided actually answering the question by saying:

"I would really rather not give figures unless one is absolutely sure… We have done all we can and we shall do all we can."[568] Do all they can to do nothing that is. As proved on 1 September 1944, when Eden told the Air Ministry not to bother planning a bombing raid of Auschwitz.[569]

Furthermore, the refusal of the Foreign Office to confirm the validity of information from Polish sources meant that knowledge was not shared with as many government departments as it should have been.[570] A blatant refusal of authentication came on 5 July 1944, when Eden told MPs in parliament (in response to their requests for confirmation of the contents of the *Vrba-Wetzler Report*): "I fear I have no definite information."[571] This was an outlandish thing to say considering the three reports making up *The Auschwitz Protocols* had been published AND literally the day before the debate, the Foreign Office had received an eight-page summary of the exterminations at Auschwitz from the Czechoslovakian Ministry of Foreign Affairs, AND let's not forget the previous three years of information. Some may argue that Eden was being cautious because he felt the data provided was uncorroborated, but why give the Nazis the benefit of the doubt? Eden's rejection of acknowledging the deportations of Hungarian Jews was an attempt to stay in control of what the British public knew so that he could avoid any public pressure to bloomin' well do something already. Pleasingly no one took much notice of what Eden didn't say and on July 7th, two newspapers (*The Polish Jewish Observer* and the *Jewish Chronicle*) reported on the debate and the 400,000 Hungarian Jews killed at Auschwitz and the BBC broadcast that Oswiecim was a place of extermination.

In a joint action, the Foreign Office and Home Office made sure visa applications to Palestine were turned down despite there being 34,000 out of 75,000 still available in 1942.[572] I mean… who the hell were they saving them for?

The Home Office, like the Foreign Office, also withheld information and prevented publication of the atrocities in the press. A British Ministry of Interior memo in July 1941 stated that: "Sheer 'horror' stuff such as the concentration camp torture stories… repel the normal mind. A certain amount of horror is needed but it must be used very sparingly and must deal always with the treatment of indisputably innocent people. Not with violent political opponents. And not with Jews."[573] The tone of this memo is shamefully anti-Semitic. Was the killing not bad enough to use the word *horror* without implying this was a subjective opinion with the use of quote marks around the word? Most shocking is their suggestion the Jews were not "indisputably innocent" simply because they were Jews. Appalling. Or as the British would put it, 'appalling'.

The Home Office prevented publicity of the atrocities due to their "intelligence" report which indicated that any talk of Jews would fuel British anti-Semitism. This then led to the Ministry of Information telling the British press to not publish news of Jews being killed. The Home Office believed it upset and offended people to hear any sort of information about Jews and therefore news about them being killed was assumed to have a negative impact. Which doesn't even make sense because if the Brits were so anti-Semitic then surely such news would have lifted their spirits? This "intelligence" also allowed the Foreign Office to claim *they* weren't the problem – the anti-Semitism of the British public was. Which is ridiculous as an excuse when you think about it because anti-Semitism is wrong, was wrong at the time, and should have been challenged by those in charge. It would be like the government today hiding stories about racist attacks because they thought if they acknowledged it, people would be more racist. Nonsensical.

The chief rabbi of British Jewry, Dr Hertz, commented on the negative impact of British censorship in 1942 and again in a speech on 29 February 1944, calling British policy: "a virtual endorsement of Hitler's doctrine".[574]

Anti-Semitism was also present in the PWE.[575] This branch of government had a huge impact because they controlled the BBC's European service and had some impact on the BBC Home Service, which meant they could stop news stories about the Jews from reaching the wider public. The decision to disregard news about the Jews was a general policy adopted by the British government[576] and it directly impacted the (lack of) broadcasts on the BBC Hungarian service. Which stinks of anti-Semitism – why else would you not warn the group most at risk that they were at risk? Even when reports did make it into the news, the Foreign Office and PWE made sure Jews were not referred to as Jews and were instead described based on their nationalities. Ergo there were not *Jews* being killed by the Nazis – there were Poles, Romanians, Czechs, French etc. Another outcome which was the result of the assumed British anti-Semitism from the Home Office's report.

This powerful, elite anti-Semitism (prejudice held by those in the top jobs) did the most damage and has been described as "disabling"[577] by Holocaust specialist Michael Fleming, and it seems the Foreign Office are the most guilty. By marginalising news stories, they hindered public awareness. By casting doubt on the credibility of sources, they stopped resources being diverted towards plans of action. By preventing appeals getting through to the intended audiences, they thwarted other people's rescue attempts (a real evil move considering other people's actions would have cost the British government nothing). By softening the genocide to become a "refugee crisis" they downplayed the seriousness of the situation and created fear of an unmanageable immigration disaster. By shutting down bombing requests of Auschwitz, they allowed the Nazis to expand their operation and make Auschwitz the main killing centre of Jews. By withholding information from MPs and the British public, they destroyed lobbying attempts which consequently meant the government weren't pressured to act. Most significantly and most disturbing of all, by ensuring Jewish visa applications into Britain and Palestine were turned down and by convincing their European Allies to do the same at the Bermuda Conference in 1943, the Foreign Office, led by Anthony Eden, caused the deaths of at least half a million people. [578]

What was Britain's role in the Holocaust?

The Nazis were only able to conduct their Final Solution due to collaboration with other anti-Semitic governments and civilians. This collaboration enabled trains to transport Jews from all over Europe to the death camps in Poland as well as giving the Nazis extra people to employ as train drivers or heavies to round up Jews from their homes. However, collaboration doesn't have to be this explicitly direct to be considered collaboration. Britain's inaction and withholding of information ultimately helped the Nazis achieve their goal of annihilating the Jews. Their lethargic and apathetic attitude also delayed the response of other countries, after all if Britain, as one of the leading Allies, were not willing to take steps to save Jewish lives, why should any other country act?[579]

No one could express this sentiment better than Szmul Zygielbojm. Jewish man Zygielbojm was a Polish political activist who became one of the most important sources of information about the Holocaust for Britain during the war. In May 1943, he committed suicide in protest at the inaction of the Allies. The last straws being the complete travesty that was the Bermuda Conference and the deaths of his family in the Warsaw Ghetto Uprising, both of which occurred in April 1943. His suicide note explained:

> *"The responsibility for the crime of the murder of the whole Jewish nationality in Poland rests first of all on those who are carrying it out, but indirectly it falls also upon the whole of humanity, on the peoples of the Allied nations and on their governments, who up to this day have not taken any real steps to halt this crime. By looking on passively upon this murder of defenceless millions tortured children, women and men they have become partners to the responsibility."580*

Britain had a role in the Holocaust. Their lack of action trying to stop it combined with too much action preventing safe refuge for European Jews makes them partially accountable for the loss of six million lives.

This is Torture

"The action or practice of inflicting severe pain or suffering on someone as a form of punishment or in order to force them to do or say something."[581]

It is unknown which society invented torture,[582] but the earliest records come from around 5000 BCE when civilisations began forming. There was no motive for torture until civilisation began – cavemen certainly had no need for it. The interrogation and responses would have been much like the soundtrack at Wimbledon – just one grunt after the other.

How has the Law changed?

Until the 20th century, there was no international condemnation of torture and countries were left to their own devices. Kicking change off was Article IV from The Fourth Hague Convention of 1907, which made torture of captured soldiers and civilians illegal in 43 different countries. When this failed to put off the likes of the Nazis and the Japanese in WW2, a second international agreement was made on 12 August 1949, called The Geneva Conventions: "No one shall be subjected to torture or to cruel, inhuman or degrading treatment or punishment."[583] To date, all 196 countries of the world have signed and agreed to this. Has this stopped torture? Has it hell.

To date, torture has been used openly in at least one-third of these countries,[584] and the 1970s has been described as the: "darkest era of torture in the history of the West."[585] Anyone who thinks incidents of torture lessened because of this international agreement is darking up the wrong tree.

England outlawed torture yonks before the world clued up on their human rights. In 1215, article 39 in the Magna Carta dictated that: "No freeman shall be arrested or imprisoned or disseised or outlawed or exiled or in any other way harmed. Nor will we [the king] proceed against him or send others to do so..."[586] Basically saying you can't torture someone or get others to do it for you. The Magna Carta laid down a set of 63 rules which EVERYONE, including those in charge (imagine that?!) had to follow, and it came about due to the desperate need to limit the power of the King of cock-ups – King John[3]. The Magna Carta (meaning "Great Charter" in English, but no one cool spoke English back then, so Latin was used instead) birthed the English Parliament. A Great Council of Barons (wealthy landowners) was established, which evolved into the institution we know today; with the word *Parliament* coming into use in the 1230s thanks to the French word *Parlement* which means "to speak" (see previous brackets of how English wasn't cool yet). Aside from this momentous shift in power and government, the Magna Carta was hugely significant for prohibiting the use of torture and any legal procedures that may use it to force confessions, it was ruled to be opposing to English Common Law. Incidentally, the Magna

---

[3] Such as when he fell out with the Pope which led to all English churches closing their doors for five years. Rather than enjoy their Sunday lie-in, the public were mightily annoyed by the fact they couldn't get married; have funerals (relatives were dumped in badly dug pits instead); baptize their children; or be forgiven for drunkenly punching Dave on Friday night. Bad times all round. Especially for Dave.

Carta is the closest thing England has to a written constitution so it's pretty damn good that torture was declared off limits early doors.

The Magna Carta limited the use of torture in England for a whopping 60 years. While it remained illegal, the interpretation of what counted as torture changed. Out went obvious physical painful methods and in came lengthy extreme pain, or as the cool kids called it at the time – *peine forte et dure.* This interpretive loophole was found thanks to the efforts of King Edward I (best known as the killer of Mel Gibson/Braveheart). Edward, who ruled England between 1272 and 1307, was mightily unhappy that his prisoners had the right to refuse to plead to charges and so torture was revived to force them into saying something. More subtle methods were used and because it didn't *look* like traditional torture and wasn't aiming to force a confession, it was OK. This full-of-holes loophole was hole-heartedly used by the Tudor monarchs who clearly weren't paying attention during their Year 7 history lessons about the Magna Carta. Henry VIII believed that torture was only torture if it was used to force confessions, therefore if it were used as a sanction or to bring about someone's death, it was legal. Happy days for Henry. Not so happy days for the 72,000 people[587] who were convicted and executed during his thirty-seven-year reign. A fact which you won't find in school history textbooks thanks to Protestant England's shit-hot propaganda machine telling us it is his Catholic daughter, "Bloody Mary", who is the evil Tudor for burning 287 people during her five-year reign.[588] Incidentally, while not so keen to use her father's re-interpretation of religion, Mary was more than happy to accept his re-interpretation of torture being legal if it were not trying to draw information and so tortured Protestants as a punishment for withholding evidence. The evidence that they then provided because of this torture was, of course, *completely* coincidental. Bloody cheeky was Bloody Mary.

Elsewhere in medieval Europe, rulers were not quite so into their loopholes. Twelfth-century Russia, for example, had hoops rather than loops – such as the rule that you had to first get the approval of the local prince if you wanted to torture someone. The theory being this bureaucracy and red tape would stop people Russian into things. If you were tortured without the torturer going through the proper procedure, then you were allowed to sue for compensation. So that's quite nice if you ignore the legality of torture itself. And if you live to see the other side of course.

The Age of Enlightenment (17th-18th centuries) brought a new wave of thinking about everything… bar sexism and racism… let's not get too carried away. The Enlightenment period is when people started to look for scientific and/or logical explanations i.e., what they could see happening, instead of relying on religion to explain everything. It is in this era that torture was outlawed (again), and with it came the realisation that torture was: "…rather a trial of patience than of truth."[589] The concept of "innocent until proven guilty'" (which was first mooted by the Babylonians in the 18th century BCE) soon found a receptive audience in the CE version of the 18th century and was written about by Italian philosopher Cesare Beccaria: "…torture becomes useless… if he be not guilty, you torture the innocent, for in the eyes of the law, every man is innocent whose crime has not been proved."[590] In England, King Charles I (1625–1649) closed the torture loophole that existed in the Magna Carta and specifically barred torturing prisoners into confessions. England therefore outlawed torture in 1640. Scotland followed in 1708. Outlawed, that is, unless the monarch was at risk and treason was suspected. And unless the process was classed as *peine forte et dure,* which wasn't abolished until 1772. And unless the accused was a woman charged with witchcraft. Unfortunately for Charles I, such enlightened thinking on crime and punishment failed to save him from being usurped by his own parliament and beheaded. But still, at least you could say England was heading (unlike Charles I) in the right direction.

The first European country to ban *all* types of torture, whatever the purpose may be, was Sweden in 1734. After this, Prussia (modern-day northern Germany) made it illegal in 1754; Britain in 1772; Austria by 1776; Italy in 1786; the Netherlands by 1794; Russia in 1801 and Spain in 1812,[591] which is also the year they abolished the Spanish Inquisition which had been going since 1484. Big year for Spain. Over in America, once the law makers had done the important stuff like making sure everyone could carry a gun, they enacted the eighth amendment in 1791 which banned the use of torture as a punishment. This was further strengthened by the fourteenth amendment, but it wasn't until they signed up to the Geneva Conventions, the Convention Against Torture, and the International Covenant on Civil and Political Rights in the 20th century that America outlawed torture of prisoners for *any* reason. These international laws came about because of the post WW2 trials which revealed the depths of human depravity. The year 1948 was a massive turning point for human rights. Because we got some. In the same year as McDonald's were cooking their first burger in the USA and the NHS opened its doors in the UK, the newly formed United Nations established worldwide human rights which included your right to not be tortured. So, with the whole world in agreement, and the atrocities from WW2 fresh in people's minds, there was no more torture from this point on.

Just kidding.

As history likes to do, there was a repeat of what happened when the Magna Carta banned torture in England in 1215 and torture was conveniently deemed not illegal if used against "enemies of the state". Torture didn't stop. It just went underground and became the remit of the secret services rather than those in the government and justice systems. It moved location so it didn't happen in the country the torturers were from. It became a service for hire so those who were behind it did not have to be in front of it.

One year into the 21st century and there was a massive U-turn on the anti-torture "gains" of the 20th century thanks to 9/11. Guess what the CIA blamed for the 9/11 attacks? Well, obviously the Iraqis and Afghans… but they also blamed human rights. They thought that *if only* they had been able to torture the people responsible in the first place, they would have discovered the plot. In reality, the CIA already had enough information about the planned attacks to stop them,[592] *if only* they had had the intelligence to link these facts together.

The 9/11 terrorist attacks, as well ending our right to carry more than a thumb of liquid onto airplanes, also ended human rights and came with a side of "F You" to the Geneva Conventions as America made torture legal again. It was now deemed "necessary" because the great and almighty America were under threat. President George W. Bush certainly thought it was the right decision: "Had I not authorised waterboarding on senior al-Qaeda leaders, I would have had to accept a greater risk that the country would be attacked."[593] Cofer Black, the head of CIA counterterrorism, described this turning point as: "The gloves come off."[594] But this openness and honesty did not go down as well as they hoped. Bush faced huge pressure from the human rights groups Amnesty International, Human Rights Watch, and Human Rights First, following a host of damning reports about torture at American hands in Afghanistan and Iraq. In a stunning PR move, on the International Day in Support of the Survivors of Torture on

26 June 2003, Bush denounced torture.[595] The fact this had already happened in 1948 was Bushed under the carpet. Along with the statement itself, which ended up having a huge impact on nothing. FBI memos from 2005 revealed torture was very much still ongoing in Guantanamo, Iraq, and Afghanistan, a fact which was also confirmed by the International Committee of the Red Cross.[596]

Laws don't change behaviour; they just make the behaviour more secret. Torture is still ongoing around the world, but it has undergone massive changes in motive and methods since its inception 7000 years ago.

Motives and methods – how and why have they changed over time?

Motive One: Punishment

In the 21st century, the whole point of torturing someone is to extract information, but torture did not begin with this motive in mind. Torture developed from the need to punish people. The first recorded use of torturous punishments begins in the 32nd century BCE and comes from the ancient civilisations around the Mediterranean such as the Egyptians, Eshnunna, Babylonians, Assyrians, Hebrews, and Greeks. These societies did not have specific torture devices *per se,* but they did have punishments that were tortuous *per sure.* Traditional weapons such as whips and knives or items that were readily available such as rocks were used instead. The Egyptians, for example, punished men who cheated on their wives by whipping them. One thousand times. A woman guilty of the same crime was physically mutilated in some way – most commonly her nose was cut off; I guess because no one would even want to look at her, let alone do the hanky-panky with her but it still seems a scentless act of violence.

The punishment motive for torture was soon established into law, such as the Code of Hammurabi (circa 1745 BCE) and the Mosaic Code (1200 BCE). The Hammurabi Code, which was only discovered in 1901, is pretty cool because not only did it aim to "prevent the strong from oppressing the weak"[597] it was also the first legal text to promote the "innocent until proven guilty" theory with every law referring to the accused using the word *if*. Fun Fact: the Hammurabi code also protected people against being mugged off by dodgy builders. Named after its creator, Babylonian King Hammurabi, who ruled central Mesopotamia (modern-day Iraq) from 1792–1750 BCE, it is also hugely significant in the history of crime and punishment because it is the first legislation to be set in stone. A four-ton, 2.25-metre-tall pillar made of a black stone to be precise. There are 282 laws and punishments in the Code of Hammurabi, 30 out of the 282 required the punishment of death, the other 252 crimes demanded fines or a torturous punishment such as the removal of the convict's tongue, breasts, eye, or ear. Talking of which, it is from Hammurabi that we get the idiom "an eye for an eye" because that was literally their 196th rule: "If a man put out the eye of another man, his eye shall be put out."[598] You can definitely see (unlike the convict) how fairness inspired such a law.

Punishment was also the motive for torture for the next law makers on the scene – the Hebrews. The Hebrews created the Mosaic Code (named after the man – not the fancy floor) with honourable intentions, but it was extreme in implementation with basically every type of torture known to man included.[599] While whipping still featured heavily as a method (limited to 40 lashings) other new methods were created such as: burning; being thrown from a high cliff; being thrown from a tower into a pile of ash and buried alive; being sawn in half; being buried up to their necks and having ploughs driven over them (literally up to their necks in bad times); and crucifixion, which, incidentally, had a 100% success rate until Jesus came along. The method of stoning someone to death (rocks not drugs) originates around this time and gained popularity in the ensuing ancient Greek and Roman cultures before spreading into the Muslim world where it remains a method of execution in Iran; Pakistan; 36 states of Nigeria; Saudi Arabia; Somalia; Sudan; the United Arab Emirates; and Yemen.[600] For the Hebrews, stoning someone to death had a strict protocol to follow. Firstly, it had to take place in a specific location, and there was a special area outside the city walls with a pile of rocks waiting patiently for their big moment. Secondly, the person who brought the charge against the convict had to wear a fancy outfit – a white fringed robe which presumably made them look like an angelic cowboy of death. And lastly, the fancy outfit wearer had to throw the first stone before all those who had come for a 'fun' day out had the chance to join in and get their rocks on.

Crucifixion as a method of torture was made famous by the Romans. Although not the inventors of it, this was adopted as their main method of torturous execution by the time of the Empire in 27 BCE. Contrary to most depictions of Jesus on the cross, there was a little platform to stand on, and the person was tied to it using rope – the nails through their hands were there for pain purposes only. If they had solely nailed people to the cross, then their body weight would have ripped through the nails, and they would have fallen off before they died. However, the platform was only meant to be used occasionally – prolonging life and prolonging pain were the aim here – and those who dared to stand on it too much had their knees smashed in. The whole thing was agonizingly slow – a person may die from dehydration, heatstroke, or suffocation, which was brought on by their diaphragm tearing due to all their weight hanging off their outstretched arms. It was a popular method because it was also open to the public;

the crosses were on display so people could see for themselves what punishment lay in wait for them should they dare defy Roman law.

There's always someone who takes it too far and in the context of torturous punishments it was the ancient Greeks. These dudes were the first to move away from traditional tools such as whips and rocks and come up with specific torture devices. The ancient Greeks are well known for their philosophers, government, maths, and olive oil, but it is also from them we get the term *draconian* (meaning extremely harsh laws) due to their tyrannical leader Draco, who decided in 700 BCE, that *all* crimes should be punished with a torturous death. J.K. Rowling certainly knew what she was doing when she chose this name for her antagonist in Harry Potter. Draco's draconian laws meant a sharp increase in the number of criminals needing to be torturously killed, and with all this extra demand, it wasn't long before imaginative devices such as the Brazen Bull, the Iron Maiden, and the Rack were created.

The Brazen Bull was invented as a way for one bloke (Perillus) to impress another bloke (dictator Phalaris). The result is terrifyingly imaginative. To get started, all you need is a hollow, bronze sculpture of a bull with holes for the nose and mouth and a raging fire. Obviously, your bull needs an opening in the side to put the victim in and then you're good to go! The person is trapped in the bull's belly and slowly cooked via the blazing inferno underneath, which is *so* hot, the bronze sculpture turns red. Happily for all the sickos watching, the screams can be easily heard thanks to the aforementioned nose and mouth openings. In places where bronze sculptures were harder to come by, actual animal corpses were used instead. For example, one woman had her body sewn into a donkey carcass with her head deliberately left out so she could fully experience the horror of her, and the donkey's, slow decomposition. We don't know what killed her – the heat, the dehydration, or the bugs and animals who were attracted to the rotting animal, but it seems the Greeks took a liking to the latter fate as they also came up with the idea of covering people in milk and honey and leaving them for 20 days confined in the pillory (hands and head through the wooden T-shape thing). What with karma being a bitch and all – Perillus was not rewarded for his Greek variety of Red Bull because Phalaris was not a fan of bum-lickers. But Perillus did get the honour of being the first person to try out his invention. Perillus business this torture malarky. And in an appropriate twist of fate, Phalaris was also killed this way thanks to an angry mob in 563 BCE.[601]

The Iron Maiden, used widely by the Germans in the medieval era, originated with Nabis who was the ruler of the 'ard as nails lot – the Spartans – between 205 and 194 BCE. Nabis was inspired by his wife and wanted to build an iron statue of her. Which sounds all lovely and romantic until you open "her" up to be confronted with a set of spikes. Who knows, maybe it was an homage to her spikey personality or the fact she had to do all the ironing… her opinion on being immortalised as a deathly torture device has not been recorded. Nabis was not famed for his sense of humour, but he liked to jest that his *Iron wife* would "persuade" a person to give an answer. Obviously, he was not famed for his foresight either because once inside, the person was unable to give any sort of answer. The spikes had persuaded them to die instead.

The Rack began life in the ancient period, and the Greeks have the earliest records of it being used as a punishment. It basically looks like a giant ladder, and a person would be stretched out with their hands tied to one end and their feet to the other; the ropes were then attached to a crank at either end of the rack. The victim would then suffer being stretched as the cranks were turned via a handle at the bottom and the rope was pulled taught. Shoulders, hips, wrists, ankles, and elbows were dislocated due to the stretching and success could be measured by a delightful popping sound. Muscles, ligaments, and tendons were also commonly torn in the process. But this was not all it was racked up to be as being tied up also allowed for other tortures to take place as well, such as whipping, burning the person's feet or legs, tearing off their nails, or placing hot coals between their toes.

Torture methods continued to change as new empires came up with adaptations and their own ideas such as the Wheel, which was adapted to be more horrific by the Romans. It is also known as the Breaking Wheel or the Catherine Wheel – so called in honour of eighteen-year-old Saint Catherine of Alexandria. Catherine was meant to be torturously killed on the Wheel for the crime of converting people to Christianity in c.305 BCE. Legend has it that then when she was brought to the spiked wheel and touched it, it shattered, meaning she had to be beheaded instead (she apparently bled a milky white substance instead of blood).[602] Whatever happened, she certainly caused some fireworks.

The Wheel could be used exactly as it was or it could be customised to have spikes. Another version saw it mounted onto a base in the ground so that it spun like a roundabout in a kid's playpark which allowed other tortures to take place at the same time, such as their skin being ripped off using pincers, or their bones broken one-by-one with a mallet. On the non-pimped-up version, the convict was attached and literally taken for a spin until they died from choking on their own stomach contents, a multitude of broken bones and bleeding, asphyxiation, a heart attack, or a messy combo of all four. The Roman adaptation saw the wheel thickened up, so it more resembled a barrel and had spikes on the outside, it was then mounted about a foot from the floor on a frame like a Ferris wheel and there were also spikes stuck into the ground. The unfortunate was attached to the outside of the barrel and then spun around, meaning they were slowly ripped to shreds by the spikes above and below. The spikey Ferris wheel did not catch on though and it is the original version that has been wheely popular through the ages and across the continents. In America it was used as a method of execution for seven slaves in 1730;[603] with the last recorded use of the Wheel coming from Prussia in 1841.

The Romans weren't just responsible for adapting methods, they also brought a new motive to the torture table – fun! While their early Republic days (until the 1st century BCE), were geared towards punishments fitting the crime, this all changed once the republic died a death with the advent of dictator Julius Caesar in 44 BCE; (he also soon died a death due to being stabbed 23 times and is today remembered as a salad). After this, it was free rein for the subsequent emperors to be as terrifying as they could imagine and torture became a leisure activity. There were special events put on at the Colosseum where Romans could go and watch Christians being tortured in various ways. Emperor Caligula (37 – 41 CE) liked to torture people as part of the entertainment at his diner parties. A real whining and dining experience.

Sometimes methods did not require a physical invention – *Scaphism* was a torturous method of execution used by the Persians (559 BCE – 330 BCE) and it relied upon food rather than tools. *Scaphism* saw the accused caged in a boat or trapped between two wooden logs and force-fed milk and honey. Where's the torture in that I hear you cry! Well… nothing but milk and honey soon led to diarrhoea and the explosion was contained in their enclosure. While covered in excrement, the person would continue to be force-fed milk and honey and soon enough they reeked of rotting milk, sickly sweet honey, and poo. Every bug's dream dinner! Worms and parasites bred in the excrement and burrowed into the person's bowels while thousands of insects bit their way into the person's body through their ears, eyes, nose, and mouth. It was only a matter of time before the person died of dehydration, exposure, bites, or stings. Over the years, this method has been adapted and used by various civilisations based upon their local wildlife and resources. In England it might a be a bear who was attracted to the honey, although sadly for the victim it was not Winnie the Pooh who turned up for dinner.

Whereas in the ancient cultures torture was a means to an end (the end of a life), the medieval era saw a transition where the person was meant to live. Not for any kindly reason, of course; the thinking was the person would act as free publicity for a monarch's power and create fear among the other plebs. In England, this transition began under the rule of King William I (aka William the Conqueror – the guy who won the 1066 Battle of Hastings). William I was crowned on Christmas Day and just like the Queen gave a Christmas Day speech: "I forbid that any person be killed or hanged for any cause."[604] A very respectable start but things quickly went downhill with his follow up statement: "Let their eyes be torn out and their testicles be cut off."[605] Torture to him meant the most painful way to maim someone, but it was important they lived on because then they could act as an example to everyone else. They certainly wouldn't have the balls to try anything again, that's for sure.

But all this good Will didn't last and by the time of King Henry VIII (1509-1547), it had become common practice to torture people to death as punishment again. Not because it had been made legal all of a sudden, it's just Henry VIII loved a loophole almost as much as he loved choosing a wedding venue. And so the prohibition in the Magna Carta was bypassed because Henry wasn't trying to extract information – he was trying to kill. In 1531, having been inspired by the crime of Richard Roose, Henry decreed boiling to be his favoured execution method. Roose was the cook of the Bishop of Rochester and had attempted to poison the bishop's household and thus it was deemed appropriate to cook him too. Therefore – just like how your nan cooks broccoli – Roose was slowly boiled to death over two hours.

A new way of torturously killing people was invented in the reign of Henry VIII – The Scavenger's Daughter. This was created by Leonard Skeffington, lieutenant of the Tower of London. The device looked like giant letter *A* and was locked around the person's neck, wrists, and ankles which forced them into a doubling over position. It killed the victim by dislocating their spine and crushing their body until they "popped" and spewed blood from all their orifices. This daughter really did bleed you dry. Henry also liked to torture his convicts as they awaited their execution. Some may be kept in a special room at the Tower of London called "Little Ease" which was so small a person had to crouch the whole time; alternatively, there was "The Dungeon Among the Rats" which was crammed with, yep you guessed it, a shit ton of rats. However, unlike the Bushtucker Trials in *I'm a Celebrity,* these rodents were not well fed beforehand, and the unfortunates sharing a room with them were forced to play hide and squeak to avoid being nibbled away.

From the Middle Ages until the 18th century, criminals were often tortured using heat. One method involved holes bored through their bodies using a blazing hot piece of metal; thieves and drunks were considered particularly ear-itating and thus were treated to holes burnt through their ears. Those caught lying or blaspheming (e.g., saying "Oh My God" before it became OMG) had their tongues burnt while other criminals were restrained and had the soles of their feet flame roasted. Those guilty of heresy (not following the religion the government said you should be) were burnt at the stake – a torture which could last as long as 45 minutes such as with Rev. Dr John Hooper, Bishop of Gloucester, in 1555. Hooper suffered slowly; first his face burnt so badly it turned completely black and his lips dissolved into his gums; then, due to him ferociously beating his chest with it, one of his arms completely fell off; this was soon followed by his other arm melting through his fingertips which had become five waterfalls of water, fat, and blood. By this point, all the skin on his lower body had burnt away but, before he died, his body had one last surprise for the spectators – with no skin left on the outside to hold his insides in – his bowels fell out.

While Hooper's story is pretty impressive, this isn't the longest someone has lived through a torturous punishment. Over in the Netherlands, when Protestant Prince William of Orange was assassinated in 1584, the Catholic perpetrator Balthazar Gerard went through 18 days of torture. This assassination was significant because it was the first time a head of state (Catholic King Phillip II of Spain) had successfully instigated the murder of another head of state (Prince William of Orange). Fun fact: this was the first assassination using a gun thanks to the recent invention of the pocket-size wheel-lock pistol.[606] Obviously, Phillip II did not do the dirty work himself and a reward of 25,000 crowns was offered to anyone who could do it on his behalf. Gerard did not live to enjoy his reward money, but he did seemingly get to enjoy his torture. Over the 18 days, he never showed any inkling of pain, but boy-oh-boy did they try to wipe that smug smile off his face. Gerard's torture began even before he was arrested thanks to an angry mob who beat him up and then added salt to his wounds (literally). On day one, the hand which had caused the death of William of Orange was plunged into a pot of boiling oil. The next day the offending hand was lopped off – Gerard's reaction? Well, he didn't want to give his torturers the upper hand as well as his *actual* hand, so he nonchalantly kicked his burnt stump away. Gerard was racked every day during the first 11 days, during which time his skin was peeled off strip by strip using sizzling hot pliers. On the eighteenth day (I mean… wow… respect to the guy for lasting this long) he was burnt at the stake. But only for a few minutes, just long enough that his body blackened like a BBQed sausage and he was then strapped to the Wheel to have his bones broken over the next six hours. But still, he refused to die and, in the end, had to be strangled. I really hope the audience gave him a round of applause for this breath-taking performance.

Torturous punishments were not the sole remit of Europeans; in Asia they continued until well into the 20th century. Reports from India in the 19th century reveal punishments such as the Rack; branding with hot irons; dipping limbs into boiling oil; crushing people between two weighty boards; squeezing their testicles; and repeatedly pinching criminals with pincers. Indian culture also provided new methods. Yoga, which originated in India over 5000 years ago, is now famed for being a positive and relaxing experience; however, with so many years' experience of how people can bend, this knowledge was also put to torturous use. A popular punishment saw a person have their head tied to their feet with a choice for the torturer of either bending the unfortunate forwards through their knees or backwards, thus unnaturally bending their spine. Arms and legs could be twisted and tied around each other while the victim is beaten. British commissioners reported in 1855 how a father and son were tortured for six hours for not paying their land tax: "Both men (had) their legs tied together, and their heads tied to their feet in stooping posture; their hands were tied behind them, and stones placed upon their backs."[607] While the torture did not kill either man directly, the father died the following month (a much more effective way of avoiding paying tax), which was likely caused by the combination of torture and the hot sun it was performed under.

Torturous punishments were also used by the Chinese from around 200 BCE onwards. They did not have specific devices and preferred to use methods such as stretching a person until their joints popped and muscles tore, or twisting someone's ear until it came off, or cutting out select muscles from a person's body. Just like in ancient Europe and the Middle East, torture was used as a method of execution for the most serious crimes such as treason, parricide (killing your parents), or triple murder (moral of the story here is always stop after two). The most notorious of these methods was *Lingchi* i.e., "Death by a Thousand Cuts", an awe-inspiring name which sounds like a Quentin Tarantino film waiting to happen. Death by a Thousand Cuts was for those guilty of patricide (killing their father). The torturer could make *Lingchi* last as long as he wanted, or as long as the judge had ruled it should, and it took place publicly. In a fun twist, the "thousand" cuts were inflicted randomly with the order decided like the FA Cup draw. Each knife was labelled with a body part and the torturer pulled them out of a covered basket one at a time (it's likely some sort of risk assessment was done here, and the knives were positioned blade down like the scissor rack at school). Whichever body part was on the label was then removed with that assigned knife. You might get lucky and have the "Heart knife" drawn first or you may suffer as this person did (which was witnessed by Englishman Sir Henry Norman on his travels in the late

19th century): "Grasping hand-fulls (sic) from the fleshy parts of the body, such as the thighs and the breasts, {he} slices them off. The joints and the excrescences of the body are next cut away one by one, followed by amputation of the nose, the ears, the toes, and the fingers. Then the limbs are cut off piecemeal at the wrists and ankles, the elbows and knees, the shoulders and hips."[608]

In Japan, torture was once again a means to an end when lower-ranking people were found guilty of high-level crimes such as treason. Criminals among the higher ranks were not executed or tortured because they were expected to follow Japanese custom and commit suicide (*hari-kari*). The Japanese had "Death of Twenty-one Cuts" (but they promise they didn't copy the Chinese). It worked in a similar way, although witness' reports tell of a deliberate avoidance of vital organs with the focus on slicing off fleshy bits and muscles first. There was no FA Cup draw excitement like the Chinese had.

During WW2, the Japanese broke with the 1907 Hague Convention they agreed to in 1911 and punished their POWs using torture. They even had the cheek to say in the midst of their all torturing, in 1942, that they were observing the Hague Convention's laws of war[609] with the huge porky pie that their captives were getting the "best possible treatment".[610] The survivors from the Japanese Outram Road Prison told a different story: "Someone somewhere was always screaming under torture."[611] American POWS were subjected to psychological torture in the form of solitary confinement until the prison got too busy and this wasn't practical anymore. So, what does one do in solitary to stay sane? Well, the prisoners at Outram spent their time figuring out maths problems; or trying to recall every memory of every moment of their lives; people chewed and ate their fingernails until there was nothing left; or they might time how long they could go without scratching their scabies lumps. Prisoners utilised what was available to them and cockroaches, bedbugs, flies, mice, and spiders were all used as entertainment, friends, or as something to take their anger out on.

The Japanese used trained torturers called *Kempeitai* to inflict physical torture on their Allied POWs. There were tens of thousands of these men who were either Japanese officers and soldiers who had volunteered for this role instead of fighting,[612] or were Koreans and Formosans who had been recruited less willingly. The *Kempeitai* used kendo sticks, iron bars, baseball bats, and ropes with knots tied in them to hit their victims. Thumbscrews were used to crush and sever a person's fingers, thumbs, or sometimes toes, and were incredibly painful without being lethal. They used buckets and drenched cloths to recreate waterboarding; electric shocks were administered to sensitive areas such as nipples and testicles; cigarettes were used to burn people's eyes, noses, and ears; and needles and thin strips of bamboo were forced under people's fingernails. Which might explain why the prisoners were so keen to bite them off. A particularly sickening method saw the *Kempeitai* shove rice down the throat of a starving prisoner followed by litres and litres of water until the victim's stomach was at capacity (up to four litres incidentally). Once they'd reached this stage and the prisoner's stomach was nearly bursting, the *Kempeitai* would jump on their midriff and forcibly expel the contents.

Not all the torturous punishments were violent; hard labour combined with starvation rations became more common as the Japanese prisons got fuller. Food was delivered through a small opening in the cell so there was no human contact – it was a minimal amount and you had minimal time to eat it. Ten seconds for breakfast and maybe up to twenty seconds later in the day. The Americans were so hungry that when they were ordered to empty the Japanese toilets, they would sift through and sieve the faeces in the hope of finding a bean or something which had not been fully digested which they could eat. Hard labour was used alongside starvation and the POWS were put to practical use. Haruku Island housed two thousand Dutch, British, and New Zealand POWs, half of whom did not make it out alive due to the torturous work regime such as being tasked with building an airstrip on Haruku on a starvation diet of rice. Not sure I would want to rely on something built by someone who is not only physically weak but also my enemy, but there you go.

Post WW2, torturous punishments continued at the hands of European imperialists who were desperate to keep control over their empires. The Algerian War of Independence (1954–62) was fought between imperialist France and native Algerians and saw electric shock torture in the armies, police, and security forces become institutionalised.[613] Electric shocks were first approved as a torturous punishment in 1888 with the electric chair in America, but electric shocks only really generated widespread interest and worldwide usage due to the success the French had with electrocuting Algerian's nipples, tongues, and private parts.[614] They were *so* successful that a senior civil servant, Wuillaume, who had been sent to investigate the accusations of torture in Algeria, concluded that this torture method was amazingly effective and recommended electric torture should be legalised and administered professionally. Not only had this bright spark missed the opportunity to deny torture was occurring at the hands of the French, he had also seemingly forgotten all about the international ban on torture agreed just a few years earlier in 1949.

Motive Two: Force confessions and provide evidence for court

Torture is a remarkably useful tool when trying to get someone to do something. Throughout history, this benefit has been ruthlessly exploited in the justice system. While these days crime can be proved using evidence such as fingerprints (1858); blood groups (1901); CCTV (1942); or DNA (1953), for most of history a conviction relied upon a confession or an eyewitness. Both of which could be conveniently obtained through torture. The first realisation that torture could be used to extract confessions came from the ancient Greeks,[615] and the idea was praised by numerous Greek philosophers – guys who are famed for thinking about stuff. As long as stuff wasn't to do with human rights of course.

China has the longest recorded history of using torture with the motive of forcing confessions. For over two thousand years, between 200 BCE and the 20th century, the Chinese used the *Tang Code of Law* which was made up of two parts – the laws and the possible punishments. Crucial for a conviction was the establishment of guilt from the accused. This guilt had to be beyond any doubt, which is hard enough to do these days even when you can see it on CCTV, let alone 2000 years ago. However, not everyone accused was up for confessing and similarly not everyone was guilty, hence the Chinese came to rely upon torture to get an admission of guilt because justice could not proceed until a confession was obtained. Although it should be noted this was not their first choice, defendants were encouraged to confess *prior* to torture with the promise of a lighter sentence – something Western powers adopted in the modern era and called "plea-bargaining".

One way of getting this confession was the torture method "Kneeling on Chains" where the accused would have to remain knelt on sharp metal chains until they were persuaded to remember the crime they had committed. Their knees would be steadily sliced open due to the pressure of their weight and tendons were destroyed which caused irreparable damage to the knee joints. To make it even more painful, their thumbs and big toes were tied together behind their backs which made them off balance – forcing even more of their weight onto their knees. However, not everyone was allowed to be tortured; the Tang Code outlawed torture for the mentally and physically handicapped, children aged seven to fifteen, and the elderly aged 70 to 90.[616] So I guess the lesson learnt here is to wait until you're 71 before embarking on a killing spree.

Japan also used torture as a way of forcing confessions and they had a similar method to the Chinese "Kneeling on Chains", although the Japanese went with the more misleading name "Hugging the Stone". This saw the person kneeling on super sharp bits of flint with their bums resting on their feet while rocks were placed on their laps. The Japanese also recycled and renamed the Pulley method, calling it *Yet Gomon,* which involved people being hoisted into the air by their wrists (which were tied behind their backs) leading to dislocation of their shoulders and arm joints. Whipping was also used by the Japanese to force admission of guilt. But this was no ordinary whip made of boring old leather – theirs were made from sharp bamboo. It really was a cut above the rest.

If you think the Chinese and Japanese systems of forcing confessions sound unfair, then you best stay away from medieval England where the justice system was even worse. Here, the authorities didn't even bother with investigating and went with their pre-decided verdicts (guilty) instead. The prosecuting judges wanted to find the suspect guilty because guilt meant money; fines could then be levied against the convict to secure their release. This corrupt system meant not only was it necessary to torture the accused into confessing, but they also needed to grab and torture randoms off the street to be "eyewitnesses". While King Edward I (1271–1307) wasn't too happy with the lack of confessions, he also didn't like this forced witness method either and sacked everyone accused of such corruption. Only to find his new appointments acted in the exact same way. "Power tends to corrupt and absolute power corrupts absolutely"[617] but unfortunately for Edward, he was 500 years too early for this quote.

While he wasn't so much a fan of corruption, Edward I (aka Hammer of the Scots), was still keen to hammer away at torturing people. However, the need to get away with it in these early days after the Magna Carta meant that methods changed to be more subtle. Rather than remove body parts (pretty hard to cover up when their time came to go to court), Edward chose to chain people face down to a dungeon floor. They would then be starved into submission with alternating days of dirty water and mouldy bread. He also pressed them into pleading. Literally. The prisoner was turned over and heavy items were balanced on their chests, making it hard to breathe and often breaking their ribs. Painful, but also undetectable from the outside. This torture continued long after Edward I and was suffered by Margaret Clitheroe in 1586 as the authorities tried to get her to confess to hiding a Jesuit priest (a Jesuit is a specific branch of Catholic Jesus lovers). She was spread-eagled and tied to the floor and 900lb of weights were loaded onto her torso. She lasted 15 minutes. But the authorities did not get their confession – instead her ribs burst out of either side of her body, and she died. Clearly learning from their mistakes, a more successful pressing took place in 1776 when Thomas Spiggot was pressed with just 400lbs of weights leading to him keeping his ribs *and* giving his confession, resulting in this method no longer getting a bad press.

This form of "acceptable" torture with the motive of forcing confessions became the go-to for the English legal system for the next 300 hundred years.[618] Queen Mary I (1553–1558) was keen to convict non-Catholics of heresy and so employed her Bishop of London, Edmund Bonner, to torture witnesses at court who weren't as forthcoming as she would have liked. Witnesses were charred into compliance by a lit candle burning their hand until the skin turned black. Bonner was well up for this – he loved a bit of torture – so much so, he built a private torture chamber at his house, much like the sort of place you'd see in a *Saw* movie. And yes, this was illegal because they were torturing people to get information, but no one was really up for challenging the guy who tortured people as a hobby and was called "The Devil's Dancing Bear" (probably not to his face though). The Rack was also a popular choice to force confessions due to how it could be carefully controlled to keep the person alive long enough to give in. Guy Fawkes, the guy we have fireworks night for, was tortured into confessing and giving the names of his fellow conspirators using the Rack. However, by 1605, torture was not routine in England and a special warrant from King James I was needed. Clearly a fan of oxymorons, James advised: "…the gentlest tortours are to be first usid unto him".[619]

Post-reformation Europe ushered in a new type of confession – witchcraft. The Puritans, aka the extremists of Protestantism, ruled England between 1649 and 1660 and colonised the British section of America in the 17th century; their vigour in torturing women into confessing to be witches in one part of the USA is known as the Salem Witch Trials. Their purpose was double-edged – force a confession of guilt and reveal "accomplices". The Rack was the most used method, but it was essentially a pointless task because the unfortunate "witch" was going to be found guilty whatever she said. This was clear from the fact authorities started compiling a list of the accused's possessions as soon as they were arrested so that they could work out the value of the conviction and start divvying up their profits – these items were taken by the church or state once the "justice" process was completed.

Torture was helpful for the authorities because each successful admission made them look Right and Powerful. While Catholics and Protestants and all their extremists disagreed over symbology and semantics – witch-hunting was a common enemy. Across Christian Europe and America, regardless of whether your church had stained glass windows or not (FYI Catholics did, Protestants didn't), you were at risk of being called out as a witch. There was even a handy guidebook! While each denomination insisted on having different versions of the Bible, they were both happy to use the same witch-hunting book – the *Malleus Maleficarum* meaning Hammer of Witches in English (sounds much cooler in Latin though).

In England, the celebrity of the witch-hunting world was ex-pub landlord Matthew Hopkins. While pulling pints, Hopkins became friendly with one of Henry VIII's spies and got wind of the anti-witch zeitgeist and, sensing an opportunity, he decided to move on from the business of beer into the business of fear. A common method of torture to test if someone was a witch was to repeatedly stick a needle into their body and gauge their level of pain. Incidentally, feeling no pain means you're a witch so if you're ever accused, make sure you scream. A lot. Hopkins invented his own needle – a retractable one. Hopkins' invention made it seem like the needle went all the way in and yet because it was a trick – the person felt no pain. Armed with his new invention Hopkins, unsurprisingly, became an incredibly successful witch hunter in England. But he didn't just stop there with all his entrepreneurial spirit – he also tried sleep deprivation – a method used in India for centuries, although it would take a few more centuries for the West to realise this inexpensive method of causing confusion was more effective than pain. After torturing Rev. John Lowes, Hopkins wrote: "We kept him awake several nights together while running him backwards and forwards about his cell until he was weary of life and scarce sensible of what he said or did".[620] The realisation that lack of sleep made people speak gobbledygook did not matter; it certainly did not prevent the person's confession being accepted as truth. Lowes ended up confessing to giving birth to four baby demons and then suckling them on his man nipples. Sure.

Hopkins charged by the head and had taken 300 female ones in just nineteen months of "investigations" between 1645-1646[621]. Luckily, he died in 1647 and despite leaving a legacy with the publication of his book *The Discovery of Witches* in 1647, the witch-hunting motive for torture craze faded away by the early 18th century. The last execution for witchcraft in England was in 1716 when Mary Hicks and her ten-year-old daughter were hanged. In Scotland the last execution was in 1727, but you could still be arrested for witchcraft well into the 19th century. Across Europe, the overall toll of witches found guilty ranges from 200,000 to 1 million,[622] witch as a ratio of population could mean up to one in every 200 people could have had a place at Hogwarts.

India followed the same trajectory as Europe in using torture as a way of helping people "remember" that time they witnessed a crime; their methods relied on psychological techniques, local resources, and ancient classics. Psychology began in the late 19th century, but even before it got a name and was accepted as a science, Indian authorities had figured out the value of psychological threats and manipulating a person's love for their family. In one case, a potential witness had his baby son tossed into a sack with a very angry cat. The father was told they would beat the sack with bamboo poles if he did not give evidence. Obviously, the cat was good to go for another eight sackings, but babies are not known for having nine lives and so happily for all, the man "remembered" what he had seen and agreed to testify.[623]

The Indian climate afforded opportunities not available in Europe. For a start, any torture inflicted outside would be made a whole lot worse by the heat of the sun, and the environment gave a more diverse range of speedy flesh-eating insects. Whereas in Europe a person covered in honey or milk may eventually attract a bear or a wolf, in India, a person suffering the same torture would be lucky to last a day thanks to the presence of carpenter beetles and red ants who, apparently, are highly skilled at munching through human flesh. These scratching and nibbling insects were deliberately captured and also used by placing them on vulnerable body parts such as the belly button or a man's scrotum. Other animals were used as well; a person might be sewn into the corpse of a water buffalo, or an elephant might be used to drag someone along the ground – considering an elephant's leg weighs three times the amount of an average man, this could pull the person's leg right off. And just when you think you've seen ivorything – you could also be sentenced with "execution by elephant" which involved your head being stamped on or sat on. Local crops also had a part to play in Indian torture with chillies stuffed into eyes, noses, or any of your down below orifices. An Indian adaptation of the ancients' suspension torture saw those with moustaches hung in the air by it – which you gotta admit is a fan-tash-tic use of natural resources. All these tortures were described in an 1855 British report sent to parliament. By this point, torture was no longer used in the British justice system and therefore criticism of others (who now do what we used to do), provided a wonderful justification to enforce British rule in India.

By the 19th century, the motive of forcing a confession became less common in Britain following changes to the judicial systems. Gossip became less acceptable as evidence; torture to elicit a confession had been outlawed (again); and most importantly there was no *need* to force a confession anymore. By

1827 there was no more use for pressing the defendant into entering a plea because, for the first time, "not guilty" was allowed to be registered for a person refusing to plead either way.

However, this wasn't the case for those living in the British Empire and the 20th century saw a resurgence in the use of torture to force confessions as the British government endeavoured to uncover rebels. After World War Two, imperialism became seriously uncool and European empires began crumbling under independence movements. Broke from war, countries like Britain lacked the finances to deal with these pesky people demanding their country back, and so torture was used to identify those most responsible. Barack Obama's grandfather was tortured by British forces in Kenya. Hussein Onyango Obama was arrested in 1949 after getting involved in the Mau-Mau independence movement. His previous service with the British army in Burma during WW2 counted for nothing and did not save him from two years imprisonment and torture. Hussein returned to Kenya after the war and, like many others, was hopeful that their contribution to the war effort would see them rewarded with independence (they had been colonised by the British in 1895 and fully immersed as a country in the British Empire in 1920). His relative Sarah Onyango tells how: "The African warders were instructed by the white soldiers to whip him every morning and evening till he confessed."[624] Confessed to being a member of a group the British didn't like that is. He was subjected to a multitude of violent torture methods, possibly including "castration pliers" which were described by other survivors; all of which left him psychologically scarred.

Motive Three: Religion

Religion as a motive for torture is first recorded with the Assyrian King Antiochus Epiphanies' torture of the Jewish

Maccabees. Antiochus wanted to Hellenize his kingdom – not, as the name suggests, turn it into the fiery pits of hell – but rather make it more Greek by doing away with the culture and religion of the non-Greeks who lived there. The Assyrians (2500 BCE – 612 BCE) were neighbours to the newly free Hebrews, but in true neighbourly fashion, the two did not see eye to eye. Especially after Antiochus sacked (invaded and looted) the Hebrew capital city Jerusalem in 167 BCE and enforced Hellenization. The Jews were forced to forfeit their doctrine and all Jewish rites were forbidden. The Jews were not about to take this lying down and so organised a revolt, with the rebels calling themselves the Maccabees (not to be confused with the indie band from the early noughties).

Antiochus was rather annoyed with the Maccabees to say the least, he had expected the Jews to just accept defeat. You know, like the French. So those who rebelled were tortured to death. Captives were boiled or put to the Wheel. When one Jewish boy refused to eat pork (part of Jewish doctrine but it has logical origins… no fridges back then to keep it), Antiochus had the boy tied to a Wheel which was above a floor of burning coals. When the Wheel turned, his joints dislocated and when it was turned again, they were broken. While he was up there, and because breaking all your bones while burning alive is not bad enough, his flesh was also ripped apart using boiling hot pincers. There was so much blood pouring from his wounds the fire was extinguished. In another case, seven brothers and their mum were tortured for refusing to relinquish their Jewish beliefs and eat pork. The first got the Wheel treatment; the second had his arms and legs cut off before his still living-and-breathing torso was cooked in a huge pan; the third was skinned alive and disembowelled; the fourth had his tongue cut out and was then spit roasted much like Antiochus wanted pigs to be. Possibly running out of ideas by the time he got to the fifth brother, Antiochus, "merely" burnt him to death, but the sixth found himself thrown into a tub of boiling water, at which point the seventh just threw himself in voluntarily. Water a way to go. The mother was later burnt too. Seven years after the sacking, Antiochus won against the Maccabees and the Jews found themselves stateless by 63 BCE, a situation which continued until the creation of Israel in 1948.

Christianity began around 300 years after Jesus' death at the hands of the Romans. With no sense of irony, the Romans made Christianity the empire's official religion in 323 CE. However, before they became Christians, they tortured them. One of the most infamous Roman emperors was a chap called Nero. Nero had a thing for torturing Christians, an obsession which began after he needed someone to blame for the great fire of Rome in 64 CE and, what with there not being enough Jews around to pin this one on, another minority group – the Christians – were chosen as the scapegoats instead. Nero made a whole show out of it called "The Games" which took place in the Colosseum – the Roman equivalent of Wembley Stadium. Those paying to watch were treated to various tortures such as Christians being attached to a stake, covered with oil, and then set aflame; or they may be strung up by their thumbs and cooked over a fire. Christians might be dressed in animal skins and set upon by dogs; they could be crushed in-between a wine press; forced to wear chain mail armour which had been heated up so hot it had turned red; or dismembered using weapons or animals. The Romans also liked to cook Christians either by frying them in a giant pan or boiling them to death in cauldrons. To make sure the crowd could see the full horror, Nero kindly lit human-sized candles at night. Human-sized because they were literally humans.

The motive of torturing people due to their religion continued in the Roman world after Nero started the trend.

Christians from the Empire were tortured in various ways as they became bothersome to the Roman rulers in the 2nd and 3rd centuries. St Lawrence the martyr was roasted on a giant BBQ in the year 258, and the Rack was used against St. Vincent in c.304 who, while being stretched, also suffered his skin being torn off and his open wounds rubbed with salt. Keen not to discriminate between religions, the Romans also tortured the Jewish population of Palestine. General Titus invaded Jerusalem in 70 CE and went on to crucify 500 Jews a day – a number so huge they ran out of wood to build all the crucifixion crosses from, which undoubtedly made him very cross indeed.

It wasn't just the Romans who tortured Christians. The Japanese mass-executed a bunch of Christian converts in 1612 by throwing boiling water on them over a series of days. The victims' burns never got a chance to heal, and with each day bringing a new dousing, they slowly succumbed to the pain and died.

The motive of religion became the biggest influence on torture once the ancient era came to an end (traditionally dated as 476CE with the fall of the Roman Empire). To start with, the Christian religion had a positive impact on torture in Europe. The Catholic church promoted forgiveness and made a lot of money dishing it out to the vulnerable sinners in the form of indulgences (when you pay the priest to say "I forgive you") or penance (when you do something to make it up to God, like starve yourself for a week). Therefore, there was little need for torture under church law because people believed punishment resided with God. God will deal them later – much like the classic "you wait till your dad gets home" type thing. Plus, in the early centuries of Catholicism, before corruption took hold, the religious leaders genuinely cared about not violating Christian doctrine. For example, Pope

Nicholas I sent an angry letter to the ruler of the Bulgar people (whose homeland is modern-day Kazakhstan) in 865 CE telling him off for using torture to get confessions out of people.[625] But religion could not stay on the moral high ground forever and following the Protestant Reformation, which began in 1517, people became more divided, and the fear of "others" and their religion led to the need to uncover these heathens. The only solution was to torture these people into converting or confessing their sin of reformation. Top of the class for torturing people into changing their religion were the Spanish; between 1481 and 1808 at least 290,000 people were tortured and imprisoned.[626] This IS the Spanish Inquisition.

The Spanish Inquisition used various methods of torture already in existence as well as inventing new methods and devices to uncover heretics and force people to convert back to Catholicism. Although all of this was in the name of preserving Catholicism, once again the Pope did not approve. Like any Karen worth her salt, Pope Sixtus IV expressed his distaste via a strongly worded letter to Spanish King Ferdinand in the 1470s, calling the whole thing a "scandal".[627] What impact did this letter have from one Catholic to another? Nun. The Spanish policy continued for another 330 years.

The Spanish Inquisition did give their victims the chance to avoid torture – people were firstly shown the devices which would be used in the hopes they may confess their guilt early. One device was The Pear which was inserted into mouth, anus, or vagina and then opened wider and wider causing whatever orifice it had been put inside to split apart. They also used The Boot, which was a metallic boot-shaped cage placed over the foot and crushed so hard, bone marrow squeezed through the cage. The ancient method of the Pulley was adapted and rebranded as the *Strappado* or *garrucha*. Like the original, the accused had their hands tied behind their back with the rope hung from the ceiling and the person was hoisted up into the air and hung from their arms. Sometimes, the torturers might choose to be jerks and jerk the person up and down to pop shoulders out of their sockets. But rather than dropping the person onto rocks below like the ancients did, the inquisitors brought the rocks to them – hanging rocks of up to 250lbs from the person's feet. And in a weird coincidence 250lbs is how much *The Rock* (aka Dwayne Johnson) actually weighs.

Having inquisitive minds, the inquisitors also came up with new ways to torture Protestants. The Inquisition chair was used to interrogate people – the chair was covered in spikes and there was also a spiked board which was pressed down onto the person's thighs. But it didn't stop there, once strapped in, a fire might be lit underneath, or the person's feet might be gradually cooked – a slow pace they achieved by smearing the feet in oil first. The Inquisition chair was very popular across Europe and was still being used in the 18th century. Also new on the scene in the Inquisition period was the Cauldron – a technique famous in popular culture due to George Orwell's *1984*. A few rats or mice were placed inside a cauldron type bowl which was then placed upside down on the person's stomach. A fire was lit on the upturned base of the cauldron – the trapped rodents then got so hot they began eating through the person's torso to escape. Another successful method they clocked onto was the Pendulum. This device used a clock's pendulum which had been adapted to have a weighted blade attached to the end. As time ticked away, the pendulum was lowered towards the victim, allowing them to see their impending death and giving time for them to retract their religion – before they got slowly sliced in half – one swoop at a time. Using rope, the *Porto* torture involved the person being tied to a wooden plank with the ropes looped through well-placed holes. The rope was then pulled tighter and tighter and could cut through skin all the way down to the bone. Another variation saw the ropes attached to loops in the wall, and the person would be suspended as the ropes bored through their flesh until the victim was ready to cooperate.

The final device to come from the Spanish was the Judas Cradle. This was a pyramid-shaped block upon which the victim was balanced with their anus or vagina on the tip of the pyramid and their hands and legs tied up so they could not redistribute their weight. They were then steadily impaled upon the pointed top of the pyramid with their orifice being stretched and ripped open until it went so far, internal injuries killed them. This might last anywhere between a few hours to a few days and could be considered an excellent method of torture up to a point.

The two most popular methods for the inquisitors were the *garrucha* and the Funnel. In this second torture method, a funnel was forced down the victim's throat and water relentlessly poured until their stomach was full and water gushed out of their nose. It could be followed by hanging the victim upside down so that they vomited all the water out, or by rolling them across the floor, thus putting pressure on their water-filled stomach. This was used against Englishman William Lithgow who was accused of being a spy. A variation on the Funnel was the *Tormento de toca,* which involved someone being strapped down and a piece of cloth stuffed into their nose and mouth. Water was then poured onto the cloth and moisture slowly seeped through, making breathing difficult as well as imitating the feeling of drowning. The cloth would then be pulled back out, questions resumed, and the whole process began again until the inquisitors got the response they were looking for. Eyewitnesses describe how the cloth was often covered in blood and the sensation was: "like pulling his bowels through his mouth."[628] And if you're thinking this method sounds familiar then you are already one step ahead of the American interrogators in the post 9/11 wave of torture who thought they had come up with "waterboarding" all by themselves.[629]

The Spanish Inquisition was not limited to Spain. During this era, the Spanish royal family – the Habsburgs – were not just busy fornicating with their own family, they were also busy keeping control of their European empire. The Austrian branch ruled Spain and the Holy Roman Empire (modern-day Romania, Hungary, and Austria). The Spanish branch ruled Iberia, Burgundy, Netherlands, and parts of Italy. The Habsburgs took charge of the Netherlands in 1556 and wasted no time in massacring and torturing the locals who had converted to Protestantism in the previous decades. One method of torture was suspension. We've seen people be strung up by their wrists, ankles, and even moustaches before, but the Spanish took it to another level by suspending men by their genitals and women by their breasts. The Dutch were also branded, burned, and the weighted Pulley was also frequently used.

The Spanish Inquisition did not make it over to England, but Catholic Queen Mary I had a good go at using torture to stop the spread of Protestantism. In one instance a Protestant minister was charged with having "scandalous books" and was whipped, locked in a pillory, had one ear cut off, the side of his nose split open, and was branded on one cheek. Hopefully for the poor guy, all of this took place on the same side of his face so at least he could turn the other cheek and look normal. But this was not enough for the torture enthusiast Bonner who brought the minister back for more tortuous punishment after a week. He branded the other side of his face this time and then whipped him so much on his back that the flesh hung off like strips of wallpaper.

The whole Protestant vs Catholic thing was not unique to the Reformation era of the 16th and 17th centuries. The Troubles in Northern Ireland (late 1960s – 1998) was also a conflict between Protestants and Catholics and had *so many* troubling elements of torture, Amnesty International made a report on it in 1975. This was the time of kidnapping, unmarked cars, and mysterious disappearances of people at the hands of groups who were immune to the law. Immune to the law because they *were* the law. The Amnesty report found that the British government arrested and imprisoned (without trial) 342 people as part of Operation Demetrius in the summer of 1971.[630] Fourteen of these people received "special treatment" which meant they were taken to a specific interrogation centre where they were beaten; threatened with death; forced into stress positions; subjected to constant white noise; and deprived of sleep, food, and water. The psychological impacts of this were huge; one of the men revealed he tried to kill himself by repeatedly banging his head against the metal pipes in his cell. These 14 men are commonly known as the "Hooded Men" because they were forced to wear a hood over their heads, blinding them, and were then flown around in low-flying helicopters. Not knowing the height at which they were flying, these men then suffered the trauma of being flung from the helicopters to the ground below. Incidentally, none of the "Hooded Men" was ever convicted of a criminal offence. Neither were the perpetrators. The case to bring prosecution to someone responsible was still ongoing in 2021.[631]

Motive Four: Extract information

Aristotle (famous for inventing logic and writing about ethics) thought torture was an ideal method for getting information. Evidently all his writing about ethics didn't lead to him possessing any. But the logic bit comes through all right – torture *does* lead to information.... it just might not be truthful information. Aristotle was oblivious to the possibility that people say whatever it takes to get the torture to stop, and instead insisted that information resulting from torture had: "absolute credibility".[632] He was, however, the first guy to identify dolphins, so at least we know he wasn't oblivious to everything.

Torture devices intended to extract information arose during the Roman era due to the rise of dictators combined with the rise of engineering. Dictators tend to be super paranoid and their need to get information about plots against them meant that there was now a need for those accused to feel enough pain and live long enough to give such information. Rome began life in 752 BCE, and was a joyfully democratic republic until Caesar came along and declared himself "dictator for life" in 44 BCE Which, in the end, turned out to not be such a momentous statement as he only lived one more month. However, his declaration did lead to a series of dictatorial emperors following his ideology for the next 400 years with the Rack being used to extract information, such as in 65 CE when Epicharis was tortured to reveal information about the plot to kill Emperor Nero (the Pisonian Conspiracy). Despite all her limbs being dislocated, she did not reveal the names of the conspirators and managed instead to rack her brains and find a way out of the situation by strangling herself on a loop of rope that hung from the back of the Rack on day two of her torture.

In order to extract information, the Romans adapted some devices to be more torturous than straight-up deadly. The Wheel, for example, was suspended over a fire so that when it turned the victim (who was precariously attached like a cheap hub cap) could be roasted – in both senses of the word. They also adapted some of their building tools; as big builders of big things, the Romans had a giant pulley (much like the modern-day crane) to lift heavy stones into place and this was soon put to work as a torture device. People were hauled up in the air and then dropped onto the rocky ground, the process could be repeated as many times as necessary with each drop resulting in more broken bones and more broken resolve. Another adaption from the building yard saw a person attached to *four* different pulleys, and as they were hoisted upwards, all their limbs were torn off. There really was no limb-it to their ingenuity.

Much to Aristotle's dismay, it turned out that torture does *not* have a 100% success rate in extracting decent information, a fact which was discovered during the colonisation of the New World (North and South America). Armed with two millennia of torture experience on their CVs, the Europeans were proper keenos in using their skills in the New World once Columbus had found "India" there in 1492. Fun fact: this geographical mistake is why the Caribbean islands are also known as the West Indies. The first victims were the Aztecs at the hands of the Spanish. The Aztec empire of Central America was conquered by Cortez in the early 1520s and the Inca Empire of southern America was conquered in 1530 by Pizarro and his 168 men (yes, they did really conquer the Incas with this few… mainly because the Incas believed them when they said they were on a peaceful mission). Unfortunately for the locals, Pizarro did not bring a cheesy stuffed crust as his name implied and delivered a slice of torture instead. Obsessed with finding gold, the Spanish tortured the Incas to discover how much they had and where it was located. However, as we know, people will say anything to get the torture to stop (shout out to the four suckling demons); and it seems like the Incas might have, maybe, just slightly, exaggerated the amount of gold they had to get the Spanish off their backs. You may have heard of the search for *El Dorado* – the Inca city made from gold. Except it wasn't. Because it didn't exist. But at least it kept the Spanish busy as they searched for it.[633] Comedy gold.

The use of torture to extract information peaked in England during the reign of Elizabeth I, [634] although some credit should be given for the fact it was in her era that the last person was hanged, drawn, and quartered. You win some, you lose some. Exact numbers of those tortured in the Golden Age are not known but considering around 800 people[635] were executed every year (daddy's girl for sure), it's likely the number is in the thousands with the Rack being put to good use having first come to the Tower of London in 1420. Despite having 2,000 pairs of gloves to keep her hands clean, Elizabeth did not do the dirty work herself. Just like her big sis, Bloody Mary, Elizabeth had a man for that – Francis Walsingham.

As her spy master, Walsingham uncovered five major plots against Elizabeth's life and torture played a big part in his success, such as when Charles Bailly was caught in Dover in 1571 with incriminating letters detailing the Ridolfi plot. He was racked at the Tower of London, and it was soon revealed that Pope Pius II and the Spanish King Phillip II were financing the plot to replace Elizabeth with her Catholic cousin, Mary Queen of Scots. [636] Then, in 1583, torture was used on Throckmorton, and the warrant for his interrogation didn't even *try* to cover up the illegal nature of the act: "to assay by torture to draw from him the truth of the matters."[637] Thanks to the persuasive powers of the Rack, Throckmorton spilled the beans on the involvement of French, Spanish, and Mary Queen of Scots. In 1594, Lopez was racked and revealed a plan to kill the Queen by poisoning her with exotic and foreign drugs; he also exposed the role of the Earl of Essex, and financing of 50,000 crowns which was provided by Spanish King Phillip II (this guy is persistent to say the least). Remember the loophole whereby monarchs insisted torture wasn't illegal if it helped them survive? Well, evidently the Elizabethan public didn't. So to help them remember this convenient caveat, a propaganda leaflet was published explaining how torture was "necessary" in cases of treason. This document is significant in English history as it was also the first to praise the work of "secret intelligence". From the late 16th century onwards, a new loophole emerged whereby torture was acceptable if undertaken by an intelligence agency. A new era had begun.

In the 20th century, extracting information became the most common motive for torture. This was used by extremist groups such as the Nazis, imperialist European nations such as Britain in Kenya and France in Algeria, and superpower states such as America. The Nazis often tortured Jews they found in hiding or on the run because they wanted to know where others were hiding or if they had connections to resistance movements. Harry Blumenfracht was caught while trying to steal weapons from a Nazi officer's apartment in the Polish city of Sosnowiec, he was then tortured as the Nazis tried to find out who his accomplices were. They put chips of wood under his fingernails and set them on fire so that his fingernails slowly burnt and melted. They hung him on an iron net for 48 hours and even brought in his mother, who cried and begged for him to say something to shorten his own suffering, but still he refused. They kept him alive for two weeks before secretly hanging him. The Nazis normally hanged people in public and forced all the Jews to watch but with Harry they were afraid his strength would inspire others; so, they did it before dawn, during curfew hours, so that no one saw him in his last moments.[638] Incidentally, Harry never betrayed his friends.

World War Two made America an economic superpower… and arrogant as hell. The end of war celebration party had an unfortunate gate crasher though – the Cold War. This was basically 45 years of nuclear threats and "mine's bigger than yours" banter between the USA and USSR. There were 45 proxy wars of the Cold War (1947–1991); proxy in this instance meant the battles and bombs did not take place in either USA or USSR. Another country is destroyed instead. This method of outsourcing destruction was about the only thing the two enemies ever agreed on. As well as the proxy wars (such as Korea and Vietnam), billions of dollars were spent building nukes which they didn't want to use. Deep within this MAD philosophy (this one isn't actually a bad joke – it's a genuine acronym meaning Mutually Assured Destruction) was a smidge of logic – these nukes could be used as a deterrent to stop one of them doing something really silly like dropping a nuke on a country to force their surrender during a war.

Oh… wait.

This toxic combination led to America sticking her nose into everyone's business for the second half of the 20th century because their economic supremacy and capitalist ideology needed to be protected. You see, communist governments were awfully selfish about sharing their resources and refused to allow American companies in to profit off their possessions. They were also unwilling to buy American goods and this sort of crazy nationalism (where a country pits the rights of *their* citizens above the profits of *American* businesses) just would not do. Therefore, torture was needed to extract information about communist opposition and to contain the spread of communism before it became a threat to America's position as the world's leading economic power.[639]

Torture with this motive occurred in Vietnam between the late 1960s and early 1970s and then in Latin America during the 1980s – 1990s. Problem was, the USA agreed to not torture people in 1948. Luckily, the CIA were there to help in this awkward situation. The CIA were formed in 1947 during the "Red Scare" era when loads of people were randomly accused of being communist, including lots of Hollywood actors such as Charlie Chaplin who was banned from coming back to America in 1952. Sticking to their brief, the CIA were awfully good at operating secretly and thus were able to avoid following annoying things like international laws which protected human rights.

The CIA began torturing people at the age of three. They started small with secret interrogation centres in Germany, Japan, and Panama in the 1950s before moving onto multiple torture centres in 1960s Vietnam. However, from the 1970s onwards, they suddenly got all shy about it and moved to torture by proxy – which meant the CIA paid other people to do it for them and got to keep their hands clean Lady Macbeth style. Torture by proxy was used all over South America and with Iraqi and Afghani detainees from the 1970s until the 2010s. The CIA still had ultimate authority over this process; they would supply the questions,[640] sometimes ask questions themselves, and sometimes supervise the torture to C (IA) if it was being done right.

Operation Phoenix was an interrogation and torture programme launched in 1968 during the Vietnam War (1963–1975) in an attempt to uncover and destroy Vietnamese Communists. Vietnam had been a colony of the French since 1858 but during WW2 the Japanese invaded and took over; once Japan lost and were taking the walk of shame back home, France moved back in to claim "their" territory. After nine years fighting, the French were defeated at the Battle of Dien Bien Phu in 1954. Which seems like it should be the end of the story and the perfect time for Vietnam to become independent. Yeah… as if. The issue was, this independent Vietnam was looking to be ruled by the Indochinese

Communist Party led by Ho Chi Minh and there was no way America was gonna let this happen. The new kids on the block – The United Nations – stepped in to help America out and temporarily split Vietnam in two in 1954. The north was to be ruled by Ho Chi Minh, and the south ruled by a Vietnamese man who was friendly to American interests – puppet ruler Ngo Diem. Thinking America would respect a democratic process, Ho Chi Minh planned an election for 1956 – an election he was set to triumph in. But the USA did not respect this democratic process. Democracy is only fun when you're winning. And so, as the natural thing to do when you are *such* a vocal advocate of democracy – America prevented the elections from happening. Vietnam remained divided, and with his legal and democratic plans scuppered, Ho Chi Minh gave orders in 1959 to begin a terror campaign in the south to win back control. Then someone assassinated Diem in 1963 and the shit really hit the fan. Puppetless, and 8,854 miles away, power was slipping away from America's grasp as Ho Chi Minh was looking even more likely to take control. America began sending "advisors" and troops to Vietnam, with their official line being they were there to protect the South Vietnamese from the evils of democracy. Oh wait, sorry, the evils of *communism*…

Vietnam did not go well for America. Despite dropping 7.5 million tonnes of bombs (double the amount dropped in WW2), sending 2.7 million people to fight, and spending $120 billion – they failed to win the support of the South Vietnamese. A failure that probably had a lot to do with their Search and Destroy tactic, which saw American soldiers burning down the houses of the South Vietnamese in their hunt for communists. Or maybe it was due to their use of chemical weapons such as the 82 million litres of Agent Orange which decimated agricultural land and poisoned crops and water supplies. Or maybe it was their use of napalm, which burned civilians' skin down to the bone at temperatures of 800°C. Or maybe it was down to the massacre at My Lai in 1968 where American soldiers went on a rampage and murdered everyone in the village. Even the babies. For some reason, unfathomable to the Americans, the Southerners just didn't understand the USA were there to protect them. So instead, they protected the communist guerrilla soldiers. By 1968, the Americans were rather ticked off by their lack of progress in hunting down the enemy and so tactics changed to torture.

Operation Phoenix was run by American man Bill Colby (as a civilian ambassador) between 1968–71. Having no sway in the north, the USA constructed their torture chambers in all 44 provinces in South Vietnam.[641] Operation Phoenix killed at least 20,000 Vietnamese.[642] A former CIA officer said few survived the interrogation process of Operation Phoenix, with most dying from the torture itself and those who didn't were later thrown from helicopters.[643] One victim was Ms. Nguyen Thi Nhan who was arrested in 1969 and tortured at Saigon police headquarters with electric shocks and an iron rod being violently forced into her vagina. Three CIA agents watched the process, and one ordered needles should also be inserted under her fingernails.[644] In another example, Mrs Nguyen Thi Bo was tortured at Danang police station in 1969 and she too had an implement forced up her vagina. Thi Bo also suffered having her head held down in a toilet filled with faeces before being beaten and questioned by five US agents in green uniforms.[645]

Electric shocks, suspension from the ceiling, and water torture were the most common methods in Operation Phoenix. The French method of electric shocking (developed in Algeria in the decade prior) was taught to US Marines. They were trained to use the TP 3-12 field telephone: "and put the connecting wire to it, then take the other end of the wire and attach it to a person's testicles and crank it -- this causes a high-voltage shock, there is no amperage behind it, just voltage, but it is extremely painful."[646] In the end, torture was unsuccessful in extracting information about communist opposition and America left Vietnam in 1973 as losers. Vietnam swiftly united and became communist in 1975. I'm sorry to say that this clear failure of the use of torture had zero impact on America's use of it elsewhere.

In a lovely example of irony, Latin American countries such as Guatemala, Nicaragua, Honduras, Brazil, and El Salvador were veering towards communism after WW2 due to capitalism. The devastating impacts of American businesses taking over their resources meant the local populations were forced into poverty. In Honduras, two-thirds of the country's natural resources (bananas and coffee) and one million acres of farmland[647] (the best farmland of course) were controlled by the American Vaccaro brothers and the American owned United Fruit Company. By the 1980s, 70% of the rural population lived in desperate poverty and 80% were malnourished.[648] In El Salvador, the economic takeover by America meant that by the 1930s, thirty-forty families owned nearly everything while 74% of the population lived in absolute poverty.[649] In Guatemala, the native Mayan population, who made up 80% of residents (80% of whom were also severely malnourished and illiterate[650]), owned very little of their own land because 70% of the country was owned by 2% of the population who were prioritising American needs over theirs.[651]

This move towards communism needed to be contained. Accordingly, America helped displace the offending governments in a series of coups. For example, the CIA directly organised and carried out the Guatemalan coup of 1954 and the El Salvador coup of 1979 had US Presidential approval from Carter and Reagan. Reagan then also funded the Salvadorean government to help them keep control (via torture) in the ensuing civil war.

In Brazil, in 1964, America helped remove president João Goulart and replace him with a military dictatorship. US Official, Dan Mitione, under the cover of "Public Safety" (aka keeping money safe) then became the advisor to the Brazilian police, which basically saw systematic torture brought to the country.[652] The Honduras coup of 1963 was a bit less black and white as President Kennedy opposed helping with the coup yet the Honduran military undertaking it were confident America would support them anyway. Which, after Kennedy's assassination in November 1963, the new president Johnson, did. America were too late for Nicaragua as the Sandinista Revolution overthrew pro-American dictator Debayle in 1979. So, in this case, the USA funded and armed the people who fought against the Sandinistas (the Contra guerrillas) as well as assisting with torturing captured Sandinistas. In at least 20 different cases from Sandinista survivors,[653] they state a North American man was present in their torture chambers, either supervising, observing, or suggesting questions.

It is worth pointing out that a lot of the leaders who were overthrown were known for being dictators so on the surface it looked like America were doing the honourable thing. Yet conveniently these "honourable intentions" were only acted upon in countries where communism looked like it might triumph. America was less proactive when Zaire, Indonesia, Philippines, Pakistan, and Zimbabwe, to name but a few, were suffering under non-left-wing dictatorships in the second half of the 20th century. Funny that.

America embarked on torture in Latin America with three motives in mind; firstly, to contain communism; secondly to ensure whatever result they wanted from a coup was the result that endured; and thirdly because they were obsessed with getting information about communist Cuba. Cuba was the first regional domino to fall to communism in 1959 when

Fidel Castro had the audacity to have a revolution which rejected the dictator America had propped up since 1934. Castro wasted no time telling American businesses like The United Fruit Company to "do one". With this trauma fresh in their minds, America was keen to ensure other countries did not follow suit. All those suspected of opposing the American backed government, or belonging to peasant unions, or getting involved in political activities, or refusing to accept their capitalistic fate of poverty, were tortured to reveal the names of their colleagues and leaders. The CIA tortured people from all over central and southern America to find out more about Cuba and the communist Sandinistas of Nicaragua.[654]

America had, by the 1960s and 1970s, moved onto torture by proxy. One of their torture apprentices from Honduras – Florencio Caballero – confirmed that America was aware of everything that was going on but "did not do anything" [655] to stop the violations of international law. An Intelligence Oversight Board report in 1996 revealed that in Guatemala between 1984-1986, the CIA used numerous "assets" and knew that these people were "credibly alleged" to be violating the human rights legislation by torturing people.[656] One asset – Alpirez – was paid $44,000 by the CIA in June 1992 to supervise the torture of a man named Everardo.[657] This whole set-up was so widespread that the guy who oversaw intelligence in Guatemala said: "it would be an embarrassing situation if you ever had a roll call for everybody in the Guatemalan army who ever collected a CIA paycheque."[658] The CIA and Guatemalan army were officially cheque-mates.

An important aspect of proxy torture was giving people the tools they needed to do it themselves. Teach a man to fish and all that. To this end, America provided money to train interrogators; teach torture methods; fund the salaries of those interrogating suspects; provide weapons and tools; and buy equipment needed for the day-to-day running of such an operation such as petrol and vehicles. In Honduras, America began sending money in 1980 ($3.9 million) and by 1984 were spending $77.4 million to help torture people.[659] In Guatemala, America spent $135 million between 1984 and 1986[660], as well as lifting an arms embargo and supplying $6.3 million worth of helicopters[661] so that people could be thrown out of them after being tortured.[662] These investments led to 200,000 people "disappearing" in Guatemala during the 1980s.[663] In El Salvador, Reagan was happy to spend a whopping $1.85 billion between 1980 – and 1985 on their torturous information quest. Reagan was so committed to this cause that even when the Salvadoran military raped and murdered four American churchwomen, the American money was halted for less than a year in a classic case of "I'm not angry… just disappointed." And where's this money coming from? Well, the poor of course! Reagan cut taxes for rich American citizens and raised them for the poor in his ridiculous policy narcissistically named *Reaganomics*. He thought the benefits of the rich having more money in their pocket would at some point trickle down to the poor. Like never in history. It's no surprise that this bozo left America in $1 trillion of debt[4] by the end of his eight-year tenure.

Keen to show off the psychological methods they had recently learnt in Vietnam, America took charge of the training in Latin America. Lessons on how to torture and most effectively violate people's human rights were undertaken at training centres such as the School of the Americas (SOA) using specially made torture textbooks.[664] The SOA first opened in Panama in 1946 before moving to Fort Benning, Georgia, in 1984. It shut down in 2000 after 54 years of

---

[4] Steve Waugh and John Wright, *The Development of the USA*, (Hodder Education, London, 2016), p. 61

training at least 57,700 people.[665] More accurately, the SOA has been dubbed a bit of a SOD (School Of Dictators) as 10 of the alumni graduated to become tyrannical leaders in South America. Sometimes torturers were trained in CIA stations such as in Honduras where the CIA, along with other American intelligence and military officials, trained the notorious Battalion 3-16.[666] Battalion 3-16 were a unit from the Honduras army responsible for torturing and killing political opponents of the new capitalist friendly government post the 1963 coup. They were taught psychological methods such as "hooding" which caused the victim to suffocate; sleep deprivation; using rats placed on a person's body; electric shocks; temporary drownings; and threatening the victim with hurting their family. Journalist Oscar Reyes, who dared to criticise the government was kidnapped and tortured along with his wife, Gloria. He was stripped naked and hung from the ceiling to be beaten "like a piñata" while she received electric shocks to her genitals.[667] Andrés Pavón Murillo was captured in 1983 and he was choked, beaten, and strung up by his arms. They never turned off the light in his cold cell, he was denied food for a week and his mother was threatened.[668] Battalion 3-16 also abducted attorney Inés Murillo in March 1983 and tortured her for 78 days. She was drowned; beaten; shocked; starved; kept naked and tied up in painful and unnatural positions; not allowed to go to the toilet; terrorized by aggressive dogs; her family were threatened with death; and she was deprived of sleep by having freezing water thrown in her face every 10 minutes.[669]

Dan Mitrione was a key individual in this Latin American learning journey. Mitrione was first sent to South America in 1960 as part of the State Department's International Cooperation Administration (as in the forced through torture sort of cooperation). His role was to teach advanced techniques such as understanding your target (by determining his physical state and his degree of resistance through a medical examination);[670] and methods which did not cause death, because, as he explained: "'A premature death, means a failure by the technician."[671] Mitrione certainly got around – he firstly worked with the police in Brazil before spending some time in the Dominican Republic following their coup in 1965 and then onto Uruguay in 1969. Mitrione went on to work for the CIA as part of the International Development's Office of Public Safety (OPS), (as in you're not safe unless you support America sort of public safety). In Uruguay he organised and led the torture training as well as visiting and supervising the ongoing torture. Mitrione taught basic anatomy to help the Uruguayan torturers hit the right spots; he recommended: "The precise pain, in the precise place, in the precise amount, for the desired effect."[672] In one of his lessons, four homeless people were brought in to be tortured as part of the student's learning. None of the four survived the class[673] which seems to me like the sort of lesson that OFSTED would judge "requires improvement" considering Mitrione had said this outcome was a failure. The influential Mitrione went out with a bang in 1970… well a double bang to be precise (and he does like being precise) with two bullets in his head courtesy of the opposition guerrilla group, the Tupamaros.

Don't be thinking the Americans took a back seat after their lessons and left everyone to it – with such vested interests and so much money spent, they wanted to be sure the torture was effective. Americans were often present to advise on questioning and in some cases took part in the actual torture, such as with María, Jose, and Marco. María Lorenzo Guardado was abducted in broad daylight in 1980 because she was working with a group fighting for peasant's rights. The Salvadoran security forces beat her up, gave electric shocks to her breasts and genitals, raped her, and forced a stake so far up her rectum she bled and passed out. When she woke up at another building, an American took charge and organised the order of events and questions. In this torture session her kneecaps were stamped on, they jumped on her back and fractured her spine, broke her wrist and ribs, and burnt her arms and legs.[674] An American advisor helped administer 200-volt electric shocks to Jose Ruben Carillo Cubas' back and ears when he was being tortured for the "crime" of visiting someone who lived near the barracks of an opposition group. A North American man was also present for the torture of "Marco" (an alias name), telling others what to ask and suggesting how to push the torture further, such as using his injuries against him. Marco's open wounds were scraped roughly to cause immense pain and, when the wound got infected and infested with maggots, the torturer pulled a maggot out and placed it just out of Marco's reach – on his chest – telling him to eat it. He was then kicked and given electric shocks when he couldn't reach it due to being tied up and all.[675] Between interrogations, Marco was hung from the ceiling by his wrists; he could not touch the ground because if he did, the pointy device which had been put in his rectum would have impaled him.

Psychological and less physically brutal methods became trendy in this latter half of the 20th century because the overall aim was to "break, not kill". One effective method of psychological torture was threatening the accused's family. No one was off limits – in Iraq, the interrogators abducted the seventeen-year-old son of their captured Iraqi military general. The son was drenched in water and kept in extreme cold temperatures while his dad was made to watch. Once again, the aim was to break not kill – they wanted to "soften up" the father for questioning.[676] Other psychological methods used were mock drownings; suffocating someone in a hood soaked in pesticide; held for long periods of time in tiny cells; threats of sexual assault (and/or actual sexual assault); mock executions using an unloaded gun fired at their head; being left in a room filled with so many ants it was dangerous for people to open their eyes; and electrical shocks to sensitive areas like testicles and armpits. In Guatemala, Santiago Cabrera López (who fought against the government during the post-coup civil war) was tortured with this aim of break not kill. His "breaking" involved him being hung from a hook and beaten so hard on his feet that his toenails fell off. He had the electric shock treatment to his genitals; was buried in a pit and chained to a bed for months.[677] Electric shocks were originally administered using cattle prods but from the 1970s, the *picana* was used, having originally been created in Argentina in 1932.[678] The *picana* was able to deliver high-voltage shocks (12–16,000 volts) but at a low current, meaning it was less likely to kill the person. Exactly what was needed.

Waterboarding was also used against Latin American victims, but they weren't the first people America had used waterboarding against – they had first put it to use in the Philippines against Filipino rebels[679] after they had defeated Spain and taken over the islands in 1898. And it's not like the USA even tried to keep this method of torture a secret – a drawing of American troops carrying out the waterboarding torture was pride of place on the 22 May 1902, front cover of *Life Magazine*. Due to the US general of the Philippines – William Taft – approving of its use, why bother with the secrecy! Taft was the general between 1901 and 1904 and then president of the USA between 1909 and 1913. He's the only man to have held both top jobs in American politics successively, and so his opinion carried more weight than he did (and he weighed 350 pounds so that's saying something).

While waterboarding originated in the late medieval period, it became a favoured technique of the CIA due to the fact it was psychically exhausting and psychologically damaging because the victim is deprived of oxygen while thinking he's going to die. The CIA strapped the person down and pushed him under water until he lost consciousness, which this was all perfectly fine and didn't count as torture in the official's eyes because there was no visible serious injury. If you can't see it, then it doesn't exist. Unsurprisingly, the Latin Americans who endured this torture did not share this opinion and instead described it as one of their worst memories.[680] In 1999, US President Clinton issued an apology for the whole coup, torture, and civil war thing in Guatemala, which thankfully made up for everything.

The use of psychological torture using the proxy method did not decrease in the 21st century, in fact it got worse due to the presidential approval given by President George W. Bush. Approval which lasted until January 2009 when President Obama signed an executive order banning torture and cruel treatment of detainees, thus ending the post-9/11 torture program.

Back in 2001, Bush thought it would be a good idea to extend the powers of the CIA following the 9/11 attacks; this meant the CIA were now able to hand over suspects to foreign security services to be tortured into revealing information *without* the risk of prosecution. No matter about the international laws against it, White House counsel Alberto Gonzales even went so far as to describe the fifty-three-year-old Geneva Conventions as "quaint"[681] and advised that they could be set aside in this War On Terror. This illegal policy got a misleadingly ambiguous name: "extraordinary rendition". It was certainly extraordinary in its blatant flouting of the law because this was nothing more than a flowery way to describe kidnap. Those behind it didn't see it that way of course. In fact, according to CIA official Peter Probst, kidnapping and secret imprisonment was "absolutely legal".[682] This was an extraordinary porky pie to tell, considering it was written down in US Criminal law that it is a crime for any US official to conspire to torture a person abroad, a crime which carried a prison sentence of 20 years.[683] But all this legality went out the window when the Americans were armed with their motive of extracting information about who was responsible for 9/11.

Just as in South America, the CIA had authority over the paid torturers and supplied the questions in these cases of extraordinary rendition.[684] While the United States National Security Advisor, Condoleezza Rice, was insistent at the time that America were NOT secretly torturing people, a CIA agent clearly did not get the memo and eloquently explained: "We don't kick the shit out of them. We send them to other countries so they can kick the shit out of them."[685] Capitalism as its finest – why do it yourself and scuff your shoes when you can pay someone else to scuff theirs. Even more backwards were Bush's insistences that the information gained from these torture sessions was 100% the truth. Aristotle would have been so proud.

This new method of capturing suspects in one location and then taking them to another location to be tortured saw the CIA take hundreds of people to be locked up in secret jails or military prisons such as Guantanamo, and hundreds more sent to be tortured by the intelligence services in Egypt, Morocco, Uzbekistan, Pakistan, Jordan, and Syria.[686] These places were chosen because they were known for their brutal interrogation methods. In 2004, journalists uncovered the fact that the American government and CIA had financed at least 300 flights using a leased plane to drop off the accused (who were often sedated with drugs and gagged for the entire flight), to one of 49 different locations around the world.[687] One such victim was Saudi citizen Abu Hamza al-Tabuki who was arrested by American officials in Afghanistan in December

2001and then flown to Jordan to be tortured. Al-Tabuki was held for around a year. Without charge of course (yes, they can jail you for *not* committing a crime, but *they* cannot be charged or jailed when there's actual evidence of the crime of torture). The suffering he and others endured at the hands of the Jordanians (working on behalf of the CIA) was documented in a report released by the group Human Rights Watch as well as being described by al-Tabuki himself:

> *"And from the first day, they began to interrogate me using the methods of terror and fear, torture and beating, insults and verbal abuse, and threatening to expose my private parts and rape me. I was repeatedly beaten, and insulted, along with my parents and family. Every time they took me, they blindfolded me…As soon as I reached the torture room, the torturers began to violently beat me. They would tie my feet and beat me with a heavy stick. After which, my flesh in my feet would tear apart, they would untie the rope and order me to run across the courtyard, over saltwater. Throughout this, they would throw questions at me and demand answers to them, while kicking and beating me all over with sticks, including my sensitive parts.* '[688]

Investigations beginning in 2004 revealed widespread use of torture throughout US bases in Iraq and Afghanistan[689] as the CIA desperately sought information about al-Qaeda and the location of Osama Bin Laden. Soldiers who were later caught and charged with torture of prisoners said they had been following orders from CIA and military intelligence officials. Much like the Nazi soldiers' defence in the post-WW2 Nuremberg Trials. But there was some truth in this defence because while it may have seemed like the soldier's motive was cruelty and personal pleasure (which it still may have been), the methods they used proved that these low-level soldiers were not the masterminds.[690] There's no way an 18-year-old American soldier would know about "the Vietnam", which had a victim hooded on a box with electric cables attached to his finger, toes, and penis. This method was not in the military training manual. But it was in the CIA bookshelf. This was torture conducted by the American military using CIA methods.

In Afghanistan and Iraq, therefore, the proxy-ness of torture was less about the torturer themselves and more about the location. And so, following the American invasions in 2001 and 2003 respectively, torture of the citizens wasn't solely done by paid natives – it was also done by the American military. In 2002, *The Washington Post* revealed how Afghan prisoners were beaten, blindfolded, tied up in painful positions, subjected to loud noises, deprived of sleep, and had cold water thrown over them in low temperatures.[691] One person in the Bagram compound had his hands chained to the ceiling for so long they turned black. Some Afghans, like eighteen-year-old Jamal Naseer and twenty-two-year-old Mr Dilawar, died because of their torture at the hands of the Americans.[692]

In Iraq, people were kept either at "the Pit" (CIA's interrogation centre in Kabul), at Abu Ghraib prison, or in shipping containers – which was a torture method without even trying due to the Middle Eastern climate making it sweltering hot inside.[693] At Abu Ghraib prison, inmates were terrorized and bitten by ferocious dogs and Marines subjected youth detainees to mock executions.[694] Special Operations Agents attached electrodes to prisoners to give electric shocks and shoved lit cigarettes into their ears, others were denied the right to use a toilet.[695] During one torture session, US soldiers broke a chemical light and poured the liquid over one prisoner and then used either the frame of the light, or a broom, to sodomise another prisoner. Prisoners at Abu Gharib were also sexually humiliated and made to do things that were sacrilegious in their Muslim faith, such as being forced to masturbate in front of everyone or made to engage in homosexual acts. Photographs and stills from CCTV showed all these things happening while US soldiers stood over them, giving thumbs up and saying cheese to the camera.[696] In April 2004, CBS TV broadcast a photo from Abu Ghraib prison with "Iraqis naked, hooded and contorted in humiliating positions while US soldiers stood over them smiling."[697] But the photos were never intended to be viewed by the world – they were part of the psychological torture and were used as threats against the prisoners – the Americans said they would show the photos to prisoners' families unless they gave some decent information.[698]

Guantanamo Bay was also used as a proxy location for torture. Guantanamo was an American military base in Cuba, the land had been rented since 1903 with the Americans retaining use of the grounds after Cuba's communist revolution. With proxy torture in full swing by 2001, this base became a prison run by Americans where they could freely torture the inmates because it was not on their soil (because a crime isn't a crime if it's not in your country, remember). At Guantanamo, prisoners were "short shackled" (sat in a chair and chained hand and foot to the floor) and then left for at least 24 hours to endure strobe lighting, loud music, extreme temperatures, and no access to a toilet. Sometimes the American tight arses didn't even provide a chair and people were just laid down and chained to the floor. Other methods used were solitary confinement, threatening dogs, rape, sleep deprivation and frequent searches of their anus[699] (presumably to see if they were hiding Osama Bin Laden up there). There were also reports of female interrogators sexually assaulting prisoners by rubbing themselves against them and flicking menstrual blood in their faces.[700]

It only took 10 years of torturing thousands of people to get genuinely useful information from Guantanamo prisoners which helped lead the Americans to Bin Laden. However, such success often wasn't the case because like many others throughout history, the CIA captives were made to say stuff that wasn't true so the proxy interrogators could justify their poxy paycheque. Al-Tabuki, for example, stated how: "They even forced me, through torture, to make up fictitious targets, about which they could report to the Americans."[701] A similar incident occurred with Salem Saleh Aboud, who was arrested in Iraq after he reported a suspicious car to the Iraqi police. Yes, you read that right. He tried to help the police and was arrested and tortured for it. If there was an award for the ability to turn neutral civilians into enemies, the Americans would win hands down. He was given to the Americans at Abu Gharib and suffered various tortures such as being tied up with his arms and legs behind him in what's known as the "scorpion" position, subjected to deafeningly loud music for hours and hours, mercilessly beaten, and chained to his cell bars for 23 hours without being allowed to go to the toilet. In the end he ended up admitting *he* was Osama Bin Laden.[702] A confession so outrageous that not even the Americans could accept this as true.

Motive Five: Experimentation

Science overtook religion in popularity for explaining things around the mid-18th century, and experimentation became a new motive for torture between 1939 and 1945. World War Two provided the ideal cover for Japanese and Nazi doctors to try out their barmy ideas; test the limits of human endurance;

gain answers to medical questions about disease, fertility, and racial supremacy; or help their nation's war effort. All these experiments were carried out using the POWs or Jews held captive in their camps. There were more than seven thousand victims of Nazi medical experiments[703] whose victims included Jews, Poles, Roma (Gypsies), political prisoners, Soviet prisoners of war, homosexuals, and Catholic priests. In the Japanese camps, at least 3,500 POWs died[704] (this represents 10% of all the POWS they held during the war), but it is unknown how many of these were as a direct result of the experiments or due to other mistreatment or illness.

Some torturous experiments were motivated by medical research such as the infamous Dr Mengele's experiments on twins at Auschwitz. Mengele was tasked with studying hereditary abnormalities, weighing up the impacts of environment versus human hereditary factors, as well as taking specimens of eyes, heads and blood to be sent back to the Kaiser Wilhelm Institute in Berlin. Records show he experimented on at least 732 pairs of twins.[705] Some experiments included dissections while the person was alive, injections to see if he could change eye colour, or injections of diseases such as Noma to study if the effects were the same in both twins.

Interest in blood and injecting people with diseases were common denominators; in Japan, research was conducted on Allied POWs to see what happened to a human if you took all their blood out and replaced it with horse blood (spoiler alert: you die). Further experiments saw the head doctor at Shinagawa, Tokyo, inject POWs with castor oil, urine, or caprylic acid because he was curious to see the effects. This guy was a proper sicko – he enjoyed seeing people in pain – one such painful experiment involved bleeding men to death in a long-drawn-out process to collect plasma.[706] Over in Nazi Europe, SS First Lieutenants Weber and Munch carried out experiments where they would inject malarial parasites, pure carbolic acid, and air into people's blood.[707] The Japanese were also keen to study the impact of various diseases, and men were infected with the plague, syphilis, or cholera, before being dissected to see what happened in their body during the various stages of these diseases. They were alive during these dissections. These experiments brought a new motive of fame and glory due to the possibility of discovering something new – at Rabaul on New Britain, a doctor deliberately injected POWs with malaria because he thought some people were immune to this disease and he would become a "very famous man".[708] Infamous more like. The Nazis also deliberately infected their prisoners (mostly Jews and Soviets) with diseases that were endemic in their Nazi-occupied countries such as typhus to find out how best to save their "superior" Aryan race from succumbing to these diseases. Clearly this "superiority" did not stretch to having hygienic conditions, without fleas, which would have prevented typhus in the first place.

Completely obsessed with creating a master race and expunging all those who did not fit the Nazi ideal, the Nazis conducted a series of experiments into fertility during WW2. The Third Reich had been sterilising "undesirables" in Germany for years but were keen to find new ways of doing this to people. In July 1942, Himmler led a meeting in Berlin where it was agreed to begin medical experiments on the Jews at Auschwitz, with fertility and sterilisation their priority. One such experiment involved fifteen girls aged 17 and 18. The girls were placed in an ultra-short-wave field and electrodes were placed on their abdomen and vulva; their bodies completed the electric circuit and electric rays were then focussed on their ovaries. The result was shocking in all ways – each of the girls' ovaries were burnt and destroyed inside their bodies. The burns were not restricted internally either – faulty doses led to serious burns on the girls' lower torsos and vaginas. One girl died as a result of her burns alone. But this was still not the end of the experiment; the Nazis wanted to see the lasting impact, and so the survivors were put to work at Auschwitz for a month before a review was done. The review showed that all the girls had gone through monumental physical change – they looked like old women. The Nazis had caused significant hormonal changes and forced menopause onto these youngsters. Nothing is known about if any of them survived the war, but we do know that several, at least, died of sepsis brought on by their wounds in the months afterwards.[709]

Some experiments had a learning element to them. Anatomical demonstrations and experimental operations were performed on Japanese prisoners and POWs with the motive of teaching Japanese medical students. Experimental surgeries were carried out, such as parts of people's brains or livers being cut out to see how long they could live without said part and intestines were sewn together to see what would happen. Surgery was also used to practice – limbs were amputated, and teeth, appendixes, testicles, and brains were removed. On Guadalcanal, two prisoners were chosen because they tried to escape – they were firstly shot in the feet to stop them moving – and then were dissected while still alive. All in front of a live studio audience. One student, rather than acknowledge the wickedness he had witnessed, wrote in his diary about how great it had all been: "For the first time I saw the internal organs of a human being. It was very informative."[710]

In Nazi camps, there were experiments with the aim of learning about bone, muscle, and nerve regeneration. Up to 20 young Polish women from Ravensbrück Camp were forced to undergo the experiment of removing muscle and bone between 1942 and 1943.[711] There were also bone transplant experiments; arms (including the shoulder blade, muscles, and nerves) and legs (at the hip) were removed from healthy inmates and then transplanted onto other victims. In the bone transplantation experiment, 10 "feeble minded" were selected and whole limbs were transplanted from one to another before the experimental subjects were then killed.[712] The doctor in charge later admitted that the experiment was little more than fancy torture as regeneration was "not checked at all".[713] He also said everything was done under anaesthetic, which obviously makes it completely OK.

Some experiments were tailored towards the war effort and involved war type injuries. In the Japanese camps, victims were burned with flamethrowers or blown up with the shrapnel deliberately left in their wounds so they developed gas gangrene (severe pain, swelling, odour, fever, discolouration of skin, and an altered mental state) which could be studied. In the Nazi camps, experiments revolved around finding ways to improve the survival rate of the German air force, navy, and army. Though I'm pretty sure not invading USSR in 1941 would have been a far more effective way of improving their survival rates.

In Dachau concentration camp, doctors carried out a series of high-altitude experiments for the *Luftwaffe* (German air force) which were ordered by the head of the SS, Heinrich Himmler. Dachau was the main camp for experiments – over 300 Polish priests died in medical experiments or by torture here.[714] Their brief was to find out what a German pilot might encounter when falling from a height of 68,000 feet.[715] With a parachute, I hasten to add. They weren't *that* stupid. There were four different types of experiment – two were investigating the experience when falling with a parachute open – one with oxygen and one without; the other two simulated a free fall before the parachute opened, again, one with and one without oxygen.[716] These took place between March and August 1942 and involved 200 randomly selected prisoners. Seventy-eight of them were killed because of these experiments. The subjects were locked into an air-tight round pod and the pressure was changed to represent the 68,900 feet height required. Continuous experiments above 34,600 feet resulted in death after about 30 minutes. The eight doctors involved (only two were actually convicted) insisted that these experiments were not akin to torture and even tried to convince the court at the post-war Nuremberg Trials that the experiments did not cause pain. A claim quickly shown to be complete and utter nonsense when the plentiful photographic evidence showing spasmodic convulsions and tortured expressions was presented.[717]

Freezing experiments were also done on behalf of the *Luftwaffe* and took place between August 1942 and May 1943 at Dachau. The motive was discovering how best to warm up pilots who had crashed into cold seas and treat those fighting in freezing temperatures. Between 280–300 prisoners were subjected to 360–400 different experiments following one of two methods – cold water freezing and dry freezing.[718] It would have been far easier to just give their troops winter clothing for fighting the USSR in winter, but – due to their arrogant belief that the June 1941 invasion (Operation Barbarossa) of the USSR would be completed well before temperatures plummeted – they were now forced to play catch up. The experiments killed between 80 and 90 people. They were placed in a wooden basin 2m by 2m which was raised off the floor by about 50cm. The basins were filled with water and ice was added until they reached 3°C. They were dressed either in a flying suit or naked (clearly some poor Nazi sods didn't get any uniform at all, let alone a winter coat). Obviously, the Nazis couldn't take the temperatures of the victims in a normal non-torturous manner, and these were measured rectally or through the stomach. Survivor Walter Neff described the experience as: "terrible"; he revealed how: "at 32°C the subject lost consciousness…Went down to 25°C and heart failure killed a person."[719] The worst experiment Walter witnessed involved two Russian officers being placed naked in these basins for five hours. It was so torturous that at hour three, one said: "Comrade tell that officer to shoot us."[720]

Sea water experiments were done for the *Kriegsmarine* (navy) and *Luftwaffe.* Their motive was to develop a method of making sea water drinkable, and the experiments were conducted, mostly on Gypsies, between July and September 1944 on forty-four subjects aged 16–49.[721] The victims were put into four groups – the first received no water at all; the second drank ordinary sea water; the third drank sea water processed using the Berka method – *Berkatit*; and the fourth group drank sea water with the salt removed. The first group, aka the "Thirst Group" also received no food because presumably the Nazis had NO IDEA what might happen if you give someone no food or water. The others had Sea Emergency Rations of one ounce a day of biscuits (not the *Nice* ones) and fats like butter or chocolate. Subject Karl Hoellenrainer explained in court on 27 June 1947, that after a couple of weeks of no food: "Then we began to drink sea water. I drank the worst kind that was yellowish. We drank two or three times a day and then in the evening we drank the yellow kind… After a few days the people became raving mad; they foamed at the mouth. The doctor from the *Luftwaffe* came with a cynical laugh and said, "Now it is time to make the liver punctures."[722] Why? Well, he wanted to see if the salt would come out of the liver. Karl also revealed how one man (who managed to sneak a drink of water which was not of the sea-sort) was punished by having his mouth sealed up with tape; another who refused to drink was forced via a long tube stuck down his throat. The Nuremberg Trials proved that the victims in this experiment suffered excruciating torture:

diarrhoea, convulsions, hallucinations, foaming at the mouth and eventually, in most cases, madness or death.

Some experiments were just plain cruel and came from a twisted and sadistic curiosity about human endurance. In the Japanese trials, some prisoners were put into huge spinning machines, called centrifuges (much like a kitchen blender but without the blade) and then spun to see how long they lived. Others were forced into sealed containers where the pressure would be increased to see how long it took for their eyes to fall out of their sockets. The Japanese also subjected prisoners to an obscene number of X-rays to see when it became lethal. Other experiments with electrocution, dehydration, being frozen and being boiled alive also took place.

The weirdest experiment was the Japanese investigation into who has the biggest penis. Yes, this really was a pressing concern for the Japanese in the midst of World War Two. At Moji on Kyushu Island, they diligently measured willies of prisoners from all nations. They even had a column on their data sheet to note down the erect size; however, the grower or shower debate was seemingly not of interest to the researchers, and none were recorded.

Why, and to what extent, has torture changed?

There has been considerable change in regard to the motives for torture. It began 7000 years ago to brutally punish people and gained traction as rulers realised torture created a climate of fear which in turn helped them keep control. This quest for power and dominance, spurred on by the paranoid dictatorial elements of the Roman Empire, then led to authorities discovering the use of torture to extract information. Namely, information about any opposition and plots against them. The Roman period also saw a transition from punishment to pastime as emperors used torture to entertain dinner guests as well as entertain the masses with "The Games" at the Colosseum. After antiquity, Europe went through the Dark Ages which actually weren't as bleak as the name suggests in terms of the development of courts of law and justice systems. What *was* pretty dark, however, was how prior knowledge of the effectiveness of torture to extract information was exploited to induce the motive of forcing confessions and eyewitness testimony. A motive which the Chinese had been using to justify their torture procedures since 200 BCE. The need to torture people as a punishment or to force them into confessing crimes faded away by the time of the Industrial Age of the 18th century due to developments in laws, rights of prisoners, prisons, education, police, and use of evidence (science). Which was pretty handy considering torture had been made illegal across most of Europe by this point. But the advent of science wasn't good news for everyone as this newly founded scientific curiosity accidentally led to the most recent motive for torture – experimentation.

There are two motives which refuse to quit: extracting information and religion. To this day, the need for authorities and governments to discover opposition and plots is employed to justify their flouting of international law and use torture. Religion as a motive for torture has been around since antiquity and began with the Assyrians torturing the Jews in the 2nd century BCE and has most recently been seen in use against the Jews in the twentieth century via the Nazis. Either tortured as a punishment for their religious choice, or tortured into recanting their beliefs, this has been the longest-running motive.

The methods used have seen considerable change. This change began with the ancient Greeks thanks to the enthusiasm of a few sickos which led to new devices such as the Brazen Bull and Iron Maiden being invented. The Greeks moved methods on from those which caused a slow and painful death (burning, boiling, stoning, the wheel, impaling, and dropping from a great height) to methods that caused slow and painful revelations (such as the Rack) due to approval from philosophers who praised the virtues of torture for extracting information. Advancements in engineering and the rise of paranoid dictators led to new torture devices such as the Pulley coming along in the Roman Era. Religion then inspired more twisted methods as the Spanish inquisitors not only tried to force confessions, recantations, and conversions – they also wanted to punish people for the incorrect choice they had made of wanting to read the Bible in their own language rather than Latin.

The rise of science in the 19th century caused the most significant change to torture methods. The new scientific discipline of psychology was immediately put to work in the field of torture, meaning sleep deprivation, food deprivation, sensory deprivation, sexual threats, threats to family, use of scary dogs, and near-death experiences became the go-to methods of the 20th century. From 1950–62, the CIA spent $1 billion on secret experiments in human consciousness,[723] which led to the first breakthrough in torture since the Spanish Inquisition – they discovered hands-off torture with a psychological twist was more difficult to endure than physical pain. They experimented with hallucinogenic drugs (well, that was their excuse anyway), electric shocks, and sensory deprivation. These methods were published in the CIA's *Kubark Counterintelligence Interrogation Manual* in 1963. Psychological torture became part of US Foreign policy as they went off and practised with real victims in Asia, Latin America, and Central America between the 1960s and1990s. They were happy chappies because psychological torture meant no external wounds. No external wounds meant deniability. Which was much needed since they had agreed to follow the international laws against torture in 1948.

The need to be deniable led to the proxy method used by America from the 1970s until the modern day. It was now a private function that was outsourced by the secret service. The need for torture to be invisible led to psychological and electric shock torture becoming favoured methods from the 20th century onwards. Amnesty International report that the sale of electric shock batons is still big business.[724]

The longest-running methods have been the Rack and the Pulley. These guys became the popular kids at torture school during antiquity and retained this status for around 2000 years until the 19th century. There was no need to develop new methods as these two were incredibly effective in getting the desired result (information or a confession) without necessarily killing the person. After all, it's much easier to charge someone with a crime when they're alive to attend the court hearing.

According to victims, observers, and science, the worst method of torture is the psychological sort. A view conveniently not shared by those most responsible. American lawyers for the government advised in 2002 and 2003 that psychological torture was baloney unless it resulted in significant harm for a prolonged period of time. There was no recognition of harm to a person's psyche or mental health. Observers of the psychological torture of sensory deprivation disagree and say that this was, actually, the cruellest method; a British journalist who saw it taking place in Northern Ireland described how it was: "the worst form of torture… provokes more anxiety… leaves no visible scars and therefore, is harder to prove, and produces longer lasting effects."[725] Scientific research also points to this method as being the most damaging. For example, a team of Danish doctors studied 200 victims of this torture and found 57 of the 76 who had been isolated for up to fourteen days still had mental issues; while out of the 101 people who had been blindfolded, 73 were left with mental issues.[726]

The Spanish Inquisitors and the CIA are the worst in terms of longevity and number of victims but perhaps those who did it for fun – the Roman emperors and the Japanese and Nazi doctors – should also share this crown. The worst period for torture has to be the 20th century due to the hundreds of thousands tortured during WW2, the Vietnam War, and in Latin America. Overall, America should be judged the worst due to their huge influence and how they spread psychological torture methods around the world. Dictatorships in Asia and Latin America became trained in the practice, and even though they may not be directly behind it, American training programmes have also spread to the third world. Amnesty International have been tracing torturers for the last 40 years and they are basically following the CIA's schedule.[727]

While modern torture is now largely the remit of secret services this does not make it any more acceptable. At the end of the day, the torturers have decided that THEIR cause is more important than a person's human rights. Just as Elizabeth I deemed it necessary to overrule the Magna Carta to protect her position, modern governments deem their existence and future safety important enough to overrule the Geneva Convention of Human Rights. Nothing has really changed except the methods. At whatever point in time you look at the use of torture, it always boils down to the same thing: power. Whether that be the maintenance of, increasing of, forced acceptance of, or show of, it still revolves around that basic concept. Humanity hasn't changed in thousands of years. We just got better at hiding our depravity.

How to get away with torture (American style)

1. **Hide your victims.** The CIA was able to deny torture because in some cases the prisoners never existed. They

were known as "ghost prisoners" because they were never registered. Perhaps learning from the Nuremberg Trials, where the Nazis were held accountable for 6 million Jewish deaths due to their meticulous record keeping, the CIA simply didn't bother. No body, no proof, no crime. At Abu Gharib in Iraq, some people detained by the CIA were never registered as being there and then were moved around so as not to be noticed by the Red Cross or other observers. Incidentally, this wasn't a secret from everyone – Secretary Rumsfeld gave authorisation for the whole thing.[728]

2. **Lead all the investigations into your wrongdoings.** When the US Army (who are suddenly detectives now) investigated the CIA ghost prisoners, they found just eight examples. Yet the guy who oversaw the investigation, General Paul J. Kern, later testified that the number was "perhaps up to 100".[729] Perhaps even more – considering he already lied once for the original report, I don't think we can really trust *anything* he's saying. Similarly, the 1996 report by the Intelligence Oversight Board (IOB) managed to evade all the issues it was meant to investigate and was conveniently unable to find evidence of *intentional* participation[730] (UK government report of 2021 into racism finding zero racism ring a bell?).

3. **Get good lawyers and reinterpret the law**. America got clever with semantics and convinced themselves and others that they weren't breaking the law. Justice Department attorney, John Yoo, wrote to President Bush on 9 January 2002, explaining how they could evade the Geneva Conventions completely. He advised that the protections afforded by the Geneva Convention did not apply to al-Qaeda because they were a violent political group rather than a nation, and they should not be

considered POWs because of the "novel nature of this conflict".[731] Like, what the hell? It's a war. Therefore, the captured enemies are POWs. The only thing novel about the US invasion of Afghanistan was the inexplicable link to Afghanistan from the 9/11 attackers. Secondly, lawyers advised in August 2002 and March 2003 that the Americans could argue they were not breaking the law because their primary goal was not to torture – it was to gain information. Then the American government decided that "moderate or temporary pain" didn't count as torture. The level of pain they plucked from the air to define torture must be equivalent to "organ failure… or even death."[732] Essentially meaning you gotta commit a worse crime (murder) for the first crime (torture) to count as a crime. Criminal.

4. **Remove POW status of your intended victims.** In January 2002, the White House applied the Geneva Conventions to the war itself but stripped the Taliban and al-Qaeda of POW status. In the internal memos of the American Justice Department, they agreed that the rights afforded POWS and citizens of the world in the Geneva Conventions were not applicable to Afghans.[733]

5. **Get medical experts to state your torture methods do no harm.** Post the 9/11 attacks, waterboarding was declared legal by the Department of Justice and CIA lawyers because, as Bush explains: "medical experts assured the CIA that it did no lasting harm."[734] While agreeing "no doubt the procedure was tough", President Bush, the CIA, and the American justice system did not see waterboarding as torture. Something which the dictionary, and the victims, wholeheartedly disagree with.

6. **Bully other countries.** Bush pushed for bilateral immunity and threatened to cut off aid to any country

which did not promise to give America immunity from International Criminal Court prosecutions. "Status of forces" agreements were made with foreign governments, which gave American personnel and anyone they hired to do their dirty work immunity from prosecution.[735]

7. **Deception.** Congress and the American public were deliberately kept in the dark. For example, extraordinary rendition was authorised by President Bush in a secret (at the time) directive.[736] Being blatantly illegal would have made it hard to be approved by Congress. The 1996 IOB report confirmed that the CIA had operated a large group of well-paid torturers and then lied about their human rights abuses when reporting back to Congress.[737]

8. **Deny. Deny. Deny.** Their proxy torture and porky-pie-policy meant the CIA could not be proven to be breaking international or American laws. Seemingly if you *say* you haven't done it then you're not breaking the law. Innocent until proven… oh… wait… there's no trial either. While America was busy capturing suspects and transporting them elsewhere to be tortured post 9/11, Secretary of State Condoleezza Rice insisted that the United States: "does not transport, and has not transported, detainees from one country to another for the purpose of interrogation using torture."[738] Rice try, Condoleezza, but unfortunately for her, history is not so good at lying, and now, 20 years later, there is a whole host of evidence from survivors, witnesses, perpetrators, as well as photos of everything she insisted *wasn't* happening, happening.

9. **Give legal protection to those responsible.** Individuals like Jenifer Harbury have attempted to bring those responsible to justice by prosecuting them through the civil court. Jenifer's husband Everardo was tortured and killed by the CIA while the American government denied

this was happening (step 8) and hid the documents (step 7) which proved he had been tortured and killed. Civil lawsuits such as hers, which were brought against American officers and CIA staff, were easily shut down with government red tape, which ultimately gave those responsible protection from the law. In Afghanistan and Iraq, the CIA agreed to torture people personally so long as they were protected by the Bush administration. Which it did.

Elizabeth I, Queen of Propaganda

Personal life		Political life
Elizabeth is born at Greenwich Palace to parents Henry VIII and Anne Boleyn.	**1533**	
Elizabeth's dad has her mum beheaded	**1536**	
Her dad, King Henry VIII, dies	**1547**	Elizabeth's 9-year-old brother becomes King Edward VI
Orphan Elizbeth goes to live with her step mum Catherine Parr and Catherine's new husband Thomas Seymour.	**1547–48**	Seymour tries it on with Elizabeth numerous times and makes a play for her hand in marriage
Elizabeth is sent away from her step-parents' house for a period of seclusion	**1548**	
	1549	Seymour is executed on 33 counts of treason

Personal life		Political life
Elizabeth's best friend – Robert Dudley – marries Amy Robsart	**1550**	
Her brother, King Edward VI dies	**1553**	Her sister becomes Queen Mary I
Elizabeth is imprisoned in the Tower of London for two months.	**1554**	Wyatt rebellion. Elizabeth is accused of being involved in the plot to depose Mary I
Her sister, Queen Mary I dies Dudley is made *Master of the Horse* (a role which means he gets to touch her a lot)	**1558**	Elizabeth becomes Queen of England on November 17th at the age of 25.
Spanish King Phillip II proposes marrying Elizabeth	**1558–59**	Elizabeth cautiously rejects the offer of marrying her dead sister's powerful husband.
King Eric XIV of Sweden proposes to her	**1558**	She officially rejects the marriage proposal in 1560
Rumours begin circulating that Elizabeth is in love with Robert Dudley.	**1559**	Elizabeth enacts *The Middle Way* (a mix of Protestantism and Catholicism)

Personal life		Political life
Dudley's wife Amy is found dead at the bottom of the stairs at their home	**1560**	Elizabeth orders all paintings must show her in a positive light – beautiful, divine, and pure
	1560s	Elizabeth helps establish the African slave trade
A baby born at Hampton Court Palace was given away (see 1587)	**1561**	
Elizabeth nearly dies from smallpox and make Dudley Protector of the Realm	**1562**	
	1563	Statute of Artificers limits people's wages
Marriage to Archduke Charles considered	**1567**	
Elizabeth's Catholic cousin, Mary Queen of Scots, flees Scotland and arrives in England	**1568**	Elizabeth imprisons Mary and then steals 400,000 gold coins from the Spanish
	1569	Rebellion of the Northern Earls thwarted (plot to depose Elizabeth and replace her with Mary)

Personal life		Political life
Elizabeth declares her wish to marry, Henri, Duke of Anjou is suggested	**1570**	Pope Pius V excommunicates Elizabeth and orders English Catholics not to obey her
Henri decided he didn't want to marry Elizabeth anymore	**1571**	The Ridolfi Plot thwarted (Spanish army to overthrow Elizabeth and replace her with Mary)
	1572	Elizabeth rules actors will be punished as beggars
	1576	First English theatre opens
	1577–80	Elizabeth gives money for Francis Drake's circumnavigation of the globe and knights him
Dudley secretly marries Elizabeth's cousin: Lettice Knollys	**1578**	
Elizabeth publicly announces she intends to marry Francis of Anjou.	**1579**	
	1580	The Pope announces killing Elizabeth is not a sin

Personal life		Political life
Elizabeth pulls out of engagement to Francis	**1581**	
	1582	Duke de Guise Plot on Elizabeth's life is thwarted
	1583	The Throckmorton Plot is thwarted (to replace Elizabeth with Mary using Spanish support)
	1584	Walter Raleigh establishes Virginia – a colony in North America, named in honour of Virgin Queen
	1585	English army sent to help Dutch fight the Spanish. Philip II begins planning invasion of England
	1586	The Babington Plot is thwarted (assassinate Elizabeth I and put Mary on the throne) Nine new warships are built for English navy

Personal life		Political life
A man turns up claiming to be the son of Dudley and Elizabeth. Robert Devereux becomes Elizabeth's new favourite and is appointed *Master of the Horse*	**1587**	Execution of Mary, Queen of Scots Francis Drake launches a surprise attack on the Spanish fleet at Cadiz
Robert Dudley dies	**1588**	Spanish Armada (invasion of England) fails
	1589	Elizabeth launches counter-armada against Spain
Elizabeth sends her favourite, Devereux to lead the forces in Ireland.	**1594**	Elizabeth sends 55,000 men to quell a rebellion in Ireland. Succeeds in 1603 but costs £2 million
	1596	Second Spanish Armada fails
	1597	Third Spanish Armada fails
	1598	Elizabeth enacts the Poor Law
	1599	Globe Theatre opens

Personal life		Political life
Robert Deveraux and Elizabeth fall out after he makes peace with the Irish behind her back and then bursts into her bedroom and catches her without her wig and make up	**1601**	Robert Deveraux is banned from court and plans a rebellion against Elizabeth. He is discovered and executed
Elizabeth dies of old age (aged 69) on March 24th. She ruled England for 44 ½ years	**1603**	

Ah, the Virgin Queen! What a noble woman she was.

Elizabeth is another monarch who is known more commonly by a moniker than her regnal number – she is known as the Virgin Queen. A status which, in 1559, Elizabeth publicly declared: "And to me it shall be a Full satisfaction…., it be ingraven upon my Marble Tomb, "Here lieth Elizabeth, which Reigned a Virgin, and died a Virgin."[739] Well, Elizabeth, I'm afraid that this engraving is not fully satisfactory as evidence for the rest of us…

Was the Virgin Queen *really* a virgin?

Highly unlikely.

She had several relationships, at least one baby, and refused a post-mortem because it would have revealed her lies. History textbooks like to focus on Elizabeth's suitors as an enquiry for students to evaluate which man would have been best matched for her. While there may be some ambiguous reference to Robert Dudley as her "favourite" – there is no enquiry into her dealings with each man, or how she played them like a fiddle, because this goes against the long-established view that she was an honourable Virgin Queen.

Hilariously, while in the modern age Elizabeth's virginity is accepted, during her time in the 16th century, no one actually believed her! Probably due to all the blatant relationships she was having. Her first attachment was with an entirely unsuitable suitor. After the death of her father, Elizabeth went to live with wifey number six, Catherine Parr and her new husband – Thomas Seymour. Catherine was below Parr on the standard time for grieving for a dead spouse and married Seymour in April 1547, just three months after Henry VIII died from a rotten leg. From Elizabeth's perspective, Seymour was her half-uncle and stepfather. Also, from Elizabeth's perspective, he was rather fit. He was tall with an athletic frame and by all accounts he had an exceptionally fine beard. We have it on record and confirmed from three people (including Elizabeth herself) that inappropriate things were going on with Seymour. Things like him entering her room to say good morning and hitting her on the "buttocks familiarly,"[740] you know, as any normal stepfather would do. On another occasion he entered her room with nothing on his bottom half bar his bottom. Catherine was not oblivious to what was going on and bizarrely there's even two occasions where she acts as his wingman. The first time, Catherine joined him in Elizabeth's bedchamber to "tickle" the girl and the second time Catherine held Elizabeth down in the garden while Seymour cut her dress into a hundred pieces. But one thing Catherine did make clear was that it was only OK to sexually harass her stepdaughter in her presence. After catching the pair kissing and hugging in a room on their own – Catherine sent Elizabeth away.

Catherine died on 7 September 1548, and left all that she had to Seymour. He seemingly took this to mean Elizabeth as well and started making enquiries about how to Seymour of her in the form of a marriage. When asked by the Privy Council if she would marry him, Elizabeth said: "When that comes to pass, I will do as God shall put in my mind." [741] While she might have preferred to say, "GOOD GOD NO", this was likely the only polite way she could express her refusal. Interestingly, she did not take the opportunity to state her intention of remaining a virgin as a way of explaining her refusal. That excuse came later. Seymour never came again.

Seymour was arrested on 17 January 1549, and was charged with 33 charges of treason – two of which concerned his dalliances and future plans with Elizabeth (charges 19 and 20).[742] It is possible that Elizabeth was not a willing party to these encounters, and she was sexually abused by Seymour; however, she never accused him of such a thing – even when he had been arrested and she was directly questioned as part of the process of convicting him.[743] Meanwhile others in her household, including Elizabeth's Lady-in-Waiting (Kat Ashley) really let the Kat out the bag by confirming a relationship of sorts existed between the two and that Seymour and Elizabeth had been attracted to each other.[744] Seymour was executed on 20 March 1549. When informed of his death, Elizabeth was still rather positive about his charm: "This day died a man of much wit, but very little judgement."[745] None of this evidence suggests Elizabeth was a victim of sexual abuse, but Elizabeth's refusal to confess what had *really* happened[746] does imply there was something to hide.

Her second relationship was with her childhood friend Robert Dudley. Although many at the time said it would never work (for starters he was already married to Amy Robsart), Elizabeth didn't let this stand in her way, and she made sure he was always by her side with the job of "Master of the Horse". While this may seem like the tail end of all royal jobs, it actually made him the mane man as he got to lift her on and off her horse (i.e., touch her a lot).

In 1559 it was noted by other courtiers that Elizabeth was in love, and Dudley was frequently invited into her bedchamber (I guess that's where she kept her horses). Just one year after their connection had been noted, in 1560, Dudley's wife was found dead at the bottom of her stairs at home. It was ruled to be "a misfortune". But it was even more a "misfortune" for Dudley as Elizabeth *still* refused to marry him. It's likely she was up for it but there was too much opposition to the relationship from her councillors due to the fact Dudley did not have enough prestige and titles to marry a queen. Sir Robert Dudley was only minor gentry, and you have to be of Sir-ious standing to marry a queen. Of course, she didn't tell him this straight away. Instead, six months after his wife died, Dudley was given an apartment with rooms adjoining Elizabeth's which meant they could go back and forth without anyone seeing. Misfortune had become his fortune. And I'm sure this whole secret back-and-forth malarky would have worked perfectly if only not *everyone* knew he had moved in. Even her ladies of the chamber said that the queen: "shows a liking for him more markedly than is consistent with her reputation and dignity."[747] Another one of her ladies (Bess of Hardwick) was less subtle when describing the sort of things Elizabeth got up to. Over the next 20 years (after Dudley), Bess reckoned Elizabeth also had sexual encounters with Sir Christopher Hatton, the French envoy Simier, and Francis, Duke of Anjou.[748] A claim which really Bess-ed up Elizabeth's supposed virginal status.

Her time with Seymour and Dudley did nothing to help her virgin claims. Elizabeth had been told to reign it in or marry by no less than everyone else alive. The English nobility, the foreign nobility, foreign monarchs, English priests, and her own loyal group of ladies had all recommended she change her way of life, proving she held no virtue of virginity or chasteness that we now believe her to have had. In short, her claims are simply virgin on the ridiculous. People of the 16th century believed a lot of weird things (such as rubbing a shaved chicken's bottom on your skin would cure the plague) but abstinence for the sake of it wasn't one of them. In Tudor times it was believed that sexual activity was necessary for the wellbeing of men AND women. Being a virgin was literally bad for your health, (I wonder how often doctors used this as their diagnosis to get someone into bed?!) This didn't mean being the village bike was your aim in life; and so a different word was used to instruct girls' behaviour so there was no confusion for their little lady brains. Girls were meant to be *chaste*. Basically, keep your legs shut long enough to get married but make sure you do get married else you'll die from lack of sex. "Chastity was the equivalent of virtue."[749] Virginity wasn't.

The existence of relationships doesn't, of course, prove Elizabeth engaged in a bit of *nug-a-nug* (1505 term for sex) but the appearance of her and Dudley's secret love child sure does. There are two times Elizabeth is believed to have been pregnant. While the first occasion is admittedly a bit of a push (!) for the imagination – the second time is far more believable, and the child was reported at the time as being hers.

The first maybe-baby dates from spring/summer 1548, aka the Seymour times. Elizabeth had been sent away from her step-parents' house but as soon as she arrived at her new dwelling, she went into seclusion. Gossip started straight away that her seclusion was not down to illness (as she and her ladies claimed) but rather due to Elizabeth being with child. A story from a local midwife kept the gossip juices flowing; she claimed she had been blindfolded and brought to assist a "very fair young lady" who was in labour while staying "in a great house".[750] She said a baby had been born and then killed. There's no good reason to kill a baby but even less so in the 16th century with infant mortality as high as it was. Therefore, they must have needed to kill the baby for a bigger reason than it just being born out of wedlock. Being born to the unmarried sister of the king with your father being the king's uncle should do it.

The second occasion dates from around 1560 aka friends with benefits time with Dudley. In 1587, 27-year-old Arthur Dudley appeared on the scene and presented himself as Elizabeth and Dudley's son. His story is convincing. Firstly, his age matched to the time when Elizabeth was in seclusion with a "swelling illness" (must try this excuse when I put on a few pounds at Christmas). At least on this occasion she came up with a *slightly* better cover story than the mysterious nine-month illness of 1548.

Secondly, Arthur was able to name a key person in the Elizabethan court who would not have been widely known; a man named Robert Southern. Southern had raised Arthur after being summoned to Hampton Court in 1561 and told he had to take the child. He was informed that a lady at court had had the baby and it would bring "great shame on all the company"[751] if it were to be found out who she was. Southern revealed this story to Arthur when he was dying in 1585, and when Arthur pressured him about who his parents were, Southern admitted they were Elizabeth and Dudley. He had nothing to gain on his deathbed with these admissions and explained he wanted to clear his conscience by being honest.

Thirdly, and probably the best evidence of all, Dudley confirmed that the boy was his. This was after meeting him for the first time at Greenwich Palace in 1587.[752] Perhaps it could have been his son with another lady at court, but if this were the case, Dudley had nothing to lose in 1587 by admitting who the mother was. If anything, it would have helped Elizabeth's reputation if he *had* named another woman. After his meeting with Daddy Dudley, and perhaps sensing the animosity from Elizabeth, Arthur fled England for Spain. The Spanish took him in, interrogated him and found him to have: "the air of a noble" but "he is thought to be a spy".[753] They weren't sure what to do with him and so kept him locked up for a couple of years before he simply disappears from all records, which was incredibly fortunate for Elizabeth. Ultimately, what is most revealing about this whole soap opera drama was the readiness of Dudley to agree that Arthur was Elizabeth's son. Had he forgotten that Elizabeth was a virgin?!

Uncertainty wasn't just restricted to Dudley. Elizabeth's local government law-enforcers were in such doubt about whether she was a shagger or a blagger that in 1560–61, the Earl of Oxford needed to write to William Cecil (Elizabeth's main advisor) to ask him if he should punish a man who was claiming the queen had a bun in the oven. He needed to ask because he was genuinely unsure if the man's claim was right or wrong! So much for the Virgin Queen. The religious crowd, possibly based on their own debased experiences, were also doubtful of her virginity. Sir Henry Sidney said to the Spanish ambassador de Quadra in January 1561: "Even preachers in the pulpits spoke of it, not sparing even the honour of the queen."[754]

Propaganda is all there is to support Elizabeth's claim of being a virgin. Well… that and her saying it. The idea of her being a devoted virgin is more of a cult than a reality. While the repected historian David Starkey believes her protestations of virtue were exposed as a "sham"[755] by 1549; Elizabeth clearly felt there was still enough wool to pull over people's eyes on the matter (wool did make up 90% of England's trade so she's not wrong there). And so, from the mid-1560s onwards (after having a baby and all that) the wool was spun, and the Virgin Cult propaganda began. Depictions of Elizabeth were instructed to show her like a goddess so that people associated her with being divine and pure. She was always dripping with pearls because they symbolised chastity (at least *something* about her did). In plays and pageants, she was represented as the most famous virgin of them all – the Virgin Mary (and I mean that one was pretty suspicious too, right?). All this propaganda combined with Elizabeth remaining unmarried soon warped people's brains into believing she really was a virgin. And with the average life expectancy at only 30, it didn't take long for people to die and take their memories of the babies and her "riding below the crupper" (1578 term for sex) with them.

Elizabeth's refusal to allow a post-mortem is a clear sign that things downstairs were not as virginal as she claimed. The Virgin Queen left specific instructions that she was *not* to be disembowelled and embalmed as kings and queens before her because a post-mortem examination would have raised further questions (read: answers) about her virginity. It would have revealed her reproductive organs, and they were knowledgeable enough to know what they should find – it would have been clear if she had carried a baby. If she were a virgin, this would have been the perfect time to get evidence; she had maintained she was a virgin all her life and now in death she was able to prove it. But she didn't. Because all it would have proved was that she was a liar. By refusing to allow the queen's corpse to be opened and embalmed, the ladies of her bedchamber were being loyal to the Virgin cult. They allowed her to remain "Regina intacta"[756] because she was no longer Vagina intacta.

Virgin or not, she chose to remain unmarried because she was so duty bound to England. That's very noble surely?

Elizabeth stated at the age of eight that she would never marry. I stated at the age of eight that I was going to be a clown and join the circus. My point is you say a lot of crap when you're eight, and Elizabeth's statement should not be used as evidence that she made a noble choice and stuck to it. The truth is she used the idea of marriage to get what she wanted from parliament – she would promise them marriage was "just around the corner" to get whatever money or agreement she needed at the time. And it wasn't just her own people she dangled a potential wedding in front of, she also successfully bluffed her way through most of the bachelors of Europe. She exploited the fact that everyone assumed she would marry at some point; she was a woman after all – what else was she going to do with her life? And so, the late 1550s was all about marrying the Spanish king; the 1560s saw her "consider" proposals from Scotland, Austria, and Sweden; and the 1570s were consumed with thinking about her French fancies. By the 1580s she was past her Best Before End date and the offers dried up much like her quaint (1598 term for lady bits).[757]

But then there's the actual shocking truth of the matter – she tried to get married twice. That's right… twice! So much for that codswallop in 1588 where she stated: "I have already joined myself in marriage to a husband, namely the kingdom of England."[758] This fabricated explanation of her being *too* devoted to England to marry is what is taught in schools to nice and tidily explains why she didn't marry (even though she tried to… twice). There is no mention of her two attempts to marry in the textbooks because this would prove that her "devotion" was, in fact, nonsense. Keen to promote this poppycock, Elizabeth wore her coronation ring on her wedding finger – she liked it, so she put a ring on it hundreds of years before Beyoncé had the idea. In fact, she was *soooo* committed to marrying herself to England her finger skin grew around the ring, meaning it had to be filed off in her later years.[759] The ring literally became part of her, such was her devotion. Gross. Most of us can't even wait long enough for our skin to form a scab before we pick it off, let alone be patient enough for our skin and jewellery to turn into a "2 become 1" Spice Girls tribute. Respect for that if nothing else.

At the grand old age of 37, and while her ring and finger were still two separate entities, Elizabeth declared that she was: "determined to marry."[760] Obviously, this sensible statement from a mature woman has been overlooked by historians in favour of what her eight-year-old self once said. After all, a middle-aged woman getting married is nowhere near as exciting as a woman so traumatised by her childhood experiences that she chose to remain unhitched.

Following this declaration in 1570, a match with the French king's younger brother was swiftly proposed. Henri, Duke of Anjou, was deemed suitable because it would secure an alliance between France and England and mean they could put up a united front against the almighty Catholic Spain. There was just one teeny-weeny little problem… Henri was a teenage transvestite, probably a bisexual and worst of all… he was still a bit Catholic. On top of this, he, like everyone else in Europe, had heard the tales of Elizabeth's sexual encounters: "So much has he heard against her honour… that he considers he should be utterly dishonoured and lose all the reputation he has acquired if he was to marry Elizabeth."[761] What "reputation" he's talking about is anyone's guess considering the cross-dressing orgy-filled stories that were circulating about *him* but still. Harsh. Negotiations continued throughout the year because, let's be honest, love had nothing to do with royal marriages, let alone actually liking the person. However, by October 1571, Henri had changed his mind and was refusing to marry her under any circumstances. He was too committed to remaining a Catholic and wanted to avoid marriage to a *putain publique* (translation = public whore – his words, not mine). And so, the truth of her not marrying is not because of some trauma or her deep commitment to England. It's because the first man she agreed to turned her down. Savage.

Fast forward seven years and a French marriage was back on the table, but this time with a different brother of the French king – Francis. Although he was still young – a mere 24 years compared to her 43, at least he wasn't a teenager, or a Catholic, and he didn't dress in female clothes – so things looked promising. The two began dating in 1579, although being royal this took the form of sending ambassadors on their behalf much like the school playground version of "my friend likes you". In summer 1579, the two met in person and Elizabeth bestowed him with a pet name; he was her "frog".[762] It hadn't become a racist slur yet (give it two hundred years) and so this was seen as *a nice thing* and a sign of their love. In another clear sign she was serious, on 20 November 1579, Elizabeth instructed her privy councillors to draw up a draft marriage treaty for the two of them – who gets to wear the crown on Tuesdays and other important stuff like that.

On November 22nd, when everyone was at Whitehall to celebrate Accession Day, Elizabeth publicly declared her plan to marry. She then kissed him on the mouth and gave him her ring[763] (still not part of her finger yet, so this was possible). A year or so passed and then suddenly Elizabeth changed her mind. She cited it was due to opposition from her councillors, but the fact that it was acceptable for monarchs to ignore conciliar advice regarding marriage (e.g., like her sister and her father) suggests this was a weak excuse. It's more likely that she cancelled the wedding because by 1581 she was past childbearing age. Not only would the failure to produce children remind everyone how old she was, but it would also have caused problems with who succeeded her because the French Royal family would now have a claim. She had played her hand well and just as long as she needed to.

Ultimately, for Elizabeth to say she remained unmarried to do good by her country is total twaddle. What's even worse is that many in the modern day have fallen for this line! Look at how her decision is described in an article by *The Independent*: "The choice she made was courageous and revolutionary, and, in the long run, the right one for England."[764] Let's not forget the choice she ACTUALLY made in 1570 and 1579 was to get married. And also, let's not forget the "short run" was not such a great time seeing how an unmarried queen heightened people's fears about England's future, especially when the queen is the last of a dynasty – a fear which was made worse by Elizabeth continually refusing to name a successor. Elizabeth had no immediate family left, and so her female cousins Mary (as in Queen of Scots) and the Grey girls (the two who didn't already have a go at being queen and lose their heads Lady Jane Grey style) and their offspring were the next in line. The issue with the cousins was that Mary was part Scottish, part French, and a big fat Catholic. Literally the three things the English hated the most in the 16th century. The Grey girls, while being Protestant, were further down the succession line than Mary and so if they did claim the throne, war against France and Scotland was likely. This is certainly not good in the long run or the short run for little ol' England. Elizabeth's attitude also ran counter to society expectations because "women who did not submit to male authority were a potential source of disorder."[765]

It is possible Elizabeth was traumatised into not wanting to marry due to the terrible outcomes she had witnessed as a child. Marriage, in her eyes, led to divorce, death, war and/or alienation. It is also possible that she'd rather commit herself to her country rather than a man. But it is now clear that these two things were more of a convenient excuse than a real justification. She was willing to marry. Marry anyone it seems. She agreed to marry a teenage French Catholic, for goodness' sake! A marriage that would have likely ended with divorce, death, war, *and* alienation. Elizabeth did not remain unmarried for the best of the country; it was for her own benefit. Nothing wrong with that, all power to her, but nowadays, where women are allowed to make decisions like this without judgement, there's no need to continue with an explanation that isn't true.

Isn't her reign known as the Golden Age?

It is true that this period is known as the Golden Age. It is false to think this was all thanks to Elizabeth. The only reason it's known as "A Golden Age" is because the Victorians idealised the Elizabethan era (probably due to all the long dresses and hidden ankles) and then after that, it's like no one bothered to check. History textbooks teach children that this era was Golden due to cultural developments in the arts and the improvement in the standard of living. The public are fed the same line, such as this from the *Encyclopaedia Britannica*: "The long reign of Elizabeth I, 1558–1603, was England's Golden Age... 'Merry England', in love with life, expressed itself in music and literature, in architecture and in adventurous seafaring."[766] I mean come on, guys, at least *try* to seem impartial!

"*Merry England*" they say, and yes, I'm sure it felt very merry for those at the top of the social scale. It's surprisingly easy to be merry with a belly full of wine and pockets full of coins. Most people would not have been *in love with life* because they were more preoccupied with not fainting from starvation and then falling down a well while trying to fetch their water (which would inevitably give them cholera). Elizabethan England, for most people, was all about poverty, unemployment, and 400% inflation[767] (prices not wages of course). Despite this glaring negative, most textbooks will try to convince you that the lower classes were loving life because this era saw the beginnings of government intervention for the poor such as the 1563 *Statute of Artificers*. This fixed wages for the common people. Sounds great on paper, but we're not talking about a minimum wage here – this act fixed a MAXIMUM wage which nicely ensured that no one at Pleb level was getting a pay rise. Ever. And don't go thinking that maybe she and her advisors lacked understanding of economic factors such as inflation because they didn't. Alongside fixing maximum wages, she made sure to raise all the rents on her land… in line with inflation. So, while her income increased by 50%, her legislation held down wages and caused a growth of poverty and beggars.

So, what did *Merry England* do to help those most in need? Well, mostly flogged them, burnt them on the ear, or hanged them. The act of 1572 helpfully gave a limit on how many times a person was allowed to be visibly impoverished: "if they were caught begging three times they were to be executed;"[768] and records from various English law courts show that this punishment was actually applied. Yet for some strange reason, the threat of death did not stop people being poor. So, in 1576 an act was passed that would at least remove the stinking paupers from the streets (the rich were finding their existence rather off-putting). The 1576 act required two Houses of Correction to be built in each county where poor people could be sent. Extracts from Norwich city records show what life was like in these houses: "The Prisoners shall work for their meat and drink for at least 21 days. They shall work 15 hours a day in the summer and 14 hours in the winter…" Note their wording – "prisoners" – Elizabeth had made it a crime to be poor.

Between 1594 and 1597 *Merry England* suffered a socio-economic crisis. There were four failed harvests, consistent bad weather, frequent outbreaks of the plague, and high taxes so she could fund a military campaign against the Spanish in the 1580s and also to control Ireland in the 1590s (spoiler alert… it wasn't controlled). All of this led to food becoming 75% more expensive. 75%!! These days there's uproar when they add a penny to a pint – can you imagine if things suddenly nearly doubled in price! Agricultural workers (pretty much everyone) saw their wages go down as the weather stalled job opportunities – no harvests = no jobs. Many families couldn't afford food and resorted to begging but lots would have starved to death. More needed to be done and it was here, right at the end of her reign that she enacted the 1597 Poor Law Act. It set into law a much-needed distinction between those who were too young, old, or ill to work, and those who were unwilling. And yes, this is better than lumping an orphaned child in with a lazy sod, but it still didn't lead to the poor being able to *love life* because the causes of poverty were not solved; the law only helped with the consequences. Her short-term fix made her look good; the fact that poverty continued to rise didn't matter to her or her sycophantic fans as they now had a piece of legislation that showed she *tried*. And while I agree there's not much a monarch can do to help the weather, they can make plans to store grain for times of starvation. They can set limits on the price of essential goods, and they can set a minimum wage. Clearly *Merry England* was not intended for everyone.

One thing the *Encyclopaedia Britannica* did get right is the flourishing theatre, music, and literature. It really was a Golden Age for culture. But don't get too excited. Theatre flourished *in spite* of Elizabeth and her government not *because* of them. In truth, the authorities were fearful of the theatre, and they tried to restrict plays in the early days of her reign for fear it might give the crowd ideas. Dangerous ideas such as "life's not fair" and "why not kill the upper classes?" In 1572, Elizabeth even went as far as to rule actors should be punished as vagrants, which really beggars' belief.

The first theatre in England since the Roman times was opened in 1576 in Shoreditch and they must have spent ages coming up with the name; it was called… drumroll please… "The Theatre". The most famous of all theatres associated with the Elizabethan Golden Age – The Globe – was actually really late to the scene, opening in 1599 just four years before Elizabeth died. This theatre was where the first performance of Shakespeare's plays happened, and it's mainly down to him and other famous playwrights such as Christopher Marlowe that we have this impression of it being a Golden Age.

Shakespeare wrote at least 38 plays, most of them during Elizabeth's reign, but this doesn't mean she should be credited with all this culture. It would be like saying Boris helped the rise of grime music in the UK just because he was in charge when it happened. While we now have freedom of speech for artists to express themselves and tell us the truth (just listen to Stormzy's 'Vossi Bop' to see what I mean), back in the Elizabethan Age, playwrights had to produce plays that would be pleasing to the monarch. The only reason Elizabeth softened towards Shakespeare is because he was an excellent brown-noser as seen in his eulogy of the "Virgin Queen" in *A Midsummer Night's Dream*, where Oberon describes her as "a fair vestal throned by the west".[769] So, while there were new entertainments and plays covering a variety of themes such as tragedy, history, and comedy, they were all still part of the propaganda machine Elizabeth had cultivated. Her influence actually *stopped* the truth being told in Shakespeare's historical play *Richard III*. While Richard is portrayed as a murderous hunchback, Elizabeth's grandfather (Henry VII) is shown as a saviour but in reality, Henry was a devious usurper. Firstly he had the weakest claim to the throne ever seen since William I usurped King Harold Godwineson in 1066. Henry's claim came through his mother's line – a big no-no due to her being a female and all but even without the sexist dimension the royal link was weak to say the least having come from King Edward III's third son's third marriage. In fact, the only reason he was able to use this claim was due to his mother's family (the Beauforts) having been granted honorary Lancaster family (i.e. royal) status back in the fourteenth century by Pope Boniface and King Richard II. Henry VII became king of England because he invaded and got lucky on the battlefield (Richard was betrayed by some of his men and then charged at Henry with no back up meaning he was swiftly killed). Not that any of this truth made it into Shakespeare's plays. In fact, *Richard III* was so influential in shaping people's opinions that even today, Richard is known as the bad guy. And here's the real punchline – Elizabeth never even went to the theatre! Turns out, the most significant work of fiction to come out of the "Golden Age of Theatre" is the story about Elizabeth being a patron of the arts.

This is considered a Golden Age for architecture because there were some pretty nice mansions built in Elizabeth's time that nobody's ever heard of, such as Hardwick Hall or Burghley House. Fireplaces were now accompanied with chimneys and thus the path for child labour and exploitation was set, or as the Tories would say, "job opportunities were created". Another positive in this Golden Age of Architecture was window cleaners finally had something to do because windows now had glass in them. Some people point to the Globe Theatre as another Golden Age example of architecture because it was an exciting shape (circular); but in reality, the only golden thing going on in this building were golden showers of pee as the audience were forced to relieve themselves where they stood due to a lack of facilities. Though to be fair, the Globe did deserve its *golden* moniker in 1613 due to all the flames burning it down to the ground. While textbooks lead us to believe English architecture flourished, the reality is less about iconic buildings that still stand today and more about changing building materials such as using brick rather than wood. But even that change wasn't noticeably big – just look at the Great Fire of London 63 years after Elizabeth's reign; wood you believe that 13,200 houses were destroyed because London's buildings were still mostly made of... yep, you guessed it, wood.

Overall, like most good things in life, this Golden Age of Architecture was limited to the top levels of society. The fourth sort (where most people slotted in) might have had some of the Golden Age architecture rubbed in their faces as they cleaned it, but they certainly weren't able to enjoy it. And beware of any books trying to convince you that having cutlery made of pewter instead of wood counts as a Golden Age for the poor. For Forks sake!

The prize for the biggest load of baloney has got to go to the phrase *adventurous seafaring* because this is essentially a highly misleading way of saying "Piracy and Slave Trade". Ironically enough it is this *adventurous seafaring* which had the most input from Elizabeth in all the Golden Age criteria. As part of her efforts to cash in on the Spanish seafaring success, she paid a quartet of sailors to attack and loot the Spanish fleet.

These men were Sir John Hawkins, Sir Francis Drake, Sir Martin Frobisher, and the guy who made smoking cool – Sir Walter Raleigh. Together they were known as "The Sea Dogs", a name likely inspired by the wuff seas they sailed upon. In the 16th century there were two types of sea thieves: those not working with the government (Pirates) and those working on behalf of the government (Privateers). Elizabeth's group were in the privateering category as she asked them to do it and they agreed to share whatever bounty they got. This was a big moment in history as it has been the only time a bounty was fought over instead of being the last one left. Traditionally, privateering was only a thing when two countries were at war with each other but trivial things like rules didn't matter to Elizabeth, and she gave the Sea Dogs the legality they needed to rob the Spanish ships. And they were pretty good at it too. In 1572, they seized silver worth around £30 million in today's money. In 1577, Drake began his quest to circumnavigate the globe and even while busy with this world-first, he managed to squeeze in five months plundering Spanish ships up the Pacific coast. Elizabeth loved it! She knighted him in 1581 for all his actions and happily shared in the profits of his voyage. To be fair, Drake being the first sailor to circumnavigate the globe was pretty cool, and this event does rightfully earn a title of *adventurous seafaring*.

Outside of Drake's achievement, I guess it could be seen as *adventurous* to begin the Atlantic slave trade because ferrying people across the sea to become enslaved on another continent hadn't been done before. The Atlantic slave trade began during the Golden Age, and Elizabeth helped it happen.

England had failed to successfully set up a settlement in the New World, and when I say failed, I mean, like, totally 100% ballsed it up. The only settlement created by the English in Elizabeth's reign was a place called Roanoke, and it went so badly there's now an episode on *American Horror Story* named after it (spoiler alert – everyone dies). Because the English couldn't maintain a settlement, they instead wormed their way into the New World under the cover of "trade". Portugal and Spain were the *conquistadors* in the Americas, and they had been looting, plundering, and destroying the many settlements of the Mayans and Incas for most of the 1500s. Annoyingly for the *conquistadors,* they didn't have enough people to extract the resources they wanted to steal, and the locals were just *soooo* unhelpful by sabotaging their efforts. On top of this, they needed people to farm the various sugar, coffee, and tobacco plantations they wanted to set up. Various labourers had been tried – the natives to start with but rather inconveniently they kept rebelling or dying from the European diseases. Prisoners brought from Europe worked reasonably well but there weren't enough of them, and you had to let these guys go after they had served their time. But then John Hawkins came along to help them out.

Hawkins had already, independently of Elizabeth, captured 300 people from Sierra Leone in Africa and traded them with the Spanish for goods like pearls and sugar. Now, here were three things that Elizabeth really liked: sugar (she would rub it in her teeth), pearls (because they implied she was a virgin) and getting one up on the Spanish (Phillip had banned trade with the English). So, she supported Hawkins. She sponsored his future voyages and gave him ships, supplies, and guns. She was in no doubt as to what was entailed in making someone a slave, as evidenced by the unique coat of arms she gave him which had a picture of a bound slave in the middle. Hawkins led three major slavery voyages in the 1560s. He, with the help of Elizabeth, created the Slave Triangle which dominated the slave trade for the next 250 years. England went on to lead over 10,000[770] slave voyages and was responsible, along with other European powers, for displacing around 12.5 million people, and for enslaving the 11 million survivors of that harrowing journey over to the Americas.

So, was it really a Golden Age? It was a Golden Age of Piracy for sure. A Golden Age for affluent white Europeans as they enslaved black Africans. A Golden Age for the arts and the creative people. But it was not a Golden Age for England. It was the age that England immersed herself in the slave trade. It was an age of political instability, growing poverty, religious uncertainty, and financial difficulty. The Elizabethan era became known as a Golden Age because firstly, the people writing the histories were the rich, and secondly, because of what happened in England *after* her reign. The 1600s saw an attempt to blow up parliament and kill the king (the Gunpowder Plot of 1605); then witnessed the English Civil War, which ended with the *actual* killing of the king and end of the English monarchy; then Christmas was cancelled for 16 years (yes, there were years worse than 2020); then there was another round of the plague; and finally, London was consumed by the fires of hell in 1666. Having lived through all that, and then looking back and comparing to the Elizabethan period, definitely made her era seem pretty golden.

Didn't she lead the English to Victory over the Spanish Armada?

Oh yes, the infamous Spanish Armada.

You know, it's only in the English-speaking parts of the world that this event is seen as an English victory. This first line of an article from History.com is typical of how the story is told: "Off the coast of Gravelines, France, Spain's so-called "Invincible Armada" is defeated by an English naval force."[771] Wikipedia tells a similar tale on their Spanish Armada page:

"An attempt by Philip II of Spain to invade England with the Spanish Armada in 1588 was famously defeated." In English history textbooks, the Spanish Armada is taught in terms of causes, events, and why the Spanish were defeated. The causes given are the ambitions of the Spanish, the war in the Netherlands, and the actions of English privateers – all of which are fair enough, but there is no coverage of Elizabeth's provocations. The events are accurately covered, but the textbook timeline stops without explaining why the English ships did not continue to chase the Spanish ships. Simply by phrasing the enquiry question of "why Spain lost", children are led to believe that England outright won and are not taught what happened after 1588 (beyond some mocking references to Philip trying and failing again). What happened with the Spanish Armada is a tale that has been cleverly constructed and controlled since 1588. Such is the power of Elizabethan propaganda that even now, in the age of limitless knowledge, we believe this was an English victory.

A more realistic summary of events goes like this: Elizabeth started the beef, then antagonised the Spanish some more, Spain retaliated with the launch of the Spanish Armada, and then this was followed by Elizabeth starting some new beef, which she lost.

Starting the beef with Spain wasn't too hard. After Elizabeth made it clear that she wasn't interested in marrying her dead sister's ex-husband (Phillip II of Spain), personal relations became a little strained to say the least; but at least they still had their mutual hatred of the French to bond them together like a knock-off Pritt Stick. However, when Elizabeth set up her little Sea Dogs posse – the cheap glue began to unstick. After years of being looted, the Spanish hit back in September 1568 and John Hawkins' fleet was attacked at San Juan de Ula (Mexico), causing him to lose four ships out of six and most of his men; only 80 men out of 400 made it back to England alive.[772] Following this attack (but according to history textbooks not linked at all… yeah right) Elizabeth changed tactics – why go all the way to the Americas when you can steal from them much closer to home!

Her chance came in November 1568, as Spanish ships were on their way to deliver 400,000 gold coins to a Spanish commander, the Duke of Alva, in the Netherlands. The journey was not going well – not only were they being chased by English privateers, they were also being battered by storms (I guess God was on someone else's side that day). So, the Spanish ships sought shelter in the ports of Devon and Cornwall. Incidentally, the 400,000 gold coins they were carrying were a loan from Genoese financiers – because it wasn't *strictly* Spanish money, Elizabeth didn't consider it as stealing from the Spanish – she was stealing from the middleman – which is obviously just fine and dandy. However, unlike Robin Hood, this money was taken from the rich and kept by the rich – more specifically – Elizabeth. After lightening the Spanish load, she kindly allowed the ships to continue their journey which most historians see as evidence that she wasn't trying to stir things up. Now I'm no expert in 16th-century diplomacy but I'm pretty sure stealing 400,000 gold coins has never been the best way to keep the peace. Even if you do let them keep their boats. Being too early to read these historians' biased interpretations of events, the Spanish *did* see the theft as 100% stirring things up. Repercussions were immediate. It was ordered that all English ships and property in the Netherlands were to be seized, to which the English retaliated by seizing all Spanish property in England. And so, with everyone in a foul moo-d, the beef began.

More provocation didn't happen until 1585 but when it did occur it was serious stuff as she literally began a war – the

Anglo-Spanish war (1585–1604). It began when Elizabeth decided to supply English troops to fight against the Spanish in the Netherlands, a country which Spain had gained control of in 1556. By this point, Spain was well and truly the superpower of the world, but all this superpower was starting to go to Phillip's head, and he thought it would be a marvellous idea to destroy all Dutch heritage and make the Netherlands a Spanish colony. Shockingly, the Protestant Dutch did not see it as quite so marvellous an idea to learn Spanish and revert to Catholicism and so things had been kicking off there since 1566. Elizabeth had refused to militarily help her Protestant ally in the previous 19 years, but then the Spanish started doing rather well and the Dutch leader was assassinated. Her decision to intervene was cemented after English shipping was once again seized in Spanish ports. The *Treaty of Nonsuch* saw her agree to send money, 5000 troops and 1000 cavalry under the command of her BFF Dudley. Which turned out to be Nonsuch a good idea.

Their armies were now fighting a proxy war in the Netherlands which is all the more impressive considering the term *proxy war* hadn't even been invented yet. Unfortunately for England, this expedition went very badly and unfortunately for Elizabeth this was all her fault. She had chosen the wrong man to lead the troops – Dudley was neither a soldier nor a military administrator and yet she had tasked him with both. A more suitable candidate, a chap called Pelham, was suggested – but Elizabeth refused to let him go because he owed her money. Priorities and all that. Dudley then (maybe taking the lead from Elizabeth's "skill" of job delegation) chose a Catholic (whaat?!) to take charge of a newly captured town – Deventer. And in a move everyone could see coming… the Catholic promptly gave Deventer back to the Spanish. Despite this setback and out of sheer desperation (he was the only leader the Dutch Protestants had), Dudley became the Governor-General of the Netherlands. Rather stupidly though, he didn't check with Elizabeth first and then she got angry at him thinking he was the big man about town and so she refused to answer any more letters. Or send any more money. Which really helped the English win that war.

The final nail in Elizabeth's coffin of blame are the revelations of Phillip's plans. Yes, he was trying to gain control of the Netherlands, but in 1587 his instructions to his military commanders show he had plans for peace with England. Yes… actual peace! He wasn't looking to add England to his empire (we had nothing worth taking bar eight million sheep and it would have taken ages to catch them all). Phillip's peace terms were reasonably fair; he wanted an English withdrawal from the Netherlands and for English Catholics to be tolerated in England. However, due to Elizabeth's military involvement (what a peace of work she was turning out to be), his non-aggressive plans changed to a full-on aggressive plan to invade England – aka *The Spanish Armada.* Ironically enough, her military intervention *did* help the Netherlands stave off a complete Spanish takeover because Phillip was now more focussed on taking down England than quelling the Dutch rebels. Accordingly, in 1587, the Duke of Parma was instructed to stop fighting the Dutch and wait to hook up with the impending Spanish Armada. Elizabeth had temporarily saved the Netherlands but sacrificed the safety of England in the process.

So, what *really* happened during the Spanish Armada of 1588? The Spanish Armada launched from Lisbon in May 1588 with the overall aim of deposing Elizabeth and replacing her with a Catholic – probably Philip's daughter Isabella. They were already a year late – the plan had been to launch in 1587 but Drake had put a stop to that by sabotaging the Spanish fleet while it was still in the Spanish Port of Cadiz. The fleet consisted of 130 ships, and it carried up to 8000 fighting men. There were also 180 priests and 14,000 barrels of wine on board just in case any of the 8000 had second thoughts.

The first lesser-known fact is there was never meant to be a naval battle. The plan was for these 130 ships to sail to the Spanish Netherlands where they would meet the Duke of Parma and the rest of the Spanish army – around 17,000 men. The Armada was then meant to protect these men as they crossed the channel on flat bottomed barges and launched a land invasion of England. They, like Elizabeth who was waiting in Tilbury, Essex, with her 16,500 men, expected a battle on land. The Armada, although a great and impressive fleet was only ever intended to be the transportation and protection element.

The reasons why the Spanish plan failed have nothing to do with Elizabeth. It's not like she had been busily preparing the navy by investing in a large English fleet. Oh no, the English navy actually only had 34 ships to call their own. Luckily for her, other people in England *had* bothered building ships, and she was able to use Drake's 20 and take 140 merchant ships to be converted into battle ships. The "victory" had barely anything to do with the English navy either. In reality, the weather had the biggest part to play and second on the list was the incompetence of the Spanish leaders. The Duke of Medina Sidonia was chosen to lead the planned invasion because he was a high-ranking nobleman – not because he was good at commanding ships. He was about as far as you could get from someone suitable for leading a fleet of ships – he got seasick! Even the guy's mother commented that he was not the right man for the job, and you can normally rely on your mum to support you on anything (just ask Richard I). But even she didn't have his back.

Once the Armada arrived off the coast of England, the navy chased the Spanish up the channel and then sent in some fireships while the Spanish were docked at Calais overnight. Fireships sound awesome but they were not some fancy new weapon – they were literally English ships which had been deliberately set on fire. The hope behind this half-baked strategy was that either the wind would carry the flames over to the Spanish boats and they would be destroyed, or that the sight of flaming fleet would scatter the Spanish ships and thus make them more vulnerable to an attack. The English got the second aim as the fireships caused a bit of panic and did lead to the Armada losing their defensive formation. But by the end of this heated encounter, the Spanish had lost zero ships. The English lost eight ships. Why? Oh yeah, because we set them on fire.

The next day (8th August) there was an actual battle – the Battle of Gravelines. The battle lasted nine hours, during which time the English sunk one Spanish ship. Two other Spanish ships ran aground on the sandbanks. So, I guess if you're feeling kind, you could say three ships were lost at the hands of the English. Out of 130. Wow. And the only reason the battle stopped was because the English ran out of ammunition. Not exactly the stuff of legends, is it? On the 9th of August, the weather took control of the situation – the wind changed which meant the ships had no choice but to sail north. The British continued to chase the Spanish into the North Sea and they kept on their tail right up to the border of Scotland until August 12th whereby the English turned around. While up north, a storm hit (well it is grim up there) and shipwrecked around 44 Spanish ships off the coast of Scotland and Ireland.

But why did the English turn back? This part of the story also eludes history textbooks. It wasn't because they had seen the weather forecast and knew the impending fate for the Spanish – the English sailors turned back because the conditions on board were so dire that they needed to get onto land before everyone died. They had only lost 50–100 men in battle, but the English navy went on to lose 7000[773] men due to diseases such as typhus and dysentery. Oh yeah, and they also hadn't been paid. The commander Lord Howard was forced to use some of his own money to pay his men after many were only given enough to get them home; he said: "I would rather have never a penny in the world, than they (his sailors) should lack…"[774] If only Elizabeth had recently acquired a decent amount of money… ooh let's say 400,000 gold coins… I'm sure she would have paid them herself.

And it's here, in 1588, that the English history textbooks leave the tale, a victory for England over the mighty Spain. Oh, what a great tale of the Golden Age! The truth is rather less golden; the English actively avoided combat in the open sea knowing that their ships would not stand a chance against the Spanish, and instead went for an underhand tactic of fireships in the night. The one battle led to the loss of one ship and then they got lucky with the storm.

Even more embarrassing than only winning due to the weather was Elizabeth's counterattack in 1589 – unimaginatively named the *Counter-Armada* at the time and now ambiguously referred to as "The Drake-Norris expedition". Elizabeth herself financed a small part of the fleet and private investors funded the rest (most likely under strong persuasion). Sir Francis Drake was put in command of the fleet of ships and Sir John Norris was in charge of the army troops on board. Her aim was for the English to go to Santander (as in the Spanish city – not to rob the bank… though she does have previous for this sort of thing) and destroy what was left of the Spanish fleet. What she hadn't bargained for was Drake producing his own plan – he fancied going to Corunna instead (the place, not the pandemic). So, what was so bad that this event has literally been wiped from English history? I guess it's the fact it completely failed.

The English arrived at Corunna on 4 May 1589, but the fourth definitely wasn't with them as 1300 of their men were killed in the first 15 days. They had to give up on Corunna and went to attack Lisbon instead – but they couldn't get this right either. Drake and Norris couldn't agree on a plan, and for reasons unbeknown to ANYONE EVER, Norris chose to land 80km away from Lisbon and *walk* his troops there. Drake sailed a bit further on and decided to wait for Norris and his walkers, despite having enough men on his ship to launch an attack without them. By the time the others had completed their 80km trek they were rather worse for wear, having been hounded by the Spanish the whole way. The Spanish troops wisely remained in Lisbon and thus avoided having to meet Drake's fleet out at sea. On June 3rd, the English were attacked in their camp from three different sides and were forced to flee. They tried using their fire trick again – this time by setting fire to the woods they were running through, but this was even less successful than the fireships incident as trees that are still alive tend to be a bit too wet to set ablaze easily. The English troops got to their ships on June 15th and were chased away by the Spanish galleons (sound familiar?). The story gets even more like for like as the English were then beset by bad weather and illness on board. The casualties suffered by the English in this counterattack were strikingly like those suffered by the Spanish in 1588. In the original Armada, the Spanish lost 51 ships out of 130 and somewhere between 11–20,000 men were killed (the Spanish say 11,000, we say 20,000). In the counterattack the English lost 40 ships out of 150, and out of a total of 23–25,000 men who set sail, only 3722 men survived to claim their pay (which they actually got this time).

Philip dispatched two more Armadas in the 1590s but they too were scattered by storms. The Spanish Armada did fail in its aims which could therefore be seen as an English victory by default. But this failure was not due to the "Might and Strength of England" as we are led to believe. The only reason England was faced with the Armada in the first place was because of Elizabeth's poor decision making and constant prodding. And her counterattack, which she helped finance, was as much of a loss as the Spanish experienced in 1588. Elizabeth didn't lead the English to victory at any point. The wind should get more credit than her. And that must really blow.

In true Elizabethan "wool over the eyes" style, once she learnt the terrible truth of the expedition, Elizabeth prohibited any publication about it. Instead, she allowed a few pamphlets to be published which implied it was a favourable outcome; what we would now call "Fake News". Alongside this, records and sources were conveniently "lost" and the records that remained differ in basic facts such as the number of English men involved. Elizabeth was playing this misinformation game long before Orwell created the Ministry of Information in *1984* which did the same thing. These propaganda pamphlets were taken as "reliable sources" by subsequent British historians. Luckily for us, England weren't the only ones keeping records and while this *Counter-Armada* is largely ignored by the English, it has been the subject of various books in Spain. And just in case you were in any doubt as to how this event is viewed outside of England, the author of one of these books, Luis Gorrochategui Santos, titled his work: *The English Armada: the greatest naval disaster in English history.*

The Virgin Queen moniker, Good Queen Bess image, and the idea of an Elizabethan Golden Age have stuck around longer than any of her heirs would have. This is more the result of propaganda (at the time and now) than as a result of the truth. Virgin Queen she is not, but Queen of PR – yes, definitely. Something which she got stuck into straight away – just five years into her reign, Elizabeth issued a proclamation to curtail the "grievous and offensive errors and deformities'" in visual depictions of her. Which basically meant you couldn't paint a realistic portrait of her. By printing pamphlets that told her version of events and losing records that didn't match up to this approved version, she was able to control information and hide the truth. While we may shout about how she was THE VIRGIN QUEEN in our English textbooks, in other countries she is remembered a little differently. "The Whore of Europe" was one name fondly attributed to her by the French. And yes, maybe that was a bit inaccurate (there was no *Europe* then) but it does demonstrate the strength of English propaganda which has protected her image for the last 500 years. Elizabeth's best PR stunt of all was the protection of her virgin status – protected even from her deathbed! Ultimately though, if she wanted to be believed to be a virgin, then she should have really behaved like one. Good try with the inscription on the marble tomb though, nearly had us there...

Weird Sex

Incest

Most cultures throughout most of history have abhorred incest with prohibition beginning around 3000 years ago with the Assyrians. However, this aversion has not been carried through into the 21st century and incest between consenting adults is legal in a whopping 25% of European countries. These mofos are France, Belgium, Netherlands, Latvia, Lithuania, Luxembourg, Portugal, Russia, Serbia, Slovenia, Spain, and Turkey. The same is true in other countries around the world, such as Argentina, Japan, Ivory Coast, Brazil, and Thailand. In some nations, such as China, Israel, and the Philippines, incest is legal, but there are restrictions on the closeness of the relatives involved and the couple are not able to marry each other.[775] Where incest is illegal in the 21st century, punishments range from prison time (up to two years in the UK) or death (UAE, Saudi Arabia, and Iran).

The first civilisation in ancient Europe – the Egyptians (3100 BCE-312 BCE) – allowed incest. In fact, they saw incest as a *necessity* for the ruling royals because it prevented the transfer of power and money (likely made through pyramid schemes) from their family to someone else's. Egyptian pharaohs often married their sisters and/or daughters, and in the families of the Pharaohs Seqenenre Tao II and Ahhotep I, the royal daughters soon got themselves a dad reputation because they were *only* allowed to marry their fathers.[776] Nevertheless, there were clearly problems with these close relations having children and so some pharaohs used non-royal women to have their children. This didn't result in any loss of power to the glorified surrogate because the status of women was not equal to men; meanwhile the pharaohs were able to keep control of their daughters, and their money, by preventing them from marrying anybody else, which doesn't seem that pharaoh deal really.

Aside from the royal practicalities, incest was also viewed as A-OK because it was part of Egyptian mythology. Isis, before becoming an extremist terrorist group, was a goddess responsible for separating heaven from earth and giving languages to the world. She also married her brother. Her brother was Osiris, the Sun God, and apparently, she had loved him since they shared the womb together. And who said young love doesn't last?! Osiris was later murdered by Set, the god of darkness, and bits of him were subsequently scattered all over Egypt. Such was Isis' love for Osiris that she searched and located every part of him… except the one bit she needed the most… his penis. But, being a goddess, she was able to build a working replica and bring Osiris back to life so he could use it (batteries weren't invented until 1800); they went on to produce a child – Horus. As with all myths, the ancient Egyptians cherry picked which bits they wanted to follow and were clearly in de-Nile about the fact the incestuous Osiris ended up dead; instead, they went with celebrating incest and honouring Isis as a symbol of renewal.

Two of the most famous ancient Egyptians – Cleopatra and Tutankhamun had incest in their blood. Born in 69 BCE, Cleopatra's parents were brother and sister, and she honoured the Ptolemy family tradition by marrying her ten-year-old brother when she came to power aged 18. Obviously, their parents taught them how to share properly because she later went on to marry her other brother too. Her first hubby-brother, Ptolemy XIII, ended up betraying her, which led to a civil war where she teamed up Roman general Julius Caesar to defeat him. Seemingly owing Caesar one, she definitely gave him one, and they had one (son) – Caesarion. Cleopatra then married her twelve-year-old brother Ptolemy XIV, but while she publicly referred to him as her husband,[777] it is unlikely this was a genuine marriage. It was only needed because Egypt was not a big fan of lone female rulers. Wishing her son Caesarion to become co-ruler with her, she wisely had hubby-brother-version-two killed before he could protest. She did not have any children with her brothers but went on to have three more children with husband number four – the Roman Mark Antony. Some researchers believe that one of the physical impacts of inbreeding on Cleopatra was obesity. Yes, shock horror, she was not the slim beauty she has been portrayed as in films. But I imagine this obesity was more the result of too much bread and beer (the staple diet of Egyptians at the time) than it was the result of too much of the family birds and the bees.

One of the most famous pharaohs of them all – King Tutankhamun – also came from an incestuous pairing. Modern-day research and DNA scans of his mummified remains have revealed that he is a product of "high level incest;"[778] and researchers hypothesized that King Tut's mother is probably his dad's sister.[779] The effects of inbreeding are visible in Tutankhamun's many ailments. Researchers have found incest made him physically frail and sickly (he had a persistent case of malaria), as well as causing him to inherit a cleft palate, a club foot, and a misshapen skull (it was excessively long). He had trouble walking and needed a cane; he was even buried with lots of these walking sticks to ensure he could get about in the afterlife. While it has long been believed King Tut must have had an accident or been murdered due to his young age at death (19), it is now believed that incest was the real killer. A combination of his club foot slowly dying (necrosis) and his compromised immune system being unable to deal with the four strains of malaria found in his body caused him to die in his ninth year of ruling in 1324 BCE.

Due to the prevalence of the Isis myth, ancient Egyptian incest was not just restricted to the royals – it was common among every group in society. By the time the Romans came and conquered the Egyptians in 30 BCE, it was standard procedure for women to marry their brothers or fathers – in the cities it has been recorded that one-third of all men married their sisters.[780] In the city of Arsinoe the frequency was even higher, and basically *every* man with a younger sister married her, thus saving her time trawling through Tinder every night. When the Romans arrived, although officially against the practice, they got stuck right in with adopting the local culture and for the first 200 years of Roman Egypt, there were loads of sibling marriages involving Roman and Egyptian commoners.[781]

The Romans were not so keen on a bit of "how's your father" with your father because they wanted to be different from their Egyptian neighbours and because by the 4th century CE they had adopted Christianity which banned the practice. It's also possible they opposed the custom due to their bad experience with the incestuous and insane Emperor Nero. While it is only rumoured that Nero had sex with his mother, it is fact that he himself was the result of incest – his parents were two Roman aristocrats – Claudius and his niece Agrippina. Nero's crazy actions sure helped give incest a bad name in the Roman world – if it wasn't him setting people on fire so that he could have some light in his garden; it might be him creating a festival to celebrate being able to grow a big-boy-beard at the age of 22 – which swayed it for people. Thus, in ancient Rome, marriage between family members was banned and sex between a parent and child was viewed as horrifying.[782] But it was hard work trying to change the Egyptian culture – incest was such an ingrained part of their society that in the end, it took the Romans 300 years to stamp out these sorts of Rome-ances.

But the Romans were not the first in the ancient world to condemn incest. Death was the prescribed punishment in the civilisations of the Babylonians (1895 BCE–539 BCE); Hittites (1650 BCE – 1178 BCE); and Assyrians (900 BCE – 600 BCE). For the Babylonians, incest was such a terrible crime that *all* involved had to die to appease the lawmakers – even if one of them was not a willing party. Therefore, a girl raped by her brother or father had to drown or burn to death alongside him.[783] And there's us thinking equality is a good thing.

Like the Egyptians, the people of ancient Persia (modern-day Iran) also had incestuous relationships with no qualms; it was seen as a good thing and was practised by royals, religious leaders, and commoners. While the ancient Persians had few other sex laws, they made sure to rule *in favour* of incest. Before Islam came to the region in the 7th century, people followed the Zoroastrianism religion between 600 BCE to 600 CE. Chapter eight of the Zoroastrian Middle Persian texts promoted incest as the most virtuous act a person could do: "Blessed is he who has a child of his child… pleasure, sweetness and joy are owing to a son that begets from a daughter of his own, who is also a brother of that same mother… the family is more perfect."[784] So perfect it seems that the happy couple's fluids were even deemed to have medicinal powers. For example, if you mixed their urine together, that could be used to purify a corpse-bearer.[785] So long as the local wildlife didn't get whiff of this and maul him to death first of course. The Persian's belief that incest resulted in perfect families was *so* strong that if a man married someone outside of the family unit, this was deemed a sin that would result in "damnation in the highest degree."[786] Women who refused were condemned to have a snake crawl in and out of their mouth for eternity – a genuine hiss and her policy.

Denunciation really took off when religion began. Religious condemnation of incest began with the Hebrews and was set down in Leviticus (the third book of the Jewish *Torah)* between 538 BCE – 332 BCE. God advises in chapter 18 of Leviticus that he would "vomit you out"[787] if you were to have sex with your relative. Likely aware of how such things could be misinterpreted, God made it quite clear what he meant by using the whole of chapter 18 to go through *every* possible family pairing there could be accompanied with the phrase "don't do this".[788] These denunciations are incredibly ironic considering Judaism's most important prophet, Moses,[789] was himself the product of incest. Exodus 6 describes how his father was his mother's nephew.[790] Conveniently, God's punishment of vomiting them out was not applied to these two. But Moses doesn't get away quite so cleanly and he was punished for their actions by suffering some bad weather later in his life.[791] So, I'm guessing the moral of this particular Bible story is to make sure you buy an umbrella and a decent coat.

Christianity adopted the same five books of the Torah for their Old Testament section of the Bible and thus Christians also condemned incest. However, it seems like the writers must never have had a meeting to decide their stance because the Bible and the Torah ended up being consistently inconsistent about incest[792] and are littered with examples of incest from their celebrity characters who escape the wrath of God for their acts. Ever wondered how we all came from Adam and Eve? Yep – incest! Cain and Abel were born to the naughty exiled pair, but did you know there was also a third sibling? There was a sister called Awan, and in the Book of Jubilees it is stated that

Cain married his sister.[793] Once more there were no vomiting repercussions. Instead, Cain goes on to murder his brother Abel – an act which *did* get God's attention and saw Cain punished with a lifetime of wandering… leaving us all wandering how serious God's prohibitions in Leviticus really were. Another tale of incest appears in Genesis 19:30-38 where it is described how Lot was "seduced" by his two daughters. Naturally, this was presented with the females at fault; poor Lot was the victim of a conspiracy between his two daughters to get him drunk and make babies to continue the family name. Lot (apparently) "perceived not" when one night his eldest seduced him – a quite remarkable feat of ignorance considering the one part of him needed for this action is the first to flounder when drunk. Even more remarkable was how the EXACT SAME THING happened the following night with his younger daughter.[794] While God was happy to burn down their village as punishment for all the homosexuals living there, once again incest was left unchecked.

Throughout history it is within royal families that incest has been most common. The idea of using incest to keep money and status within the family was first documented with the Egyptian pharaohs but has also been long practised by the Persians, Japanese,[795] European, and Inca royal families. For the Incas of Peru (13th – 16th century CE) it was standard procedure for the king to marry his sister. They, like the ancient Egyptians, were fixated on ensuring their royal blood remained pure as well as making sure no one else got their hands on the family fortunes. In another similarity, the Incas also got their justification from mythology where the sun married his sister, the moon. And because Inca kings claimed to be descended from these celestial bodies, they felt they should act just as their ancestors did. Apart from the whole never-being-seen-in-the-same-place thing of course. But there was no favouritism; if the first incestuous pairing produced no children, the king would keep marrying his sisters until children were produced.[796] They insistered upon it.

Out of all the inbreeding royal families of Europe, the incestuous Habsburgs have definitely got the prize for taking it too far.

It literally killed them.[797]

Throughout their history, the Habsburg royal family tried to keep it, well, in the family. Keen to avoid wars of succession and potential loss of power to other European royals, sixteen generations over 600 years married each other instead. Approximately 9% of the genes found in a Habsburg were identical because they came from the same ancestor.[798] While they were wrong in their methods, they were at least right with their fears because as soon as the last Habsburg died there *was* a war of succession (the Austrian War of Succession in 1740).

The Habsburgs began in Switzerland in the 11th century CE, and they went on to rule most of Europe. The Austrian Habsburgs were Emperors of the Holy Roman Empire (central Europe) until the 20th century, and the Spanish Habsburgs were kings of Spain and Portugal up until the turn of the 18th century. They were the big dogs of Europe and a thorn in the side for our much beloved Tudors (apart from Mary I, aka Bloody Mary, who only went and bloomin' married one – the Spanish Habsburg Phillip II of Spain). However, Mary was unable to have a child and died four years into the marriage which was most un-four-tunate for the non-incestuous future of the Habsburg family tree. Phillip then, obviously sensing the error of his ways, married his fourteen-year-old niece.

It was all going so well until the last eight generations, beginning with Joanna and Philip I of Castile marrying in 1496. By this point, the Habsburg gene pool had been so badly decimated, the frequency of impairments such as epilepsy and insanity sharply increased. The most obvious defect caused by inbreeding was facial deformity,[799] i.e., massive chins, big humpy noses with a hanging tip, and lips which were basically inside out. The proper term for this is "mandibular prognathism" but at the time it was known simply as the "the Habsburg jaw" – much like "The Kardashian butt" of the 21st century. Except the Habsburg's enlargement was real.

These deformities were seen in Charles I, Phillip IV, and Charles II – all three kings had five of the seven features of mandibular prognathism which was more than any other family members. It all began with Charles I (also known as Charles V of HRE) who lived between 1500 and 1558. Charles I was described at the time by the (very brave/foolish) Italian diplomat Antonio di Beatis in 1517 as having: "a long, cadaverous face and a lopsided mouth (which drops open when he is not on his guard)."[800] And this effect was with a relatively (pun intended) low inbreeding coefficient of .038. In comparison, his great-great-grandson Charles II had the highest inbreeding score of all the Habsburgs with 0.2539.[801] And if you look at their portraits, you can see the different scores written all over their faces….

Charles II of Spain was the last of the Spanish Habsburgs and is a great example of what inbreeding can do to a person. His mother was also his cousin because Charles' father (Phillip IV) had married his niece (Mariana of Habsburg). As a result of this pairing and all the years of incest prior, poor Charlie was the same level of inbreeding as a child born of two siblings and thus was physically and mentally disabled.[802] Obviously, neither of these deficiencies stopped Charles from finding a wife. Or two. But what really takes the biscuit is that he broke with family tradition and married into the Bourbon family rather than an all-out Habsburg. In 1679 he was arranged a marriage with Marie Louise, granddaughter of French King Louis XIII and Habsburg Anne of Austria. Making Charles and Marie *very* distant cousins. Marie was not keen to say the least – mostly because she preferred her other cousin (the one from the less incestuous Bourbon side), but also because of Charles' "monstrous jaw". When informed of her future, she fell to her knees and cried and begged to not be sent away,[803] but to no avail. The pair were unable to produce a child, a failure which Marie blamed on Charles' premature ejaculation. Considering Charles was unable to father children in either of his two marriages,[804] it seems likely Marie had come to the right conclusion. Unfortunately, just like Charles, she was a bit premature with thinking people would accept a woman's explanation over a man's, and she was blamed for the malfunction and made to undergo various "fertility" treatments which did nothing but wreck her insides.[805]

Charles' nickname was *El Hechizado*, which means "the bewitched". This was inspired by his epileptic fits and his difficulty talking (due to a humungous tongue) which made him seem somewhat possessed. His deformities and ailments were no secret; one contemporary described him as: "short, lame, epileptic, senile and completely bald before 35, always on the verge of death but repeatedly baffling Christendom by continuing to live".[806] Foreign observers did not mince their words either; in 1679, the French ambassador wrote: "... he is so ugly as to cause fear and looks ill".[807] In 1700, British envoy Alexander Stanhope (the guy we had over in Spain keeping an eye on things) described Charles as: "He has a ravenous stomach, and swallows all he eats whole, for his nether jaw stands so much out, that his two rows of teeth cannot meet."[808]

By the grand old age of 39, Charles couldn't even do this sort of eating anymore and he died just five days short of his big 4-0 party. His autopsy record reads like a horror story and goes a long way to explain why he was mentally challenged and unable to produce a child: "his body did not contain a single drop of blood; his heart was the size of a peppercorn; his lungs corroded; his intestines rotten and gangrenous; he had a single testicle, black as coal, and his head was full of water."[809] Researchers say that this terrifying result is likely due to the effects of the disease hydrocephalus, which comes from having measles as a child, as Charles did.[810] Put *that* on the MMR vaccination posters and we may get some more take up.

While the Spanish failed to see the links between incest, chins, and death (incidentally, in 2021, incest between siblings is STILL legal in Spain), England and Wales made incest illegal for the first time in 1908 with The Punishment of Incest Act. The act explicitly stated that it was against the law for a man to engage in sexual intercourse with his female granddaughter, daughter, sister, half-sister, or mother and it was banned on genetic grounds.[811] Gene-ious idea.

But this was seven years too late to protect the descendants of Queen Victoria who had married her first cousin, Prince Albert. While they did not suffer the deformities which plagued the Habsburgs, her children and grandchildren did inherit the blood disorder haemophilia which prevents blood from clotting. One of her children and five of her grandchildren died due to complications brought on by haemophilia.

Our current Queen, Elizabeth II, is also a guilty party – she married her third cousin, Philip, in November 1947. Although to be fair, according to British law, it is not actually illegal to marry your cousin (who knew?!). Interestingly, this was completely her choice – she was not forced into an arranged marriage, as was the case with other historic royals. As a result, her son and heir to the British throne, Prince Charles, has an inbreeding coefficient of 0.004.[812] While this clearly isn't the worst case of incest, it still doesn't sit right with those of us not descended from royalty, a feeling backed up by science, which has shown cousin-inbreeding can cause defects in any children which are produced.[813] Elsewhere in the world, cousin relations are not so acceptable; for example, it is illegal in China, Taiwan, North Korea, South Korea, the Philippines, and 24 of the 50 states of America. Europe, with its long history of royal inbreeding, stands with the UK on permitting it.[814]

Outside of royalty, there are some famous faces who have married their cousins, such as President Franklin Roosevelt, actor and EE promoter Kevin Bacon, dictator Saddam Hussein, and Charles Darwin (who clearly didn't read his own books).[815] Albert Einstein also married his cousin – Elsa – proving his famous theory wasn't the only thing to be relative. While in the UK there was no law against it until 1908, it was still not OK to shag your sister. Instead, it was viewed as a religious offence (i.e., God will deal with you later) and therefore punishable by penance rather than the penal system.[816] The tide started turning in the 1880s as it became obvious to social reformers and children's rights groups, such as the NSPCC, that the victims of incest were often young girls.[817] The 19th century also brought with it scientific developments, such as Darwin's Theory of Evolution which highlighted the dangers of incest and encouraged legislation to prevent it.[818] The law was updated in 1979 and statistics show that since 1979, about 300 cases of incest are reported every year in England and Wales with half going to trial.[819] In 2003 it was updated again to include adoption and fostering counting as incestuous relationships.[820] But your cousin is still fair game of course. Britain might be dragging its feet on this one because if cousin marriage were made illegal, then that makes the Queen a criminal. Besides, all her kids turned out just fine…

Bestiality

In the modern day, bestiality is viewed as disgusting or used as a joke against the Welsh. But the truth is it was far more common than just one part of the UK. These days, bestiality is illegal in most countries; although as recently as 2014 (Sweden) and 2015 (Denmark), you were able to book a holiday to either of these places with the sole purpose of copulating with an animal because their laws allowed it. The Danish Ethical Council for Animals stated in 2015: "There are frequent reports of the occurrence of organised animal sex shows, clubs, and animal brothels in Denmark."[821] FYI, all of this was "fine" so long as the animal did not suffer as a result – something which I'm assuming the animal was able to confirm after firstly ringing the police.

Then, of course, there's NASA helping Margaret Lovatt masturbate a dolphin named Peter in the 1960s. It's worth pointing out that this hand-party was not NASA's aim – they were funding the experiment in order to find a way for humans to communicate with dolphins. Which… I guess… in a way they did?! Margaret explained: "He (Peter) would rub himself on my knee, or my foot, or my hand… I allowed that. I wasn't uncomfortable with it, as long as it wasn't rough. It would just become part of what was going on, like an itch – just get rid of it, scratch it and move on… It wasn't private. People could observe it."[822] The experiment came to an end after six years and, because Peter wasn't house trained, the two had to be separated. Peter did not take this well and committed suicide (by deciding not to take another breath and sinking to the bottom of the water). It's a shame the Swedish law of suffering wasn't applied in this case because while Peter was clearly heartbroken, Margaret described her feelings as: ""I wasn't terribly unhappy about it."[823] Seemingly remembering what their name stood for, NASA then focussed on space stuff and got to the moon three years later, hoping that this would overshadow their dolphin dalliances of earlier years.

In the ancient Mediterranean world, sex with animals was common.[824] Once again, Egypt was at the extreme end of acceptance. Around 1000 BCE, sex with goats was viewed by Egyptians as a form of devotion to the god Pan. This belief was so strong there were even specially trained goats available at the temples for women to use in their "worship"[825] and was written about at the time by the ancient historian Herodotus. In fact, bestiality was so acceptable in ancient Egypt, it was used as a punishment as well as a godsend. A man committing the crime of damaging stone property markers (i.e., trying to move them to steal land from his neighbour) was forced to hand over his wives and children to be raped by donkeys.[826] Yes, that's right – he wasn't even the one who faced this beastly punishment, which must have been a real kick in the teeth for his family.

However, while the ancient Mediterranean world clearly had the practice, they also were the first to rule against it. The ancient Hittite kingdom (1600 BCE – 1179 BCE), located in modern Turkey, had four laws against bestiality in their "sexual offences" category (Laws 187, 188, 199, and 200a). But there was no blanket ban on the practice and particular animals were singled out to be more acceptable partners than others – the reason why some got this special treatment is unknown.[827] Law 187 concerned the cows; Law 188 was about sheep; and Law 199 protected pigs and dogs – anyone caught fornicating with any of these beasts "shall die" or was "put to the death".[828] Conversely, Law 200a threw horses and mules under the bus by stating: "If a man sins with a horse or one mule: there is no offence."[829] It was still regarded as a sin, but only got you banned from becoming a priest or approaching the king.

Really life-changing stuff, sure, but at least you got to have a life to change. The Hittites also ruled, as part of Law 199, that if an ox were to jump on a man "in sexual excitement" the ox must be killed, along with a random sheep too (baa-d luck for them). Meanwhile pigs were held in the highest regard. If a man were raped by a pig, this was not an offence for which the pig was punished (regardless of how dis*grunt*led the victim may be). However, should a man initiate sex with a pig, the man was put to death.[830] Who squealed on who first was undoubtedly paramount.

Ultimately it was religion which changed bestiality into an offence. Bestiality started to lose favour when the new kids on the Mediterranean block – the Hebrews – were trying to establish themselves as different from their neighbours (no Jones' to keep up with yet.) It is unlikely they were influenced by the Hittite's previous rulings[831] as evident from this passage in Leviticus: "Do not defile yourselves in any of these ways, because this is how the nations that I am going to drive out before you became defiled."[832] Therefore, in a classic case of last but not beast, the Israelites banned incest because they wanted to define their identity in opposition to the Canaanite people who had inhabited the land prior to the Hebrew's arrival.

These prohibitions were set down in the first five books of the Hebrew Bible (known as the Torah), and because these books were later shared by the Christian and Muslim faiths, religion was responsible for changing attitudes across Europe and the Middle East in the first millennia CE. There are four prohibitions against bestiality in the Hebrew and Christian Bibles. The first is found in Exodus: "Anyone who has sexual relations with an animal is to be put to death".[833] The second was in Deuteronomy: "Cursed is anyone who has sexual relations with any animal".[834] Interestingly this reference does not attribute any punishment to this sin or make it a capital offence as Exodus did. The third and fourth references are in Leviticus which was basically the rule book section of the Bible. It first stated: "Do not have sexual relations with an animal and defile yourself with it. A woman must not present herself to an animal to have sexual relations with it; that is a perversion."[835] Which is nice in the way it recognises women but not so nice in the way it assumes the woman is asking for it and hasn't been "jumped on" Hittite style. The fourth entry is the most detailed of all: "If a man has sexual relations with an animal, he is to be put to death, and you must kill the animal. If a woman approaches an animal to have sexual relations with it, kill both the woman and the animal. They are to be put to death; their blood will be on their own heads."[836] Condemnation of bestiality was clearly not meant to be one of those things open to interpretation.

While religion put a stop to bestiality being morally and legally acceptable, the capital punishment of death prescribed in the religious texts was rarely meted out to Christian zoophiles. This is because there were no government laws yet (secular law only began in the 13th century and didn't completely take over from religion until the 16th century). Thus, the people of Europe were punished according to the religious Penitentials which were based on canon law (church laws based on the Bible) but did not follow it to the letter. The Penitentials originated in the 6th century and at first bestiality was treated like masturbation. One Penitential advised that bestiality should stop once a boy reaches adulthood, thus implying for boys it was an acceptable and common thing to do. The punishment also reflected this belief as a boy got 40 days penance while an adult man was penalised with one year.[837]

These rule books clearly contained punishments for those guilty of bestiality, but they weren't overly harsh because there were seriously blurred lines between animals and humans in the medieval era. For starters, people were with their animals as much as they were with their human loved ones – it was normal to sleep with your beasts in your one-roomed hut to keep them safe from theft or wild animals, and so a close bond would have developed. Then there were statements in the Penitentials which basically *recommended* bestiality, such as the idea that men were better off having sex with a pig than a bit of back door action with their wife. The medieval justice system didn't exactly help matters either by allowing animals to be taken to court and tried for a crime just like a person might be. In France, for example, a sow was convicted of biting a child in 1386. Not content with just hanging the sow for its misconduct, the courts also had the animal dressed in female clothing for the event.[838] If the law was treating animals as humans, why shouldn't the public?

By the end of the 13th century, England had a law – *Fleta, xxxviii.*[3] – which prescribed live burial as a punishment for those engaging in bestiality. However, bestiality rarely led to punishment, let alone the death penalty[839] in England or Europe because there were so many ways to get away with it. Even if they were caught, people could avoid punishment and keep their place in heaven by paying off the local priest. Animals meanwhile were not so lucky. Because they could not pay for their sin in cold hard cash, it was ruled animals should pay with their lives: "animals polluted by coitus with men are to be killed and their flesh thrown to dogs".[840] Being young brought you a lesser penalty, and another way to get away with some cheeky creature copulation was to have a "valid" reason for it, such as Simon in 15th century Venice who was caught having sex with a goat. Having suffered an accident which rendered him unable to perform with women or masturbate, Simon said animals were his *only* option. (Erm… ever heard of abstinence, Simon?) The Venetian authorities, rather than, you know, do their job and convict him of the crime he had been caught doing, chose to investigate Simon's downstairs issue. Firstly, they enlisted the help of a surgeon who concluded Simon's member was mostly normal (a glowing evaluation) but confirmed he was unable to feel sensation or finish the job. Then the authorities employed two (human) prostitutes to use all their skills to test the man and his manhood. Poor Simon. Such suffering. In the end, Simon was judged to be telling the truth, his excuse was accepted, and he got to keep his life. But not his right hand,[841] meaning he was left to enjoy more animal relations. I guess I must have missed that bit in the Bible where it says a man's need to orgasm trumps the ban on bestiality…

It seems the only time in the medieval era bestiality did lead to the death penalty was if you were Scottish or if the law was *misapplied*. Scotland (not to be united with England until 1707) had no state laws against bestiality, but they did prosecute people using the Bible's condemnation. In 1654, John Muir was seen getting it on with a mare and, seemingly having a truth attack, he later confessed that was *actually* his sixth time. In the same year, William MacAdam was found to be violating a cow. Both men and both animals were killed as the Bible stipulated they should be.[842] When it came to misapplication of the law – the English channelled their anti-Semitism. This meant the crime of bestiality was charged against people who had relationships with Jews; i.e., Jews were put in the same category as animals: "Coition with a Jewess is presisciely (sic) the same as if a man should copulate with a dog."[843] In England, in 1222, an Oxford deacon was charged with bestiality after he married a Jewish woman. But while, in reality, if he *had* copulated with a dog, he would have faced one year penance and/or a large fine, the authorities chose to go with the Bible recommendation he was burned to death. Barking mad.

It was not until the 16th century that bestiality turned a corner from blind eyes to all-out public executions. This change occurred due to the Protestant Reformation which led to state law eclipsing church law. The opportunity for governments to create new laws saw bestiality featuring more prominently than in the Penitentials. The Holy Roman Empire led the way in 1524 with a law prescribing death for those engaging in "impurity with a beast". In England, it was part of Henry VIII's 1533 Buggery act which stipulated: "abominable Vice of Buggery committed with mankind or beast... offence be from henceforth ajudged Felony".[844] However, Henry's act had minimal impact on convictions and there are only a few recorded prosecutions of bestiality in England from 1533 until the late 19th century.[845] This was because although his law made it a capital offence, there was no distinction between bestiality and sodomy (male-male sex), and in practice, when the authorities did get round to enforcing the law from the 17th century onwards, they were more concerned with homosexual sex than crimes against nature. That being said, there were some cases that made it to court – such as when Thomas Skinner was convicted of having sex with a mare in 1820. But there was still no conviction because, in an age before weird human talents could be showcased in TikTok challenges, the prosecution was unable to believe Skinner managed the act of copulating with a "high spirited horse" while standing on the rim of a bucket with a "gammy leg".[846]

This minimal conviction rate was not the case over in the European states which had converted to Protestantism (Switzerland, Sweden, the Germanic states, Netherlands and France). Here, the Protestant Reformation caused their law makers to come down harshly on bestiality in law AND in life. French philosopher Voltaire commented at the time: "There is hardly a tribunal in Europe which has not condemned to the fire some miserable ones convicted of this turpitude."[847] As in the Dark Ages, the main perpetrators of bestiality were young peasants who Voltaire sympathetically described as "scarcely differ from the animals with which they couple".[848] In Sweden, between 1630 and 1770, at least 600 men were executed for bestiality[849] – a stark contrast to their *laissez-faire* attitude of the 21st century. And it wasn't just the European Protestants who were more on it than the English – in Catholic Spain and under the influence of the Spanish Inquisition, hundreds were executed for bestiality. One case saw nine Spanish peasants burned alive at the same time for raping mules and donkeys.[850] In fact, there were so many people to burn – the authorities ran out of wood that day. Perhaps they should have asked the notorious nine to help… clearly there was no issue for *them* getting wood.

Proving any crime is difficult, but the European courts found proving bestiality was especially tricky considering only one of those involved could talk. So, the authorities had to be crafty. When French girl, Claudine de Culam, was accused of fornicating with a dog in 1601 but denied the charge, she and the dog were made to prove their innocence. They were both taken to court (the dog wore his birthday suit), and as part of the trial they were made to go into a separate room where Claudine was made to get undressed. The dog's reaction was all the court needed to convict her – he leapt on Claudine and attempted to have sex. Like, real sex. Not dog-awkwardly-humping-your-leg sex. In fact, doggo was *sooo* enthusiastic the court recorded: "he would have perhaps accomplished had we not prevented him".[851] Having successfully proven they were not barking up the wrong tree, Claudine and her dog were strangled, burnt, and their ashes discarded so that no trace remained. But the courts weren't always so "logical" with their efforts to prove guilt. In a few cases the authorities thought it would be wise to ask the animals to confess their crimes. Their method was akin to torture as the accused beast would be held over a fire – if it squealed it was taken as a confession. Unsurprisingly, using this method of squealy hot fire, every animal ended up "confessing" and is perhaps where the expression "to squeal on someone" comes from.

While the emergence of state law was a big factor in formally prohibiting bestiality, it also became seriously uncool in the early modern era due to this being the age of superstition. Europeans suddenly became obsessed with a belief in the devil and the need to hunt down witches, and between 1450 – 1750, sixty thousand people were executed in Europe on the charge of witchcraft, 80% of whom were women.[852] Bestiality was closely linked to witchcraft and the devil in people's minds, especially when goats were the partner of choice because the devil was said to appear as "a great Black Goat with a Candle between his Horns"[853] and since the 11th century a goat head had been used to depict Satan. This figure was known as Baphomet.

Bestiality was considered a form of devil worship, so much so, people even used this as an excuse! Those caught in the act would claim they had seen the devil who then, at some point during their titillating conversation, turned the chat to request they copulate with an animal. For example, in 1718, when Scottish man David Malcolm was caught having sex with a beast – he claimed Satan had forced him to do so. Although off to a good start with his story, he didn't exactly do himself any favours when he then revealed he had tried to have intercourse with the animal numerous times (Malcolm and Satan must have talked a hell of a lot), but this was the first time he had been successful. Sometimes the devil used his powers of persuasion for good, as seen in Switzerland in 1595 when a peasant admitted to the authorities that he and a cow had had sexual relations. Apparently, Satan had visited him after the event and told him that this act had ruined his soul and he needed to confess and repent. While his confession may have saved his soul from eternal damnation, it failed to moo-ve the courts towards forgiveness. He, along with all his family, was killed for his sin.

You may have been lucky enough to have seen pictures of "animals who look like people" as clickbait on various trashy sites. The implication being a human and animal have copulated and produced a child. The science says this isn't possible. But for people living before science, the possibility of "huminals" (my word) was a genuine concern and was why the newly founded British colonies in America began clamping down on bestiality. In New Haven, in 1642, a sow birthed a piglet who looked uncannily like the guy who worked at the farm. George Spenser apparently had "whitish and deformed" eyes[854]... and so did the piglet. Coincidence? Well, yes. But unfortunately for George, he *had* actually been having sex with the sow, something which he later admitted (after denying it under oath, twice) and was executed for. Quite why he admitted to going further than hogs and kisses is beyond me, considering there were no witnesses, but perhaps he genu-swine-ly loved her and wanted to save his lover from being tortured into a confession like previous pigs had been.

A similar case occurred in Plymouth (the American version) a few years later. In 1647 a sow gave birth to a deformed piglet who had "faire and white skin" – just like the guy who worked at that particular farm. And I kid you not, this man was called Thomas Hogg. People really *can* live up to their names. In this case, the authorities had to be more imaginative to get to the bottom of it all because Hogg didn't admit diddly-squat. So, what do you do? Get the pair together to see what happens of course! It's remarkably easy to prove a crime when you make the accused commit said crime in front of your eyes. They went to the sow's barnyard and ordered Human Hogg to fondle Animal Hog. The records state that: "immedyatly there appeared a working of lust in the sow, insomuch that she powred out seede before them".[855] Yes, he made the pig climax. Obviously, they had to prove this was because the two had been at it before and not just because Hogg was the Dr Doolittle of animal orgasms, and so he was ordered to fondle another sow. (Why commit one crime when you can commit two?!) The second victim was indifferent and thus the courts had their "proof". But because different colonies had different laws (like modern US states), Hogg was not executed. He was charged with "filthyness" (pig pens aren't famed for being clean), whipped, and then sent to prison.

Just like the people engaging in bestiality, the crazy stories kept on coming. In Massachusetts, when the authorities were unable to find out which sheep had been used for Thomas Granger's bestial pleasure, they staged a line-up.

Yes, really.

Similar to a modern-day criminal investigation where look-a-likey criminals are lined up against a height chart behind a screen, the local sheep were rounded up (literally… cos they're sheep) and put in a row for Granger to pick out the ones he had been intimate with. What Granger was looking for i.e., whether the sheep were ordered to face forwards or backwards is unknown. Nevertheless, Granger managed to pick out five sheep, and the violated animals were killed in front of him before he was also killed. I like to think that Granger actually picked five sheep he didn't get on with, or those that he'd had a baa-d romance with, in order to let his animal lovers live. Turns out Granger wasn't the fussy sort – he was also charged with copulating with "five sheep, two goats, two calves, a mare, a cow and a turkey".[856] All that was missing was a partridge in a pear tree. But I bet he would have screwed that too if he could have found one.

The last known prosecution for bestiality in the New England colonies of America was in 1681. Once again, the man in question lived up to his name – Thomas Saddeler was accused of copulating with a mare (a female horse). Again, evidence was lacking, and in the end, he was charged with "attempted buggery" – a crime which got him whipped and humiliated with a *P* branded onto his forehead (P= Pollution). He was then banished from the colony, free to saddle up with other mares out of sight. But the prosecutions didn't stop because bestiality became rare, in fact it was the opposite. It was *soooo* common the courts didn't have time to pursue all the offences! The commonality of the act was even used as a defence by Massachusetts man William Hackett in 1642, who claimed, when caught, that bestiality was "perfectly normal back home in rural England".[857] And it seems he was onto something as the frequency of the offence meant the Puritan authorities (the religious types running the colonies) soon became desensitized to the issue and didn't see it as a big deal. Which isn't exactly the best attitude towards crime, is it.

Over in Europe, more leniency towards bestiality emerged in the 18th century as the witchcraft/devil obsession faded away. Some people were still burned at the stake but not as many as before because Europe had largely reduced penalties from death to short jail terms, such as in 1791 when an Englishman was imprisoned for just two years after being caught copulating with a cow.[858] In a twist towards animal rights, some courts even started treating the animals like the victims they were. In France, in 1750, Jaques Ferron was charged with bestiality with an ass, but the court was presented with a petition, signed by various religious and civil officials which stated the ass: "is in a word and deed and in all her habits of life a most honest creature".[859] Ferron was executed but the ass was acquitted. Ferron went from feeling the ass to feeling like a right ass. Shame for Ferron that he didn't live 40 years later as after the French revolution in 1789, France's new civil code made no mention of bestiality as a crime. Bestiality was even decriminalised completely in some Catholic states such as Bavaria in 1813.

This leniency was reflected in the emergence of a new bestiality outlet in the 18th century – animal pornography. Bestiality porn remained legal in the UK until 1959. The Victorian era, although assumed to be an age of prudishness, was awash with pornography of all types; and those making it were keen to appeal to as many fantasies as they could. Pamphlets such as Edmund Curll's 1710 report on an Irishman who "fornicated with a cow and other creatures" commanded a high price – 1 shilling[860] (roughly one day's wage). Pornographers discovered that men liked to imagine women and animals together, particularly if it involved pet cats and dogs, proving that men can be domesticated when they want to be.

Henry's 1533 Buggery Act was not updated until 1861. This change occurred as part of the 19th century age of revolution – a time when the world witnessed massive changes in industry, science, education, and politics (there were a whopping 186 different revolutions[861] around the world in this 100-year period). Following the trend, in Britain, there was also a revolution in animal rights and the RSPCA was formed in 1824 over a cup of coffee. Known at the time as just the SPCA (Queen Victoria added her Royal seal of approval in 1840), this group reflected the change in attitudes about cruelty towards animals. A change which 37 years later led to the 1861 Offences Against the Person Act which ruled: "Whosoever shall be convicted of the abominable Crime of Buggery, committed either with Mankind or with any Animal, shall be liable, at the Discretion of the Court, to be kept in Penal Servitude for Life or for any Term not less than Ten Years".[862] While the act still deemed bestiality just as horrific as homosexual sex, the penalty had been reduced from death to imprisonment. But it still took another 20 years or so for the Home Office to really start hunting down these zoophiles; their oldest record of a bestiality case dates from February 1888 with George Miller's conviction of getting it on with a female sheep.[863] Ewe, gross.

The classification of bestiality being in the same league as homosexual sex came to an end with the Sexual Offences Act of 1967 whereby homosexual sex was decriminalised;[864] but there were no further updates to the prohibition on bestiality until the 21st century. Section 69 (wahey) of The Sexual Offences Act of 2003 made everything much clearer than before and most possibilities were covered, although amusingly there is the loophole of claiming you didn't know it was an animal: "if he knows". [865] The only thing left out of the law was necrophilia with a dead animal – hopefully because this was unheard of rather than tacitly being approved. If convicted, a person could be imprisoned for up to two years. Between 2005 and 2019 (the latest statistics currently available) a total of thirty-five[866] people have been convicted of bestiality in England and Wales (thirty-one were in England and four were in Wales).[867] We better rethink all those Welsh jokes…

Interestingly, while the 20th century saw progress in bestiality legislation in Britain and Nazi Germany in 1935 (the latter due to Hitler being a lover of animals… though I think the world would have fared better if he had focussed on people instead); other European countries went in the opposite direction and made it legal! Russia legalised zoophilia in 1903; Denmark in 1933; Iceland in 1940; Sweden in 1944 (being neutral in WW2 obviously meant they didn't have much going on); Hungary in 1961; West Germany in 1969 (this is the capitalist bit by the way, even the communists in the East with all their 'everyone's equal' malarky did not stretch to include animals); Austria and Finland in 1971; and Norway in 1972. One reason why these nations made the change was due to a desire to move away from morality-based legislation[868] i.e., they didn't want to convict people based on opinions of what was right and wrong and therefore bestiality was deemed illegal if it could be proved the animal was harmed.

The practice of bestiality is thousands of years old and has roots in spiritual ceremonies as well as practical needs to fulfil sexual desires. Religion has initiated the biggest change in condemning the practice, but it still goes on because ultimately, some people like weird sex. Currently in Europe – Hungary, Finland, and Romania are the only countries where bestiality is not illegal[869] because the 21st century saw most countries re-criminalise the act, with France leading the way in 2004[870] (they had no prohibition against it since the 18th century) and Denmark being the most recent in 2015. Of course, not everyone was happy about this, least of all German man Michael Kiok when Germany re-criminalised the act in 2013. When the new law came in, Michael publicly stated he would appeal the change (he didn't win) because he didn't think laws should be made based on people's squeamishness. At the time he was the midst of an eight-and-a-half-year relationship with an Alsatian named Cessie, but he revealed the two don't have penetrative sex because "she doesn't like it".[871] So at least he's not a rapist too. Similarly, over in Canada, when Brian Cutteridge was found guilty of bestiality in 2012, he protested that the law was wrong because his constitutional rights to equality were being ignored.[872] People like Michael and Brian feel justified in their choices thanks to validation from some sex therapists. One therapist stated: "The accusation 'that a dog who licks peanut butter off your hand is getting a treat, while the same dog licking peanut butter off [your genitals] is being sexually abused' is absurd."[873] Not as absurd as likening those two events as similar situations that's for sure. Let's see how she likes it when she's innocently licking a lolly only to discover there's a penis inside.

Cannibalism*

Cannibalism is "the practice of someone who eats human flesh"[874] but this chapter will really get under the skin of the issue and explore how and why people have been eating *all* human parts for thousands of years.

Cannibalism is one of the ultimate taboos, and it has been this way since the 8th century BCE thanks to Homer (as in the ancient Greek writer, not the Duff-drinking yellow man) who preached against it in *The Odyssey*. Since then, and thanks to stories from Shakespeare; the Brothers Grimm; Daniel Defoe's *Robinson Crusoe*; Freud's *Totem and Taboo;* and Thomas Harris' *Silence of the Lambs* *shoutout to Hannibal Lector*, it has become associated with depravity, savages, and sickos. It even features in fairy tales, for example the original story of *Snow White* (written by Charles Perrault) has a scene where the queen eats a bit of what she thinks is Snow White's heart. A scene which, for some reason, Disney leaves out of their 1937 animated version. Similarly, *Hansel and Gretel* has an underbelly of cannibal bellies – the pair were abandoned by their parents due to an ongoing famine, and the witch so desperately wanted them because she wanted to eat them. Famines spell trouble for witches too, you know.

The truth is, cannibalism is not unique to wicked individuals or works of fiction; it has existed longer than us

_____
*Do not try this at home.

Homo sapiens have (cannibalism began with our ancestors – the Homo antecessors) and it is more common throughout history than we'd like to stomach. Archaeological and anthropological studies have proven that people have been eating people since people walked this earth.[875] It's been a real bone-anza for cannibals since day one. From the archaeological side, human bones have been found which show evidence of being deliberately de-fleshed (the muscle and skin have been carefully stripped away), a process that can *only* be completed by another human. Meanwhile, anthropological studies have revealed cannibalistic practices in our genes. Apparently, it is an evolved human trait to turn to cannibalism in crisis times because our overriding instinct is to survive to fulfil our reproductive role. Just don't expect the defence of "I ate him to ensure I could have a baby later in life" to work in court.

Even Jesus told us to eat him! "Anyone who does eat my flesh and drink my blood has eternal life… For my flesh is real food and my blood is real drink."[876] Maybe this is meant to be metaphorical but if that's how we're meant to interpret the Bible, how come all the "women are inferior to men" parts weren't seen as metaphorical by the exclusively male Christian clergy?

People who eat people have not always been called cannibals, and until the 16th century they were known as *anthropophagi*. The term *anthropophagi* was created by the ancient Greeks, a civilisation famed for creating long and difficult words along with other more useful things like democracy. The term *cannibal* comes from a mix of European prejudice and geographical location. In the 1490s, Columbus discovered the Caribbean islands, home to the Caribe people who were infamous flesh eaters. The prejudicial descriptions which then flooded back into Europe heralded these Caribe people as dogs ("Canis"). This then merged with Columbus' description of the Caribe people in his diaries as *Canibales*[877] and thus a new word was formed.

There are four main types of cannibalism – survival, ritualistic, medicinal, and just plain psychotic. There are also different classifications. Endocannibalism is eating those within your culture group; exocannibalism is eating people outside of your group; homicidal cannibalism is doing it for "fun"; and auto-cannibalism is to consume yourself in some way. Disturbingly we all fit into this last category because sucking that cut on your finger, biting your nails, and even eating your bogies all count as eating yourself. You cheeky little cannibal, you.

Prehistoric origins

Europe has the fun claim to fame of having the oldest evidence of cannibalism; remains found in Spain and France date back at least 150,000 years. The Homo antecessors were the first guys on the scene for the human race over 530,000 years ago and evidence proves the Homo antecessor was a cannibal.[878] A pit excavated in northern Spain between the 1980s and 1990s (known as *Sima de los Huesos*, aka Pit of Bones) contained human bones with scrape marks on them made by tools designed to cleanly remove the flesh. In France in 1991, palaeontologists (like Ross from *Friends*), discovered 100,000-year-old bones from six Neanderthal victims at a cave known as *Moula-Grecy*, which showed similar evidence of cannibalistic activity. Marrow had been scraped out of their bones; brains had been removed from the skull; their bodies had been cut at the shoulder to make them easier to carry; and cut marks left on the bones suggested, just like in Spain, filleting had taken place using tools.[879] While this could be deemed circumstantial evidence, if you've ever seen a dog try to carry a long stick through a doorway, you'll appreciate the unlikeliness of an animal thinking to neatly cut up a body to make it easy to carry. Let alone ignore their razor-sharp teeth in favour of creating a scraping tool.

Interestingly, these human OGs ate each other not because they needed to survive. They did it because they liked it. Ian Tattersall, head of the Anthropology Department at the American Museum of Natural History, confirms that: "the environment was pretty rich, and you wouldn't necessarily need to practice cannibalism to make your metabolic ends meet".[880] At a time when urbanisation was not a thing (though they could probably just about say "ur"), animals were ten-a-plenty and there would be no issue finding a meaty dinner. Therefore, the cannibalism which took place was more likely out of choice than necessity.

After the Homo antecessors and Neanderthals died out, the prehistoric (48,000–10,000 BCE) Homo sapiens used cannibalism in a more pragmatic way – to get rid of dead bodies.[881] While there is evidence that human burials began with the Neanderthals around 130,000 years ago,[882] it was still hazardous if you did not bury the body deep enough because it attracted predators. Following a variety of meetings and a thorough risk assessment (maybe), the Homo sapiens chose to avoid this danger by eating the dead person. There was, of course, zero acknowledgement of cannibalism being "wrong" – after all there were no laws against it, or religion to guide people at this early stage in our development. Not that Christianity would have helped anyway, considering Jesus' blasé attitude to the whole thing.

However, pragmatism wasn't always the motivation in prehistoric times. In Britain there is evidence of cannibalism occurring 14,700 years ago, and archaeologists have proved that they, too, were people eaters out of choice rather than necessity. People now known as the *Cro-Magnons* came from Western Europe to live in Britain after the last ice age finished and, after passing their citizenship test, they settled in Cheddar Gorge,

Somerset. In the 1980s, archaeologists excavated Gough's Cave, located in Cheddar Gorge, and discovered dozens of bones which showed cut marks resulting from cannibalistic practices. Dr Silvia Bello of the Natural History Museum has studied the cut marks and found that the bones were stripped of all their muscle and then deliberately broken to get to the marrow inside. Brains, tongues, and eyes were all systematically removed. Why? Well, the Brits love a drink don't they! Without Ikea to supply some funky rainbow-coloured beakers, the prehistoric people had to fashion their own. From someone else's skull of course.[883] Scientists from the Natural History Museum established that skulls were also used as bowls based on how the brains were expertly scooped out leaving a bowl shape. They theorised that if prehistoric people wanted just the brain, then there were much quicker ways of getting to it – such as simply smashing the skull to smithereens. Dr Bello confirmed that this process was deliberate and not linked to starvation: "We don't see any traumatic wounds in these remains which would suggest this violence was being inflicted on living people. This was some kind of cultural process that they brought with them from Europe."[884] Bet Nigel Farage and co. wish they had known *that* fun fact for their Brexit campaign.

Thanks to the British weather, this gorging at the Gorge only lasted a mere few thousand years. Around 10,700 BCE, temperatures in Britain plunged back to ice-age levels and the population fell as people "went back to where they came from" in search of sunshine, sangria, and presumably more skulls to drink it from.

Survival

Survival means you've done it, so you don't starve to death. The earliest recorded example of survival cannibalism comes from China and occurred in 594 BCE during a war between Ch'u state and Sung state. In the capital city of Sung, people avoided starvation by eating children. They did at least have the decency to not eat their own children, though, and thus began an exchange programme where instead of going to live with another family for a week or so, children went to another family to ensure *the family* lived another week or so. This was so successful that in 205 BCE, it was made legal in an imperial edict (a law made by the emperor).[885] Children got a bit of a break during a war in 259 BCE when soldiers defending a castle in Chao firstly ate servants and concubines (a woman who is living with a man as his bit-on-the-side)… before moving onto children, then women, with men of low status becoming the last supper factually and figuratively. Historian Key Ray Chong has discovered 153 separate incidents of war-related survival cannibalism and 177 incidents of natural-disaster-related survival cannibalism from the last 2600 years of Chinese history.[886] This might not sound like a lot, but it works out as happening roughly every eight years which is more regular than the census. The Chinese potentially eight people for dinner on eight different occasions.

The ancient world also saw incidences of survival cannibalism in the Middle East and Africa. In the Old Testament of the Bible, written sometime between 1200 BCE and 165 BCE (by persons unknown), cannibalism was undertaken by the besieged citizens of Jerusalem and Samaria. Jerusalem was obviously the place *not* to be because cannibalism was again later reported due to the Roman's siege in 70 CE.[887] The logistics of survival cannibalism were revealed by a man credited with being the first historian – the ancient Greek Herodotus – aka "The Father of History". In his book *The Histories* (5th century BCE), Herodotus explained how the starving men involved in King Cambyses's exploration of

Ethiopia chose who would be eaten in such a time of crisis by drawing lots. The unlucky one-in-every-ten to draw the short straw then became dinner for the other nine.[888] The plan worked to keep most men alive (yay for them), but not so great for the rest of us left having to deal with all the discarded straws clogging up the seas.

Survival cannibalism came to England because of William the Conqueror (the dude who won the Battle of Hastings in 1066). Prior to 1066, the north of England was pretty tight with the Danes, and so they weren't too keen on this random bloke from France taking over and claiming to be their king. After William paid the Danes to leave England and allow him to get the cool "conqueror" bit added to his name (you can appreciate his need for this considering he was previously known as William the Bastard), he was left with the Yorkshire locals to deal with. Unfortunately for them, William was not up for watching *Emmerdale* with a cup of tea, and instead retaliated with an early form of scorched earth policy – a military strategy whereby anything useful to the enemy is destroyed. This act is now known as the "Harrying of the North" and his men set about burning down people's homes and scorching their fields of crops. An act which the French nuns, who recorded William's ventures into England, proudly sewed into the Bayeux Tapestry for all to see. The result was starvation for the survivors with 75% of the Yorkshire population wiped out.[889]

To ensure future recovery was impossible, and because he was still a bit of a bastard, William had the soil salted so that it was too poisonous for crops to grow in the coming years. Symeon of Durham said that the countryside remained empty and uncultivated for nine years. The Domesday Book recorded one-third of the available land in Yorkshire was still wasteland by 1086: "*vasta*".[890] There's no doubt William completely salted out the opposition, but as a result, survival cannibalism began in northern England during the winter of 1069/70. John of Worcester, a 12th-century chronicler, reported: "… men were driven to feed on the flesh of horses, dogs, cats, and even of human beings". [891] If old John, living 165 miles away in Worcester, doesn't strike you as a reliable sort of chap, then there's also the findings of modern historian Jay Rubenstein who discovered that cooked human flesh was sold at the markets during this time as a sort of fun takeaway option. [892] Available with a side of Lord of the Fries.

About 30 years after William made the north eat itself, survival cannibalism next made a European appearance during the Crusades. The Crusades took place between the 11th and 13th centuries; they were basically a series of religious wars between Christians and Muslims – both of whom wanted to claim and keep the Holy Land (Jerusalem) as their own. These wars were encouraged by the Pope and fought by Christian soldiers, members of the public, and children who fancied a gap year abroad. And no, it wasn't the enemy Muslims who were doing the eating – it was the supposedly saintly Christians who are recorded (by their own people) as turning to cannibalism after capturing the Syrian city Ma'arra, and then again during a siege in Antioch.

There are three eyewitness accounts from Europeans of what happened. The first account explains how the Christian Crusaders ate Muslim buttocks and the author even had the cheek (like the Crusaders *literally* did) to finish with a criticism of the quality of cooking: "…very many of our people, harassed by the madness of excessive hunger, cut off pieces from the buttocks of the Saracens already dead there, which they cooked and chewed, and devoured with savage mouth, when insufficiently roasted at the fire".[893] The second account confirmed the cannibalism but also added a delightful anecdote about the Christian soldiers hunting through the guts of the dead to find a gold or silver coin: "…So, they ripped up the bodies of the dead, because they used to find bezants hidden in their entrails, and others cut the dead flesh into slices and cooked it to eat."[894] The third account of Crusader cannibalism explains how, even though the bodies were visibly decomposing in this pre-fridge age, Christian soldiers were not put off by them being past their best before date: "Meanwhile there was so great a famine in the army that the people ate most greedily the many already fetid bodies of the Saracens which they had cast into the swamps of the city two weeks and more ago".[895] But at least it's good to know the soldiers would have been swamped with choice.

The Pope was told all about the cannibalism in a letter signed by three of the most prominent crusade leaders in September 1099. In the letter, the men describe how at Antioch and Ma'arra: "some might scarcely refrain themselves from eating human flesh".[896] There is a disparity in the reports about how much the leaders approved of such a thing, but it's likely they supported it because you can't win a crusade if your army have starved to death. Plus, there was the added benefit of cannibalism making them look 'ard to the enemy Muslims. Problem was, back home in Europe, such tales of cannibalism were harmful because people in the Middle Ages were led to believe only certain people committed such acts. You know the ones, the falsely accused go-to scapegoats of history: Jews, witches, and pagans (people with no religion). But seeing how *Sky News* weren't around to report on such atrocities, it was relatively easy to cover up and just not talk about it. Even the accounts which were written down could not have been read by the uneducated masses. Illiteracy was a real blessing in disguise for these Christian Crusaders.

War continued to be a cause for cannibalism into the 20th century where civil war (caused by the communist revolution) led to survival cannibalism in Russia between 1921–22. Russia converted to communism in the 1917 October Revolution[5] – an event organised by Vladimir Lenin – who the Germans thoughtfully helped get back into the country after Russia had kicked him out for being a troublemaker. The revolution occurred due to poor leadership from Tsar Nicholas II and their disastrous experience in WW1. Unfortunately, the Tsar had not inherited the good-at-ruling gene from his British grandma Queen Victoria, and he left important decisions, like arming the army, to his wife. Or when she wasn't available, he deferred to the hedonistic madman Rasputin (nowadays more widely known as "Ra-Ra-Rasputin, Russia's greatest love machine"). To be fair, it *was* difficult to rule Russia because it was just so bloomin' huge! The land covered one-quarter of the world and by 1914 had a population of 130 million, 60% of whom unhelpfully only spoke Russian as a foreign language.[897] Huge losses and embarrassing defeats in WW1 further turned public support away from the Tsar. Defeats which were caused by the fact Russia did not get the memo that machine guns were in – and cavalry, lances, and sabres were out. Even when the Russian troops did get guns, they had to share one between three.[898] By the end of 1914, in just four months, Russia had suffered one million casualties; by 1918, their total casualty rate was a whopping 76% compared to Britain's 36%.[899] And so, in the least violent revolution ever (only six people died[900]) the Tsar was deposed, and communist rule began. Lenin promptly got his coat and left the WW1 party early, on 3 March 1918, and charged straight into a civil war – fought

---

[5] The October revolution actually happened in November, but the Russians were so (literally) behind the times having not yet updated their calendar to the Gregorian version, that for the rest of us, it happened in October. And the name stuck.

between communist supporters (come on you Reds) and Tsarist supporters (the Whites).

It was the impact of the Russian civil war which directly led to cannibalism. Outdated farming methods (horse-drawn ploughs and manpower rather than machines) meant Russia was already producing less than was needed, but the advent of communism meant the food that *did* exist was taken away from the peasants who grew it – to share it out equally. As is the communist way. Feeding Red Army soldiers took priority over feeding the families that birthed them. This meant that when a famine hit in the Volga region in 1921–2 there were no stores of grain to make up the shortfall. Famines were not a rare occurrence – there had been four in this district in the last twenty years alone, but this time, with no stores in place, five million people ended up dying of starvation.[901] By spring 1921, one-quarter of the peasants in Russia were starving and the famine had spread from the Volga region to seven other districts. To make matters worse, they were trapped in these famine ridden regions because the government stopped all trains in an effort to prevent the spread of cholera and typhoid. Evidently communist equality doesn't stretch to sharing disease. These people were beyond hangry, as evidenced by the story of one woman with her child at the Simbirsk train station in spring 1921: "The child cries, asking for food… this seems to drive the woman mad… She rains blows with her fist on its little face, on its head and at last she throws it upon the floor and kicks it with her foot."[902]

Hangry soon turned to Cangry (cannibal hungry) and survival cannibalism became a remarkably common choice with thousands of cases reported in the worst affected areas.[903] Much like the meat markets in 11th century northern England, local cafés had human flesh on the menu and young children were literally served up on a plate.[904] Children were a frequent feature because they were often the first to die, so this was practical in a way, but they were also (apparently) the yummiest because their flesh tasted sweet. One man who was convicted of eating children justified his actions by explaining: "In our village everyone eats human flesh."[905] Obviously, he had never heard the mum classic of "would you jump off a cliff if everyone else did?" He wasn't the only one to feel it was OK to eat people. Interviews from other corpse-consumers show how they rationalised the process as *not* being a criminal act because the soul had already departed the body and it would be wasteful to not take advantage and instead leave it "for the worms in the ground".[906] Reasoning which allowed them to worm their way out of feeling guilty.

Cannibalism really took off in the winter of 1921 when snow and ice covered up all the food substitutes such as grass, weeds, moss, leaves, and tree bark. People who died were not buried, instead their corpses were stored in barns to be later cut up, boiled and consumed by their surviving relatives. Those that had been previously buried were dug up to be eaten – this became such an issue that armed guards had to be placed at cemetery gates to try and prevent it happening. There are even stories of families not waiting for natural causes to take its toll on their weakest members and killing their youngest children, usually the girls (ladies first and all that), to feed the rest of the family. Relief workers and police did travel to the region to try and stop such practices but didn't think to bring food with them and were strangely unsuccessful. In one case they arrived in Ivanovka to find a woman mid-way through eating her dead husband. She was not a happy bunny and shouted at them: "We will not give him up, we need him for food, he is our own family."[907] Disturbingly, cannibalism soon became comparable to a can of pringles – once you pop you can't stop, and doctors working in the region described: "the insuperable and uncomfortable craving" they developed to eat more people once they'd had a taste.[908] Which, incidentally, is the exact same excuse vampires use when questioned.

Cannibalism became such a common occurrence that a new crime of murder-for-meat emerged. Gangs would attack and either eat the victim themselves or sell the body parts to others. In Pugachev it was too dangerous for children to go out after dark (just too darn tasty); conversely in the Novouzensk area it was too dangerous for everyone else to go out as gangs of children roamed the streets killing adults to eat. These kiddie gangs had their own "moral" code and were often married with kids of their own, and three murders under their belt by the age of 12. Girls as young as seven were prostitutes and many were alcoholics or addicted to heroin or cocaine.[909] Which if they chose the latter might at least alleviate some of those hunger pangs.

Communism made the famine worse and thus increased the levels of survival cannibalism. In a classic example of communist censorship, Lenin's government denied there was a famine and reported that all was well. A claim they were so desperate for others to believe they exported MILLIONS OF TONS of their cereal crops to sell to other nations![910] There are no words. Or foods.

However, from July 1921 there was no hiding away any more as an appeal for help "To all Honest People"[911] was made by the renowned Russian writer Maxim Gorky. Wanting to seem honest, America provided relief under the leadership of future president Herbert Hoover. By summer 1922, American aid was feeding 10 million Russians every day as well as supplying tools and seed to help the Russians help themselves. As a way of saying thank you to America for their $61 million worth of assistance, the Bolsheviks (the name for the Russian communists) accused them of spying, seized their supplies, and arrested their relief workers.[912] Sensing they weren't welcome, American help ended in June 1923, but luckily, they had done enough to ensure 1922 and 1923 saw bumper harvests and the famine and cannibalism ended. For now.

Twenty years later, courtesy of World War Two, cannibalism returned to USSR (they got their fancy new name in 1922). This time it was caused by the Nazi siege of the city of Leningrad, which lasted for 872 days, from 8 September 1941, to 27 January 1944. Between 632,000 and 1 million people died during the siege.[913] Food was rationed and centrally stored but when the Nazis bombed this storage facility, people had to take desperate measures to survive. Resident writer, Tikhonov, recorded how workers ate grease from machine bearings and drank oil found in their factories,[914] and another survivor recounted how her mother used glue to make soup more filling, which doesn't sound particularly tasty but at least this mum wasn't stuck for ideas.

Survival cannibalism in Leningrad saw some continuities in behaviour – such as digging up dead bodies and targeting women and children, but it also brought a new option to the table – eating bits of yourself. Viktor Koslov remembers: "People were cutting off and eating their own buttocks,"[915] which must have really bummed them out. Just as in the 1920s famine – graveyards became supermarkets with one woman recorded as being arrested on her way back from the cemetery with the bodies of five dead children in a sack.[916] Children who were still alive were at huge risk of being grabbed and gorged because "their flesh was so much more tender"[917] and obviously when you're starving, taste is super important. Women were targeted because of the extra fat Mother Nature decided to plant on their bodies. Edith Katya Matus survived the siege and recalled: "I remember a neighbour, a woman, used to come knocking at the door of our apartment shouting at mother, 'Let me in!' And she would run through the door, because her husband was trying to kill her to eat her".[918] Women were also able to award people with the booby prize: "Women's bodies with breasts cut off, which people had taken to eat."[919]

For those who didn't fancy eating their own bum, just as in the 1921 famine, there was also the option to buy human flesh at the market. While the label might have said dog, cat, or horse (wink wink Tesco), it was actually human meat. Many survivors claimed that burgers made from minced human were available to buy as early as November 1941.[920] The streets of Leningrad were soon carpeted with rotting and dismembered corpses; severed legs were found with the meaty bits chopped off, and scraps of bodies were found dumped in bins. All of this was, of course, hidden from the world at the time. Can't have communism getting a bad rep and all that. Leningrad was even named "Hero City" for the behaviour of its citizens once World War Two ended as a thinly veiled attempt to make the residents keep schtum. Stalin conveniently purged the evidence of cannibalism from the records just as he was happily purging all those captured USSR soldiers who returned home (his rationale being that if you got captured then clearly, you're not a good soldier). But in 2004 the truth was revealed by the NKVD, aka the People's Commissariat for Internal Affairs. Their report stated that around 2000 Leningraders were arrested for cannibalism during the siege and many were executed for their crime.[921]

It wasn't just in Russia that survival cannibalism made an appearance during World War Two, the Japanese also resorted to this. And they nearly ate future American president George H. W. Bush! The man famous for fathering President George "dubya" Bush and taking credit for ending the Cold War (by being the one to announce it was over in 1989), narrowly escaped becoming a victim of Japanese survival cannibalism in

September 1944.[922] The Japanese were quite au-fait with the process of cannibalism from their historic ritual of feeding on their foes, and thus when Japanese soldiers found themselves starving on the island of Chichi Jima, their Lieutenant General Yoshio Tachibana saw no problem with eating their American detainees. He ordered the execution of a group of eight imprisoned American pilots and medical staff were then asked to cut their livers out to be dished for dinner. There should have been nine livers on the menu that night, but Bush senior had somehow been the only one to avoid capture and was saved by an American submarine. Bush was definitely living life on the hedge with this last-minute escape.

While war has been the cause of survival cannibalism thus far, in some cases in the modern era it has been driven by bad weather. Most recently this occurred in 1972 when the Uruguay rugby union team plane crashed in the Andes. Of the 45 people on board, only 16 survived, and those that did managed to do so because they ate the bodies of their deceased teammates. One survivor, Roberto Canessa, explained his role in the whole thing: "We had to eat these dead bodies, and that was it. The flesh had protein and fat, which we needed, like cow meat. I was also used to medical procedures, so it was easier for me to make the first cut."[923] They justified their decision by agreeing *their* bodies could be used in the same way if they died. They also used the Jesus Justification in what is now known as the "communion defence" or as the cynics would call it "good PR". Survivor Pablo Delgado helped the aghast public understand their thinking by telling everyone how the Lord's Supper had been their inspiration, essentially because Jesus had shared his body with his mates, it was OK for them to do the same.[924] It worked, and with everyone seeming to forget how "metaphorical" that bit in the Bible was meant to be, the top Archbishop in Uruguay publicly forgave them of their sins.

A more infamous tale of bad weather survival cannibalism is that of the Donner Party. This was a group of 87 American pioneers (people trying to settle across America) who in 1846–47 got stranded in the Sierra Nevada mountains while trying to reach sunny California. The group was a mix of families – there were 29 men, 15 women and 43 children; they ended up being stranded for a total of five months, with 45 people surviving.[925] Two families out of 12 had all members make it through – the Reeds and the Breens.[926] Mr Breen kept a journal beginning 20 November 1846, and he described how *others* resorted to cannibalism but insisted his family had not – presumably they had managed to survive on thin air: "Mrs Murphy said here yesterday that thought she would commence on Milt. & eat him… The Donnos told the California folks that they commence to eat the dead people 4 days ago…"[927] Fun Fact: President Abraham Lincoln (famous for winning the American Civil War, ending slavery, being assassinated at the theatre, and wearing a big hat) would have been on this doomed trip too if it were not for his wife, Mary Todd, putting her foot down, saying: "I don't think so, matey, you just got elected to Congress and we got two kids." Or something to that effect.

While bad weather was ultimately to blame for their cannibalism, human error also played a big part in this group's fate. Their piss-poor planning meant they were the last of the season's pioneer groups to leave in May 1846 (they should have left in early April to avoid winter in the mountains). Admittedly, the snow was early that year, BUT the group still would have made it over the mountains if they hadn't made the ludicrous decision to try a shortcut called the Hastings Cut-off that no one had tried before. Literally no one. Not even the guy who said it existed had tried it. But they thought they would be the first – pioneer by name, pioneer by nature, I guess. The 125-mile "shortcut" added an extra month to their journey and the only thing cut short was their lives. The group split into two but even the faster-paced group of 59 did not make it through to civilisation before five feet of snow fell on Halloween night. They were forced to turn back and take shelter in some dilapidated cabins around Truckee Lake while the other 21 slower members took shelter eight miles back in the Alder Creek Valley.

Survival cannibalism began with a breakaway group of ten men and five women who left to find help after one month of eating horses; boiled leather; tree bark; animal hides; mice; and their dogs (paw things). They were so keen to eat each other that the idea was first mooted before anyone had even died! They considered drawing lots or having two men (yay for sexism!) fight to the death to decide who would be eaten first. However, it did not come to this as three of the group succumbed to the freezing conditions just two days later and their bodies were promptly cooked and eaten by their companions. But soon enough they were hankering for more food. Thirty-year-old William Foster, a carpenter by trade, was keen to kill and eat three of the women, because, you know, sexism (I'm assuming he liked the other two… you'd certainly hope so considering one was his wife), but this was not agreed upon by the others. Undeterred, Foster then suggested they eat the two natives – Salvador and Luis, because, you know, racism. These two had joined the Donner Party just before they became snowbound but upon hearing Foster's plan, they legged it. Two days later they were found, and by most accounts, Foster shot both in the head (the only case of murder for meat that took place) and they too were eaten.[928] Foster, who survived the journey, was never prosecuted for this. A total of eight people died on this journey; historian and Donner Party researcher Kristin Johnson states there is: "no question"[929] that all but one of the deceased were eaten by their comrades. This fuelled two men and all five of the women (Mother Nature's fat stores, remember) to complete their journey, arriving at a ranch in California in January 1847 when rescue attempts began.

The rescue missions revealed the existence of survival cannibalism, as well as the sad fact of people having to eat their own family members and the alarming case of one individual who seemed to quite to like it. There were four rescue missions in total; the second attempt failed and saw two families having to be abandoned at "Starved Camp" – three of whom died (the survivors ate their dead relatives)[930] before the rest were saved a few weeks later. James Reed, the leader of the second relief mission, observed that when arriving at Truckee Lake: "Among the cabins lay the fleshless bones and half eaten bodies of the victims."[931] As well as describing how: "The mutilated body of a friend, having nearly all the flesh torn away was seen at the door… half consumed limbs were seen concealed in trunks. Bones were scattered about."[932] Even the namesakes of the whole expedition did not escape a cannibalistic fate; as the second relief mission arrived at Alder Creek, they found Jacob Donner's children feasting on their father's roasted liver and heart. Their faces were apparently stained with blood, and they didn't even notice the rescue party arrive so engrossed were they in dining on dad. Evidence (i.e., bones) also suggested they had previously consumed four other bodies.[933] Mrs Tamzene Donner was eaten by German emigrant Lewis Keseberg, who was the last to be found by the fourth rescue party in April 1847. Right from the start, Keseberg was a big red flag disguised as a man – he was abusive towards his young, pregnant wife, Philippine, (buy one get one free in cannibal talk) and disrespectful towards the natives by looting their burial sites as the group travelled. Keseberg was located with a cauldron of cooked human chunks and surrounded by human bones. Some of the surviving children said that Keseberg hadn't even waited for natural causes to give him his dinner; one night he had taken a young boy under his wing to "comfort" him, which in Keseberg world actually meant killing him. In the morning, the child was found hanging from the wall of the cabin like slaughtered cattle, before being eaten.[934] Keseberg himself had no issue with admitting to his cannibalism, and he revealed that for two whole months all he had eaten were humans.

Subsequent archaeological digs have revealed the extent of cannibalism in the Donner Party. Thousands of bones have been discovered at the sites by archaeologists, and 362 of the bones showed the flesh had been deliberately removed i.e., cannibalised. Around one-quarter of them had evidence of being smashed and others had been smoothed around the edges due to being stirred in a pot during the cooking process.[935] While the snowstorms and freezing temperatures had caused the marooning, it ironically also helped people survive because the surroundings became a freezer for their human meals. Parents deliberately placed dead bodies under the snow and ice to preserve them for later.[936] That's why mums go to Iceland!

In 20th century communist China, human error once again led to survival cannibalism. Russia was not the only communist nation where people were forced to eat each other to survive. (Sidenote: this should have been the content of all those anti-communist posters in the Cold War, right? The Americans really missed a trick there focussing on "the Red menace" rather than "they're gonna eat you".) China fell victim to survival cannibalism during the Great Leap Forward (1958–1960) and the Cultural Revolution (1966–1976). Incidentally, both events have entirely inappropriately positive names – the only thing *great* about the Great Leap Forward was the fact it led to the greatest famine the world has ever seen – between 20 and 45 million people died.[937] The other claim to fame is no better – the Great Leap Forward led to the biggest number of cannibalism related deaths ever recorded in China.[938] There was also no culture to be found in the Cultural Revolution where between 400,000 and 20 million people died.[939] The death tolls in both events have a huge range between the lower and higher estimates because lots of deaths went unreported, lots were covered up, and China, for some reason, has been reluctant to fully research either event.

The human error factor came from Chairman Mao Zedong, who converted China to communism in 1949. His first big idea, after communism, was the Great Leap Forward which was intended to industrialise China and move people away from a rural and agricultural lifestyle. Which it did. A bit *too* well. Because unfortunately for the Chinese civilians, Mao had not clicked about the link between agriculture and food... and a famine soon ensued. *Gazetters* were used to record information and their accounts stated: "people ate each other... exchanging children and eating them" and "people ate each other to the point that close kind destroyed each other".[940] However, some scholars say that only a few people were truly eaten.[941] Apparently, these statements from the *Gazetters,* whose sole purpose is to record what they see, are all metaphorical. That old chestnut again.

A mere six years after Mao failed to Leap, he had another go at making China more communist – a thorough bodge-job which saw him become the face of the proverb: "those who cannot remember the past are condemned to repeat it".[942] Yep, he caused another famine and another episode of survival cannibalism. He thought this "cultural revolution" would be a good idea because Chinese communism was going in the wrong direction (not enough left turns), and he wanted to purge the "impure" parts of the regime while also improving his personal reputation. The Chinese people were urged to rid China of the "Four Olds": old customs, old culture, old habits, and old ideas. So, naturally, they went after the old people. This vigilante group was mainly youngsters and students because Mao had closed the schools so they could focus on this sort of culture (murder) instead.

There were murders across China during the Cultural Revolution, but it was only in Guangxi region that cannibalism occurred with 421 cases recorded in thirty-one of the seventy-five counties of Guangxi.[943] Cannibalism took place in Guangxi for over a year and has been described as "state sponsored" due to the fact the leaders of the Revolutionary Committee and local militia organised the armed forces to engage in this kind of behaviour.[944] Systematic murder and cannibalisation were carried out in the name of political revolution and "class struggle".[945] Those selected were landlords, rich peasants, ex-members of the opposition KMT party, and any communist who didn't fully agree with Mao's policies. Senior party historians corroborated allegations of cannibalism,[946] and more accounts can be found in the official *Cultural Revolution Annals* of Wuxuan County, Guangxi Autonomous Region in the South of China, such as: "On July 10, 1968… Liao Tianlong, Liao Jinfu, Zhong Zhenquan and Zhong Shaoting were beaten to death. Their bodies were stripped of flesh, which was taken back to the front of the brigade office to be boiled in two big pots. Twenty or thirty people participated in the cannibalism. Right out in the open, they boiled human flesh in front of the local government offices."[947]

What was different about survival cannibalism in the Cultural Revolution was the element of theatre and enjoyment. The atrocities sometimes occurred as entertainment: "Feasts of human flesh, at which people celebrated by drinking and gambling, were a common sight."[948] A report from the *Annals* highlights the numbers of people involved being akin to a festival: "And they just kill those victims and they cut their chests they prise the hearts and livers out and just eat them. At least 10,000 people participated."[949] Those participating were clearly looking to enjoy their meal, and cooking was not rushed with the desperation of near death but instead: "all their body parts – heart, liver, gallbladder, kidneys, elbows, feet, tendons, intestines – were boiled, barbecued or stir-fried into a gourmet cuisine…"[950]

All instances of survival cannibalism explored have not resulted in mass prosecution and condemnation. Partly due to cover-ups and lost records but mainly because it seems to be understood that this was a desperate measure. Even after the Cultural Revolution, where there was clearly a different vibe to previous examples, those caught were later released. Between 1981 and 83, an investigation was sent to Guangxi County, and just like Santa, they made a list of those who had been naughty and who had been nice. Fifteen people were jailed and 130 were expelled from the Party. But in reality, these sanctions were all just an elaborate cover-up and the punishments were withdrawn; the authorities did not want the document detailing the convictions slipping out to Hong Kong (located in China but ruled by the UK at this point) and likely being revealed to the world.[951] This was cancel culture in the truest sense of the term.

Medicinal

Medicinal cannibalism refers to the use of human body bits as treatments or preventions for illness. Europe, the continent with the oldest archaeological evidence of cannibalism, suddenly got all classy about it in the 17th century and turned to medicinal use. They had to. Because brutish cannibalism was the charge they levied against the people of the New World and Asia as their justification for invasion and forced conversion to Christianity. This European hypocrisy is clear from the definition of *anthropophagi* in a 1538 dictionary: "people in Asia, which eate men".[952] Obviously, the Europeans weren't as well educated in their own history as they were in their xenophobia. Classy cannibalism meant pretending you were eating someone for medicinal purposes in order to validate the weirdness, a bit like how alcohol was prescribed by American doctors during the Prohibition era (when alcohol was illegal) because calling it medicine was the only way people could legalise their drinking. While medicinal alcohol only lasted 13 years (1920 – 1933), medicinal cannibalism lasted for hundreds – really taking off from 1680[953] and lasting into the 20th century.

While it might not have been trendy in Europe until the 17th century, medicinal cannibalism can be traced back to the ancient Greek, Roman, Mesopotamian, Arabian, Egyptian, Chinese, and Indian civilisations. In the Roman era it occurred after gladiator fights. One account from the Colosseum in 25 CE describes a man slurping the blood straight from the sliced throat of a fallen gladiator. He does this because drinking blood is a "well known" cure for epilepsy and those afflicted were advised to use the gladiators as "living cups".[954] The fact that, by this point of the battle, the gladiators were factually *dead cups* is probably why this cure failed to work. Among other reasons. Chunks of gladiator liver were also used to treat epilepsy – the recommended dose being nine pieces – which is weirdly precise. A Roman doctor named Scribonius Largus (his handwriting as a new-born baby must have been huge to warrant that name) described how the spectators of a gladiator battle would: "step forward and snatch a piece of liver from a gladiator lying gutted in the dust".[955] Handily for all this snatching business, the liver's texture is a bit like jelly, so hands were sufficient tools for the job. Gladiators were the preferred source because they were strong, healthy, and courageous, and it was thought these traits would transfer into the liver and thus into the cannibal patient. Plus, logistically, their bodies were in plentiful supply. However, they weren't the only option in the Roman world; for example, one medicine contained: "man's marrow and infant's brains".[956] I hate to think how long you had to wait in line for *that* prescription to be filled.

In China, the first documented use of medicinal cannibalism occurred during the later Han period (25–200 CE). It reached peak popularity around the 7th century CE during the Tang Dynasty and, following the trend, Ch'en Tsang-ch'i became the first Chinese doctor to prescribe human flesh in the 8th century. There are, however, some important differences between Chinese medicinal cannibalism and that practised in Europe. Firstly, in China, the person whose body part is to be eaten must remain alive. Secondly, they had to "do a Katniss" and nominate themselves as tribute. Thirdly, the cannibal and volunteer victim had to be closely related, and fourthly the cannibal must not *know* they are eating human flesh and so it should be disguised in a soup or stew. All these requirements were necessary for the medicine to work. And if it didn't – there were four things to blame (other than the "medicine" itself of course). The third and fourth caveat must have been particularly tricky to achieve considering mums' superpowers of spotting a tiny love bite from a mile away. Good luck hiding your missing arm.

In Chinese medicine, the bones, hair, gall bladder, toes, nails, heart, liver, milk, urine, placenta, and flesh were all used.[957] Menstrual blood was the remedy for fevers and delirium while regular boring blood treated diseases which caused people to spit up blood and was also given to women who had lost blood giving birth. So at least there was some logic in all this bloody mess. The gallbladder provided bile which was thought to cure muscle wastage. Finally, in a clear F -You to the carrots of this world, the Chinese used liver to treat night blindness.[958] Which, by the way, I'm pretty sure is not an illness –it's hard to see at night due to the lack of light, not lack of liver.

Doctors are to blame for encouraging medicinal cannibalism. Galen was a Roman doctor from the 2nd century CE and boy has he got a lot to answer for in this regard. Not least because his ideas were blindly followed for around 1500 years (they obviously didn't try the Chinese liver idea). Galen encouraged the practice of consuming humans based on the pharmacological belief that: "the human body and its by-products possessed an extraordinary medicinal and curative power"[959] which, in hindsight, would be better known as a pharmaco-illogical belief. As a result, not only did he recommend using body parts, but he also promoted using bodily fluids such as breast milk, blood, urine, menstrual blood, and faeces. Seemingly also oblivious to the fact that if that last one on the list was a liquid, then you should really be getting some treatment instead of donating it to medicine. Galen was on the right track with a few things, though, such as acknowledging the brain (not the heart), controlled speech; urine was formed in the kidney; and his discovery that arteries carried blood (wouldn't have liked to be the guy he tested *that* theory on).

However, Galen was wholly on the wrong track with advice such as drinking "burned human bones" to cure epilepsy and arthritis.[960] His mistakes have had a long-lasting impact because he widely published his findings and made everyone think humans looked the same on the inside as a monkey or frog. No one had the chance to challenge this view since the church opposed human dissection. Galen's "evidence" that God created all beings using the same blueprint was all they had to back up their biblical claims, therefore the church insisted that all anatomical studies had to agree with Galen and ergo support the Bible as a factual source. As a result, this inaccuracy remained until 1543 when Andreas Vesalius had the bright idea to, you know, dissect a human. This was during the Renaissance era – a time between 1500 and 1700 where people revived classical wisdom i.e., experimented and thought for themselves; but unfortunately, so much thinking for oneself did not lead to a happy ending for cannibalism. In fact, Vesalius' accurate knowledge of the human body made the whole thing a lot worse as this awareness was soon put to good use by body snatchers and grave robbers who were now able to locate specific organs and remove them, whole and undamaged, to sell for medicinal use. Medicinal cannibalism was now big business.

Books are to blame for bringing the delights of medicinal cannibalism to England. Pharmacological beliefs made their way to England through the published work of ancient blaggers/doctors such as Galen and Paracelsus. Later European medical books, such as Marsilio Ficino's *De Vita,* then continued with such advice as sucking milk directly from a lactating woman (presumably a willing party) or sucking blood directly from a youth (presumably an unwilling party) to revitalise oneself.[961] Not to be outdone by those across the narrow sea, in 1618, the *Pharmacopoea Londinenis* was published in England and became the country's most significant text on the topic of medicinal cannibalism. It even got the royal seal of approval from King James I (like the Queen approves of Heinz ketchup), who recommended all pharmacists should hurry up and embrace the idea of eating people for medicinal purposes.[962]

The *Pharmacopoea Londinenis* recommended human blood and mummy as medicines. Yes – they really thought they were onto something good in the early modern era (roughly 1500–1750) by eating little bits of pulverized mummies imported from Egypt, which was known as *mumia*. That's right, we were mummy eaters, and we didn't stop until the 20th century – there was a German Pharmaceutical company still selling mummy medicine in 1908 for the bargain price of 17.5 marks per kg.[963] Obviously, it couldn't just be any old mummy – the mummy had to have suffered a violent death because otherwise "the occult qualities of Medicines"[964] would not exist. Mummies were *so* popular that a fake trade began, and these counterfeit mummies (who were actually dried bodies of victims of desert sandstorms in Northern Africa)[965] were sold in London shops until the late 18th century. Hilariously, NONE of this mummy madness should have happened and only *did* happen in Europe due to a misunderstanding. The Arabs used tar or bitumen to glue wounds together and stop bleeding and they called this substance mumia. This was also the word they used to describe the mummies they discovered after taking over Egypt in 6th century CE because they mistakenly believed bitumen had been used to preserve them. By the 11th century, the Arabs were promoting this bituminous substance and also any other part of the mummy as medicine. Arab doctor Avicenna (980–1037) was pushing mumia as a treatment for: "abscesses and eruption, fracture, concussion, paralysis, hemicrania, epilepsy, vertigo, spitting of blood from the lungs, affections of the throat, cough, palpitation of the heart, debility of the stomach, nausea, disorders of the liver and spleen, internal ulcers, also in cases of poisons".[966]A bit like how Calpol made everything better when you were a kid (and tasted so damn good). Not knowing the Arabs had misunderstood the bitumen and mummy thing, when the

Europeans found out about this wonder drug, they just copied their work.[967]

Nothing was without a potential use but human blood and fat were the most used substances. Blood was sometimes dried into a powder form but mostly it was drunk, best served while still hot, such as immediately after a beheading or even while the donor was still alive. English doctors were still prescribing blood as a remedy for illness until the mid-18th century.[968] It was not uncommon for poor people to attend a beheading with a little cup to collect the blood from the criminal, and executioners could make a pretty penny by charging for such a thing. It didn't have to be main body blood either, menstrual blood was also collected and used as a treatment. Bearing in mind this sort of blood does not come gushing out, this process must have entailed the sporadic wringing out of a filthy rag before drinking. Gross. Fat was thought to be good for healing skin and bandages were soaked in melted human fat before being applied to a wound. Rubbing fat into areas afflicted with gout was also believed to be a remedy. Fat chance of that!

Aside from bones, blood, and fat, early modern medicine also contained hair, liver, brain, skin, heart, urine, semen, nails, earwax, saliva and even, wait for it… poo.[969] The body parts required for such a high demand could be obtained from donors but were mostly acquired from criminals' dead bodies or were simply stolen such as mummies from their Egyptian tombs or skulls directly from their graves. The prospect of being stolen was so real that Shakespeare's 17th-century gravestone has a warning to all potential body snatchers: "cursed be he that moves my bones".[970] Stealing bodies from graves was such a good money maker by the 18th century that booby traps were sometimes installed on people's graves to prevent it; for example, on one grave there was a gun hooked up to a tripwire.[971] Which must have been great news for the next body snatcher who came along – steal one – get one free!

The fun thing about medicinal cannibalism was that it was open to all. Going to see a public execution became a trendy way to spend your day off as people realised they could buy the offcuts of the criminal. A description from 1660s London tells how the accused had: "his privy members cut off before his eyes and his bowels burned" before he was decapitated, and his body cut into quarters to maximise its resale value.[972] While the poor might get their fix from the quack (fake doctors) at the market or the criminal on the stand, the English monarchy were also getting involved. The second and third Stuart Kings of England (1625–1685) are pretty well known; Charles I caused the English Civil War and is the only English king to be executed, and good-time-party-guy Charles II was on the throne during the Plague and Great Fire of London. Their links to medicinal cannibalism are, however, left out of the school history books. Charles I became corpse medicine when those attending his beheading dipped their handkerchiefs in his blood with the view to suck on it later; and Charles II made his own corpse medicine.[973] Charles II would drink "The King's Drops", which was human skull mixed with alcohol.[974] Skull was the ingredient of choice for a headache (because… say what you see) and the bones would be crushed and ground to become ingestible. Considering the other common remedy for a headache was trepanning (having a hole cut into your skull to "release the evil spirits" without the use of anaesthetic), I can totally understand why drinking skull juice was so popular.

Think we're past these ridiculous days? Think again. While Chinese medicine used human placenta to treat impotence and insanity, these days the placenta is still held onto as having health benefits for those that eat it. If you're interested, there are various recipes online advising how to cook up this organ into a tasty meal. However, please proceed with caution. There is little proof that eating your placenta will make you healthier yet plenty of proof it can spread blood-borne diseases like AIDS and Hepatitis. Placenta to think about before tucking in.

Ritual

Ritualistic means you've done it because your culture believes it has a purpose and has become part of your way of life. But why has such a ritual come about in all continents across the world? And why, if it has been part of their culture for thousands of years, did it come to an end? Some practice cannibalism because it has a basis in their belief system; some have it as part of their wartime ritual; some use it as a funeral ritual; some as part of their sacrifices, and some have cannibalism as part of their punishment rituals.

Belief system

A belief system is a set of principles that form the basis of a religion, philosophy, or moral code of a country. China has the longest documented history of ritualistic cannibalism[975] with a basis in their belief systems. In China, they had two influential belief systems – Confucianism from 6th century BCE and Buddhism from 1st century CE; both of which had allowances for cannibalism. In Buddhism there is the idea of self-sacrifice, and in Confucian philosophy there is the belief in filial piety, which means younger family members must show deference, compliance, and care for their elder family members. Which all put together basically meant some young people were expected to sacrifice themselves for the benefit of their family. There are at least 766 recorded cases of filial piety cannibalism in China over a period of 2000 years.[976] When elders were hungry, the youngsters would "cut off parts of their body and make them into soup to please family members, particularly their parents".[977]

And you thought *your* parents were demanding.

There were even specific names relating to the choice of body parts donated: *Ko-ku* is the ritual of cutting flesh from a thigh or arm and *Ko-kan* is when part of the liver is removed. Unsurprisingly, thighs and upper arms were the most popular choices. There are even cases of children volunteering their breast, their finger (that kid's tight or what), or their eyeball. This was common enough for an edict (a law) to be made in 1216 which specifically banned cutting out livers or plucking out eyeballs.[978] Eye imagine the aim here was to ensure the children liver another day, but it didn't put a stop to the practice.

Ritualistic cannibalism became a part of Chinese culture because their belief systems had so many justifications for it: "hate, love, loyalty, filial piety, desire for human flesh as a delicacy, punishment, war, belief in the medical benefits of cannibalism, profit, insanity, coercion, religion, and superstition".[979] While women with big feet were abhorrent (google foot-binding and prepare to gag), cannibalism was not viewed with the same horror. Chinese culture allowed it, and there are numerous examples of emperors and other high society types in the imperial court casually eating people for dinner. Writer T'ao Tsung-yi, who was alive during the Yuan dynasty (1271–1368), clearly had enough of a taste to provide a review: "children's meat was the best food of all in taste"; he ranked women second and men third.[980] Which is a convenient conclusion for an adult male to make. Outside of the ruling class, up until the 19th century, it was common practice for executioners to eat the hearts and brains of the prisoners they had slayed and then make a bit extra cash by selling off the rest as sloppy seconds. There are lots of recipes in Chinese literature with ideas on different ways to cook people (just in case you're interested – baking, roasting, broiling, steaming, boiling, smoke-drying, sun-drying and made into dumplings).[981] Nigella, eat your heart out. They certainly will.

Wartime

War rituals are the most common form of ritualistic cannibalism, and it has been documented across the world over thousands of years. In the ancient Greek and Roman era there were various reports from the two historians of the time (Herodotus and Cassius Dio) of ritualistic wartime cannibalism. Herodotus wrote in *The Histories* (450s to the 420s BCE) about how the Scythians of modern-day Siberia enjoyed smoking weed and drinking the blood of their first kill. Probably in that order too. The Scythians were also pro-recycling – enemies' heads were hollowed out and used as drinking cups; severed right hands were stripped of their skin and nails and used as coverings for their arrow quivers; and human skin was flayed off the body and stretched across a frame to be carried around on their horses as a trophy. These were known as napkins and the man with the most napkins was judged to be the greatest[982] – the napKing presumably. Cassius Dio stated that the Bucoli (an Egyptian tribe) killed and ate two Roman officers as some sort of ritual which ended with them swearing an oath over their spilled intestines.[983] Which you gotta admit, takes guts.

When the Europeans began exploring the world, they discovered a whole host of wartime cannibalistic rituals. The Carib people: "…eat human flesh when they are at war and do so as a sign of victory, not as food".[984] The New World was discovered by the Italian explorer Christoffa Corombo, but you were likely taught about Christopher Columbus because this way little kids are fooled into thinking he was British… ergo Britain must have been important. Incidentally, Columbus was also a bit of a blagger and called the native people he encountered "Indians" because India was where he was *trying* to go, and there was no way he was gonna admit making a mistake with directions. Columbus' four voyages between 1492 and 1504 brought to Europe lots of tales of ritualistic cannibalism as well as a variety of fun things such as potatoes, pineapple, peppers, peanuts, and syphilis. Incidentally, the natives weren't giving out necklaces made of eyeballs and testicles as the explorers touched down – Columbus and his men only discovered cannibalism after the natives astutely realised these newcomers were not the friendly sort and had run for their lives. Dr Diego Alvarez Chanca describes what they left behind: "He (the captain) found much cotton, spun and ready for spinning and provisions of food… he likewise brought away with him four or five bones of the arms and legs of men."[985] It didn't take them long to cotton on the fact they were on the Carib islands whose inhabitants ate flesh.

Spanish, English, French, and Dutch explorers described cannibal rituals among the Aztecs, Venezuelan, Caribbean, and Brazilian tribes which saw enemies captured as trophies and then eaten as part of their war ritual. The Piritu of Venezuela dried out their enemies' hearts and turned them into powder to be added to chicha, a fermented drink. It was also observed in the "friendly" Arawak and Tupinamba tribes.[986] Englishman Sir Walter Raleigh, famed for being the first person to circumnavigate the globe before being executed for treason, wrote about Arawak Indian cannibals during his exploration of Guiana in 1595. He described how they: "beat the bones of their lords into powder, and their wives and friends drink it all in their several sorts of drinks".[987] Interestingly, while these are clearly wartime rituals, they also had a medicinal base. Just like the Romans, the New World cannibals believed they were gaining vitality, strength, bravery, and wisdom of those they had consumed, and numerous sources describe the Caribs eating their enemies because they believed this would give them the powers their enemies possessed. The fact they had beaten them, and their enemies clearly did not possess qualities such as strength or wisdom, was very much the elephant in the room.

However, the extent of this practice is in some doubt. Cannibalism soon became a handy "observation" to make due to the advice from Columbus' benefactor – Queen Isabella of Spain. She instructed the conquerors to be kind and considerate to the locals… unless they turned out to be cannibals. Which is a pretty random clause to add considering phrases such as "unless they turn out to be violent" were available. In addition to this small print, there was also the incentive to label the locals as cannibals when they were being terribly unhelpful helping Columbus find the stacks of gold he expected to. Directions were not the only thing Columbus was bad at – he also thought gold was magically created in hot climates, therefore there *must* be some in the New World. When he and his mates failed to find it: "why God our Lord has concealed the gold from us,"[988] the indigenous population were deemed no longer "friendly" and labelled as gold-hiding cannibals instead. Consequently, "sightings" of cannibalism changed according to what the Spanish wanted at any given moment. For example, Trinidad was supposedly full of cannibals in 1511, but when reports of gold on the island surfaced in 1518, it magically wasn't. Why? Because now the locals were needed alive to put them to work extracting it. Once the Spanish realised they had been mugged off, Trinidad suddenly became cannibalistic again, and orders were given to colonise the island (European code for killing), and within 100 years the indigenous population on Trinidad had halved.[989]

In addition to these selective labellings and helpful "observations", Europe became gripped with propaganda touting the indigenous people of the world as savages who needed European guidance. The White Man's Burden of correcting All Others had begun. Some guy who had never been to the New World, or met any locals, considered himself expert enough to write a book about them. Touted as factual but blatantly fiction, *De Orbe Novo* (On the New World) became a 16th-century bestseller alongside the similarly nuanced Bible. The author, Peter Martyr, was certainly a martyr to the cause of prejudice and exaggerated the already exaggerated accounts from those who visited the Americas. So, while Dr Chanca described *one* hut used for cannibalistic rituals, Martyr turned this into *numerous* huts, each with a kitchen where: "human bodies were fixed on spits, ready for roasting".[990] And it's not even like Dr Chanca was a reliable source to begin with! He was dodgier than the Artful Dodger eating a Jammie Dodger in a dodge car. For starters, Chanca didn't even see these cannibalistic sights for himself and relied on others' stories while he went off looking at all the flowers (he was compiling a book about the flora and fauna). Then there's the fact Columbus *needed* this description of cannibalistic behaviour from a respected professional to get permission to take over – Chanca being the doctor to the Spanish monarchy fitted the bill perfectly. And then to top it all off, once the letter was written, Columbus sent an accompanying note asking for the doctor's pay to be increased. Lots to be gained for both men with these "observations". Which is totally not suspicious at all…

So, were the people of the Americas cannibals?

Yes, they were.

We all were!

The existence of ritualistic cannibalism has been confirmed by Cristo Adonis – an ancestor of the indigenous people and the current spiritual leader of the Trinidadian Amerindians. Cristo states that endocannibalism was practised for religious reasons, and exocannibalism was used to gain strength from their defeated enemies.[991] His evidence is the verbal history passed down through generations of indigenous people. Which, OK, isn't the best sort of evidence but equally this is also not the sort of thing most people would want to admit. Were they any worse than their European critics? No. But by the 16th century, Europeans had moved on to using human parts as medicine so they could claim superiority over these "savages".

The practice of eating your enemy, reported from the New World, was not unique in this location. Warfare cannibalism was common in tribal societies because what else were they meant to do with them?![992] Captives take up space and they're pretty annoying to have around, what with all their complaints about loss of freedom and all that. In Africa, particularly tribes in the Niger and Cameroon areas, prisoners of war were also eaten. Sometimes the process was quick like a McDonald's drive thru (on a good day), but in other instances, the process was long-ed out. Either way, the victim would have parts of their body cut away, bit by bit, and made to watch as the captors chomped down on their cooked flesh and muscles.[993] This ritual died out as societies got more organised in their agricultural production (less need for captives as food) and with economics becoming a thing – the prospect of exchanging captives for money or goods made them more valuable alive.[994]

However, not all tribal rituals of killing an enemy ended with cannibalism. Pacific explorer Captain James Cook of "oh look, there's Australia" fame was killed by Hawaiians on Valentine's Day 1779. They (lovingly, I hope) removed all his bones, cooked him up, and then gave a piece of him back to his fellow explorers – a true piece offering. But the Hawaiians did not eat him. And the islanders were shocked when the receiver of the cooked bit of Cook asked them if they had eaten the rest of him.[995] From their perspective, it was the Europeans who were the cannibals (which they were) for even thinking of this.

There have even been cases in the 20th century. During World War Two, the Japanese were reported to have chosen one Allied prisoner a day to have one limb cut off while he was still alive, which was then cooked and eaten. It was also discovered to still be happening in the 1960s by anthropologist Pierre Clastres during his time in Paraguay.[996] As the saying goes, you should keep your friends close and your enemies closer… and it doesn't get much closer than in your stomach.

Funeral rituals

This category of mortuary cannibalism refers to the consumption of the dead during their funeral. Like, instead of crying into your whiskey and saying a few nice words about the deceased, people ate them. The Melanesian people of the Bahamas; the Wari' people of the Amazonian rainforest in Brazil; and on the Pacific islands of Fiji, Papua New Guinea, Vanuatu, and Solomon Islands cannibalism can be found as part of their funeral rituals.[997] It is even practised in the 20th century in the Eastern Highlands Province of Papua New Guinea and the Brazilian and Peruvian Amazon. But there's no need to be repulsed at the idea of eating dear old nanny because, apparently, this is: "an act of affection and respect for the dead person, as a well as being a means of helping survivors to cope with their grief".[998] Love made you do it type thing.

The motives behind mortuary cannibalism vary from tribe to tribe; some believed it would give them health benefits while others believed it would help with their grief or was a good way to honour the dead. The Bahamas-based

Bimin-Kuskuskin people practised mortuary cannibalism because they believed it would keep them fertile. And so as early advocates of the idiom "you are what you eat" – the Bimin-Kuskuskin would eat a person's genitals when they died. If your husband or wife died then you were expected to eat their penis, uterus, or vaginal canal (an expectation which at least could be used as a decent excuse when you're asked for the thousandth time why you haven't got married). Even the infertile elderly did not escape this fate, and tribal elders would feast on the reproductive organs of other dead elders with the belief this act would redistribute their prior reproductive abilities to the remaining community.[999] With female elders it was again their uterus and/or vaginal canal, which was selected to have this power of recycling; however, with the old men it was ticker over tackle. Seemingly, shrivelled sausage with a side of nuts just wasn't gonna cut it and a heartier meal was required to fulfil the ritual's purpose.

The Melanesians ate small portions of their dead relatives because they believed the spirits of the deceased would be transferred to them and it would help their soul leave the body. The Wari' also ate small portions but they added honey to make them sweeter (try babies instead, guys). The theory for the Wari' was eating their dead beloved would help deal with their grief because the corpse was no longer around to remind them of their loss.

In New Guinea, the Fore people, who inhabited around 170 villages, used mortuary cannibalism as a way of honouring their dead. This practice was observed by Australian officials after WW2 and anthropologists Ronald and Catherine Berndt. The Berndts arrived in New Guinea in 1951 and reported there was "plenty of cannibalism" and "dead human flesh to these people is food, or potential food".[1000] Their funeral ritual saw the dead body placed on edible leaves before being cut up and placed in piles to be divvied out to the dead person's relatives. The bigger bits were sliced and stuffed into bamboo containers which were then cooked and shared. The head was cooked to remove the hair, the skin was peeled off and the brain was then removed and cooked because brain was considered a local delicacy.[1001] Much like the Scythian recyclers of history, nothing was wasted and bones were dried and ground into powder to use in cooking; but the ritual which is hardest to digest is how the Fore also made sure to scrape any remaining poo out of the intestines to eat.[1002]

In a far more disturbing scene (yes, it can get worse than pooey-pieces), Ronald described how a Fore man was having sex with a dead body while his multi-tasking (and incredibly forgiving) wife was chopping up the same dead body for dinner. Things obviously got entwined, and the wife ended up "accidentally" cutting off her husband's penis. Her reaction was not one of sorrow or horror, she instead put the severed member in her mouth and ate it.[1003] His reaction is unknown, but I'm guessing he didn't indulge in a quick snack as she did. Scientific research into the prevalence of the disease *Kuru* (which had been annihilating the indigenous population) also backs up the Fore's cannibalistic rituals. Doctors and neurologists who researched the spread of disease concluded that it spread through the practice of cannibalism. It was supposedly mostly women and children who engaged in cannibalism, and by eating contaminated human parts, such as the brain, Kuru was transmitted into the consumer.[1004]

Sacrifice

Sacrificial cannibalism means you've done it because your culture believes it has meaning – it is a ritual, but this is the hardest type of cannibalism to prove because archaeological evidence does not uncover the purpose behind the cannibalism. It has been somewhat evidenced in Britain and in Mesoamerica.

Did you know human sacrifice is recommended in the Bible? Which, by the way, I have come to conclude should really have an 18-rating attached to it. God told Abraham to sacrifice his only son Isaac: "Take your son… and offer him there as a burnt offering on one of the mountains".[1005] The sacrifice of your first-born son was thought to be the best gift to God (hard guy to buy for… doesn't wear socks). Luckily for all the first-born sons of Christians out there, this story was taken to be of the metaphorical sort and people chose to sacrifice animals instead. But still. Wow.

Recent discoveries by the University of Bristol revealed that the Celts (the people who populated Britain before the Roman invasion 2000 years ago) indulged in human sacrifice and they ate their sacrifices too.[1006] This took place between 800 BCE and 100 CE during what is known as the Iron Age (the era of zero creases in your shirt). Human remains discovered in a cave at Alveston, South Gloucestershire, were studied, and after excavating just 5% of their findings, a human femur bone was discovered with all the hallmarks of cannibalistic activity – marrow, flesh and muscle expertly scraped from the bone.

In Mesoamerica, human sacrifice and cannibalism were fairly common; it was most popular in the Aztec civilisation, peaking in the 15th century, just before the Spanish conquistadors arrived.[1007] This process of human sacrifice is evidenced by the racks of skulls in their cities which held over 100,000 different human heads[1008] and the 20–80,000 victims' remains discovered at their main pyramid, Tenochtitlan.[1009] The Aztecs believed human sacrifice was necessary to avoid destruction by the gods – providing the Sun God with energy (human blood) would ensure they would be saved.[1010] Sacrificial victims were mainly enemies captured in war but sometimes slaves, and their own children were used when a specific purpose called for it. Children were required for things like ensuring a good maize harvest and were chosen according to the astrological significance of their birthday before being offered to the god Tlaloc. The children's throats were slit, and they were killed, but there is no evidence they were cannibalised.[1011]

The ones who were sacrificed and then cannibalised were war captives. The sacrifice itself involved the person being stretched out over a stone table at the top of a pyramid and held down by four priests, the fifth priest then cut out the heart and held it up to the Sun God. The body was then unglamorously pushed down the steps of the pyramid where those at the bottom would chop the limbs up for people to eat while the torso was sent for the animals at the local zoo.[1012] (A zoo? The fun never stops with these guys.) The limbs were then delivered to the soldier who had captured the victim and they were made into a stew flavoured with peppers and tomatoes.[1013] I'm sure the victim would have been happy to know people were enjoying every part of them "from my head to-ma-toes".

The reasons why the Aztecs cannibalised their sacrifices are unknown. One theory was it was a rational and practical choice – it was due to a lack of protein (no cows *and* no shakes) in the Mesoamerica area but no shortage has actually been documented.[1014] Maize was their main crop, and this was vulnerable to drought so it could be linked to survival: "for the necessary satisfaction of essential protein requirements, cannibalism was the only possible solution".[1015] However, lower-class people were forbidden to eat humans, so clearly this was not *that* necessary a process. It's also possible that cannibalism existed with the purpose of stimulating war – the prospect of getting dinner may have enticed people to fight.

What seems most likely is that Aztec sacrifice and cannibalism was all a big power play by the priests. Performing the ceremony was the only way to prove their usefulness – and then they maintained the ritual to preserve their usefulness and position of power. It was a very clever system. If food was short, then the priests said it was because they needed more sacrifices (the idea that *they* had clearly failed to persuade the gods to give rain was, of course, never an option). And so, off the soldiers would trot, to initiate war with another region, and gain some captives to be sacrificed; people were happy to go because taking a captive led to elevation of status.[1016] With this elevated status they could then eat future captives.

Once the sacrifice was complete, suddenly there was no issue of food anymore. Which of course was all thanks to the priests and nothing at all whatsoever to do with the resulting cannibalism and raiding the enemies' crops stores while they were there.

There are many rumours that the Mayans sacrificed people and ate them too but, according to modern-day Mayan ancestor Frank, this is not the case.[1017] And FYI he gets *very* angry when people suggest otherwise. Hollywood has done them a dirty with implying this was common practice and, quite frankly, most modern literature agrees with him.

Punishment

In East African tribes, cannibalism was not just reserved for prisoners outside a tribe. Forced cannibalism was a punishment meted out to those guilty of adultery (sex outside marriage) Saying " and "nice to meet you" swiftly turned into "nice to eat you.". The pair were tied to stakes facing each other a few feet apart and not given any food over the proceeding day or so. They were allowed water but in a particularly cruel twist in the burning climate, this was salty water leading to both cheating parties becoming even more desperate. The taunting question "would you like something to eat?" was then posed. When one of the pair said, "bloody hell, yes of course I do," those inflicting the punishment would slice off a body part from the other victim (like a breast) and force feed it to their lover. They were careful not to let either person bleed to death too quickly, and the wounds were swiftly cauterised to this end. The process would be repeated back and forth until one of them died. And in a touching tribute, the other was then allowed to survive as long as they could by eating the remains of their dead partner.

Why has ritualistic cannibalism ended?

Ritualistic cannibalism was brought to a slow end due to European imperialism, beginning in the late 15th century with the Spanish conquistadors in the New World. In reality, this part of the world (North and South America and all the Caribbean islands in between), was as "new" as cannibalism itself; but not wanting to break their ignorant stride, the saintly Europeans condemned a custom as old as humanity and criticised the natives for their war rituals. A hypocrisy which was picked up by Michel de Montaigne in 1580: "I am not sorry we note the barbarous horror of [cannibalism], but grieved that, prying so narrowly into [the Tupinambás'] faults, we are so blinded in ours."[1018]

Enslavement then prevented the indigenous population from enacting any of their freedoms – including their rituals. Spanish Queen Isabella, who obviously had already decided all locals were cannibals, later advised in 1503: "If such cannibals continue to resist and do not wish to… be in my service and obedience, they may be captured… and be sold."[1019] Weirdly, the natives were not up for just giving over their land and being in the service of a foreign ruler they had never met, which meant Isabella got her way and the gold diggers turned to people trafficking and slavery. This enthusiasm occurred because, despite there being a shit ton available in the New World, no one wanted to be paid peanuts.

Christianity also brought about an end to ritualistic cannibalism because this came as part of the crappy imperialism package. Tribal belief systems and their accompanying rituals were replaced with Catholic (in southern and central America), and Protestant (in Northern America), belief systems and rituals. The indigenous people were "re-educated" by meddling officials sent by their overseas overlords. For example, the Wari' people of the Amazon rainforest were made to change their funeral ritual of eating the corpse because the Europeans found this disgustingly morbid. (The Wari' would have been better off letting the corpses stew for thousands of years and become mummified and *then* eating it… as was the European way). Natives were instead forced to follow the Christian ritual of burying them six feet under to slowly rot away. A process which the Wari' found equally disgusting. All of this was helpfully sanctioned by the Pope who, in 1510, decreed cannibalism was a sin (he must have skipped those Jesus bits in the Bible). Pope Julius II said that Christians were doing "the right thing" by physically punishing those practising such rituals. This allowed other European explorers and nations to then claim they NEEDED to invade and conquer to remove these terrible people from the planet. All the while drinking their skull juice and munching on dried mummies of course.

Overall, it was European imperialism that ended ritualistic cannibalism. Firstly, their condemnation and Christian colonisation forced a change of culture which removed the rituals in a practical and visible sense. Secondly, the rituals ended because quite simply there was no one left to keep it going. The invading colonists rather casually caused the "greatest act of genocide in recorded history"[1020] – another fact you're unlikely to learn in your history lessons on Empire. Due to Columbus' "discoveries"; Queen Isabella's guidance; Dr Chanca's "observations"; Pope Innocent IV's decree; and Martyr's fiction, the New World native population was decimated with the justification of eradicating the cannibal threat. Between 60 and 80 million people died, either through Pope-sponsored direct murder (approximately 2–15 million people), the effects of enslavement (justified due to cannibalism), or through the spread of European diseases such as measles, flu, and smallpox. Poxy lot these Europeans.

Psychotic

This type of cannibalism is the one most prevalent in the modern day. In most parts of the world, sacrificial and ritual cannibalism have been replaced with civilisation, religion, and law. Survival cannibalism is much rarer because famines are less common thanks to improved farming methods and the backup of trade with other nations. Medicinal use has been substituted with actual medicine. Which actually works. But what hasn't changed is the existence of disturbed and criminally minded individuals.

Psychotic cannibalism has existed throughout history. One of Herodotus' more infamous tales was about the psychotic cannibalism of King Astyages, the last ruler of the Median empire. Astyages killed and cooked the son of his ex-favourite general – Harpagus, after learning that 10 years prior Harpagus had disobeyed his orders to kill his grandson (he wanted the new-born grandson killed because of a weird dream he had… a perfectly natural reaction in the ancient world). Astyages invited Harpagus and his son over for dinner, with the son arriving first to find he WAS the dinner. His body was chopped up, with some parts being roasted and the tougher bits going into a stew. While everyone else at dinner was served mutton,

Harpagus was given his son to eat. Seemingly not noticing his son wasn't there (he won't be winning any father of the year awards that's for sure), Harpagus tucked in and gave the meal a 5-star rating. Astyages then told Harpagus to open a basket and take what he liked from it, in a "have some pudding" sort of set-up. But instead of pudding, Harpagus discovered his son's severed head, hands, and feet. In an equally psychotic move, Harpagus did not react with a torrent of vomit and Astyages, thinking Harpagus didn't get the "joke", asked if he knew whose flesh he had eaten. Harpagus replied: "Yes. I know: whatsoever my lord the king does is pleasing" and he took the basket and went home.[1021] If that story sounds familiar it's because Shakespeare took it as inspiration for his play *The Tragedy of Titus Andronicus,* where Titus kills the two sons of his enemy Queen Tamora and bakes them into a pie which is later served to Tamora and her husband. Being a tragedy, that story didn't end quite so amicably, and Titus finishes the meal by killing Tamora; her husband then kills Titus; and Titus's son then kills the husband. A plot line which I'm sure we'll see in a Christmas Day *EastEnder*s at some point.

One of the most notorious stories of psychotic cannibalism from the 20th century is that of American man Albert Fish. He didn't have a great childhood – at five he was put in an orphanage and was traumatised early on by childish bullying over his given name of Hamilton Fish (he was called "Ham and eggs") and about the fact that when he was whipped, he liked it so much he got excited in the downstairs department. Fish later became a painter and decorator and in 1898 married and went on to have six children. His wife left him after he began to self-harm by inserting needles into the space between his rectum and balls – the perineum. When this was later investigated and x-rayed, police discovered 29 needles.[1022] What a prick.

Even more prickish than this – Fish admitted to killing and eating children. The first description of which came from a letter he wrote in 1928 using the pseudonym Frank Howard. He began by explaining how his inspiration for cannibalism came from a neighbour who had tasted human flesh when he got stuck in Hong Kong in 1894 during a time of famine. The neighbour, John, had eaten young boys and girls and described how "all children under 12 were sold for food in order to keep others from starving."[1023] John also revealed: "A boy or girls' behind which is the sweetest part of the body and sold as veal cutlet brought (sic) at the highest price".[1024] When John returned to America, just as the doctors described in the cannibalistic times of 1920s Russia, he found he had acquired a taste for children. Rather than ignore it, he set about finding his own human dinner and stole two boys aged seven and eleven. Keen to have the best taste he could, John: "spanked them – tortured them – to make their meat good and tender. First, he killed the 11-year-old boy, because he had the fattest ass… He was roasted in the oven (all of his ass), boiled, broiled, fried, and stewed. The little boy, next, went the same way".[1025] Rather than react as any sane person would – with horror and a swift phone call to the police – Fish decided to give it a go for himself.[1026]

Fish's first victim was a little girl called Gracie Budd, whose mother was also the recipient of the sickening confessional letter described above. Luckily for her, she couldn't read, and it was passed to the detectives investigating Gracie's disappearance. Fish knew the family and had been over their house that day, ironically enough, to bring food. He told her mother he wanted to take ten-year-old Gracie to a party but instead took her to an empty house where he, in his own words: "choked her to death, then cut her in small pieces so I could take my meat to my rooms. Cook and eat it. How sweet and tender her lite (sic) ass was roasted in the oven. It took me 9 days to eat her entire body".[1027]

After Fish had been captured, his photo was published in the news and another cannibalism incident was brought to light. A man who worked on the Brooklyn trolley line (like a tram line) recognised his face and told police about having seen Fish in February 1927 dragging a little boy off the trolley. Under questioning, Fish admitted what he had done to this boy, Billy Gaffney. After kidnapping him, he stripped, bound, and gagged the boy and left him overnight at a dump. The next day he "cut off his ears, nose, slit his mouth from ear to ear. Gouged out his eyes. He was dead then. I stuck the knife in his belly and held my mouth to his body and drank his blood."[1028] After cutting the boy up and carrying him home, he described what happened next: "I had the front of his body I liked the best. His monkey and pee wees and a nice little fat behind to roast in the oven and eat. I made a stew out of his ears – nose – pieces of his face and belly… It was good."[1029] Obviously keen to get his five-a-day, Fish then added onions, carrots, turnips, celery, salt and pepper. But that wasn't the end of it. He proceeded to slice the boy's buttocks open and lay bacon over the top before roasting in the oven: "I never ate any roast turkey that tasted half as good as his sweet fat little behind did… His little monkey was as sweet as a nut."[1030] But not everything was tasty: "his peewees I could not chew. Threw them in the toilet".[1031] When convicted of his crimes (at least 10 children across 23 states), he was *not* deemed legally insane and instead was judged a "psychopathic personality without a psychosis".[1032] In the most understated statement of the 20th century, Fish himself said he was not "altogether right".[1033]

Psychotic cannibalism is not relegated to history. In 2001, the case of German man Armin Meiwes shocked the world not only because he had killed and eaten a man but also because the man-who-became-a-meal was a willing victim. Like a lot of modern love stories, they found each other on the internet. Unlike lots of modern love stories, these guys opted to use an online food delivery service (not quite "Deliver*you*" … it was called "The Cannibal Café") with Meiwes posting an advert looking for a "young, well-built man who wanted to be eaten".[1034] Meiwes described the taste as: "like pork but stronger".[1035] As is the 21st century way, Meiwes filmed the whole thing[1036] which led to his original 2004 conviction of manslaughter (I mean… what?) being overturned and he was sentenced to life imprisonment in 2006. Unable to get such strong pork in prison, Meiwes has since become a vegetarian.[1037]

Final thoughts

Fun Fact – cannibalism is not illegal in the UK. You could be charged with murder, but there is no specific law against cannibalism (it's definitely frowned upon though).

Essentially cannibalism began because, well, why not?! Europe has the oldest archaeological evidence, while China has the longest documented evidence. Overall, war has been the biggest cause of cannibalism. It led to the ritual of eating your enemy across American, Pacific, and African tribes, as well as leading to survival cannibalism in Europe and Asia. Human arrogance (the theory that we are so powerful that we must be able to produce our own medicine) combined with a lack of *any kind* of anatomical and scientific knowledge then led to medicinal use. It only became a taboo from the 16th century onwards, and even then, this only related to ritualistic use by foreigners.

There's a lot of take home from the history of survival cannibalism. Firstly, you're more likely to survive a famine if you're female… in terms of a natural death. This is because females burn protein slower than males while needing fewer calories to survive. Women also have bigger fat reserves than men making them literally born ready for a crisis, (incidentally another study has shown that women who carry a little extra weight also live longer than the men who mention it). However, women's chances of survival don't look so good if their town turns to survival cannibalism, but it's nice to have some sort of silver lining. Interestingly, married men should aim to keep their wives alive in such cannibalistic times because, believe it or not, marriage reduces your stress levels which helps men live longer. Unfortunately, no one told the Leningrad husband that fact before he tried to eat his wife. The expert's advice on how to avoid falling victim to survival cannibalism is: "The best thing to be is a member of a family group, and not be too young or too old".[1038] Oh, and make sure you hide your delicious kids.

Endnotes

Churchill's not so finest hours

1   Alan Brooke and Alex Danchev, *War Diaries*, 1939-1945 (Berkeley: University of California Press, 2001), p 451
2   "Churchill, 'Greatest' PM of 20th Century", *BBC Politics,* (4 January 2000)
3   "Churchill voted Greatest Briton", *BBC News*, (24/11/2002), http://news.bbc.co.uk/1/hi/entertainment/2509465.stm, (accessed 09/08/2020)
4   "*BBC Newsnight poll", BBC News*, (1 October 2008, (accessed 15/12/2020
5   "The Times's Top 50 Prime Ministers", *The Times,* timesonline. co.uk, (2010) accessed 15/12/2020
6   *Rating British Prime Ministers*, Ipsos MORI, (2004), retrieved 24 November 2015
7   Boris Johnson, 2014, cited in Harry Howard, "In Churchill's footsteps?" *Daily Mail,* (13/10/21) https://www.dailymail. co.uk/news/article-10087319/How-Boris-Johnson-channelled-lifelong-hero-Winston-Churchill.html
8   NATIONAL HEALTH SERVICE BILL, House of Commons Debate, 02 May 1946, vol 422 cc323-417, https://api.parliament. uk/historic-hansard/commons/1946/may/02/national-health-service-bill
9   Tom Pendry, Letters in *The Guardian*, 1/11/2017 https://www. theguardian.com/society/2017/nov/01/jeremy-hunt-claims-a-tory-was-the-true-founder-of-the-nhs-thats-rubbish

10　Boris Johnson cited on Tom Heyden, "The 10 greatest controversies of Winston Churchill's career", *BBC News Magazine,* (26 January 2015), https://www.bbc.co.uk/news/magazine-29701767, (accessed 09/07/2020)

11　Roy Jenkins, *Churchill,* (London: Macmillan, 2001), p. 4

12　Peter Padfield, *Hitler, Hess and Churchill,* (London: Icon books, 2013), p. 69

13　Ibid, p. 6

14　Ibid, p. 204-205

15　Charlie Duffield, "Was Winston Churchill racist? Why some people accused the wartime PM of racism after his London statue was defaced", *The i,* (June 25th, 2020) https://inews.co.uk/news/winston-churchill-racist-pm-racism-accusations-london-statue-protest-blm-explained-440668

16　Roy Jenkins, *Churchill*, p. 2

17　Roy Jenkins, *Churchill*, p. 19

18　https://www.nationalchurchillmuseum.org/winston-churchills-military-career.html

19　Candice Millard, *Hero of the Empire. The Making of Winston Churchill*, (USA, 2016), p9

20　Ibid p8

21　Ibid p11

22　Ibid p16

23　Ibid p16

24　Ibid P17

25　Ibid p18

26　Roy Jenkins, *Churchill,* pp. 38–41

27　Peter de Menddelssohn, *The Age of Churchill: Heritage and Adventure 1874–1911,* (London: Thames and Hudson, 1961), pp. 122–134.

28　Candice Millard, *Hero of the Empire*, p. 21

29　Ibid p301

30　Peter de Menddelssohn, *The Age of Churchill,* pp. 122–134.

31　Candice Millard, *Hero of the Empire*, p. 59

32　Christopher Klein, "The Daring Escape That Forged Winston Churchill," *History.com*, (updated: SEP 3, 2018, Original:

NOV 7, 2016) https://www.history.com/news/the-daring-escape-that-forged-winston-churchill (accessed 22/06/2020)

33 Christopher Klein, "The Daring Escape That Forged Winston Churchill,"

34 Roy Jenkins, *Churchill, p.* 65

35 ibid*, p.* 69-70

36 Robert Pilpel, *Churchill in America 1895-1961* (NY: Harcourt Brace Jovanovich 1976); p63

37 Roy Jenkins, *Churchill,* p. 69

38 Peter Frost, "The Horrible truth about Winston Churchill," *Morning Star*, (Jan 18 2018), https://morningstaronline.co.uk/article/truth-about-winston-churchill 02042020

39 Christopher Klein, "Winston Churchill's World War Disaster," (updated: SEP 3, 2018, original: MAY 21, 2014), https://www.history.com/news/winston-churchills-world-war-disaster, (accessed 01/07/2020)

40 https://winstonchurchill.org/the-life-of-churchill/life/man-of-action/on-the-western-front/

41 Winston Churchill, Clementine Churchill**,** *Speaking for Themselves: The Personal Letters of Winston and Clementine ... (*Random House, 1999), p.148

42 Paul Cowan, "Churchill in the Trenches", *Scottish Military Disasters*, (2020), https://www.scottishmilitarydisasters.com/index.php/titles-sp-26803/66-churchill-in-the-trenches#, (accessed 06/07/2020)

43 https://winstonchurchill.org/the-life-of-churchill/life/man-of-action/on-the-western-front/

44 https://winstonchurchill.org/the-life-of-churchill/life/man-of-action/on-the-western-front/

45 CHAR 28/120/1-2, *Churchill Archive*, https://www.churchillarchive.com/collection-highlights/churchills-first-world-war

46 https://winstonchurchill.org/the-life-of-churchill/life/man-of-action/on-the-western-front/

47 Ibid

48 Peter Padfield, *Hitler, Hess and Churchill*, p.71

49   Ibid, p.72

50   Stephen Leacock, *Our British empire; its structure, its history, its strength* (London, Right Book Club, 1941) pp. 266–75

51   Jonathan Fennell, "5 Facts About the British and Commonwealth Armies and the Second World War," *Historyhit. com* (12 Dec 2018), https://www.historyhit.com/facts-about-the-british-and-commonwealth-armies-and-the-second-world-war/ (accessed 19/06/2020)

52   Jeremy A. Crang, *The British Army and the People's War, 1939-1945*, (Manchester University Press, 2000). p. 144.

53   UK settles WWII debts to allies, *BBC News,* (29/12/2006,) http://news.bbc.co.uk/1/hi/uk/6215847.stm,   (accessed 19/06/2020)

54   Donald W. McIntyre, *The Commonwealth of Nations*, (University of Minnesota Press, 1977) p. 39

55   Yasmin Khan, "Has India's contribution to WW2 been ignored?" *BBC News*, (17 June 2015), https://www.bbc.co.uk/news/world-asia-india-33105898, (accessed 19/06/2020)

56   https://winstonchurchill.org/the-life-of-churchill/senior-statesman/the-empire-lost/ (accessed 19/06/2020)

57   Candice Millard, *Hero of the Empire,* p.18

58   Hitler talking to Hess, Cited in Henry Theophilus Finck, *A. Seidl, A memorial by his friends*, (Hardpress publishing, 2013) pp. 82-3

59   James Holland, "9 things you (probably) didn't know about the evacuation of Dunkirk", *History Extra,* (26 May 2020), https://www.historyextra.com/period/second-world-war/dunkirk-facts-history-east-mole-hitler-halt-order-douglas-jardine/ (accessed 06/07/2020)

60   Ibid

61   Padfield, *Hitler, Hess and Churchill,* pp. 70-71

62   Thomas Parker, "When Winston Churchill Bombed France: The Battle of Mers el-Kabir", *National Interest*, (August 13 2016),https://nationalinterest.org/feature/when-winston-churchill-bombed-france-the-battle-mers-el-17337 (accessed 08/07/2020)

63   Thomas Parker, "When Winston Churchill Bombed France"

64   ibid

65

66   Imperial War Museum, "The Polish Pilots who flew in the Battle of Britain", https://www.iwm.org.uk/history/the-polish-pilots-who-flew-in-the-battle-of-britain (accessed 19/06/2020)

67   Joss Meakins, "Polish Pilots and the Battle of Britain", https://www.historic-uk.com/HistoryUK/HistoryofBritain/Polish-Pilots-the-Battle-of-Britain/ (accessed 19/06/2020)

68   Imperial War Museum, "The Polish Pilots who flew in the Battle of Britain", https://www.iwm.org.uk/history/the-polish-pilots-who-flew-in-the-battle-of-britain (accessed 19/06/2020)

69   https://winstonchurchill.org/publications/finest-hour/finest-hour-145/1939-1945-polands-contribution-to-victory-in-the-second-world-war/ (accessed 19/06/2020)

70   M. Lufakharul Islam, "The Great Bengal Famine", *Modern Asian Studies 41*, no. 2 (2007): pp. 421-440

71   Michelle B. McAlpin, "Famines, Epidemics, And Population Growth: The Case Of India*", Journal Of Interdisciplinary History 14*, no. 2 (1983): p. 351, doi:10.2307/203709.

72   Lance Brennan, Les Heathcote and Anton Lucas, "War and Famine Around The Indian Ocean During The Second World War", *Research In Ethical Issues In Organizations*, no. 18, (2017), pp. 5-70, doi:10.1108/s1529-209620170000018002.

73   Shashi Tharoor, "The Ugly Briton", *TIME*, 2010,

74   J.N Uppal, *Bengal Famine Of 1943: A Man-Made Tragedy* (Delhi: Atma Ram, 1984), pp. 87-103.

75   Mark Tauger, "The Indian Famine Crises Of World War II", *British Scholar 1,* no. 2 (2009): p188.

76   Arthur Herman, "Absent Churchill, Bengal's Famine Would Have Been Worse", *Hillsdale Education*, (Oct 13, 2017), https://winstonchurchill.hillsdale.edu/churcills-secret-war-bengal-famine-1943/ (accessed 16/12/2020)

77   H. Braund, *Famine in Bengal*, Braund Archives, 09WO, 715,Eur 792/2, (India Office Library, London, 1944), https://

www.lboro.ac.uk/media/media/subjects/politics-international-studies/downloC.E.s/Alexander%20Miell-Ingram%20-%20 Dissertation.pdf

78   Amartya Sen, *Poverty And Famines*, 2nd ed. (New Delhi: OUP, 1984), p. 58.

79   Maya Oppenheim, "'Winston Churchill is no better than Adolf Hitler,' says Indian politician Dr Shashi Tharoor", *The Independent,* (27/3/2017), https://www.independent.co.uk/news/world/world-history/winston-churchill-C.E.olf-hitler-no-better-shashi-tharoor-indian-politician-post-colonialist-author-a7641681.html (accessed 19/11/2019)

80   Soutik Biswas, "How Churchill 'Starved' India", *BBC News*, (2010), http://www.bbc.co.uk/blogs/thereporters/soutikbiswas/2010/10/how_churchill_starved_india.html, (accessed 16/12/2020)

81   Michael Safi, "Churchill's policies contributed to 1943 Bengal famine – study", *The Guardian,* (29 March 2019), https://www.theguardian.com/world/2019/mar/29/winston-churchill-policies-contributed-to-1943-bengal-famine-study (accessed 09/07/2020)

82   Madhusree Mukerjee, *Churchill's Secret War: The British Empire and the Ravaging of India during World War II,* (Basic books, 2011), p. 68

83   James Felton, *52 Times Britain was a Bellend: The History you didn't get taught at School*, (London: Sphere, 2019), p. 52

84   "Did Churchill Cause The Bengal Famine*?", The Churchill Project - Hillsdale College*, (2015), https://winstonchurchill.hillsdale.edu/didchurchill-cause-the-bengal-famine/), (accessed 15/12/2020)

85   Mukerjee, *Churchill's Secret War,* p. 126

86   Shashi Tharoor, "The Ugly Briton", *TIME,* 2010,

87   Alexander Miell-Ingram, *The Dark Side of Churchill*, https://www.lboro.ac.uk/media/media/subjects/politics-international-studies/downloads/Alexander%20Miell-Ingram%20-%20 Dissertation.pdf (accessed 4/12/2020)

88   Richard Langworth, "Indians Again: No Oscars For Movies About War Criminals", (2018), https://richardlangworth.com/ starving-indians-denychurchill-oscars, (accessed 15/12/2020)

89   Sam Dalrymple, "The Shameful truth about Churchill", Cherwell.org, (23 December 2017), https://cherwell.org/2017/12 /23/churchill-and-india/ (accessed 08/07/2020)

90   Jasper Becker, *Hungry ghosts,* (London: Holt, 1996), p.14

91   Stephen Devereux, "Famine in the twentieth century", *Brighton: Institute of Development Studies*: *6.* Table 1, (2000), p. 6

92   Tom Heyden, "The 10 greatest controversies of Winston Churchill's career", *BBC News Magazine,* (26 January 2015), https://www.bbc.co.uk/news/magazine-29701767, (accessed 09/07/2020)

93   Richard Toye, *Churchill's Empire: The World that Made Him and the World He Made,* (Pan books, 2011)

94   Leo S. Amery, John Barnes, and David Nicholson, *The Leo Amery Diaries* (London: Hutchinson, 1980)

95   Martin Gilbert, *Winston S. Churchill: The Churchill Documents* (Hillsdale, Michigan: Hillsdale College Press, 2006), p. 51.

96   Arthur Herman, *Gandhi & Churchill: The Epic Rivalry That Destroyed an Empire and Forged Our Age,* (Bantam books, 2009)

97   Johann Hari, "Not his finest hour: The dark side of Winston Churchill", *The Independent,* (27/10/2010) https://www. independent.co.uk/news/uk/politics/not-his-finest-hour-the-dark-side-of-winston-churchill-2118317.html (02042020) (accessed 11/07/2020)

98   Toye, *Churchill's Empire*

99   Alexander Miell-Ingram, *The Dark Side of Churchill*, p.29

100   M. S. Venkataramani, *Bengal Famine Of 1943: The American Response* (Delhi: Vikas, 1973), p. 8

101   CBBC Newsround writers, "Who was Winston Churchill and why was he important?", CBBC, (14/02/2019) https://www. bbc.co.uk/newsround/31043477 (accessed 21/01/2020)

102   Lance Brennan, "Government Famine Relief In Bengal, 1943", *The Journal Of Asian Studies 47*, no. 3 (1988): p. 541, doi:10.2307/2056974.

103   Maya Oppemheim, "'Winston Churchill is no better than Adolf Hitler,' says Indian politician Dr Shashi Tharoor," *The Independent*, (27/3/2017) https://www.independent.co.uk/news/world/world-history/winston-churchill-C.E.olf-hitler-no-better-shashi-tharoor-indian-politician-post-colonialist-author-a7641681.html (accessed 19/11/2019)

104   Madhusree Mukerjee, "How Winston Churchill Stole From India For Britain's War", *Quartz India*, (2018), https://qz.com/india/1235178/howwinston-churchill-stole-from-india-for-britains-war/ (accessed 15/12/2020)

105   Ibid

106   F. Capie and M. Collins, *The Interwar Economy: A statistical abstract*, (Manchester: Manchester University Press, 1983) cited in Nicholas Horsewood; Somnath Sen and Anca Voicu, *Beggar Thy Neighbour: British Imports During the Inter-War Years and the Effect of the 1932 Tariff*, (University of Birmingham, Department of Economics Discussion Paper 10-31, 2008), p.6

107   Tom Heyden, "The 10 greatest controversies of Winston Churchill's career", *BBC News Magazine*, (26 January 2015), https://www.bbc.co.uk/news/magazine-29701767 (accessed 6/12/20)

108   "Roald Dahl family sorry for author's anti-Semitic remarks," *BBC News*, (6/12/20) https://www.bbc.co.uk/news/entertainment-arts-55205354 (accessed 6/12/20)

109   Cambridge English Dictionary, https://dictionary.cambridge.org/dictionary/english/racist

110   https://www.bbc.co.uk/newsround/31043477 (14/02/2019) (accessed 02/04/2020)

111   Richard M. Langworth, 'Hearsay Doesn't Count: The Truth About Churchill's "Racist Epithets"', *The Churchill Project, Hillsdale College*, July 2, 2020, https://winstonchurchill.hillsdale.edu/churchills-racist-epithets/ (accessed 10/12/2020)

112   Professor William Roger, *Churchill and the Liquidation of the British Empire*, (Kemper Lecture 29/03/1998)

113   Johann Hari, "Not his finest hour: The dark side of Winston Churchill", *The Independent*

114   Richard Toye, *Churchill's Empire*

115   Paul Addison, *Churchill, The Unexpected Hero,* (Oxford University Press, 2006) P.233

116   Johann Hari, "Not his finest hour: The dark side of Winston Churchill", *The Independent*

117   Johann Hari, "Not his finest hour: The dark side of Winston Churchill", *The Independent*

118   Richard M. Langworth, "Was Churchill a White Supremacist? *Hillsdale education,* (May 7, 2019), https://winstonchurchill. hillsdale.edu/white-supremacy/ (accessed 16/12/.2020)

119   ibid

120   Richard Dowden, "Apartheid: made in Britain," *The Independent*, (22/10/2011), https://www.independent.co.uk/ voices/apartheid-mC.E.e-britain-richard-dowden-explains-how-churchill-rhodes-and-smuts-caused-black-south-africans-lose-their-rights-1370856.html (accessed 16/12/2020)

121   Boris Johnson, cited in Peter Walker, 'We cannot edit our past': Boris Johnson's statue tweets explained", *The Guardian*, 20/06/2020

Historical Homosexuals and rise of Homophobia

122   Eric Berkowitz, *Sex and Punishment*, (The Westbourne Press, 2013), p.58

123   Sylvia Tamale, "Homosexuality is not un-African", *Al-Jazeera*, (26/04/2014) http://america.aljazeera.com/opinions/2014/4/ homosexuality-africamuseveniugandanigeriaethiopia.html (accessed 10/05/2020)

124   F.F Ruan, "China", in West D.J., Green R. (eds) *Sociolegal Control of Homosexuality. Perspectives in Sexuality (Behavior, Research, and Therapy)*. (Springer, Boston, MA, 2002) p59

125   LGBT rights by country or territory, https://en.wikipedia.org/wiki/LGBT_rights_by_country_or_territory (accessed 03/06/2020)

126   Kate Lister, *A Curious History of Sex,* (Unbound, London, 2020), p50-51

127   Kendall, ""When a Woman Loves a Woman" in Lesotho: Love, Sex, and the (Western) Construction of Homophobia". In Murray, Stephen O.; Roscoe, Will (eds.). *Boy Wives and Female Husbands: Studies of African Homosexuality's*, (New York: St. Martin's Press, 1998), pp. 234–236

128   "World's oldest dildo", *Miami Herald*, 07/02/2019 https://www.miamiherald.com/miami-com/things-to-do/article225861110.html (accessed 11/05/2020)

129   currently housed at The World Erotic Art Museum in Miami.

130   Definition' by Joshua J. Mark published on 16 June 2014 https://www.ancient.eu/Ur-Nammu/ accessed 070620

131   "China country profile". *BBC News*, 18 October 2010, https://www.bB.C.E..E.E..co.uk/news/world-asia-pacific-13017882accessed 11/05/2020

132   Louis Crompton, *Homosexuality and Civilization*, (Cambridge, MA: Harvard University Press, 2003)

133   F. F. Ruan "China", p57

134   Ibid

135   Ibid

136   Bret Hinsch, *Passions of the cut sleeve: the male homosexual tradition in China*, (University of California Press, 1990), p.77

137   Ibid pp. 77-78.

138   F.F. Ruan, "China", p58

139   ibid p58

140   *South China Morning Post* 28 Jan. 2001 Quoted in China: Information on Treatment of Homosexuals Page 2 of 5 file://I:\country\countryinfo\RIC\RIC\China\CHN01001.htm 03/05/2003, (accessed 03/06/2020)

141   F.F. Ruan, "China", p.58

142   Eric Berkowitz, *Sex and Punishment*, p.40

143   Ibid, p.27

144   Strabo observation 25B.C.E. in Eric Berkowitz, *Sex and Punishment*, p.44

145   Eric Berkowitz, *Sex and Punishment*, p.40

146   Hawass Angy Essam, "Ancient Egyptians denounced homosexuality", *Egypt Today*, 3 October 2017, https://www.egypttoday.com/Article/4/25825/Hawass-Ancient-Egyptians-denounced-homosexuality (accessed 28/12/2020)

147   "In a Time of Torture: The Assault on Justice In Egypt's Crackdown on Homosexual Conduct: II. Homosexual Conduct and the Law: The Conditions for a Crackdown". https://www.hrw.org/reports/2004/egypt0304/2.htm#_Toc63760382 (accessed 28/12/2020)

148   Neel Burton, M.D, The Oldest Gays in History; Three tales of same-sex love in Ancient Egypt", *Psychology Today*, Jul 14, 2017, https://www.psychologytoday.com/gb/blog/hide-and-seek/201707/the-oldest-gays-in-history (accessed 28/12/2020)

149   Eric Berkowitz, *Sex and Punishment*, p.81

150   Ibid p.87

151   Louis Crompton, *Homosexuality and Civilization*, p205

152   Eric Berkowitz, *Sex and Punishment*, p.80

153   Ibid, p. 81

154   Daniel Mendelsohn, "Girl, Interrupted. Who was Sappho?", *NewYorker magazine*, 9 March 2015, https://www.newyorker.com/magazine/2015/03/16/girl-interrupted (accessed 19/01/21)

155   Malcolm Brabant Lesbos islanders dispute gay name, 1 May 2008, http://news.bB.C.E..E.E..co.uk/1/hi/7376919.stm accessed 19/01/2021

156   Louis Crompton, *Homosexuality and Civilization*, pp. 99-100

157   Eric Berkowitz, *Sex and Punishment*, p129

158   Seneca, *Controversies 4,* Praef. 10

159   Amy Richlin, "Not before Homosexuality: The Materiality of the Cinaedus and the Roman Law against Love between Men," *Journal of the History of Sexuality* 3.4 (1993) pp. 562–563.

160 Eric Berkowitz, *Sex and Punishment,* p.132

161 Ibid p.132

162 Suetonius, *Life of Nero* 28–29; Williams, *Roman Homosexuality*, p. 279

163 Thomas K. Hubbard (eds), *Homosexuality in Greece and Rome: A Sourcebook of Basic Documents*, edited by, California University Press

164 "Federal Register, Volume 83, Number 141 dated July 23, 2018", https://www.govinfo.gov/content/pkg/FR-2018-07-23/pdf/2018-15679.pdf (accessed 11/02/21)

165 Jeffrey S. Jacobi, *Two Spirits, Two Eras, Same Sex: For a Traditionalist Perspective on Native American Tribal Same-Sex Marriage Policy*, (U. MICH. J. L. REFORM 823, 2006), P.823

166 Johann Hari, "The hidden history of homosexuality in the US", *The Independent*, 22/06/2011 https://www.independent.co.uk/news/world/americas/johann-hari-the-hidden-history-of-homosexuality-in-the-us-2300636.html (accessed 10/05/2020)

167 ibid

168 Bisi Alimini "If you say being gay is not African, you don't know your history", *The Guardian,* (09/09/2015), https://www.theguardian.com/commentisfree/2015/sep/09/being-gay-african-history-homosexuality-christianity (accessed 09/05/2020)

169 Donald Donham, *History, Power, Ideology: Central Issues in Marxism and Anthropology* (1990) https://www.jstor.org/stable/525135?seq=1

170 Sylvia Tamale, "Homosexuality is not un-African", *Aljazeera*, (26/04/2014) http://america.aljazeera.com/opinions/2014/4/homosexuality-africamuseveniugandanigeriaethiopia.html (accessed 10/05/2020)

171 Bernard Faure, *The Red Thread.: Buddhist Approaches to Sexuality*, (Princeton, Princeton University Press 1998), p. 215

172 Makoto, Furukawa, and Angus Lockyer. "The Changing Nature of Sexuality: The Three Codes Framing Homosexuality

in Modern Japan." *U.S.-Japan Women's Journal. English Supplement*, no. 7, [Josai University Educational Corporation, University of Hawai'i Press], 1994, pp. 99, 100, 108, 112 http://www.jstor.org/stable/42772078.

173 Tsuneo Watanabe and Jun'ichi Iwata, *The Love of the Samurai: A Thousand Years of Japanese Homosexuality*, (GMP Publishers Ltd, London 1989), pp. 47-48

174 Peter Avery, *Islam in Sociolegal Control of Homosexuality*, edited by Donald J. West and Richard Green, (University of Cambridge press, London, 1997), p. 117

175 Bernarda Reza Ramírez. "Propuesta para abatir el delito en el estado de Veracruz - Llave". (Universidad Abierta, 24 August 2007)

176 *The Shatapatha Brahmana* (2.4.4.19)

177 "Stances of Faiths on LGBT Issues: Hinduism", *Human Rights Campaign.* (Accessed 28/12/2020)

178 "Homosexuality, Hinduism & the Third Gender: An Overview," *GALVA-108 GAY & LESBIAN VAISHNAVA ASSOCIATION,* https://www.galva108.org/single-post/2014/05/15/homosexuality-hinduism-the-third-gender-a-summary (accessed 28/12/2020)

179 *Manusmriti* 11.68 and 11.175; *Artha-sastra* 4.13.40.

180 *Manusmriti* 8.370 and *Artha-sastra* 4.12.20-21.

181 Leviticus 18:22, *The Bible*

182 Eric Berkowitz, *Sex and Punishment,* p.60

183 Eric Berkowitz, *Sex and Punishment,* p.63

184 Eric Berkowitz, *Sex and Punishment,* p.59

185 Leviticus 18:3, *The Bible*

186 ibid

187 Jonathan, D Spence, *The Memory Palace of Matteo Ricci,* (Faber and Faber, London 1985), p.225

188 Dharmachari JÃanavira, "Homosexuality in the Japanese Buddhist Tradition", *The Western Buddhist Review*, Vol 3, 2001, pp. 105-33

189 Tu Weiming, Confucianism, *Encyclopaedia Britannica*, https://www.britannica.com/topic/Confucianism (accessed 30/12/2020)

190 Louis Crompton, *Homosexuality and Civilization*, p.205

191 John Drane, "The Bible", *BBC,* Last updated 2011-07-12, https://www.bbc.co.uk/religion/religions/christianity/texts/bible.shtml#:~:text=The%20Old%20Testament%20is%20the,in%20the%20first%20century%20C.E (accessed 21/12/2020)

192 Leviticus 18:22, The Old Testament, *The New International Version of the Bible*, 1973

193 1) Annals of Imperial Rome, a first-century history of the Roman Empire written around 116 C.E. by the Roman senator and historian Tacitus and 2) Jewish historian Flavius Josephus, twice mentions Jesus in Jewish Antiquities, his massive 20-volume history of the Jewish people that was written around 93 C.E.

194 Matthew 19:3 *The Bible*

195 D. Hilborn, *Homosexuality and Scripture*, (Evangelical Alliance, 2002)

196 J. Boswell, *Christianity, Social Tolerance, and Homosexuality: Gay People in Western Europe from the Beginning of the Christian Era to the Fourteenth Century* , (University of Chicago Press, 1980)

197 Mona West, "The Bible and Homosexuality", Metropolitan *Community Churches (MCC),* Archived 2012-05-08 at the Wayback Machine

198 Elizabeth Sloane, "Can We Eat Bacon Now? Leviticus Was Written for Priests, Not You, Say Scholars", 13/05/2017, *Haaretz,* https://www.haaretz.com/archaeology/revisiting-leviticus-can-we-eat-bacon-now-1.5471003, (accessed 31/12/2020)

199 Eric Berkowitz, *Sex and Punishment,* p.133

200 Leopold August Warnkonig, Flandrische Staats- und Rechtsgeschichte bis rum Jahr 1305, 3 vols. (Tiibingen: L. F. Fues, 1839), 3(2): 76.

201 N. S. Davidson, "Sodomy in Early Modern Venice", in *Sodomy in Early Modern Europe*, edited by Tom Betteridge, (New York: Manchester University Press, 2002) p. 67

202 Ibid, p. 65-81

203 Samuel Pepys, *Samuel Pepys' Diary*, Wednesday 1ˢᵗ July 1663

204 Eric Berkowitz, *Sex and Punishment,* p. 231

205 Amanda Skofstad, "Connections between Quran and Bible illuminated in new commentary", *Notre Dame News,* June 06, 2018, https://news.nd.edu/news/connections-between-quran-and-bible-illuminated-in-new-commentary/ (accessed 30/12/2020)

206 Peter Avery, *Islam in Sociolegal Control of Homosexuality*, edited by Donald J. West and Richard Green, (University of Cambridge press, London, 1997), p110

207 Ibid,

208 ibid

209 Ibid, p. 111

210 Ibid, p. 111

211 A.L., "How homosexuality became a crime in the Middle East", *The Economist*, Jun 6th 2018, https://www.economist.com/open-future/2018/06/06/how-homosexuality-became-a-crime-in-the-middle-east (accessed 02/06/2020)

212 Eric Berkowitz, *Sex and Punishment*, p.186

213 Louis Crompton, *Homosexuality and civilization*, p362

214 Peter Avery, *Islam in Sociolegal Control of Homosexuality*, p112

215 R. Levy, *A Mirror for Princes* (translation),(London, 1951), p. 78

216 ibid

217 Brian Whitaker, "Everything you need to know about being gay in Muslim countries", *The Guardian*, 21/06/2016 , https://www.theguardian.com/world/2016/jun/21/gay-lgbt-muslim-countries-middle-east, (Accessed 28/12/2020)

218 Eric Berkowitz, *Sex and Punishment*, p.140

219 Eric Berkowitz, *Sex and Punishment*, p.136

220 Ryan Nelson, "Who Was the Apostle Paul?" *Overview Bible*, 28/02/2019, https://overviewbible.com/apostle-paul/ (accessed 09/02/2021)

221 Yebamoth 76a, trans. Isaac Slotki; in *The Babylonian Talmud*, 18 vols. (London: Socino Press, 1961),8: 513.

222 Romans I, 26, *The Bible*

223 St. Anselm, *Omnes sanctissimi Pauli apostoli epistolas enarrationes* (Venice: C.E. signum spei, 1547), p. 8v.

224 St. Thomas Aquinas, *Summa theologica*, trans. Fathers of the English Dominican Province, 3 vols. (New York: Benziger Brothers, 1947-48),2: 1825.

225 Eric Berkowitz, *Sex and Punishment*, pp. 133-4

226 Edward Gibbon, *The History of the decline and fall of Roman empire*: vol II, (New York: Harper and brothers, 1840)

227 Eric Berkowitz, *Sex and Punishment*, p.134

228 Ibid p.173

229 Bonnie J. Morris, "History of Lesbian, Gay, Bisexual and Transgender Social Movements", *American Psychological Association*, 2009, https://www.apa.org/pi/lgbt/resources/history (accessed 16/02/21)

230 Louis Crompton, *The Myth of Lesbian Impunity Capital Laws from 1270 to 1791*,(Faculty Publications, University of Nebraska, 1981), p11

231 John Boswell, *Christianity, Social Tolerance, and Homosexuality: Gay People in Western Europe from the Beginning of the Christian Era to the Fourteenth Century*, (Chicago: University of Chicago Press, 1981) pp. 289-90

232 Pierre Rapetti, ed., *Li Livres de Jostice et de plet* (Paris: Didot Freres, 1850), pp. 279-80.

233 Louis Crompton, *Homosexuality and Civilization*, p363

234 David Rogerson, Samantha Ellsmore and David Hudson, *The Early Tudors,* (London, 2001), p.121

235 WALTER HUNGERFORD AND THE 'BUGGERY ACT', *English Heritage,* https://www.english-heritage.org.uk/learn/histories/lgbtq-history/walter-hungerford-and-the-buggery-act/

236 Louis Crompton, *Homosexuality and Civilization*, p. 363

237 Theodor Hartster, *Dm Strajecht der f &en Reichsstadt Speier* (Breslau: Marcus, 1900), pp. 184-85.

238 Helmut Puff, *Sodomy in Reformation Germany and Switzerland, 1400-*1600. (University of Chicago Press, 2003) pp. 32–33

239 J. Kohler and Wily Scheel, eds., *Diepeinliche Gerichtsordnung Kaiser Karls V: Constitutio criminalis Carolina* (Halle an der Saale: Verlag der Buchhandlung des Waisenhauses, 1900), p. 62.

240 Antonio Gomez, *Variae resolutiones, juris civilis, communis et regii* (Venice: Typographia Remondiniana, 1758), p. 328.

241 *Statuta prouisionesque dudes civitatis Tarvisii* (Venice, 1574), pp. 187v- 188.

242 Louis Crompton, *The Myth of Lesbian Impunity Capital Laws from 1270 to 1791*, (Faculty Publications, University of Nebraska, 1981), p. 19

243 Ibid, p. 18

244 Eric Berkowitz, *Sex and Punishment*, p.305

245 Edmond Jean Francois Barbier cited in Berkowitz, *Sex and Punishment*, p.319

246 'Charles II, 1661: An Act for the Establishing Articles and Orders for the regulateing and better Government of His Majesties Navies Ships of Warr & Forces by Sea.' In *Statutes of the Realm: Volume 5, 1628-80*, ed. John Raithby (s.l, 1819), pp. 311-314. British History Online http://www.british-history.ac.uk/statutes-realm/vol5/pp311-314 [accessed 17 January 2021].

247 Arthur Gilbert, "Buggery and the British Navy, 1700-1861," *Journal of Social History 10* (1976) pp. 72-98.

248 Eric Berkowitz, *Sex and Punishment*, p.292

249 B. R. Burg, *Sodomy and the Pirate Tradition*, (NYU press, 1995),

250 B. R. Burg, *Sodomy and the Pirate Tradition*, (NYU press, 1995), pp. 139-174

251 Eric Berkowitz, *Sex and Punishment*, p. 311

252 Ibid

253 The 1801 Census, worked out using population of 8,870,000 with 50% male and 35% of these being adult https://www.thegazette.co.uk/all-notices/content/162

254 Sexual Orientation, UK: 2019, Sexual orientation, UK - Office for National Statistics (ons.gov.uk) (accessed 02/04/22)

255 Eric Berkowitz, *Sex and Punishment*, p. 296

256 Louis Crompton, "Gay Genocide: From Leviticus to Hitler," *The Gay Academic*, ed. Louie Crew (Palm Springs, Calif.: ETC Publications, 1978), pp. 69-91; and A. Harvey, "Prosecutions for Sodomy in England at the Beginning of the Nineteenth Century," *The Historical Journal 21* (1978) pp. 939-48.

257 Louis Crompton, "The Myth of Lesbian Impunity Capital Laws from 1270 to 1791" (Faculty Publications, University of Nebraska, 1981), p.13 https://digitalcommons.unl.edu/english facpubs/59

258 "Consolidation of the Criminal Laws." 9 Mar. 1826, British Parliamentary Debates. House of Commons., pp. 1214-15

259 British Library, LGBTQ histories, https://www.bl.uk/lgbtq-histories/lgbtq-timeline (accessed 29/12/2020)

260 Hyde v Hyde (1866) LR 1 PD 130

261 ibid

262 104th Congress Public Law 199, Page 110 STAT. 2419, https://www.govinfo.gov/content/pkg/PLAW-104publ199/html/PLAW-104publ199.htm, (accessed 02/04/22)

263 Michael S. Foldy, *The Trials of Oscar Wilde Deviance, Morality and Late-Victorian Society*, (Yale University Press, 1997), p. 47

264 Oscar Wilde's testimony, 29 April 1895, Transcript of Trial, https://www.famous-trials.com/wilde/327-home (accessed 02/04/22)

265 Frank Lockwood, closing statement at the Old Bailey trial of Oscar Wilde, 25 May 1895, Transcript of Trial, https://www.famous-trials.com/wilde/327-home (accessed 02/04/22)

266 Richard Ellmann, *Oscar Wilde,* (New York: Vintage Books, 1988), p. 769

267 James Felton, *52 Times Britain was a Bellend,* (Sphere, London, 2019), p.83

268 Ibid

269 Cortez, cited in Berkowitz, *Sex and Punishment*, p. 259

270 Bonnie J. Morris, "History of Lesbian, Gay, Bisexual and Transgender Social Movements", *American Psychological Association*, 2009, https://www.apa.org/pi/lgbt/resources/history (accessed 15/02/21)

271 Louis Crompton, "Homosexuals and the Death Penalty in Colonial America," *Journal of Homosexuality* ,(1967) p. 279

272 Bonnie J. Morris, "History of Lesbian, Gay, Bisexual and Transgender Social Movements", *American Psychological Association*, 2009

273 Stephen O Murray; Will Roscoe, *Islamic homosexuality's: culture, history, and literature.* (New York, 1997)

274 Bruce W. Dunne, "Homosexuality in the Middle East: An Agenda for Historical Research." *Arab Studies Quarterly 12, no. 3/4* (1990), pp. 55-82. http://www.jstor.org/stable/41857885

275 Grant Walsh-Haines, "The Egyptian Blogosphere: Policing Gender and Sexuality and the Consequences for Queer Emancipation." *Journal of Middle East Women's Studies 8, no. 3* (2012), pp. 41-62. https://muse.jhu.edu/article/483266 (accessed 16/02/21)

276 Sayuri Yoshida, *The Collections of F. J. Bieber and the Kafa Culture: Connecting Anthropological and Archival Research,* (2019), pp.25-40

277 Bret Hinsch, *Passions of the Cut Sleeve*, (University of California Press, 1990), pp. 77-78

278 Wenqing Kang, *Obsession: male same-sex relations in China, 1900–1950*, (Hong Kong University Press, 2009), p. 3

279 Associated Press, "Rights group urges China to ban abusive gay 'conversion therapy'". *NBC News.*15/11/217, https://www.nbc news.com/feature/nbc.-out/rights-group-urges-china-ban-abusive-gay-conversion-therapy-n821031 (accessed 2/12/2019)

280 Peter Avery, *Islam in Sociolegal Control of Homosexuality*, p. 117

281 Ibid, p.112

282 Nicola Menzie, "NIV More Popular Than KJV, NLT Bibles; 11 Million Copies Sold Worldwide", *Christianpost.com,* March 26, 2013, https://www.christianpost.com/news/niv-more-popular-than-kjv-nlt-bibles-11-million-copies-sold-worldwide.html, (accessed 13/03/2021)

283 Stephen Dryden, "The Men killed under the Buggary Act*", British Library,* https://www.bl.uk/lgbtq-histories/articles/the-men-killed-under-the-buggery-act (accessed 02/01/2020)

King Richard I – more Lyingheart than Lionheart

284 Ralph V.Turner, Richard R. Heiser, *The Reign of Richard Lionheart, Ruler of the Angevin empire, 1189–1199*, (Harlow: Longman, 2000)

285 "Richard I King of England", *Encyclopaedia Britannica,* https://www.britannica.com/biography/Richard-I-king-of-England

286 Douglas Boyd, "Richard the Lionheart may not have spoken English – plus 7 more surprising facts", *HistoryExtra*, April 8th, 2020, https://www.historyextra.com/period/medieval/8-things-you-probably-didnt-know-about-richard-the-lionheart/ (accessed 6/7/2020)

287 UK GDP https://www.statista.com/statistics/281744/gdp-of-the-united-kingdom/

288 John Gillingham, "The Kidnapped King: Richard I in Germany, 1192–1194" *German Historical Institute London Bulletin*, Vol.30:1 (2008)

289 Beha-ed-Din, his account appears in Archer, T.A., *The Crusade of Richard I (*1889),

290 Roger of Howden, *King Henry the Second , and the Acts of King Richard (c. 1200)* , https://spartacus-educational.com/MED richard1.htm 03042020

291 Westminster Abbey Writers, "Richard I", https://www.westminster-abbey.org/abbey-commemorations/royals/richard-i (accessed 20/06/2020)

292   Marion Meade, *Eleanor of Aquitaine* (Phoenix publishers, 2002) p. 377

293   Livia Gershon, "Chivalry Was Established to Keep Thuggish, Medieval Knights in Check", *History.com*, 23/01/ 2019, https://www.history.com/news/chivalry-knights-middle-ages (accessed 15/08/2020)

294   ibid

295   John Harvey, *The Plantagenets*, (Fontana/Collins, 1948), pp. 62-64

296   Ben Johnson, "Richard Lionheart", *Historic UK* , 5/1//2016, https://www.historic-uk.com/HistoryUK/HistoryofEngland/Richard-Lionheart/ (accessed 10/07/2020)

297   Roger of Howden, *King Henry the Second, and the Acts of King Richard (c. 1200)*

298   Charles Scott Moncrieff, *Kings and Queens of England* (Blandford Press, 1966) p. 28

Britain's role in the Holocaust

299   Likely attributed to Edmund Burke

300   Eckhardt Fuchs, "What countries teach children about the Holocaust varies hugely", (January 26, 2015), https://theconversation.com/what-countries-teach-children-about-the-holocaust-varies-hugely-31599 (accessed 6/12/2019)

301   http://news.bbc.co.uk/1/hi/education/6563429.stm. 14/4/2007, (accessed 6/12/2019)

302   "Introduction to the Holocaust", *United States Holocaust Memorial Museum*, Washington, DC, (12/3/2018) https://encyclopedia.ushmm.org/content/en/article/introduction-to-the-holocaust

303   History.com editors, "The Holocaust", *History.com,* (29/8/ 2019), https://www.history.com/topics/world-war-ii/the-holocaust, (accessed 6/12/2019)

304   Martin Gilbert, *The Holocaust. The Jewish Tragedy,* (William Collins Son & Co. London, 1986), p. 52

305 "Einsatzgruppen", *United States Holocaust Memorial Museum,* Washington, DC, https://encyclopedia.ushmm.org/content/en/article/einsatzgruppen, (accessed 6/12/2019)

306 How many Jews were murdered in each country? Encyclopaedia of the Holocaust, *YadVashem*, https://www.yad.vashem.org/holocaust/faqs.html (accessed 17/02/21)

307 "Concentration camps", Jewishvirtuallibrary.org, https://www.jewishvirtuallibrary.org/how-many-concentration-camps, (accessed 6/12/2019)

308 Jack Fairweather, *The Volunteer*, (London, 2020), p.42

309 Ibid, p.142

310 Martin Gilbert, *The Holocaust,* p. 287

311 Michael Fleming, *Auschwitz, the Allies and Censorship of the Holocaust*, (Cambridge, 2014), p. 21

312 ibid

313 Martin Gilbert, *The Holocaust,* p287

314 "What were the extermination camps? When did they start to function, and what was their purpose?" *Yad Vashem,* https://www.yad.vashem.org/holocaust/faqs.html (accessed 17/02/21)

315 Encyclopedia.ushmm.org (accessed 12/02/20)

316 Michael Fleming, *Auschwitz, the Allies and Censorship of the Holocaust*, p. 5

317 Ibid, p.3

318 Walter Laquer, *The Terrible Secret: Suppression of the Truth About Hitler's 'Final Solution'* (Henry Holt & Co, 1998), p. 197

319 Michael Fleming, *Auschwitz,* p.10

320 Ibid

321 Richard Breitman, *Official Secrets. What the Nazis planned, what the British and Americans knew,* (Penguin books, St. Ives, 1998), p. 90

322 German Police Decodes V and VI, 25 Dec. 1939 and 14 Jan. 1940, PRO HW 16/1

323 "Ghettoes in Occupied Poland," United States Holocaust Memorial Museum, https://encyclopedia.ushmm.org/content/en/article/ghettos-in-poland (accessed 05/02/21)

324   Michael Fleming, *Auschwitz,* p. 21

325   Adolf Hitler, *Mein Kampf,* trans Ralph Manheim (Boston, 1943), p. 344

326   "Mordanschlag gegen Adolf Hitler geplant", *Volkischer Beobachter*, 21 March 1933

327   "The Wannsee Conference and Final Solution", *United States Holocaust Memorial Museum*, Washington, DC, https://encyclopedia.ushmm.org/content/en/article/wannsee-conference-and-the-final-solution (accessed 19/02/21)

328   Postal and Telegraph Censorship Report on Jewry, no.3, part 1, p.3, PRO HO 213/953

329   Information given via Holocaust Educational Trust on a visit to Auschwitz, desecrated graves were seen by myself during visit in 2013

330   Martin Gilbert, *The Holocaust*, p. 285

331   Yehuda Bauer, *Rethinking the Holocaust* (Yale University Press, London, 2001) p.219

332   Richard Breitman, *Official Secrets,* p. 153

333   PRO/HW 14/11, item 93

334   German Police Decodes V and VI, 25 Dec. 1939 and 14 Jan. 1940, PRO HW 16/1

335   Raul Hilberg, *The destruction of the European Jews* (New York 1985) p186

336   "Frequently asked question", *Yad Vashem,*, p.17, http://www.un.org/en/holocaustremembrance/docs/FAQ%20Holocaust%20EN%20YC.E.%20Vashem.pdf (accessed 6/12/2019)

337   Jack Fairweather, *The Volunteer*, pp.171-173

338   Raul Hilberg, *The Destruction of European Jews*, (Holmes & Meier Publishers Inc, 1985), p.1219

339   "Frequently asked question", *Yad Vashem,*, p.17, http://www.un.org/en/holocaustremembrance/docs/FAQ%20Holocaust%20EN%20YC.E.%20Vashem.pdf (accessed 6/12/2019)

340   German Police decodes, 4 August 1941, items 2 and 9, NA RG 457, Box 1386

341 Summary of German Police decodes, 3 July - 14 August, 1941, ZIP/MSG 27, 21 August, 1941, pp.3-4, PRO HW 16/6 part 1

342 German Police Decodes, 7 August 1941, item 24, NA RG 457, Box 1386 and Fegelein's Adjutant to Reit. Abt., 8 August 1941, NA RG 242, T-354/R 168/3818930

343 Summary of German Police decodes 275-323, 21 August 1941, p4 PRO HW 16/6 part 1,

344 David Cesarani, "Secret Churchill Papers released", *The Journal of Holocaust Education* 4, no. 2 (1995) pp. 225-6

345 Winston Churchill, Full transcript: http://preventgenocide. org/genocide/crimewithoutaname.htm

346 Richard Breitman, *Official Secrets,* p109

347 German Police Decodes 324-343 (3 July-14 Aug. 1941) pp.1 and 4, PRO HW 16/6, part 1

348 David Cesarani, "Secret Churchill Papers", p.226

349 Richard Breitman, *Official Secrets,* p.97 and p. 153

350 NA.FO 371/39014 (441)

351 FO 371/39014 (439-49)

352 "Holocaust Timeline", *Historyplace,* https://www.historyplace. com/worldwar2/holocaust/timeline.html (accessed 12/02/20)

353 "1944: Key Dates", United States Holocaust Memorial Museum, https://encyclopedia.ushmm.org/content/en/article/ 1944-key-dates (accessed 05/02/21)

354 Yad Vashem website interview with professor

355 German Police Decodes, 7 August 1941, item 24, NA RG 457, Box 1386 and Fegelein's Adjutant to Reit. Abt., 8 August 1941, NA RG 242, T-354/R 168/3818930

356 Richard Breitman, *Official Secrets,* pp. 95-6

357 Jeckeln to Kommandostab RFSS, 29 Aug. 1941, Military Archive, Prague, RFSS KDO 1A 10909 KR2

358 Richard Breitman, *Official Secrets,* p. 94

359 Walter Laquer, *The Terrible Secret,* p.68

360 Cited in Bernard Wasserstein, *Britain and the Jews of Europe, 1939-1945* (Oxford, 1979), pp.164-5

361 NA.FO 371/34552 and HS 4/210

362 Aneks 58, Kew National Archives

363 Michael Fleming, *Auschwitz*, p238

364 Ibid, pp.110-111

365 Jack Fairweather, *The Volunteer*, p.117

366 German Police Decodes, no.1 Traffic, 15 Oct. 1943, PRO HW 16/38

367 Jack Fairweather, *The Volunteer*, p.182

368 Ibid p.213

369 Ibid, p.192

370 Michael Fleming, *Auschwitz*, p.259

371 NA.FO 371/34361 (CM255)

372 Polish underground (Rowecki) AKD, Volume II, Document 401 in Fleming, Auschwitz, Appendix 1.

373 FO 371/34550

374 NA.FO 371/34552

375 Michael Fleming, *Auschwitz*, p.13

376 Ibid, p.264

377 Ibid, p.5

378 NA.FO 371/34361 (CM 255) p11

379 FO 371/34383

380 Julia Rappaport, "Where Did the Word "Genocide" Come From?" *facinghistory.org,* 3/11/2014, https://facingtoday. facinghistory.org/where-did-the-word-genocide-come-from (accessed 10/03/21)

381 The Vrba-Wetzler report, held at the FDR memorial library, http://www.fdrlibrary.marist.edu/_resources/images/hol/hol00522.pdf accessed 04/03/21

382 FO 371/42807 (148)

383 Michael Fleming, *Auschwitz*, p14

384 Ibid, p.15

385 Mary Fulbrook, *A Small Town Near Auschwitz: Ordinary Nazis And The Holocaust,* (Oxford University Press, 2012), p.218

386 Michael Fleming, *Auschwitz*, p.130

387 AAN 1325 202/I-31 (213), Microfilm 2201/9I, cited in Michael Fleming, *Auschwitz* , p.135

388 English translation of "Document appertaining to the German occupation of Poland: Poles in German concentration camps", Polish Ministry of the Interior, London (1943), PUMST A3.16 (158)

389 Michael Fleming, *Auschwitz*, p.25

390 NA.FO 371/34552

391 NA.FO 371/34550 (65)

392 Michael Fleming, *Auschwitz*, p235

393 Summary of interrogation of Barth, approx. mid Nov. 1943, in PRO HW 16/1, pp47-49

394 NA.FO 371/39014 (441)

395 Ibid

396 Jack Fairweather, *The Volunteer*, p.161

397 Richard Breitman, *Official Secrets,* p. 75

398 German Police Decodes, 11 December 1941, decode #550, PRO HW 16/32

399 Jack Fairweather, *The Volunteer*, p.174

400 Walter Laquer, *The Terrible Secret,* pp. 67 and 244

401 Ibid, p.68

402 *Jewish Chronicle,* 24 October and 7th November 1941, cited by Bernard Wasserstein, Britain and the Jews of Europe, 1939-1945 (Oxford, 1979) p167

403 Michael Fleming, *Auschwitz,* p.131

404 Ibid, p.259

405 Ibid, p259

406 Roy Greenslade, "Daily Telegraph's holocaust article in 1942 that went unheralded", *The Guardian,* 27/01/2015, https://www.theguardian.com/media/greenslC.E.e/2015/jan/27/daily-telegraphs-holocaust-article-in-1942-that-went-unheralded (accessed 03/02/2020)

407 United Nations Declaration, House of Commons Debate, 17 December 1942, vol 385, cc2082-7

408 Ibid

409 House of Commons Debate, 17 Dec. 1942, 2082-2087

410 Richard Breitman, *Official Secrets,* p. 192

411   JR(Randall) Minute, 14 Jan. 1943, in PRO FO 371/34361 (C 255/18/62)

412   The Earl of Avon (Sir Anthony Eden), *The Eden Memoirs: The Reckoning*, (London, 1965), p.358

413   Michael Fleming, *Auschwitz*, p.229

414   cited in Michael Fleming, *Auschwitz,* p.233

415   Michael Fleming, *Auschwitz,* p.247

416   *The Manchester Guardian*, 4th July 1944, page 6

417   Michael Fleming, *Auschwitz*, p239

418   BBC WAC, News, 26 June 1944 (Home Service, 6 pm. Bulletin (box 114)

419   BBC WAC, Home Service, News Bulletin, 9 pm, 7th July 1944

420   Ibid

421   Michael Fleming, *Auschwitz* , p.281

422   Ibid, p.306

423   Ibid, pp.306-7

424   Richard Breitman, *Official Secrets,* p.229

425   Michael Fleming, *Auschwitz*, p.305

426   Ibid, p.266

427   Richard Breitman, *Official Secrets,* p.94

428   Cited in Michael Fleming, *Auschwitz*, p.252

429   Michael Fleming, *Auschwitz*, p.252

430   Mindy Weisberge, Tami Davis Biddle, "Why Didn't the Allies Bomb Auschwitz?", *Live Science,* April 2020, https://www.livescience.com/bombing-auschwitz-wwii-pbs.html (accessed 3/5/21)

431   D. Allen Minute, 14 Jan. 1943 and A. Walker minute, 21 Jan 1943, PRO FO 371/34361 (C 555/18/62)

432   Richard Breitman, *Official Secrets,* p.169

433   John Mcloy and Franklin Roosevelt, cited in Michael Fleming, *Auschwitz*, p.251

434   Henryk Swiebocki (ed.) *Auschwitz 1940-1945: Central Issues in the History of the Camp.* Vol. IV: *The Resistance Movement.* Trans. William Brandt. Oswiecim: PMA-B, 2000, p.231

435   Michael Fleming, *Auschwitz*, p,234

436   Ibid, p.238
437   Breitman 2004, p184
438   Michael Fleming, *Auschwitz*, p.219
439   Ibid, p.255
440   Kinga Frojimovics and Mornár Judit, *The Righteous World,* (Ballassi Kiado, 2009), p.257
441   Henryk Swiebocki (ed.) *Auschwitz 1940-1945*, p231
442   Auschwitz Camp Complex: Maps, United States holocaust Memorial Museum, https://encyclopedia.ushmm.org/content/en/gallery/auschwitz-camp-complex-maps (accessed 12/5/2021)
443   "The Holocaust year by year", *BBC*, https://www.bbc.co.uk/teach/the-holocaust-year-by-year/zkxwgwx (accessed 13/4/2020)
444   Ibid, p.236
445   Martin Gilbert, cited in Fleming *Auschwitz*, p.249
446   NA.FO 371/42814/196, FO official advising to scrap the bombing plan, 25th August 1944
447   Gerhard Weinberg cited in Breitman *Official Secrets,* p.228
448   Richard Breitman, *Official Secrets,* p.192
449   Yad Vashem accessed 6/12/2019, p18
450   David S. Wyman, *The Abandonment of the Jews: America and the Holocaust,1941-1945 (*New York: New Press, 2007), p571
451   Durbrow Memorandum, undated but stamped received 25 Jan. 1943, NA RG 59 CDF 8600/4016/644 1/2
452   NA.FO 371/39451 (C7873)
453   Yad Vashem (accessed 6/12/2019), p18
454   "Nazi Propaganda and Censorship", Holocaust Encyclopaedia, *United states Holocaust Memorial Museum*, 15/01/21, https://encyclopedia.ushmm.org/content/en/article/nazi-propaganda-and-censorship#:~:text=Banning%20Germans%20from%20Listening%20to,Germans%20hear%20about%20the%20war. (Accessed 20/02/21)
455   Richard Breitman, *Official Secrets,* p.156

456 Political Warfare Executive, Central Directive week beginning 10 Dec. 1942, copy in NA RG 208, Entry 359, Box 831, PWE central directives 1942.

457 ibid

458 Bernard Wasserstein, *Britain and the Jews of Europe, 1939-1945*, pp.176-77

459 David Bankier, *The Germans and the Final Solution, Public Opinion Under Nazism - Jewish Society and Culture,* (John Wiley and Sons Ltd, 1996) p.145

460 NA.FO 371/39272, PWE directive, 30 March 1944

461 John P. Fox, "the Jewish Factor in British War Crimes Policy in 1942", *English Historical Review 92* (1977) p.87

462 BBC WAC European News bulletins – Polish 1943 cited in Fleming, *Auschwitz,* Appendix 9

463 HL MS 238 2/17, Hall letter to Easterman, 2 May 1944 (Foreign Office document WS 806/15/48)

464 Elie Wiesel, *Night,* (1960, Penguin, St Ives), p.41

465 Michael Fleming, *Auschwitz*, p.225

466 *The parliamentary debates, House of Lords, Fifth Series, vol. 125* (London 1943) 17 Dec 1942, cols. 609-10

467 Richard Breitman, *Official Secrets,* p.166

468 Bernard Wasserstein, *Britain and the Jews of Europe, 1939-1945* pp.176-83

469 Richard Breitman, *Official Secrets,* pp.177-8

470 Minutes of Committee meeting 31 Dec. 1942, PRO FO 371/36648

471 "Great Britain" (PDF). *Shoah Resource Center, The International School for Holocaust Studies, Yad Vashem,* p2. http://yad. vashem.org/odot_pdf/Microsoft%20Word%20-%206312.pdf (accessed 14/5/21)

472 Ibid, p.3

473 Louise London, *Whitehall and the Jews, 1933–1948: British Immigration Policy, Jewish Refugees and the Holocaust,* (Cambridge University Press, 2000)

474 *Parliamentary debates, fifth series, vol. 126*, House of Lords, 23 March 1943, 856-7

475   Draft of Churchill to Lady Reading, attached to Lawford to Brown 26 Jan. 1943 PRO FO 371/36650 (W 1409/40/48)

476   "Refugees", United Sates Holocaust Memorial Museum, https://encyclopedia.ushmm.org/content/en/article/refugees (accessed 16/5/21)

477   Johnson to secretary of State, 9 October 1943, regarding conversation with Boheman, NA RG 59 CDF 840.48 Refugees/4557

478   Winant to Secretary of State, 15 Dec, 1943, NA RG 59 CDF 840.51, cited in Bernard Wasserstein, *Britain and the Jews of Europe, 1939-1945*, p.247

479   Minutes of Committee meeting 31 Dec. 1942, PRO FO 371/366488

480   Richard Breitman, *Official Secrets, p.171*

481   Lady Reading to Churchill 16 Jan. 1943 PRO FO 371/36650 (W 1409/40/48)

482   Nunn (Home Office) to Walker (Foreign Office), 5 Jan 1943, and Walker to Nunn, 6 Jan. 1943, PRO FO 371/36648

483   Summarised in Callman to Secretary of State, 26 Feb 1943, NA RG 59, Lot File 52D 408, Box 3,

484   Richard Law memorandum of conversation with Alexander Easterman, 7 Jan. 1943, PRO FO 371/36648

485   Lady Reading to Churchill 16 Jan. 1943 PRO FO 371/36650 (W 1409/40/48)

486   "Pre-State Israel: Atlit Immigration Camp", *Jewish Virtual Library,* https://www.jewishvirtuallibrary.org/atlit-immigration-camp, (accessed 10/03/21)

487   Cited in "Churchill and the Holocaust: The Possible and Impossible", *International Churchill Society*, (02/06/2009), Churchill and the Holocaust: The Possible and Impossible - International Churchill Society (winstonchurchill.org) (accessed 11/01/2021)

488   Cohen, Michael J. "The British White Paper on Palestine, May 1939. Part II: The Testing of a Policy, 1942-1945." *The Historical Journal*, vol. 19, no. 3, 1976, pp. 727–757. JSTOR, www.jstor.org/stable/2638227. (Accessed 09/03/21)

489   Dalia Ofer, *Escaping the Holocaust: Illegal Immigration to the Land of Israel, 1939-1944 (Studies in Jewish History),* (Oxford University Press, 1991) pp. 218, 290.

490   *Anne Karpf, "Immigration and asylum: We've been here before", 7 June 2002, The Guardian.*

491   Michael Cohen, "Churchill and the Jews", *The Churchill Project*, 14/09/2017, https://winstonchurchill.hillsdale.edu/ churchill-jews-michael-j-cohen/ (accessed 10/03/21)

492   Welles Memo, 4 March, 1943, Welles Papers, Box 164, Franklin D. Roosevelt library, New York

493   Richard Breitman, *Official Secrets,* p.185

494   Richard Law to Anthony Eden, 21 April 1943, Avon Papers, PRO Microfilm FO 954, R 2, Con/43/2

495   Richard Breitman, *Official Secrets, p.194*

496   CHAR20/95A/69-71 churchillacrchiveforschools

497   Richard Breitman, *Official Secrets,* p.185

498   Johann Hari, "Not his finest hour: The dark side of Winston Churchill", *The Independent,*

499   Memo of conversation, 24 June 1943, Welles Papers, Box 164, Folder 10, Franklin D. Roosevelt library, New York

500   Berne (Norton) to Foreign Office, 8 July 1943, PRO FO 371/36663 (W9994/49/48)

501   Breitman and Kraut, American Refugee policy, p246

502   History Bergen-Belsen, Gedenkstätte Bergen-Belsen https:// bergen-belsen.stiftung-ng.de/en/history/#:~:text=When%20 the%20Bergen%2DBelsen%20concentration,thousands%20 of%20severely%20ill%20prisoners (Accessed 23/02/21)

503   Richard Breitman, *Official Secrets,* p.175

504   John Mendelsohn, *The Holocaust: Selected Documents in Eighteen volumes*, vol. 7, *Jewish emigration* (New York, 1982) p.173

505   Steven Koblik, *The Stones Cry Out: Sweden's Response to the Persecution of the Jews, 1933-1945,* (Schocken, 1987), p. 62-63

506   NA.FO 371/42809 (WR 218)

507   Richard Breitman, *Official Secrets,* p.171

508   Richard Law memorandum of conversation with Alexander Easterman, 7 Jan. 1943, PRO FO 371/36648

509   Richard Breitman, *Official Secrets,* p182

510   Michael Fleming, *Auschwitz*, p.27

511   Tuvia Ben-Moshe, *Churchill: Strategy and History* ,(Boulder, Columbia, 1992) pp.317-20

512   James Felton, *52 times Britain was a Bellend*, (London, 2019), p.33

513   Richard Breitman, *Official Secrets,* p.192

514   Churchill Speech September 8/9/1942, column 97, https://hansard.parliament.uk/Commons/1942-09-08/debates/b7ccb905-c8f0-4780-b548-e100956da6c3/WarSituation

515   British statement in parliament in NA RG 59, CDF 840.48 Refugees/3633

516   From the minutes of the Bermuda Conference in RG 59, Lot File 52D 408, box 3

517   CHAR20/95A/69-71 churchillacrchiveforschools

518   Foreign Office to British embassy, Washington, D.C, 19 March 1943, PRO FO 371/36655 (W 4236/49/48)

519   Internal memo - Reams to Travers, 15 Dec 1942 NA RG 59 Lot file 52D 408, box 3

520   Ibid

521   Pickett Journal, 15 June 1943, Pickett Papers, American Friends Service Committee archives, Philadelphia, cited in Richard Breitman, *Official Secrets,* p.193

522   Report by Stettinus, 22 May 1944, on visit to London, 7-29 April 1944, quoted in Waserstein, *Britain and the Jews*, p.326

523   Alex Weissberg, *Advocate For the Dead, The Story of Joel Brand,* (Criterion Books, New York, 1958), p.15

524   Michael Fleming, *Auschwitz,* p.231

525   Fleming, Auschwitz, p13

526   Cited in Martin Gilbert, "Churchill and the Holocaust: The Possible and Impossible", *International Churchill Society*, (02/06/2009), Churchill and the Holocaust: The Possible and Impossible - International Churchill Society (winstonchurchill.org) (accessed 11/01/2021)

527 Full transcript of speech: http://preventgenocide.org/genocide/crimewithoutaname.htm

528 Viscount Samuel, House of Lords Debate, 17 December 1942, vol 125 cc607-12, https://api.parliament.uk/historic-hansard/lords/1942/dec/17/persecution-of-the-jews-allies

529 Spencer C. Tucker; James R. Arnold; Roberta Wiener (30 September 2011). 'The Encyclopaedia of North American Indian Wars, 1607–1890: A Political, Social, and Military History, p.332

530 Ian Steele, *Warpaths: Invasions of North America*, (Oxford University Press, 1994) pp. 15, 47, 116

531 James Felton, *52 times Britain was a Bellend*, p.81

532 German Police Decodes 324-343 (3 July-14 Aug. 1941) pp.1 and 4, PRO HW 16/6, part 1

533 James de Rothschild, Palestine House of Commons Debate, 22 May 1939, *vol 347 cc1937-2056* https://api.parliament.uk/historic-hansard/commons/1939/may/22/palestine-1#column_1984 (accessed 03/02/2020)

534 Richard Breitman, *Official Secrets,* p.9

535 Richard Breitman, *Official Secrets,* p.230

536 NA.FO 371/39449

537 Michael Fleming, *Auschwitz*, p.262

538 Distribution lists appear both on the original German language decodes and on British summaries of them, from Richard Breitman, *Official Secrets,* p101

539 Jack Fairweather, *The Volunteer,* p.170

540 Jack Fairweather, *The Volunteer*, p.161

541 "Theresienstadt: Red Cross Visit", *United States Holocaust Memorial Museum,* https://encyclopedia.ushmm.org/content/en/article/theresienstC.E.t-red-cross-visit (accessed 21/4/21)

542 Richard Breitman, *Official Secrets,* p.91

543 Michael Fleming, *Auschwitz*, p13

544 Ibid, p.260

545 Toye cited in Alan Cowell, "Churchill took a swipe at Jews in 1937 article", *New York Times*, (11/03/2007), https://www.

nytimes.com/2007/03/11/world/europe/11iht-winston. 4873300.html (accessed 15/12/2020)

546 Michael B. Hammer, *The Dot on the I in History: Of Gentiles and Jews-A Hebrew Odyssey Scrolling the Internet,* (Lulu Publishing, 2017), p. 13

547 Alan Cowell, "Churchill took a swipe at Jews in 1937 article", *New York Times,* (11/03/2007), https://www.nytimes. com/2007/03/11/world/europe/11iht-winston.4873300.html (accessed 15/12/2020)

548 Cited in Martin Gilbert, "Churchill and the Holocaust: The Possible and Impossible", *International Churchill Society,* (02/06/2009), Churchill and the Holocaust: The Possible and Impossible - International Churchill Society (winstonchurchill. org) (accessed 11/01/2021)

549 Churchill 'greatest PM of 20th Century', *BBC NEWS,* (04/01/2000) http://news.bbc.co.uk/1/hi/uk_politics/575219. stm (accessed 17/11/20); and *Rating British Prime Ministers,* Ipsos MORI, (2004)

550 David Dutton, *Anthony Eden: A Life and Reputation* (London 1997) pp.35-109

551 Michael Fleming, *Auschwitz,* p.235

552 E. Thomas Wood and Stanislaw M. Jankowski, *Karski: How one man tried to stop the Holocaust* (New York, 1994) pp. 167-9

553 Foreign Office to British embassy, Washington D.C 17 March 1943, PRO FO 371/36655 (WH383/49/48)

554 Quote from Law to Halifax for Eden, 18 March 1943, PRO FO 371/36655 (WH383/49/48)

555 Richard Breitman, *Official Secrets,* p.182

556 Frank Roberts in a 1995 interview with Barbara Rogers

557 PRO FO 371/36648

558 Richard Breitman, *Official Secrets,* p.177

559 A. Walker Minutes, 28 Jan. 1943, PRO FO 371/36650 (W 1649/49/48)

560 Norton (Berne) to Foreign Office, 28 May 1943, PRO FO 371/34362 (C 6109/18/62)

561 Ibid

562 Tony Kushner, "The meaning of Auschwitz: Anglo-American responses to the Hungarian Jewish tragedy" in *Genocide and Rescue: The Holocaust in Hungary*, ed. David Cersani, (Oxford 1997), p165

563 Ibid p.162

564 Ibid, pp. 160-62

565 Jewish Telegraphic Agency, 30 June 1944, "450,000 Hungarian Jews already deported; Federal Council of Churches issues appeal", cited in Fleming, *Auschwitz*, p.243

566 NA.FO 371/42807 (97), copy of cable from Jerusalem (received 30 June 1944)

567 NA.FO 371/42807 (193)

568 Hansard House of Commons debates, 5th July 1944, volume 401, columns 1160-2 http://hansard.millbanksystems.com/commons/1944/jul/05/hungary-mass-deportations-of-jews accessed 17/04/21

569 NA.FO 371/42814/196, FO official advising to scrap the bombing plan, 25th August 1944

570 Michael Fleming, *Auschwitz*, p.260

571 "Hungary (Mass deportation of Jews)", House of Commons Debate, 05 July 1944, vol 401 cc1160-2, https://api.parliament.uk/historic-hansard/commons/1944/jul/05/hungary-mass-deportations-of-jews

572 Dalia Ofer, *Escaping the Holocaust*, pp. 218, 290.

573 Jack Fairweather, *The Volunteer*, pp.174-5

574 Dr Hertz, published in *Polish Jewish Observer*, 3 March 1944

575 Gabriel Milland, *Some Faint Hope and Courage. The BBC and the Final Solution, 1942-45* (University of Leicester, 1998), p.56

576 Michael Fleming, *Auschwitz*, p.368

577 Ibid, p.263

578 Louise London, *Whitehall and the Jews, 1933–1948: British Immigration Policy, Jewish Refugees and the Holocaust*, (Cambridge University Press, 2000), pp. 169-191

579 Minutes of 22 Dec. 1942, PRO FO 371/32682 (W17521)

580 "The Last Letter From Szmul Zygielbojm, The Bund Representative With The Polish National Council In Exile" May 11, 1943, *Yad Vashem, The World Holocaust Remembrance Center,* https://www.yadvashem.org/docs/zygielbojm-letter-to-polish-national-council-in-exile.html

This is Torture

581 Oxford English language dictionary, languages.oup.com

582 Mark P Donelly and Daniel Diehl, *The Big Book of Pain, Torture and Punishment throughout History,* (The History Press, Gloucestershire, 2008), p.27

583 Universal Declaration of Human Rights, https://www.ohchr.org/EN/UDHR/Documents/UDHR_Translations/eng.pdf

584 Eric Hobsbawm, *Age of Extremes, The Short Twentieth Century, 1914-1991*, (London, 1995) p.49

585 Ibid, p.446

586 The Magna Carta (English translation from Latin), https://www.magnacartaplus.org/magnacarta/index.htm#en2

587 Lauren Mackay, "How many executions was Henry VIII responsible for?" *History Extra Magazine*, 28/12/2014, https://www.historyextra.com/period/tudor/how-many-executions-was-henry-viii-responsible-for/ (accessed 02/04/21)

588 John Guy, *Tudor England,* (Oxford, 1988), p.238

589 Michel De Montaigne*, The Works of Michel De Montaigne,* Edited and Arranged by David Widger (Project Gutenberg eBook, 2004), https://www.gutenberg.org/files/7551/7551-h/7551-h.htm (accessed 17/06/21)

590 De Cesare marchese di Beccaria**,** *An Essay on Crimes and Punishments,* (fifth edition, Dublin: 1777), p.45

591 Donelly and Diehl, *The Big Book of Pain,* p.133

592 Jennifer K. Harbury, *Truth, Torture, and the American Way. The History and Consequences of U.S. Involvement in Torture,* (Beacon Press, 2005) p. XXVII

593 Christopher Andrew, *The Secret World*, (Penguin, 2019) p.117

594 Testimony of Cofer Black, https://fas.org/irp/congress/2002_hr/092602black.html (accessed 18/8/21)

595 Robin Wright and Glenn Kessler, "Rejection of Prison Abuses Was Sought; Administration Was Reluctant," *Washington Post*, May 16, 2004

596 Caroline Moorehead "Crisis of confidence", *Financial Times*, 18/06/2005, republished on International Committee Red Cross, https://www.icrc.org/en/doc/resources/documents/article/other/6dzk8m.htm (accessed 21/08/21)

597 History.com editors, "Code of Hammurabi", *History.com*, updated 21st February 2020, https://www.history.com/topics/ancient-history/hammurabi, (accessed 7/7/21)

598 *The Code of Hammurabi ,* translated by L.W. King, The Avalon Project, Yale Law School, https://avalon.law.yale.edu/ancient/hamframe.asp (accessed 07/07/21)

599 Donelly and Diehl, *The Big Book of Pain*, p.32

600 Emma Batha, "Special report: The punishment was death by stoning. The crime? Having a mobile phone", *The Independent*, 28/09/2013, https://www.independent.co.uk/news/world/politics/special-report-punishment-was-death-stoning-crime-having-mobile-phone-8846585.html (accessed 09/07/21)

601 Donelly and Diehl, *The Big Book of Pain,* p38

602 Léon Clugnet, "St. Catherine of Alexandria" . In Herbermann, Charles (ed.). *Catholic Encyclopedia. 3. (New York: Robert Appleton Company,* 1908)

603 Executions in the U.S. 1608-2002: The ESPY File Executions by State, p.147 https://files.deathpenaltyinfo.org/legacy/documents/ESPYstate.pdf, (accessed 09/07/21)

604 William I's inaugural speech, 25th December 1066, cited in Donelly and Diehl, *The Big Book of Pain*, p. 53

605 Ibid

606 Christopher Andrew, *The Secret World*, p.170

607 British Commissioners Report of 1855, cited in Donelly and Diehl, *The Big Book of Pain*, p.156

608 Henry Norman, *The Peoples and Politics of the Far East: Travels and Studies in the British, French, Spanish and Portuguese Colonies, Siberia, China, Japan, Korea, Siam and Malaya,* (Charles Scribner's Sons, New York, 1895), p.226

609 "Japan, POWs and the Geneva Conventions," *PBS,* (Accessed 07/08/21) https://www.pbs.org/wgbh/americanexperience/features/bataan-japan-pows-and-geneva-conventions/

610 Gavan Daws, *Prisoners of the Japanese, POWs of World War II in the Pacific,* (William Morrow and Company, New York, 1994), p.274

611 Ibid, p.254

612 Ibid, pp. 254-55

613 Eric Hobsbawm, *Age of Extremes,* p.220

614 Ibid, p.220

615 Donelly and Diehl, *The Big Book of Pain*, p.37

616 Ibid, p.149

617 John Dalberg- Acton in a letter to Bishop Creighton in 1887

618 Donelly and Diehl, *The Big Book of Pain*, p.59

619 "Torture, Trial and Execution", *UK Parliament*, https://www.parliament.uk/about/living-heritage/evolutionofparliament/parliamentaryauthority/the-gunpowder-plot-of-1605/overview/aftermath/toture-trial-and-execution/ (accessed 14/7/21)

620 Natasha Sheldon, "The Macabre Career of Witch Finder General Belonged to this Scheming Man in the 17th Century", *History Collection,* (December 1, 2018) https://historycollection.com/the-macabre-career-of-witch-finder-general-belonged-to-this-scheming-man-in-the-17th-century/2/ (accessed 15/7/21)

621 The British Library, entry for *The Discovery of Witches*, 1647, https://www.bl.uk/collection-items/the-discovery-of-witches (accessed 06/04/22)

622 Donelly and Diehl, *The Big Book of Pain*, p.123

623 Ibid, p.154

624 Owen Bowcott, "Revealed: Britain's torture of Obama's grandfather", *The Times*, 3/12/2008 https://www.theguardian.

com/world/deC.E.lineusa/2008/dec/03/obama-grandfather-maumau-torture (accessed 10/7/21)

625   Donelly and Diehl, *The Big Book of Pain*, p48

626   Ibid, p. 93

627   Ibid, p.89

628   Cited in Donelly and Diehl, *The Big Book of Pain,* p.212

629   Christopher Andrew, *The Secret World, a History of Intelligence*, p.4

630   Amnesty International Report on Torture, second edition, (Duckworth, London, 1975), P.107

631   "The Hooded Men, Torture, Lies and the quest for Justice", *Amnesty International UK*, (21/06/21) https://www.amnesty. org.uk/hooded-men-torture-uk-ireland (accessed 10/7/21)

632   Donelly and Diehl, *The Big Book of Pain,* p.37

633   Christopher Andrew, *The Secret World,* p.137

634   Donelly and Diehl, *The Big Book of Pain,* p.76

635   Ibid

636   Christopher Andrew, *The Secret World,* p.165

637   Gavan Daws, *Prisoners of the Japanese*, p.274

638   Testimony of Frieda Mazia: Eichmann Trial, 4 May 1961, session 27

639   Steve Waugh and John Wright, *The Development of the USA, 1929-2000*, (Hodder Education, 2016, London) p.21

640   Faye Bowers and Philip Smucker, "US Ships Al Qaeda Suspects to Torture Using Arab States", *Christian Science Monitor*, July 26, 2002

641   Nick Gier, "Beheading, Hooding, and Water Boarding: CIA Torture in Vietnam, Latin America, and Iraq", *University of Idaho*, https://www.webpages.uidaho.edu/ngier/torture.htm, (accessed 07/04/21)

642   Tim Weiner, *Legacy of Ashes, The History of the CIA* (Penguin, London, 2007) p.394

643   Jennifer K. Harbury, *Truth, Torture, and the American Way*, p.97

644   A. J. Langguth, *Hidden Terror* (Pantheon books, 1978), p. 225

645 Ibid, p.25

646 Darius Rejali , *ELECTRICITY: THE GLOBAL HISTORY OF A TORTURE TECHNOLOGY* https://www.reed.edu/poli_sci/faculty/rejali/articles/History_of_Electric_Torture.html (accessed 14/7/21)

647 Tom Barry and Deb Preusch, *Central America Fact Book,* (Ground Zero Books ltd, 1998) p. 253

648 Ibid, pp. 251, 264

649 Jennifer K. Harbury, *Truth, Torture, and the American Way,* p. 40

650 Ibid, p.33

651 1950 and 1964 Guatemalan census reports

652 Jennifer K. Harbury, *Truth, Torture, and the American Way,* p93

653 Ibid, p.31

654 Ibid, p.98

655 Ibid, p.53

656 Intelligence Oversight Board, *Report on Guatemala*, June 28th, 1996, p.2

657 Jennifer K. Harbury, *Truth, Torture, and the American Way,* p.36

658 Allan Nairn, "The CIA and Guatemala's Death Squads", *The Nation*, April 17th, 1995

659 Gary Cohn and Ginger Thompson, "Unearthed: Fatal Secrets," *Baltimore Sun,* June 11-18, 1995,

660 Jennifer K. Harbury, *Truth, Torture, and the American Way,* p.34

661 Ibid, p.37

662 *The Guatemalan Military: What the U.S. Files Revealed*, National Security Archive, 1st June 2000, Doc. No. 42

663 Jennifer K. Harbury, *Truth, Torture, and the American Way,* p.71

664 *Inside the School of Assassins,* video by Richter Productions, 1997, cited in Harbury, *Truth, Torture, and the American Way*, p.44

665 Richard F. Grimmett and Mark P. Sullivan, *United States Army School of the Americas: Background and Congressional Concerns,* (3/3/1994) https://irp.fas.org/crs/soa.htm (accessed 12/7/21)

666 Vicky Imerman,; Heather Dean (3/8/2009). "Notorious Honduran School of the Americas Graduates". *Derechos Human Rights*. http://www.derechos.org/soa/hond-not.html (accessed 11/07/21)

667 Gary Cohn and Ginger Thompson, "Unearthed: Fatal Secrets," *Baltimore Sun,* June 11-18, 1995,

668 Jennifer K. Harbury, *Truth, Torture, and the American Way,* p.81

669 Gary Cohn and Ginger Thompson, "Unearthed: Fatal Secrets," *Baltimore Sun,* June 11-18, 1995,

670 A.J. Langguth, *Hidden Terrors*

671 Ibid

672 Ibid

673 Manuel Hevia Cosculluela, *Passporte 11333: Ocho Años con la CIA*, (Havana, Cuba: Editorial de Sciencias Social, 1978), p.284

674 Jennifer K. Harbury, *Truth, Torture, and the American Way,* p.74

675 Ibid, pp. 78-80

676 Michael Hirsh, "Abu Gharib: 'Breaking a General'", *MSNBC Newsweek,* Sept. 6, 2004

677 Personal interviews with Santiago conducted by Jennifer Harbury, 1993-1998, cited in Harbury, *Truth, Torture, and the American Way,* p.58

678 Darius Rejali , "Electricity: The Global History of a Torture Technology", *Reed Education,* https://www.reed.edu/poli_sci/faculty/rejali/articles/History_of_Electric_Torture.html (accessed 14/7/21)

679 Christopher Andrew, *The Secret World*, p.116

680 Jennifer K. Harbury, *Truth, Torture, and the American Way,* p.16

681 Alberto Gonzales, *Memorandum to the President, Re: Decision Re Application of the Geneva Conventions on Prisoners of War in*

the Conflict with Al-Qaeda and the Taliban, 25/1/2002, https://www.justice.gov/sites/default/files/olc/legacy/2009/08/24/memo-laws-taliban-detainees.pdf, (accessed 19/8/2021)

682 Peter Probst, quoted in Dana Priest and Joe Stephens, "The road to Abu Ghraib," *Washington Post,* 11/5/2004, p.A-12

683 18 U.S.C. 2340

684 Faye Bowers and Philip Smucker, "US Ships Al Qaeda Suspects to Torture Using Arab States", *Christian Science Monitor*, July 26, 2002

685 Jennifer K. Harbury, *Truth, Torture, and the American Way,* p.2

686 Tim Weiner, *Legacy of Ashes. The History of the CIA,* (Penguin books, 2007), p.556

687 Amy Goodman, "US Operating Secret 'Torture Flights,'" *Democracy Now,* (17/11/2004)

688 Testimony of al-Tabuki, Human Rights Watch, *What Happens When the Gloves Come Off,* (8/4/2008), https://www.hrw.org/news/2008/04/08/what-happens-when-gloves-come accessed 18/8/21

689 Jennifer K. Harbury, *Truth, Torture, and the American Way,* p.16

690 Darius Rejali (expert on torture) cited in Barry, "The Roots of Torture", *Newsweek,* 23/5/2004, p.28

691 Jennifer K. Harbury, *Truth, Torture, and the American Way,* p.9

692 Ibid, p.17

693 Ibid, p.17

694 Thomas Ricks, "Documents detail Abuse of Detainees", *Boston Globe*, 15/12/2004

695 Neil Lewis and David Johnson, "New FBI Memos Describe Abuses of Iraqi Inmates," *New York Times,* 21/12/2004

696 Jennifer K. Harbury, *Truth, Torture, and the American Way,* p.11

697 Alfred W. McCoy, *A Question of Torture, CIA Interrogation, from the Cold War to the War on Terror*, (Metropolitan books, New York, 2006), p.14

698 Statement from U.S. Senator John Warner, quoted in Harbury, *Truth, Torture, and the American Way,* p.14

699 FBI memorandums obtained by the ACLU cited in Carol Leonnig, "Further Detainee Abuse Alleged", *Washington Post,* 26/12/2004

700 Carol Leonnig and Dana Priest, "Detainees Accuse Female Interrogators", *Washington Post,* 10/2/2005.

701 Testimony of al-Tabuki, Human Rights Watch, *What Happens When the Gloves Come Off,* (8/4/2008), https://www.hrw.org/news/2008/04/08/what-happens-when-gloves-come accessed 18/8/21

702 Jennifer K. Harbury, *Truth, Torture, and the American Way,* p.15

703 "Medical Experiments", *The United States Holocaust Memorial Museum,* https://www.ushmm.org/collections/bibliography/medical-experiments (accessed 11/7/21)

704 "Prisoners of War of the Japanese 1939-45", *Forces War Records,* https://www.forces-war-records.co.uk/prisoners-of-war-of-the-japanese-1939-1945 (accessed 04/07/21)

705 Andy Walker, "The Twins of Auschwitz", *BBC,* (28/01/15) https://www.bbc.co.uk/news/magazine-30933718 (accessed 04/07/21)

706 Gavan Daws, *Prisoners of the Japanese,* p.258

707 P.D.C, Mackay, member of the Royal College of Surgeons, to the British Medical Journal, 19 August 1945: Foreign Office papers, 371/50989, cited in Martin Gilbert, *The Holocaust,* p.375

708 Gavan Daws, *Prisoners of the Japanese,* p.258

709 P.D.C, Mackay, member of the Royal College of Surgeons, to the British Medical Journal, 19 August 1945: Foreign Office papers, 371/50989, in Martin Gilbert, *The Holocaust,* p374-375

710 Gavan Daws, *Prisoners of the Japanese,* p.259

711 Vivien Spitz, *Doctors From Hell, The Horrific Account of Nazi Experiments on Humans* (Sentient Publications, USA, 2005), p.116

712 Testimony of Dr. Zofia Maczka, affidavit taken on April 16, 1946, prosecution exhibit 232

713 Testimony of Dr. Zofia Maczka, affidavit taken on April 16, 1946, prosecution exhibit 232

714 Vivien Spitz, *Doctors From Hell,* p.91.

715 Ibid, pp.65-66

716 *The Medical Case*, Vol. 1, p. 104, NO-476, Prosecution exhibit 40 at Nuremburg Trials.

717 Ibid, p899, NO-610, prosecution exhibit 41.

718 Vivien Spitz, *Doctors From Hell*, pp.85 -86

719 Testimony of Walter Neff at Nuremburg Trials, December 17-18, 1946. Prosecutor James McHaney.

720 Testimony of Walter Neff at Nuremburg Trials, December 17-18, 1946. Prosecutor James McHaney.

721 Vivien Spitz, *Doctors From Hell,* p.157

722 Testimony of Karl Hoellenrainer, June 27th 1947, cited in Spitz, *Doctors from Hell,* p.165

723 Christopher Simpson, *Science of Coercion: Communication Research and Psychological Warfare 1945-1960,* (Oxford University Press, New York, 1994), p.9

724 Amnesty International, *Arming the Torturers,* (March 1977)

725 Peter Watson, *War on the Mind: The Military Uses and Abuses of Psychology,* (Basic Books, New York, 1978), pp.266-67

726 Ramussen, "Medical Aspects of Torture", p.30-31 cited in Alfred W. McCoy, *A Question of Torture: CIA Interrogation, from the Cold War to the War on Terror,* (St. Martins Press, 2007), p.18

727 Alfred W. McCoy, *A Question of Torture,* p.21

728 Jennifer K. Harbury, *Truth, Torture, and the American Way,* p.19

729 Eric Schmitt and Douglas Jehl, "Army Says CIA Hid More Iraqis Than It Claimed," *New York Times,* 10/9/2004, p.A-1

730 Jennifer K. Harbury, *Truth, Torture, and the American Way,* p. XXII

731 John Yoo, *Memorandum to President Bush, Re: Application of Treaties and Laws to al-Qaeda and Taliban Detainees,* 9/1/2002,

https://www.justice.gov/sites/default/files/olc/legacy/2009/08/24/memo-laws-taliban-detainees.pdf (accessed 18/8/2021)

732 Jennifer K. Harbury, *Truth, Torture, and the American Way,* p.198

733 Ibis, p.22

734 Bush, Decision Points, Ch 6, cited in C. Andrew, *The Secret World*, p.117

735 Jennifer K. Harbury, *Truth, Torture, and the American Way,* p.22

736 Douglas Jehl and David Johnston, "Rule Change Lets CIA Freely Send Suspects Abroad to Jails," *New York Times*, 6/3/2005

737 Jennifer K. Harbury, *Truth, Torture, and the American Way,* p. XXII

738 Human Rights Watch, *What Happens When the Gloves Come Off,* (8/4/2008), https://www.hrw.org/news/2008/04/08/what-happens-when-gloves-come (accessed 18/8/21)

Elizabeth

739 Myra Weatherly, *Elizabeth I: Queen of Tudor England*, (Compass books, Minneapolis, 2005) p.57

740 S. Haynes, *A Collection of State Papers left by William Cecil, Lord Burghley* (London, 1740), pp.99-100

741 Scott Newport, "The Love Life of Queen Elizabeth I", *Historic UK,* (accessed 06/05/2020) https://www.historic-uk.com/HistoryUK/HistoryofEngland/The-Love-Life-of-the-Virgin-Queen/

742 *ARTICLES OF HIGH TREASON AND OTHER MISDEMANORS AGAINST THE KING'S MAJESTY AND HIS GROWN OBJECTED TO SIR THOMAS SEYMOUR, KNIGHT, LORD SEYMOUR OF SUDLEY, AND HIGH ADMIRAL OF ENGLAND*, February 1549.

743 Diane L. Dunkley, "Thomas, Lord Seymour of Sudeley: Treason and power in Tudor England" (1983), p.24 *Dissertations, Theses, and Masters Projects*. Paper 1539625224. https://dx.doi.org/doi:10.21220/s2-yqse-f028

744 Ibid, pp. 25-26

745 Robert Stephen Parry, *Elizabeth - the Virgin Queen and the Men who Loved Her. Biographical Sketches from the Elizabethan Court,* (Robert Stephen Parry publishers, 2014), chapter 4

746 Thomas Heywood, *England's Elizabeth: Her Life and Troubles* (Cambridge: Roger Daniel, 1641, rpt. The Harleian Miscellany, London: T. Park, 1808-13, Vol. X), pp.225-229.

747 Viktor Von Klarwill, *Queen Elizabeth and some Foreigners... hitherto unpublished letters from the archives of the Hapsburg family,* (John Lane The Bodley Head Ltd. 1 Jan. 1928), pp.113-115

748 Anna Whitelock, *Elizabeth's Bedfellows. An intimate History of the Queen's Court,* (Bloomsbury, London, 2013) p.218

749 Ibid, p.5

750 Ibid

751 Ibid p.242

752 Ibid

753 CSP VEN 1581-91, 288

754 Calendar of state papers, Spanish ed. G. A. Bergenroth, 13 vols (London 1862-1954) in Whitelock, Elizabeth's bedfellows, p52

755 David Starkey, *Elizabeth*, (London, 2000) p. 66

756 Anna Whitelock, "Elizabeth I: the monarch behind the mask", *History Extra Magazine,* (June 1 2013) https://www.historyextra.com/period/elizabethan/elizabeth-i-the-monarch-behind-the-mask/ (accessed 04/02/21)

757 Kate Lister, *A Curious History of Sex*, (Unbound, London 2020), p.24

758 Elizabeth I, "Tilbury Speech", 9 August 1588, British Library, Shelfmark: Harley MS 6798

759 Anna Whitelock, *Elizabeth's Bedfellows*, p.334

760 Ibid, p.132

761 Fénélon, *Correspondance Diplomatique II*, pp. 178-9

762 Elizabeth I to François, Duke of Alençon and Anjou, 19 February 1579, National Archives, (SP 78/3 f.9) https://www.nationalarchives.gov.uk/education/resources/elizabeth-monarchy/elizabeth-i-to-the-duke-of-alencon/

763 Susan Doran, *Monarchy and Matrimony: The Courtships of Elizabeth I,* (London, 1996) p.187

764 "Historical Notes: Why did Elizabeth I never marry?" *The Independent,* (09/06/98) https://www.independent.co.uk/arts-entertainment/historical-notes-why-did-elizabeth-i-never-marry-1163767.html (accessed 22/04/2020)

765 Anna Whitelock, *Elizabeth's Bedfellows*, p.8

766 "England", *Britannica Student Encyclopaedia (*2020), http://www.britannica.com/ebi/article-200261 (accessed 23/04/2020)

767 David Ferriby, Angela Anderson and Tony Imperato, *The Tudors, England 1485-1603*, (Hodder, London, 2015) p.170

768 "The act of 1572", *Elizabethan England SHP Textbook* (London, 1999) p.69

769 William Shakespeare, *A Midsummer Night's Dream*, Act 2, Scene 1

770 Anthony Tibbles, *Conference Paper*, April 2000, https://www.liverpoolmuseums.org.uk/ports-of-transatlantic-slave-trade (accessed 13/04/2020)

771 History.com editors, "The Spanish Armada Defeated", *History. Com,* (25/07/2019) https://www.history.com/this-day-in-history/spanish-armada-defeated (accessed 13/04/2020)

772 John Hampdem, *Francis Drake, privateer: contemporary narratives and documents*, (Taylor & Francis, 1972), p.40

773 Ben Johnson, "The Spanish Armada", *HistoricUK,* https://www.historic-uk.com/HistoryUK/HistoryofEngland/Spanish-Armada/ (accessed 13/04/2020)

774 Ibid

Weird Sex

775 "Criminal law of the people's republic of China" (translation), criminal law of the people's republic of china (amendment) _ chinese.com (npc.gov.cn) (accessed 12/03/2021)

776 Eric Berkowitz, *Sex and Punishment 4000 years of Judging Desire*, (London, 2012) p.27

777   Duane W. Roller**,** *Cleopatra: A Biography,* (Oxford University Press, New York, 2010), p.37

778   Zahi Hawass, PhD; Yehia Z. Gad, MD; Somaia Ismail, PhD; "Ancestry and Pathology in King Tutankhamun's Family, Congenital Defects", *JAMA.* 2010;303(7), pp. 638–647

779   Byker Thanfor, "King Tut Mysteries Solved: Was Disabled, Malarial, and Inbred", *National Geographic News,* 17/02/2010, (accessed 28/8/2021) https://www.nationalgeographic.com/culture/article/100216-king-tut-malaria-bones-inbred-tutankhamun

780   Eric Berkowitz, *Sex and Punishment,* p.27

781   Allen W, Johnson; Douglass Richard Price-Williams, *Oedipus Ubiquitous: The Family Complex in World Folk Literature.* (Stanford University Press, 1996), p.28

782   Susan Treggiari. "Roman Incest." *The Classical Review*, vol. 54, no. 1, (Classical Association, Cambridge University Press, 2004), p.204, http://www.jstor.org/stable/3661907

783   Eric Berkowitz, *Sex and Punishment,* p.26

784   Zoroastrian Middle Persian (Pahlavi) texts, chap. 8 of the *Pahlavi Rivāyat* accompanying the *Dādestān ī dēnīg* (ed. Williams, I, pp. 48-61: text; II, pp. 10-17: translation)

785   Eric Berkowitz, *Sex and Punishment,* p.28

786   Ibid

787   Leviticus, 18: 25 and 18:26

788   Leviticus, 18: 7-15

789   Deuteronomy 34:10

790   Hebrew-English Bible, Exodus 6:20

791   John, Witte Jr.; Robert Kingdon, *Sex, Marriage, and Family in John Calvin's Geneva: Courtship, Engagement, and Marriage.* (Grand Rapids: William B. Eerdmans Publishing Company, 2005) p.321

792   Michael Coogan, *God and Sex. What the Bible Really Says* (New York, Boston: Twelve. Hachette Book Group., 2010) pp.112–113.

793   John Byron, *Cain and Abel in Text and Tradition: Jewish and Christian Interpretations of the First Sibling Rivalry,* Brill, 2011), p.27

794 Genesis 19:32–35

795 George Patrick Smith, *Family Values and the New Society: Dilemmas of the 21st Century*, (Greenwood Publishing Group, 1998), p.143

796 L. Van Den Berghe-Pierre; Gene M. Mesher, "Royal incest and inclusive fitness", *American Ethnologist 7.* University of Washington, 10 December 1979, pp.300–317.

797 F.C Ceballos, G. Alvarez, *Royal dynasties as human inbreeding laboratories: the Habsburgs. Heredity* (Edinb). 2013; 111(2): 114-121. doi:10.1038/hdy.2013.25 https://www.ncbi.nlm. nih.gov/pmc/articles/PMC3716267/

798 Ed Yong, "How Inbreeding killed off a line of Kings", *National Geographic*, (14/4/2009), https://www.nationalgeographic. com/science/article/how-inbreeding-killed-off-a-line-of-kings (accessed 25/4/2021)

799 Román Vilas, Francisco C. Ceballos, Laila Al-Soufi, Raúl González-García, Carlos Moreno, Manuel Moreno, Laura Villanueva, Luis Ruiz, Jesús Mateos, David González, Jennifer Ruiz, Aitor Cinza, Florencio Monje & Gonzalo Álvarez "Is the "Habsburg jaw" related to inbreeding?", *Annals of Human Biology, 2019,* 46:7-8, 553-561, https://www.tandfonline. com/doi/10.1080/03014460.2019.1687752

800 Geoffrey Parker, *Emperor: A new life of Charles V*, (Yale, 2019), p.45

801 Gonzalo Álvarez and Francisco C. Ceballos, "Royal Inbreeding and the Extinction of Lineages of the Habsburg Dynasty", *Human Heredity*, Vol. 80, No. 2 (2015), p.68 https://www. jstor.org/stable/10.2307/48513201

802 Ibid, p.63

803 Moniek Bloks, "Marie Louise of Orléans – The first wife of Charles the Bewitched", (18/12/2018) https://www. historyofroyalwomen.com/marie-louise-of-orleans/marie-louise-of-orleans-the-first-wife-of-charles-the-bewitched/# easy-footnote-1-97847 (accessed 26/4/2021)

804 Gonzalo Álvarez and Francisco C. Ceballos, "Royal Inbreeding", *Human Heredity* , Vol. 80, No. 2 (2015), p.63 https://www.jstor.org/stable/10.2307/48513201

805 Ángel García-Escudero López; A. Arruza Echevarría; Jaime Padilla Nieva; Ramon Puig Giró, "Charles II; from spell to genitourinary pathology", *History of Urology*, 2009, p.181

806 Ariel and Will Durant, *Age of Louis XIV (Story of Civilization),* (Simon & Schuster, 1963)

807 Sylvia Z. Mitchell, *Mariana of Austria and Imperial Spain: Court, Dynastic, and International Politics in Seventeenth-Century Europe* (PHD), (University of Miami, 2013)

808 Philip Henry, 5th Earl Stanhope, *Spain Under Charles the Second; Or, Extracts from the Correspondence of the Hon. A. Stanhope ... 1690-1699*, (Bradbury and Evans, London, 1844), p.99

809 P. Gargantilla *Enfermedades de los reyes de España. Los Austrias : de la locura de Juana a la impotencia de Carlos II el Hechizado* (in Spanish). (La Esfera De Los Libros S.L., 2005)

810 Turliuc, Cucu, AI "Hydrocephalus of King Charles II of Spain, the Bewitched King", *European Neurology*. 81 (1–2) (2019) : pp.76–78

811 A. H. Manchester, "Law of Incest in England and Wales", *Child Abuse and Neglect* Volume: 3 Issue: 3/4 (1979), pp. 679-682, https://www.ojp.gov/ncjrs/virtual-library/abstracts/law-incest-england-and-wales, (accessed 25/4/21)

812 Lila Thulin, The Distinctive 'Habsburg Jaw' Was Likely the Result of the Royal Family's Inbreeding, *Smithsonian Magazine*,(24/12/2019) https://www.smithsonianmag.com/smart-news/distinctive-habsburg-jaw-was-likely-result-royal-familys-inbreeding-180973688/(accessed 24/4/21)

813 Hamamy H. "Consanguineous marriages : Preconception consultation in primary health care settings", *J Community Genet.* 2012;3(3), pp.185-192. doi:10.1007/s12687-011-0072-y

814 D.B. Paul, H.G. Spencer, "It's ok, we're not cousins by blood": the cousin marriage controversy in historical perspective".

PLoS Biol. 2008;6(12) pp. 2627-2630. doi:10.1371/journal. pbio.0060320 https://www.ncbi.nlm.nih.gov/pmc/articles/PMC2605922/

815   The Ancestry Team, "9 Famous people who married their cousins", (09/06/2015), https://blogs.ancestry.com/cm/9-famous-people-who-married-their-cousins/ (accessed 12/05/2021)

816   P. Johnston, "How incest slipped from statute book". *The Telegraph*, 23 November 2002, https://www.telegraph.co.uk/news/health/3299240/How-incest-slipped-from-statute-book.html, (accessed 28/4/21)

817   A. V. John, & C. Eustace, "Shared histories – differing identities: Introducing masculinities, male support and women's suffrage", *The Men's Share? Masculinities, Male Support and Women's Suffrage in Britain, 1890–1920*, (Routledge, 2013), p.4

818   Seth J. Denbo, "Speaking relatively: a history of incest and the family in eighteenth century England", thesis for the University of Warwick, Department of History, (September 2001) p.253, http://wrap.warwick.ac.uk/2835/1/WRAP_THESIS_Denbo_2001.pdf (accessed 28/4/21)

819   A. H. Manchester, "Law of Incest in England and Wales", *Child Abuse and Neglect* Volume: 3 Issue: 3/4 (1979), pp. 679-682, https://www.ojp.gov/ncjrs/virtual-library/abstracts/law-incest-england-and-wales, (accessed 25/4/21)

820   Sexual Offences Act 2003, section 27, British Government, https://www.legislation.gov.uk/ukpga/2003/42/section/27

821   "Denmark passes law to ban bestiality". *BBC Newsbeat*, 22 April 2015, https://www.bbco.uk/news/newsbeat-32411241 (accessed 07/06/21)

822   Christopher Riley, "The dolphin who loved me: the Nasa-funded project that went wrong", *The Guardian,* (28/06/2014) https://www.theguardian.com/environment/2014/jun/08/the-dolphin-who-loved-me (accessed 28/7/21)

823 Margaret Lovatt, cited in Christopher Riley, The dolphin who loved me: the Nasa-funded project that went wrong, ibid.

824 Eric Berkowitz, *Sex and Punishment*, p.59

825 Ibid, p.41

826 Ibid.

827 Ilan Peled, "Bestiality in Biblical and Hittite Law", *The Torah. com* (2019) https://thetorah.com/article/bestiality-in-biblical-and-hittite-law (accessed 03/07/21)

828 Martha T. Roth, Laws 187,188 and 199, Hittite Laws, *Law Collections from Mesopotamia and Asia Minor,* (Society of Biblical Literature, 1997) pp. 236-237

829 Law 200a, ibid. p.237

830 Law 199, ibid

831 Ilan Peled, "Bestiality in Biblical and Hittite Law", *The Torah. com* (2019) https://thetorah.com/article/bestiality-in-biblical-and-hittite-law (accessed 03/07/21)

832 Leviticus 18:24

833 Exodus 22:18 (New International version) Bible

834 Deuteronomy 27:21 (New International version) Bible

835 Leviticus 18:23

836 Leviticus 20:15-16

837 Eric Berkowitz, *Sex and Punishment*, p.147

838 Mark P Donelly and Daniel Diehl, *The Big Book of Pain, Torture and Punishment throughout History,* (The History Press, Gloucestershire, 2008), p.62

839 Derrick Sherwin Bailey, *Homosexuality and the Western Christian Tradition*, (London: Longmans, Green, 1955), p.145

840 ibid

841 Eric Berkowitz, *Sex and Punishment*, p.176

842 Ibid, pp.232-3

843 James A. Brundage, Sex, Law and Marriage in the Middle Ages, (Variorum, 1993), p.20

844 1533 Buggary Act, British Library, General Reference Collection 506.d.33

845 A. D. Harvey, *Bestiality in late-Victorian England,* 15/11/2007, p.85 https://doi.org/10.1080/01440362108539618

846 Ibid

847 Voltaire, cited in Robert E. L. Masters, *The Hidden World of Erotica: Forbidden Sexual Behaviour and Morality,* (Lyrebird Press, 1973), p.39

848 Ibid

849 A. D. Harvey, *Bestiality in late-Victorian England,* 15/11/2007, p.85 https://doi.org/10.1080/01440362108539618

850 Eric Berkowitz, *Sex and Punishment*, p.178

851 Ibid, p.232

852 Ibid, p.235

853 Margaret Murray, Survey of The Witch-Cult in Western Europe, p. 145.

854 Eric Berkowitz, *Sex and Punishment*, p.290

855 Robert F. Oaks, Robert F. "'Things Fearful to Name': Sodomy and Buggery in Seventeenth-Century New England." *Journal of Social History*, vol. 12, no. 2, Oxford University Press, 1978, pp. 268–81, http://www.jstor.org/stable/3787139.

856 Eric Berkowitz, *Sex and Punishment*, p.290

857 Ibid, p.327

858 Ibid, p.328

859 Edward Payson Evans*, The Criminal Prosecution and Capital Punishment of Animals*, (The Law Book Exchange, New Jersey, 2006), p. 150

860 Eric Berkowitz, *Sex and Punishment*, pp. 328-9

861 "List of revolutions and rebellions" https://en.wikipedia.org/wiki/List_of_revolutions_and_rebellions#1800%E2%80%931849

862 1861 Offences against the Person Act, British Government, https://www.legislation.gov.uk/ukpga/Vict/24-25/100/section/61/enacted

863 A. D. Harvey, *Bestiality in late-Victorian England,* 15/11/2007, p.85 https://doi.org/10.1080/01440362108539618

864 Sexual Offences Act 1967, chapter 60, British Government, https://www.legislation.gov.uk/ukpga/1967/60/2004-05-01

865　Sexual Offences Act 2003, Section 69, British Government, https://www.legislation.gov.uk/ukpga/2003/42/section/69

866　FOI 201122004 bestiality convictions by court (table) - GOV. UK, https://assets.publishing.service.gov.uk/government/ uploC.E.s/system/uploC.E.s/attachment_data/file/984993/ FOI_201122004_bestiality_convictions_by_court__table_. ods

867　Ibid

868　Oliver Moore, 'Zoophiles' vow fight after Germany re-bans bestiality", *The Globe and Mail,* 14/12/2012

869　"Denmark passes law to ban bestiality". *BBC Newsbeat*, 22 April 2015. https://www.bbc.co.uk/news/newsbeat-32411241 (accessed 07/06/21)

870　French Penal Code - Chapter one: Serious abuse or acts of cruelty animals. - Article 521-1

871　Oliver Moore, 'Zoophiles' vow fight after Germany re-bans bestiality", *The Globe and Mail,* 14/12/2012

872　Ibid.

873　C. Queen, *Talking with Animals,* cited in Hani Miletski, *Understanding Bestiality and Zoophilia* (Hani Miletski, 2001)

Cannibalism

874　Definition of Cannibalism, *Cambridge Advanced Learner's Dictionary & Thesaurus* , (Cambridge University Press), https:// dictionary.cambridge.org/dictionary/english/cannibalism (accessed 24/5/21)

875　Richard Hollingham "Natural born cannibals", *New Scientist*: 30, July 10, 2004, https://www.newscientist.com/article/ mg18324555-400-natural-born-cannibals (accessed 26/08/20)

876　Jesus, cited in The Bible, John 6:53-56

877　Carmen Nocentelli, "A 16th-century comparative literature and culture scholar at the University of New Mexico, in Europe's Hypocritical History of Cannibalism", *Smithsonian Magazine* https://www.smithsonianmag.com/history/europes-hypocritical-history-of-cannibalism-42642371/ (accessed 27/08/20)

878 Bill Schutt, *Cannibalism, A Perfectly Natural History,* (Algonquin, New York, 2017), p.97

879 Ibid, p.93

880 Ian Tattersall, *The Fossil Trail, How We Know what We Think We Know about Human Evolution*, (Oxford university press, 1995)

881 Tim D White, "Once were Cannibals", *Evolution: A Scientific American Reader*, September 15, 2006, p.339

882 Nikki Withers, "When did we start burying our dead?", *BBC Science Focus Magazine*, 2021, https://www.sciencefocus.com/science/when-did-we-start-burying-our-dead/ (accessed 21/6/21)

883 Jonathon Amos, "Ancient Britons 'drank from skulls'", *BBC News*, February 16, 2011, https://www.bbc.co.uk/news/science-environment-12478115 (accessed 26/08/20)

884 Robin McKie, "Bones from a Cheddar Gorge cave show that cannibalism helped Britain's earliest settlers survive the ice age", *The Guardian,* June 20, 2010 https://www.theguardian.com/science/2010/jun/20/ice-age-cannibals-britain-earliest-settlers (accessed 26/08/20)

885 Bill Schutt, *Cannibalism*, p.198

886 Key Ray Chong, *Cannibalism in China,* (Wakefield NH: Longwood Academic, 1990)

887 Flavius Josephus, *The Wars of the Jews*, Book VI, Chapter 3, Section 4

888 Herodotus, *The History,* (Chicago press, London, 1987, trans. David Grene), book 3: 25, pp.221-2

889 "The Harrying of the North", *BBC Bitesize*, https://www.bbc.co.uk/bitesize/topics/zvhjdp3/articles/zhrysk7#zjs6m393 (accessed 26/08/20)

890 James Aitcheson, "The Harrying of the North", *History Today Magazine*, October 12, 2016, https://www.historytoday.com/history-matters/harrying-north, (accessed 26/08/20)

891   John of Worcester *The Chronicle of John of Worcester - 456 to 1140 C.E.* (accessed 26/08/20) http://www.bsswebsite.me.uk/History/JohnofWorcester/Chronicle_John2.html?t1=cannibalism#

892   Sarah Everts, "Europe's Hypocritical History of Cannibalism", *Smithsonian Magazine,* April 24, 2013, https://www.smithsonianmag.com/history/europes-hypocritical-history-of-cannibalism-42642371/, (accessed 27/08/20)

893   Fulcher of Chartres', *History of the Expedition to Jerusalem* (1100-1102) cited in Geraldine Heng, Cannibalism*, The First Crusade and the Genesis of Medieval Romance, (1998), p.103* https://www.academia.edu/318266/Cannibalism_the_First_Crusade_and_the_Genesis_of_Medieval_Romance, *(accessed 27/08/20)*

894   An anonymous crusader in the Norman army, *Deeds of the Franks and other Pilgrims to Jerusalem* (1099-1101) cited in Geraldine Heng, Cannibalism*, The First Crusade and the Genesis of Medieval Romance, (1998), p.103* https://www.academia.edu/318266/Cannibalism_the_First_Crusade_and_the_Genesis_of_Medieval_Romance, *(accessed 27/08/20)*

895   Ibid, p.104

896   Heinrich Hagenmeyer, *Die Kreuzzugsbriefe aus den Jahren 1088-1100* **,** (BiblioBazaar, 2009) p.169

897   John Wright, Steve Waugh, *Russia in Transition 1914-1924*, (Hodder, London, 2012), p9

898   Ibid, p.18

899   Encyclopaedia Britannica, "World War I, killed, wounded and missing", (20/07/1998) https://www.britannica.com/event/World-War-I/Killed-wounded-and-missing (accessed 28/5/21)

900   John Wright, Steve Waugh, *Russia in Transition 1914-1924*, p.36

901   Orlando Figes, *A People's Tragedy, The Russian Revolution 1891-1924*, (Pimlico, London, 1996), p.775

902   Cited in Orlando Figes, *A People's Tragedy*, p.777

903   Orlando Figes, A People's Tragedy, p.777

904 Ibid, p.777

905 Ibid

906 Cited in Ibid

907 Ibid

908 H. Fisher, *The Famine in Soviet Russia, 1919-1923*, (New York, 1927), p.98

909 Orlando Figes, *A People's Tragedy*, p.781

910 Ibid, p.780

911 Benjamin M. Weissman, "Herbert Hoover's 'Treaty' with Soviet Russia: August 20, 1921." *Slavic Review*, vol. 28, no. 2, 1969, pp. 276–288. *JSTOR*, www.jstor.org/stable/2493227 , (accessed 18/07/ 2021.

912 Orlando Figes, *A People's Tragedy,* p.779

913 C N Trueman, "The Siege Of Leningrad.", *The History Learning Site*, 15 May 2015. https://www.historylearningsite. co.uk/world-war-two/world-war-two-and-eastern-europe/the-siege-of-leningrad (accessed 26/05/ 2021)

914 Ibid

915 Ed Vulliamy, "Orchestral manoeuvres (part one)", *The Guardian*, (25/11/2001), https://www.theguardian.com/ theobserver/2001/nov/25/features.magazine27 (accessed 24/5/21)

916 Ibid

917 Harrison Salisbury, *The 900 Days: The Siege of Leningrad*, (Harper and Row, New York, 1969), p.479

918 Ed Vulliamy, "Orchestral manoeuvres (part one)", *The Guardian,* (25/11/2001), https://www.theguardian.com/ theobserver/2001/nov/25/features.magazine27 (accessed 24/5/21)

919 Viktor Koslov (survivor) cited in ibid.

920 Bill Schutt, *Cannibalism*, p.147

921 D. Korn, M. Radice, and C. Hawes, *Cannibal: The History of the People Eaters*, (Channel 4 books, London, 2001), pp. 83-86

922 Bill Schutt, *Cannibalism,* pp. 112-3

923   Roberto Canessa, Pablo Vierci, *I Had to Survive: How a Plane Crash in the Andes Inspired My Calling to Save Lives,* (Atria books, New York, 2017)

924   Bill Schutt, *Cannibalism,* p132

925   "Donner Party", *Encyclopaedia Britannica*, https://www. britannica.com/topic/Donner-party (accessed 20/5/21)

926   Evan Andrews, "10 things you should know about the Donner Party", *History.com*, (30/1/2020), https://www.history.com/ news/10-things-you-should-know-about-the-donner-party, (accessed 20/5/21)

927   Ed. Frederick; J. Teggart, *Diary of Patrick Breen, One of the Donner Party* (University of California Berkeley press, 1910) pp.28-29

928   Evan Andrews, *10 things you should know about the Donner Party*, History.com, (30/1/2020),

929   Kristin Johnson, cited in Bill Schutt, *Cannibalism*, p.142

930   Bill Schutt, *Cannibalism,* p.153

931   J. H. Merryman using information from a letter by James Reed (Donner Party member and leader of the second relief), 1847, cited in Shutt, *Cannibalism,* p.156

932   J. Q. Thornton, interview from James Reed, 1849, cited in Shutt, *Cannibalism,* p.156

933   Ibid

934   Michael Wallis, *The Best Land Under Heaven: The Donner Party in the Age of Manifest Destiny*, (Liveright, 2017), chapter 44

935   Bill Schutt, *Cannibalism,* p.163

936   Simon Worrell, "Beyond Cannibalism: The True Story of the Donner Party", *National Geographic,* (2/7/2017) https://www. nationalgeographic.com/history/article/donner-party-cannibalism-nation-west, (accessed 24/5/21)

937   Frank Dikötter, *Mao's Great Famine: The History of China's Most Devastating Catastrophe, 1958–62.* (Walker & Company, 2010), p. xii and p.333

938   Bill Schutt, *Cannibalism*, p.198

939   History.com editors, "The Cultural Revolution", *History.com*, 9/11/2009, https://www.history.com/topics/china/cultural-revolution (accessed 13/5/21)

940   Kathryn Edgerton-Tarpley, *Tears from Iron: Cultural Responses to Famine in Nineteenth Century China,* (University Press of California, Berkeley, 2008), p.223

941   Ibid, p.225

942   George Santayana, *The Life of Reason*, Vol 1, 1905, ebook 15000 at Project Gutenberg (2005), https://www.gutenberg.org/files/15000/15000-h/15000-h.htm, (accessed 14/5/21)

943   Jan van der Made, "Cannibalism in China 50 years on", *RFI News*, 22/5/2016, https://www.rfi.fr/en/asia-pacific/2016 0522-cannibalism-china-publication-official-records-50-years-after-cultural-revolut, (accessed 13/6/21)

944   Song Yongyi, of California State University, cited in ibid

945   Yi Zheng, *Scarlet Memorial: Tales of Cannibalism in Modern China,* (Boulder, Colo. Westview Press, 1996), p.198

946   Roderick MacFarquhar; Michael Schoenhals, *Mao's Last Revolution*. (Harvard University Press, 2006), p.245

947   Cited by Jan van der Made, "Cannibalism in China 50 years on", *RFI News*, 22/5/2016

948   Yi Zheng, *Scarlet Memorial,* pp.198-200

949   Song Yongyi, of California State University, cited in Jan van der Made, "Cannibalism in China 50 years on", *RFI News*, 22/5/2016

950   Yi Zheng, *Scarlet Memorial,* pp.199-202

951   Yi Zheng, *Hongse ji'nianbei (Red memorial)* ,1993, p.52, cited in Donald S. Sutton, "Consuming Counterrevolution: The Ritual and Culture of Cannibalism in Wuxuan, Guangxi, China, May to July 1968." *Comparative Studies in Society and History*, vol. 37, no. 1, 1995, p.136. *JSTOR*, www.jstor.org/stable/179381. (accessed 25/07/2021)

952   Sarah Everts, "Europe's Hypocritical History of Cannibalism", *Smithsonian Magazine,* April 24, 2013, https://www.smithsonianmag.com/history/europes-hypocritical-history-of-cannibalism-42642371/, (accessed 27/08/20)

953 Richard Sugg, *Mummies, Cannibals and Vampires: The History of Corpse Medicine from the Renaissance to the Victorians*, (Routledge, New York, 2016), pp.14-15

954 Ibid, p.15

955 Sribonius Largus cited in Richard Sugg, *Mummies, Cannibals and Vampires,* p.15

956 Thomas Moffet cited in Richard Sugg, *Mummies, Cannibals and Vampires,* p.16

957 D. Korn, M. Radice, and C. Hawes, *Cannibal: The History of the People Eaters,* p.92

958 Marissa Rhodes, PHD, *A History of Medicinal Cannibalism: Therapeutic Consumption of Human Bodies, Blood, & Excrement in "Civilized" Societies,* (July 12, 2020), https://digpodcast.org/2020/07/12/medicinal-cannibalism/ (accessed 20/7/2021)

959 Louise Noble. "'And Make Two Pasties of Your Shameful Heads': Medicinal Cannibalism and Healing the Body Politic in 'Titus Andronicus.'" *ELH*, vol. 70, no. 3, 2003, p.681, JSTOR, www.jstor.org/stable/30029895 (accessed 20 July 2021)

960 Owsei Temkin, *The Falling Sickness*, (Baltimore: The John Hopkins University Press, 1971), p.22

961 Marsilio Ficino, *Three Books on Life*, ed. Carol V. Kaske and John. R. Clark (Binghamton: Medieval and Renaissance Texts and Studies, 1989), p.197

962 *Pharmacopoeia Londinensis,* 1618, ed. Urdang (Milwaukee: Hammersmith-Kortmeyer, 1994), p.19

963 Louise Noble, "'And Make Two Pasties of Your Shameful Heads", *ELH, JSTOR*, p.686

964 Karen Gordon-Grube, "Anthropophagy in Post-Renaissance Europe: The Tradition of Medicinal Cannibalism", *American Anthropologist 90* (1988), p.406

965 Richard Sugg, *Mummies, Cannibals and Vampires,* p.6

966 Thomas Joseph Pettigrew, *History of Egyptian Mummies*, (London: Longman, Rees Orme, Green and Longman, 1984) p.9

967 Louise Noble, "'And Make Two Pasties of Your Shameful Heads", *ELH, JSTOR*, p.683

968 Bill Schutt, *Cannibalism*, p.212

969 Louise Noble, "'And Make Two Pasties of Your Shameful Heads", *ELH, JSTOR*, pp. 683-4

970 James Felton, *52 Times Britain was a Bellend, The History you didn't get taught at school*, (Sphere, London, 2019) p.63

971 Ibid

972 J. Lawrence, *A History of Capital Punishment,* (Citadel press, New York, 1960), p.407

973 Richard Sugg, *Mummies, Cannibals and Vampires,* p.6

974 Maria Dolan, "The Gruesome History of Eating Corpses as Medicine", *Smithsonian Magazine*, May 6 2012, https://www.smithsonianmag.com/history/the-gruesome-history-of-eating-corpses-as-medicine-82360284/ (accessed 27/08/20)

975 Bill Schutt, *Cannibalism*, pp.196-7

976 Key Ray Chong, cited in Bill Schutt, *Cannibalism*, p.204

977 Key Ray Chong, *Cannibalism in China,* (Wakefield NH: Longwood Academic, 1990), p.154

978 Ibid, pp.100-101

979 Ibid, p.2

980 T'ao Tsung-yi, cited in Bill Schutt, *Cannibalism*, pp. 202-203

981 Key Ray Chong, *Cannibalism in China,* pp.145-157

982 Herodotus, *The History,* translated by David Grene, (Chicago press, London, 1987), Book 4: 64-66, pp.303-304

983 Cassius Dio, *Roman History,* LXXII.4

984 Jacinto de Caravajal, cited in Bill Schutt, *Cannibalism*, p.111

985 Diego Alvarez Chanca, and Augustine Marcus Fernandez De Ybarra, "The letter of Dr. Diego Alvarez Chanca, dated 1494, relating to the second voyage of Columbus to America (being the first written document on the natural history, ethnography and ethnology of America)", 1907. *Smithsonian Miscellaneous Collections*. 48 (26), pp.435-436

986 Neil L. Whitehead, "Carib Cannibalism. The Historical Evidence." *Journal De La Société Des Américanistes*, vol. 70, 1984, p.69. *JSTOR*, www.jstor.org/stable/24606255 (accessed 01/07/2021)

987 Sir Walter Raleigh cited in Marissa Rhodes, PHD, *A History of Medicinal Cannibalism: Therapeutic Consumption of Human Bodies, Blood, & Excrement in "Civilized" Societies*

988 Letter from Columbus, 1499

989 Bill Schutt, *Cannibalism,* p.106

990 Peter Martyr, *De Orbe Novo. The Eight Decades Of Peter Martyr D'Anghera Volume 1 1912,* translated by Francis Augustus MacNutt, (Generic, 2019), p.50

991 Cited in Bill Schutt, *Cannibalism,* p.114

992 Marvin Harris, cited in Herbert Burhenn, "Understanding Aztec Cannibalism", *Archiv Für Religionspsychologie / Archive for the Psychology of Religion*, vol. 26, 2004, p.8, *JSTOR*, www.jstor.org/stable/23910038 (accessed 20 July 2021)

993 Mark P Donelly and Daniel Diehl, *The Big Book of Pain, Torture and Punishment throughout History,* (The History Press, Gloucestershire, 2008), p.159

994 Marvin Harris, *The Sacred Cow and the Abominable Pig. Riddles of Food and Culture*, (Touchstone books, 1987), pp.218-222

995 Ibid, p.175

996 Bill Schutt, *Cannibalism,* pp.111-2

997 Ibid, p.113

998 Sarah Everts, "Europe's Hypocritical History of Cannibalism", *Smithsonian Magazine,* 24/04/2013

999 Marissa Rhodes, PHD, *A History of Medicinal Cannibalism: Therapeutic Consumption of Human Bodies, Blood, & Excrement in "Civilized" Societies*, July 12, 2020

1000 W. Anderson, *The Collectors of Lost Souls*, (John Hopkins University Press, 2008), pp.21-25

1001 J. Whitfield, W. Pako, J. Collinge, and M. Alpers, "Mortuary rites of the South Fore and kuru", *Philosophical Transactions of the Royal Society,* V.363, (2008), pp.3721-24

1002 R. Rhodes, *Deadly Feasts,* (Simon and Schuster, New York, 1997), pp.22-23

1003 Ronald Berndt, *Excess and Restraint,* (University of Chicago Press, Chicago, 1962), p.283

1004 John D. Matthews, Robert Glasse, and Shirley Lindenbaum, "Kuru and Cannibalism", *Lancet 2* (1968), pp.449-52

1005 Genesis 22.2

1006 "Cannibals Discovered", *University of Bristol*, 7 March 2001, http://www.bristol.ac.uk/news/2001/cannibal.html (accessed 26/08/20)

1007 Herbert Burhenn, "Understanding Aztec Cannibalism", *Archiv Für Religionspsychologie / Archive for the Psychology of Religion*, vol. 26, 2004, p.2, *JSTOR*, www.jstor.org/stable/23910038 (accessed 20 July 2021)

1008 Marvin Harris, *Cannibals and Kings,* (Random House, New York, 1977) p.106

1009 Michael Harner, "The Ecological Basis for Aztec Sacrifice", *American Ethnologist 4*, 1977, p.119

1010 Herbert Burhenn, "Understanding Aztec Cannibalism", p.3

1011 Inga Clendinnen, *Aztecs: An Interpretation.* (Cambridge University Press, Cambridge, 1991), pp.98-99

1012 Herbert Burhenn, "Understanding Aztec Cannibalism", p.3

1013 Marvin Harris, *Cannibals and Kings,* p.109

1014 Herbert Burhenn, "Understanding Aztec Cannibalism", p.9

1015 Michael Harner, "The Ecological Basis for Aztec Sacrifice", *American Ethnologist 4*, 1977, p.132

1016 Ibid, pp.129-30

1017 Frank, tour guide at Chichen Itza, November 2019

1018 Michel de Montaigne, 1580, cited in Marissa Rhodes, PHD, *A History of Medicinal Cannibalism: Therapeutic Consumption of Human Bodies, Blood, & Excrement in "Civilized" Societies*, 12/07/2020

1019 Queen Isabella, 1503, in Neil L. Whitehead, "Carib Cannibalism. The Historical Evidence." *Journal De La Société Des Américanistes*, vol. 70, 1984, pp.69 -87. *JSTOR*, www.jstor.org/stable/24606255 (accessed 01/07/2021)

1020 Bill Schutt, *Cannibalism,* p.107

1021 Herodotus, *The History,* (Chicago press, London, 1987), Book 1: 119, pp.89-90

1022 Chloe Castleden, *Albert Fish, The Lying Cannibal,* (Magpie Books, Constable and Robinson, London, 2011), p.17

1023 letter quoted in Gini Graham Scott, American *Murder,* (2007), cited in Chloe Castleden, *Albert Fish, The Lying Cannibal,* p.9

1024 Ibid, p.10

1025 Ibid

1026 Ibid

1027 Ibid

1028 Quoted in Amanda Howard and Martin Smith, *River of Blood,* 2004, cited in Castleden, *Albert Fish, The Lying Cannibal,* p.13

1029 Ibid, p.14

1030 Ibid

1031 Ibid

1032 "Albert Fish", *Crime Museum,* 2021, https://www.crimemuseum.org/crime-library/serial-killers/albert-fish/ (accessed 1/7/21)

1033 Chloe Castleden, *Albert Fish, The Lying Cannibal,* p.18

1034 Roisin O'Connor, "Armin Meiwes: Interview with a Cannibal documentary sheds new light on one of Germany's most infamous murderers", *The Independent,* Tuesday 9 February 2016

1035 Ibid

1036 John Hall, "Dresden cannibal: German police worker 'obsessed' with cannibalism", *The Independent,* 29 November 2013

1037 Yvonne Jewkes; Majid Yar (eds), *Handbook of Internet Crime,* (Routledge, 2013), p.376

1038 Lewis Petrinovich, *The Cannibal Within,* (Transaction publishers, New York, 2000), p.36

Lynsey Calver is an Associate Assistant Headteacher and History Teacher at a Grammar School in Kent. She has been teaching history to ages 11-18 since 2011 and absolutely loves her job. Lynsey took a sabbatical from teaching between September 2019 and September 2020 to research and write Banned History. Lynsey lives in north Kent with her fiancée Aaron and dog Barney.

YouTube channel: TheHistoryMiss
Instagram: @thehistorymiss
Twitter: @TheHistoryMiss

9 781803 811055